To Jan

With all best wishes

[signature]

Stephen Twigg

DIANA
HER TRANSFORMATION

KINGS HART BOOKS

First published in 2012 by Kings Hart Books
An imprint of Publishers UK Ltd
6 Langdale Court, Market Square,
Witney, Oxfordshire, OX28 6FG
www.kingshart.co.uk

The information this book contains is not meant to replace
medical care. Before making any changes to your
health regime always consult a doctor.
While all the therapies in this book are completely safe
if done correctly you must seek professional medical advice
if you are in any doubt about a medical condition. Any application of the
information contained in this book is at the reader's sole risk and discretion.

Cover illustration by Hal Lever of www.lever-artwork.co.uk

Cover design: Kelly Twiggs of www.commercialcampaigns.co.uk

ISBN: 978-1906154-31-8

A CIP catalogue record for this book is available
from the British Library.

ACKNOWLEDGEMENT AND APPRECIATION

Many people are involved in bringing a book to its audience. I am grateful for the parts played by the following:

For financing the project – Angie, Barbara, Mike and Robin.

For their technical and professional expertise – Colin and Liz at King's Hart Books; Suzanne at Suzanne Evans Communications; Heather for assistance and her encouragement when I needed it.

For writing about what they knew and offering what they thought it meant – Andrew Morton, James Hewitt, Jonathan Dimbleby, Ken Wharfe, Patrick Jephson, Richard Kay, Sally Beddell Smith, Simone Simmons, Tina Brown, Trevor Rees-Jones.

For contributing, knowingly or not, to Diana's self-transformation, all the healers, especially – Chryssie Fitzgerald, Debbie Frank, Michael Skipwith, Oonagh Toffolo, Rita Rogers, Simone Simmons.

Thank you all

CONTENTS

INTRODUCTION

Health is a state of complete
physical, mental and social well-being
and not merely the absence of disease or infirmity.
World Health Organisation
(Preamble to the Constitution)

On 14 December, 1988, Diana, Princess of Wales, embarked on a process of transformation that was to see her emerge from a marriage which almost destroyed her and set out on the path she believed would bring her the love and fulfilment she desired. In the nine years of her journey she changed from a broken and desperate young woman, suffering from bulimia, depression and thoughts of suicide, to an immensely powerful individual, who strode the world stage on a self-imposed humanitarian mission. She challenged governments and ultimately caused a royal dynasty to bow to the wishes of a nation. This is the story of her metamorphosis and the part I played in it.

Like all of us, Diana was driven from within by the needs of her personality and make-up. Prominent amongst those were her desires to be understood and to help make the world a better place by caring for others. What follows will enable you to understand her. It may also help, in some small way, to make the world a better place if you can see aspects of your own life reflected in Diana's story and respond with even half the courage and determination she showed.

Famous people, like Diana, offer us more than opportunity to observe other people's lives through the screens of our televisions and computers, or the pages of our newspapers and magazines. They offer us mirrors by which we can see ourselves more clearly, if we care to notice.

Each of us views our world and the others who share it with us, through a filter made up of our own expectations and beliefs about what is right and wrong, and what people should do or should not. This is particularly the case when it comes to celebrities, those highly visible people we assume we know but who we don't, and whose circumstances we're not really aware of. They are judged like no others. Diana's situation was even more extreme than most. From the age of nineteen she had been subjected to a level of public, peer and press scrutiny unprecedented in modern times and she was constantly being judged as mad, bad or saintly on the basis of what she did, not why she did it. Without knowing who Diana was and what made her act as she did, such judgements are only useful for exposing the personal bias of the observer.

That then is why so many people have been confused by what they've heard or read about the Princess. We have always known a great deal about what she did during her life. Yet observers, writing about the same events, have each shown us a different Diana because they have offered us personal views lacking in an essential element, knowledge of *who* she was. This story provides that essential element – the part which says this is *who* Diana was – the part which brings everything you have heard into focus and enables you to say "now I understand her".

An important aspect of Diana's transformation was to understand herself so she could recognise she was a normal, healthy human-being trying to cope with burdens she hadn't learned how to deal with effectively. Many of those burdens were a matter of her perspective. What she believed about herself and how she tried to act as a result, was based on unsound information or lack of knowledge. When she finally discovered that the way she looked at the world and experienced it were normal, she was relieved of a huge amount of physical and mental stress. When she discovered that what she believed about herself and felt as a result could be changed, she was able to step away from a situation that had kept her trapped and helpless for seven years.

Diana's lack of self-understanding was not the sole reason she became stuck in a place where she had no answers to her problems. Overlaid on her confusion were the effects of a difficult childhood which gave her doubts and dark thoughts which she ignored, believing they would go away when she was married with a home and children. She was wrong and when she began experiencing the physical and emotional symptoms brought on by the painful situation in which she found herself, after marrying into the royal family, she didn't have the ability to deal with them. Instead she reacted and behaved in ways which made the problems worse and indicated to those around her that she might have serious mental problems.

Some observers, who barely met Diana and relied on hearsay, or who only came across her in circumstances that did not enable them to see all of who she was, have noted her behaviour and judged her harshly as a result. Perhaps they will alter their opinions when they discover she was almost certainly beset by a common affliction which affects nearly every one of us at some time in our lives, when our carefully nurtured expectations and assumptions are destroyed by events over which we have no control.

Post Traumatic Stress Disorder used to be considered the exclusive domain of those whose notion of reality and expectation of the future are shattered by experiences such as war or a dreadful car crash. Now we understand that there are many common real life events, such as bereavement, the breakdown of a relationship or even moving home, that can cause varying degrees of disorder to the mind and body, until a new vision of the future can be created to provide purpose and the confidence to go on. The symptoms of muscle aches, sleeplessness, anxiety, depression, alienation and eventually a sense that her life was too hard to bear finally brought Diana to her lowest ebb and caused her to seek my help.

It was her health, and the collection of painful physical symptoms from which she suffered, that prompted her most. Without sufficient knowledge to recognise the true source of her debilitating headaches and pains in her back, neck and shoulders, Diana sought relief from these without much expectation that I would be able to help with any of the other problems that ailed her. She did not realise that her physical pains, her body's distress, were a manifestation of her emotional anguish.

At the core of Diana's recovery and eventual metamorphosis, was the understanding that the human body and mind are interconnected and constantly interacting, as an integrated whole, so the quality of one is represented by the quality of the other.

The primary technique I employed in my work with clients was massage. Hands-on bodywork enabled me to alleviate physical symptoms while I acquired information about the emotional issues which underpinned them. I was then able to offer suggestions and guidance about how to improve unhelpful mind-sets using common, but powerful, self-help techniques similar to those employed by sports professionals and high achievers in business. The results were a more consistent relief from the physical symptoms and a profound change in outlook and behaviour that gave rise to better life experiences as well – the process of body-mind focused self-transformation.

My first massage session with her, however, offered us both more information than I imagined it would, and convinced her she should work with me for the next seven years.

PROLOGUE

The root of all health is in the brain.
The trunk of it is in emotion.
The branches and leaves are in the body.
The flower blooms –
when all parts work together.

Kurdish saying

4.15 pm, 14 December 1988, London, England

Good afternoon. My name is Stephen Twigg. I have an appointment with her Royal Highness the Princess of Wales.

Silently I practised the words over and over, like a mantra, as I drove slowly up the long driveway from Kensington Road to the gate in the black railings which surrounded Kensington Palace. I was trying to make myself comfortable with the strange phrase I would be using within the next few minutes.

I began musing on the person who was identified by the collection of words with which my mouth was so unfamiliar. Her Royal Highness The Princess of Wales, Diana, perhaps the most famous woman in the world. Her life was a topic for millions of words in print and poured out over the airways on an almost daily basis, her image a constant presence on TV in newspapers and magazines. Yet I had no idea what I would discover when I met her. Since making this appointment, I had made a deliberate effort to avoid preconceptions. I had fallen into that trap with famous clients before – and usually found their private persona to be very different to their public profile. All I knew about Diana was she had asked for my help and I would find out soon enough whether I might be of any use to her.

How odd that they should have a hut guarding a palace, I thought, as I brought my car to a halt beside a small wooden structure in the centre of the entrance, and lowered my window.

The hut had two windows, one to a side, each overlooking a cantilevered barrier, one to control vehicles entering, one for exits. I looked up to the IN side window. The ruddy face of a rather portly policeman peered down at me.

Straight from central casting, I thought, *not your typical SAS military type at all, and not a gun in sight. Probably plenty around somewhere though.* I should have stayed focused on my mantra.

'My name is Stephen Twigg. I have an appointment with her Royal Highness the Princess,' I stumbled.

'Which Princess would that be then sir?' quipped the bobby, 'we've got several 'ere?' Not a semblance of a smile crossed his face at the oblique reference to other members of the royal family who resided at Kensington Palace. Seen it all, got the T-shirt was the unspoken message.

'The Princess of Wales,' I finished.

The bobby checked a large ledger style book and made a short phone call, then motioned me through the barrier. 'Park anywhere you can find a space. Someone will come and get you,' as he walked from the hut and leaned on the balance weight to raise the beam for my car to pass.

I drove slowly up the drive and parked where it formed a circle alongside the fairly unprepossessing, if large, London town house with several front doors. As I lifted my massage table, then the case containing linen and oils, from my car, one of the doors opened and a young woman stood waiting for me. She turned out to be Diana's dresser with whom I had spoken briefly on the phone when arranging this appointment.

Things moved rapidly and smoothly from there. I was shown up an impressive staircase to Diana's bedroom where a massage table covered with giant bath towels was set up in readiness. We folded the table away as I chatted about my preference for using my own – it being set at the height I found ideal – but that I was happy to use the towels.

Left alone to prepare I slipped into the routine I had carried out thousands of times before in luxury homes all over the city. My ritual was well established now. It enabled me to let go of any tension I had acquired from dealing with the busy traffic and noise outside and replace it with the calm frame of mind I needed for my work. I knew the best way to relax a new client was for me to be relaxed so I deepened my breathing, and slowed my movements until I felt myself shift into the familiar state I wanted.

My bag contained thin-soled, black, Chinese slippers and I changed into them. They offered the feeling of being balanced and grounded not possible with regular hard soled shoes.

I unfolded my massage couch and flipped it upright then covered it with my own fresh linen and spread one of the huge palace towels over. A pillow for her head at one end of the table and the second giant towel arranged so she could slide under it and be warm and comfortable, and that was it.

I arranged my massage oils, creams and watch on a small side table on top of an A4 size piece of card I carried in my case to keep the oil from marking furniture which often turned out to be very expensive.

I closed the drapes on the bleak, grey London late-afternoon, noting as I did the blank brick facade and skylight windows of the building opposite, and the courtyard garden, like an oasis, below.

I switched on the bedside lamps so their glow made the large room seem warm and cosy. I glanced around and felt confident the atmosphere was just about right; not too bright and clinical but not too intimate either.

In the bathroom I washed my hands, hot water to warm them, and then I was ready. All I needed now was a body to work on. I re-entered the bedroom to wait.

I had only a little time to look around, gaining impressions of decorative round tables covered in small ornaments, a huge pile of cuddly toys of every size and many colours and a variety of paintings amongst which I noticed one by my favourite artist Robert Heindel, before my guide of earlier glanced around the door to see if I was ready and left again saying, 'Her Royal Highness will be with you shortly.'

I heard someone in the corridor outside. A heavy tread if quite an energetic one it seemed to me.

It was Diana. She entered the room – or to be more accurate she burst into the room like Tigger from the *Winnie the Pooh* stories – with a big smile, reaching forward for my hand as she strode towards me. She was dressed in a baggy tracksuit.

'Hello Stephen I hope I haven't kept you waiting. I've heard so much about you,' a breathless gush of words to go with the rush of her movements.

'All good I hope?' I responded grasping her hand firmly but briefly and smiling into her eyes. Her eyes were the most intense blue I had seen.

The first few seconds with any new client are important if they are to get the best massage possible. I knew everything I did from now on would be significant. After all I was a complete stranger about to share quite an intimate experience and it was essential that Diana felt relaxed and comfortable with me. But I'd been doing this for a long time and without realising it Diana now became both audience and participant in a performance I had enacted many, many times before.

The first thing I needed to do was to take control. Uncertainty creates anxiety. I could reduce that by telling her very clearly just what I wanted from her and what she could expect from me.

'Just sit down a minute and let's have a chat.' I gestured at the big double bed. Diana sat and folded her hands in her lap. I perched on the edge of the massage table my feet swinging, looking down on her. My attitude was intentionally relaxed as if this was the most normal situation in the world.

Keeping my voice low so she would have to concentrate I asked about any problems which might make massage therapy unsuitable and what she wanted my help with.

'I get a lot of tension in my shoulders and neck,' she reached up with her left hand I noticed and rubbed at her right shoulder.

'Is one side worse than the other?'

'No it's both sides and all up my neck.'

'Do you do any exercise?'

'I swim nearly every day and play tennis quite often. I feel it's important to keep myself fit.'

'Any injuries or accidents which might have caused the problem?'

'No. It's mostly when I get stressed out and tired. I feel it all around here,' she said, gesturing again to her neck. 'It makes me feel so down and I hate to disappoint people by not being on top of my game.' She looked down at the floor as she spoke, glancing up at me only occasionally.

We chatted on for a little longer in a conversation intended to make it clear she was now the focus of all my attention and concern. She was not as animated as some clients can be, rather she was quietly spoken and slightly withdrawn, as if shy and lacking in confidence. I found out later this was a demeanour Diana habitually took when unsure of herself, as if she would rather keep quiet than say anything for which she might be ridiculed.

No accidental trauma. Both shoulders – upper trapezius – so possible kidney issues. Maybe neck muscles – could be stomach acid imbalance. Possible low self –

esteem and the posture to go with it a factor, I noted mentally as I started to explain clearly how I wanted her to prepare for her massage.

'I'd like you to make yourself comfortable under here,' I indicated the bath sheet on the massage table, 'lying face up head on the pillow,' making the instructions almost childishly simple. I had clients, wealthy and powerful people used to all manner of stressful situations, who had become so nervous at their first massage session with me they became distracted and failed completely to hear what I said.

'I'll just go and wash my hands while you get ready. Be back in a minute.'

I returned to the bathroom and washed my hands – warm water again – the second time in the last ten minutes – giving her the opportunity to prepare herself while I was away. When I returned, Diana was on the massage table, covered from her neck down with the fluffy towel and gazing at the ceiling, waiting for me to begin.

From the moment she had entered the room I had been gathering information which might help me in my work.

News clips and photos showing her face and body shape had already led me to believe she was the kind of person who experienced the world primarily through her emotions, rather than her senses, intellect or intuition as other types do. Seeing her face-to-face confirmed this impression, as did the frequent references to her emotions and feelings when we were discussing her aches and pains and how they made her feel when they interfered with her work.

The way she moved and held herself suggested she was not comfortable in her skin, and not very confident, although she compensated for that by charging into challenging situations. Her hunched shoulders and the heavy tread I had noticed before indicated a lack of coordination. She certainly did not have the smooth and graceful movements and posture of a person fully at ease with themselves and their place in the world.

What was it I'd noticed in those eyes, so expressive and so haunting? There was something disturbing there. Was it *sanpaku*? The excess white of the eyes showing around the iris which, some say, can indicate extreme stress or anger or the possibility of great danger, as it had with Lincoln and J F Kennedy.

I couldn't put my finger on what it was that troubled me or, more precisely, I hadn't put my hands on it yet, but I knew I probably would sometime in the next hour.

As I walked across the room I let myself lapse into the state of concentration and receptiveness that would help me tune in to her better. It would also allow my intuition to guide me about where I should start work.

A sudden surprise! With no hesitation I decided to begin with her face. I almost never start the first massage of a new client with their face. There is a vulnerability associated with the face. To be touched there feels highly personal, even intimate to many people. With new clients I generally start with their feet, so they can become used to my touch applied to a less sensitive area and acquire confidence and trust in me and my techniques.

'Just lift your head a moment while I take this pillow away. Your head will go back down onto the table top. I'm going to start with your face, neck and shoulders.'

Gently, I removed the pillow and draped the small towel from beneath it around her hair to keep it from getting oily. I stood behind her then and pressed her shoulders down firmly to trigger a relaxation response, then held her face in the palms of my hands for a few moments, making my touch gently firm and unmistakably professional to reassure her and show her she was safe and could let me be in control. It also indicated where I intended to begin the massage, so the first strokes would not come as a surprise to which she would tense.

The mood, frame of mind and intention of any massage therapist are all in their first contact with their client's skin. Competence and compassion can be spelled out in the first few moves.

I turned, poured some oil into one palm and spread it on the other, held the backs of my hands briefly on her forehead to remake the contact, and then made firm but superficial movements to cover over her brow and temples, cheeks and chin, then up over her throat. The first light touches would register in her mind, telling her she was being cared for and she was literally in my hands for the next hour or so. The same movements equally served me, spreading the oil and enabling me at the same time to assess the state of the muscles and joints beneath her skin.

Her face in repose showed sadness. Her jaw and mouth were stiff and rigid. She gazed into mid-air with fixed eyes and a benign, almost blank, expression. *Curious*, I thought, *she seems resigned, as if she's not really involved. She's not engaged.* Some clients will close their eyes immediately, others keep them open but if their face is being massaged most people show they are aware of what is happening. Diana was in a daydream – in a mind space with her own thoughts – detached from the room, and from her own body.

A client will get the most from a massage treatment when they are in a light meditation state. They are then physically and mentally relaxed but aware of what is happening, and able to bring their attention to those muscles and joints being worked, able to respond to the pressure of hands and fingers, to release tension and involuntary holding patterns, without the need for words. Detachment, and worse still sleep, from which they can waken with a jolt not knowing where they are or what is happening, are not helpful.

I cast a brief glance over her. Hands on abdomen, crossed, fingers seemingly relaxed but the index finger of her right hand was being held an inch above her left. Her breathing was quite shallow and rapid and high in her chest – definite signs of unconscious tension.

'Has anyone ever taught you how to receive a massage?' I asked, removing my hands from her face and walking around from the head of the table to where she could see me at her side.

A perplexed expression crossed her face and she responded, 'No.'

I placed my palm on her abdomen – around the *tanden* – the area close to the navel recognised in all Eastern martial arts as the source of intrinsic energy and seat of power in the body.

'You're breathing high up in your chest and quite fast which is what we do when we're nervous or stressed. In most adults it becomes normal to breathe like that because of all the stresses and strains we meet every day. When you were tiny you would have naturally breathed more slowly – down here, into your abdomen – when you were asleep and deeply relaxed. Think of your babies when they slept. Breathing high and fast is a signal to your mind and body that you are ready to fight or run. You don't need to do either right now so I want you to take a deep breath and hold it for a second or two then release it in a long, loud sigh. Then continue breathing deeply and evenly down here, so your tummy goes up with each in-breath, then down as you breathe out.' She followed my directions as I spoke quietly beside her.

'Can you feel your body slowing down and becoming more peaceful?'

She nodded.

'Now while I work, try to focus on where my hands are and imagine your breath circulating there. Just relax the muscles and allow my hands deeper into them.'

Returning to the head of the table I pondered about the intensely disturbing sensations I had just felt while my hand was resting on her stomach area. In oriental medicine a person's state of health and mind are represented by the energy in this area, the *hara*. The sense of turmoil and confusion I had felt emanating from Diana was not unusual in itself. Many people, especially the young have not acquired the strength and harmony of mind and body which can be felt as a powerful calmness in the *hara*. But this turbulence was on a scale I'd rarely experienced in anyone before. There was also the incongruity between the personality she seemed to be when she entered the room, bright and cheerful, and what was going on within. She was really good at masking her true feelings. I wondered if she masked them from herself.

I oiled my hands again, re-made the contact and started work once more. Silent now, I spoke to her with my hands alone. I let my own breathing match the rise and fall of her abdomen as I worked. Gradually I slowed my hands and breathing and without realising it she followed, slipping into a deeper state relaxation. Now the treatment had really begun.

Her facial muscles gradually allowed my fingers to work deeper into them and, as they did so, I allowed my own thoughts to recede. I needed to be able to make a connection that would tell me what was happening to this woman and the rattle of my own mind would get in the way of the kind of exchange I wanted, and there it was.

After just a few minutes, I suddenly felt an overwhelming wave of sadness sweep over me. It was a strong physical reaction, as if the release of her facial muscles had allowed a tidal-wave of emotion to surge out from the top of her skull straight into my stomach area and up into my chest. I felt my throat constrict and my eyes prick with the sharp sting of imminent tears.

Well I asked for that, I said inwardly to myself allowing the feeling to pass.

Her pain was unmistakable.

Not the physical kind of pain though. No, this kind of anguish comes from deeper within, from the mind, and it gets worse with time, not better.

What else did I feel?

Fleeting sensations of fear—

Flashes of intense anger, bordering on rage—

Excruciating self-judgment—

Extreme sadness and abject loneliness—

It was becoming clearer now. Diana's distress was the kind that came from a mind tormented by thoughts and feelings that can only result when a long held dream has been shattered. Thoughts and feelings that can bring the strongest to their knees and make them weep helpless tears.

Desolation...

Despair...

I realised then that the young woman whose face I held was very close to giving up on life – that her problems seemed to her insurmountable. Merely surviving appeared a hopeless and impossible task. The dark night of the soul is the loneliest place in the universe, and my new client was there now, feeling very isolated and desperate.

The same upsurge of released emotion had swept through Diana, and now I felt and saw rapid changes overtake her. First her mouth altered as her lips lost their benign mask and started to quiver, then her skin and the muscles of her jaw all but collapsed. Grief showed itself fully to a mind which had been keeping it at bay. I knew because I felt it as well and then watched without comment as her eyes opened and focused on some inner picture, and then clouded with tears. Her breathing became uneven and she fought to regain control by holding a deep, deep breath, eventually letting it go in a ragged, chest heaving sigh.

I let the palm of one hand rest on her brow then, and cupped the base of her skull with the other.

Touch speaks an age old message of love and healing understood by hurt and damaged children everywhere. I hoped that holding her like this would speak the same gentle message to Diana, and to the hurting child within her. I lifted her head gently, replaced the pillow beneath it, then moved away. She needed time *alone* to deal with the intense emotions released by the work on her face. By moving and working a different area I would give her that space.

With fresh oil and cream on my hands I started working her left foot and ankle, allowing an element of briskness and firmness into my touch, to draw her back from the thoughts and images her feelings would undoubtedly have thrown into her mind. Automatically I put a little extra pressure to those areas of tight muscle or their attachments to bone where there would be some discomfort – just to let her know I was aware of them. Gradually, I felt her becoming more present and conscious of her situation as I worked her legs with the even rhythms of Swedish massage and the other gentle manipulations I'd made my repertoire over the years.

I wanted to help this woman, and I really would have preferred some time to establish a relationship, which would enable me to understand what was at the root of the feelings I'd just tapped into. But I had discovered the shadow of a pressing problem, and I needed to respond to it before this massage was over.

I worked her hands and arms almost on autopilot, only half engaged. There was little more to be learned from them, they just confirmed what I already knew. Work to her neck and shoulders gave me some further insights. I became convinced the tightness and tension there resulted from her distressed emotional state and the dark and painful thoughts which went with it. Perhaps the weakness in the neck muscles was associated with a stomach acid imbalance but that too was a sign of stress for some people.

I gave her shoulder a gentle squeeze of encouragement as I walked around the head of the table to stand beside her again.

'Turn over now so I can work on your back.'

She turned while I adjusted the bath sheet to keep her covered.

Now I tuned again into the natural tempo of her body rhythms and worked her back for a few minutes using soothing movements to restore some relaxation and calm within her. Work to the large muscle groups of the legs and hips confirmed there was a lack of good vibrant tone in the muscles throughout most of her body despite her regular exercise, and increased my concerns about her sense of defeat.

This was not the first time I had experienced what the body of a human being feels like when they are close to giving up on life.

I returned my attention to her back and shoulders and set about dismantling the layers of knotted and stiff muscles I felt there. As I loosened her shoulder blades and upper spine I considered the emotions I commonly associated with the muscles and structure on which I was working, and wondered how to deal with the situation revealed to me.

I concluded the massage by placing my hands on the main energy points along her limbs, back and head until I felt the flow between them gradually balance into a streaming from the soles of her feet to the top of her head. The overall level of her intrinsic energy was low and in places it took several minutes until I felt it flowing strongly. By the time I had finished I was sure the grim thoughts and feelings released in her had been largely replaced by a sense of well-being. She felt relatively at peace beneath my hands.

Just as well, I thought to myself. I wanted her to be as receptive as possible before I shared what I needed to impart. Her relaxed state would enable her mind to be more open to what I wanted to say.

She lay on her front now with her face turned away from me so I was unable to see her expression. But in that position she had a degree of privacy in which to listen. I began to speak again, calmly and quietly.

'You can change what's happening for you, if you want to,' I said.

She remained quiet for a few moments. Then answered 'What do you mean?'

Her body had tensed, and I replied without words at first, just resting my hand gently on her back over her heart area – the chakra from which love of self and others emanates.

I continued. 'I don't know the reasons you feel so angry and so desperately sad but I do know you've reached a point where you've all but given up. You don't seem to want to be here in the world much any more. I want you to know no matter how bad things look to you your situation can change if you are willing to try. I'll help you and show you how, if you want me to.'

While I spoke my hand continued to rest over her heart. Caring touch reaches deep aspects of the mind, beyond conscious doubts and concern, moving them aside, allowing more hopeful thoughts and feelings to be recognised.

I allowed my mind to fill with compassion and understanding and waited quietly hoping my state of mind would, as I knew it could, transfer to her. I hoped it would be enough, but this was her wake-up call.

First she had to discover a ray of hope in her inner world of despair. She had to decide for herself that there might be a worthwhile future for her. She had to believe that change was possible...and she had to take a step towards it.

'Tell me what I'd have to do,' she said quietly.

With that she crossed an invisible barrier and began to travel the path of her life in a different way. Diana would never be the same again. Her few simple words were an outward sign she believed she had a chance to create a future different from the bleak outlook she was living with now.

I started talking again then – telling her about how her body and mind acted together and what had enabled me to know what she was feeling, how her body responded to her thoughts and emotions.

'These muscles here,' I touched the tops of her shoulders, 'are associated with fear and anxiety when you get stressed. These here,' I touched between her shoulder blades, 'are related to anger, either at yourself or others, or at a situation you're in.'

I continued to speak about how her feelings were becoming locked into her body, affecting her health and life by imposing limitations, on how her body could function and what her mind could imagine. I talked about her surprising lack of muscle tone and strength given the amount of swimming and exercise she did, and related it to the feeling of helplessness. I spoke of her neck muscles and their connection with disturbed or imbalanced stomach acid and learned then about her bulimia.

'I make myself sick,' she said in a hushed and shameful voice.

I knew what she meant instantly but this was not the time to address it nor for Diana to dwell on something she obviously felt distressed by. I had learned long ago not to feel any judgement when a client begins to share their deepest self. Instead I explained how we all have ways of coping with life's challenges and how being sick was probably one of hers. And I talked about how together we could look for better ways to help her cope and to feel better.

I talked about how she could work with her body and mind to understand herself better and to discover a new path of her own choosing.

'Make no mistake, if you do this you will change and as a result people will change how they act towards you and your life will change. The important thing is to make the changes you want.'

She nodded, still looking down.

Later, as I drove away, I speculated on what might have brought her to her current situation. I knew the answers would be somewhere within her – concealed, probably even from herself, in her mind and body. I didn't know if I had convinced her. Certainly she had been amazed by how much I was able to learn from just one massage. I would have to wait and see if she really understood that she could change herself and her life.

I hoped I would have the chance to guide her. I knew if I did it would involve Diana changing much she took for granted about herself. Only a transformation in her self-belief would suffice to resolve the distress and discomfort she was experiencing.

It never occurred to me that I would not be able to help, nor that there might be anyone better placed than I was at that moment to show her what needed to be done. Neither did I consider that the past hour might be the start of something momentous, with implications far beyond simply helping a client to become healthier and happier.

Diana did not make a new appointment before I left. Royals don't do that. Others make their requests for them so there can be no direct rejection if they are refused.

Anyway, Christmas was coming, she was due to go away for the holidays, and I preferred that new clients had time to think for a while after their first treatment, to be sure they want to continue. If they call me back it is because they are ready to commit.

Of course, I pondered, *I might not see her again, except on TV or in the papers.*

I wondered what I would do if she did not make another appointment. I was convinced if she did not resolve the conflict within her then sooner or later something bad would happen but all that was for another day. Right then I had another client to see.

PART ONE

WOMAN IN THE MAKING

One comes to be
of just such stuff as that
on which the mind is set.

Upanishads

If we had been able, you and I, to visit Diana Spencer on the day before her nineteenth birthday, I could have shown you so many clues pointing to what would happen to her later in her life.

The date was 30 June 1980, it was a Monday. For a year Diana has been living in her own London flat at 60 Coleherne Court with a few flatmates. She is revelling in the sense of freedom it gives her after years of feeling she had little influence over her own life. Maybe we would have caught her looking from her window onto the South Kensington streets, waiting for her friends to come home, her mind drifting as it often did when she was alone.

Inevitably her thoughts turn to marriage and her own longing to be a wife and mother with a beautiful home to take care of. A sage trained in oriental mysteries would not have been surprised at the strength of her need to be married. Her face and body, rounded, not angular, soft, slightly plump, even without her penchant for eating well, and her blue eyes all speak of Water being dominant within her. Water is the most powerful of the four essential elements which influence our make-up and is about motherhood, home and emotions.

Undercurrents of deep and intense feelings do indeed ebb and flow beneath her apparently calm exterior. We see her emotions in her face as subtle shifts of expression when she responds to the thoughts in her mind. She does not experience her feelings like the other elements. She understands the world and her place in it by the way she feels. Her opposites, the stocky, chunky, solid Earth elements are uncomfortable when emotions flood them and get in the way of their hands-on, I-can-fix-it practical approach to life. They find fixing emotions difficult. And the Fire elements, short, slim, fast of mind and tongue find surges of deep emotion dampen their intuitive reactions to life's mysteries; they lose their way in feelings. Our oriental sage might wonder if Diana's height indicated the influence of Air and the intellectual, thinking nature of those who are tall and slim. But most of the time her thinking is more like daydreaming in which she explores what she is feeling. In any case Air elements are also made uncomfortable by emotions, sentiment has nothing to offer in place of their methodical reasoning.

Together the other types make up the majority and they do not understand that Diana possesses an emotional pallet far broader and more immediately useful to her than theirs is to them. Hers has tone and nuance and vibrancy. She uses her feelings as inner guides to what she should do. She experiences some as friends to be welcomed and celebrated. Others are enemies whose devastating effects on her normally calm inner world, both body and mind, must be avoided at almost any cost or diminished as much as possible. What she has never questioned is whether her feelings are the best arbiter for the choices she makes, and now they are about to lead her astray.

During her childhood years Diana's particular emotional make-up and needs were not well catered for. None of her family is a Water element, nor are they similar in many other ways. So Diana's complex nature was not understood by those who had most influence over her, and in any case they were distracted by troubles of their own. The result for Diana now is a collection of poor notions about who she is, and what she is capable of, and what she must do to be in the world. She started collecting her ideas early.

Who am I? Where am I? What must I do? What can I do? Over millennia human beings have evolved so we each must have our own answers to these questions in order to be able to function in the world. A time tested process which starts as soon as we are born provides us with the answers we need.

Helpless newborns suck in information continuously and indiscriminately and lay it down in their brains, each child building piece by piece from their own experiences a personal inner reality that will become a frame of reference for how to survive throughout their life. So young that they do not have the ability to understand what they are absorbing, except like or dislike, feels good or feels bad, feels safe or threatening, every occurrence is experienced as personal, with no wider context than their own self-centred need. They learn with rapid instinct what it is that gets them what they need. What they need are food, shelter and human contact, preferably loving, caring human contact. All they have to get these essentials at the beginning of their life is the limited repertoire of a baby's expressions and sounds.

A smile gets a smile. Crying or smiling or laughing or screaming may get comfort or food or contact. The equations are simple and work quite well to enable them to start building their essential ideas about themselves and their world and how the two interact. Every experience is a lesson in how to get what is needed from those who can provide it, how to cope in a challenging world. Every lesson is laid down in the cells and chemistry of their brain, in their mind. Every lesson forms a point of reference in the belief system they will use in the future. This is nature's way for us all. With luck negative and unhelpful ideas are exceeded by positive and the end result is constructive and useful – for Diana it was not to be.

The baby Diana incorporated her daily myriad of lessons like any other infant and, like other infants she was naturally sensitive to how those she relied upon were feeling. Their states of mind governed their responses when they were with her and directly influenced how safe she felt in turn. In her home the atmosphere was frequently disturbed by ongoing conflict between her parents. Diana sensed the agitation of the people around her. She felt the effects of their discomfort deeply as uncertainty and distress of her own and had no way to understand it properly. Instead she stored away unintended impressions that the people upon whom she relied for her needs often reacted to her with distress and that her world was not a place she enjoyed being in. From these impressions, and their associated feelings of fear, frustration and anger, she began to build the early foundations of her own personal inner reality.

The reasons for the discord in her parents' marriage are easily understood and had little to do with the Diana directly. Amongst them was their desperate desire, after producing two daughters, for a son and heir to the Spencer dynasty. Then there were the anguish and recriminations which followed the death, only 10 hours after his birth, of their first son John. Add nineteen months of anxious anticipation until Diana was born and their disappointment at the arrival of yet another girl and it can be no surprise that their marriage was strained. Three more years of arguments and reproach followed however, three crucial years of impact on Diana's emotional and psychological development, until her brother Charles finally emerged to become the focus of his parent's hopes. But even his birth was unable to heal the rift which had developed by then. The damage was done and their relationship continued to deteriorate noisily and bitterly around Diana and her three siblings.

No one around Diana then could realise how this environment was affecting her, or for that matter her brother and sisters. The custom in Diana's family home was to separate the children from their parents until the youngsters were old enough to join father and mother for meals and social occasions. The difficulties in their marriage had merely resulted in her undemonstrative parents becoming even more physically and emotionally remote and so distracted by their own troubles that they were unable to offer her what she needed. Her sisters at six and three years older, and her brother at three years younger, were all separated from Diana by that chasm of years and rivalry experienced by siblings who are undergoing different stages of development and growth at an almost frightening pace. One of her strongest beliefs now is that her parents would have been happier if she had been a boy. Not far away must be the unspoken question "How would things have worked out differently for them and her if she had been?" To Diana's earliest impressions were added the notions that she was not wanted nor cared about, was not worthy of love, and her sense of exclusion increased.

A virtual procession of nannies of varying temperaments and abilities was engaged to care for Diana and the other Spencer children during their childhoods. The constantly changing parade added to a long period of instability in Diana's young life as they came and went. The kinder nannies balanced somewhat, with their gentleness and attention, the dark impressions the infant Diana was acquiring and she was sometimes as cheerful as any child can be, but her mood was unpredictable. Even the most loving of her carers was unable to give her enough care to fill the need for attention, love and affection her volatile family life was leaving unsatisfied. Some nannies, by their harshness and insensitivity added to her growing conviction that the world was an uncertain and painful place and she was of little importance to anyone in it and she began to be wary of people and their motives. None of those with responsibility for her at that time was able to help her develop an image of herself positive and powerful enough to ensure a future less troubled than the one she would experience as an adult.

At age five she started school, or as the sensitive Diana would have experienced it, was sent away from home each day. During her sixth year her sisters were sent to boarding school, her parent's marriage ended acrimoniously and her mother left the family home to live in London. Diana's recollection of that experience is still clear and harrowing, as are her memories of her brother's tearful distress, her own feeling of helplessness that she could not comfort him and weekend trips to visit her distraught mother in London. All these events fixed more firmly in her mind her sense of insecurity and a firm conviction of her own low self-worth. She constantly sought validation from those around her and became increasingly sensitive to any signs of abandonment or rejection, or betrayal.

Plenty of those signs came during the next few years, at least in her perception. Shuttle diplomacy was called for when she and her little brother tried to share their affection between their separated then divorced parents. Diana felt the pressure of trying to do the right thing all the time, and experienced guilt and misery when she believed she got it wrong. Her confidence about the place she held in her mother's affections was dented after she remarried a couple of months before Diana's seventh birthday. Her early impressions that the world was one of uncertainty and painful emotions, and that she was helpless in it, were confirmed when at the age of nine Diana was sent away to boarding school and when her beloved grandmother was taken from her by a brain tumour just two years later. At about the same time, her mother and stepfather moved to a remote area of Scotland making Diana's frequent holidays with them more difficult. It was another example of how her life was not within her control.

A year after her grandmother's death Diana was moved to a new boarding school. Eighteen months on the whole family moved from the home she had always known, to Althorp, the stately pile they were to occupy as a result of the death of her grandfather, the then Earl Spencer, and her father's accession to the title. Add that a new woman, Raine, Countess of Dartmouth, was making increasingly frequent appearances in her father's life to distract his attention and attract an instant dislike from Diana and her siblings, and Diana had firmly established a collection of unpleasant conclusions about herself and the world by her mid teens. When her father married Raine in the same year that the seventeen year old Diana was sent away to finishing school in Switzerland her unhappy conclusions developed into a solid belief system that would not only shape her future for years to come but end up shaking a royal dynasty to its core.

You would not think, looking at her now, two years on from those events that such destructive force could lay beneath her happy and fun loving exterior. But Diana is operating with a mental frame of reference, which is constructed of poor material. From her experiences to date have come opinions about herself and the world, and a collection of beliefs and assumptions and thoughts about how they interact, that is only workable up to a point. In fact, deep down her inner reality is a shaky construction of low self-esteem and poor self-image that gives rise to an intense desire to be acknowledged and appreciated. She still needs attention and affection to make up for the feelings she is unimportant and uncared for. She is still constantly on the lookout for signs others are rejecting her. Her awareness of what they say, their tone of voice and even how they look at her, is highly developed and constantly on alert. She still believes that ultimately her world is an insecure place from which she must anticipate painful experiences and abrupt and life altering changes she feels helpless and unable to influence. She yearns for the stability of a home and family of her own. She longs for the control they will bring her.

Except for her desire for marriage, home and family Diana is not aware of all this. She does not know what is deep in her own mind. Not many of us do, especially at eighteen. The beliefs she has about herself and the world are her reality and seem to her perfectly satisfactory. She is who she is in a world the way she sees it and everything seems better than it has ever been. From her perspective it can only get better. She does not know what is really driving how she acts and the choices she makes. She does not recognise the collection of habits and automatic responses her inner mind has programmed into her everyday life so she can experience the certainty she has now.

During infancy her inner ideas about herself and her world have evolved and adapted to provide automatic responses to new situations, so she could continue to get what she needed. A smile or facial expression became the right smile or expression to the right person to get the particular thing she wanted, food, comfort or a touch, and a rudimentary influence over her environment.

Words and then speech, movements and then mobility, gave a wider repertoire of reactions and more certainty that her needs would be met. To food, shelter and human contact were added other symbols representing the love, caring and acceptance she desperately needed. Pets, toys but above all more attention and their attendant emotions of pleasure and satisfaction were Diana's rewards if she was successful; distress and displeasure were the result if she failed. Successful responses were validated and reinforced, unsuccessful ones were abandoned rapidly. The little girl was learning how to avoid the discomfort of unpleasant feelings. As she became older her mental images of herself and the world were refined by increasing amounts of information. From them she assimilated more sophisticated strategies for gaining what she needed and producing outcomes which were more predictable. As Diana grew her collection of available responses to her world grew and so naturally did her desire for more influence over her life, for nothing could make her life more predictable and secure than if she controlled it herself. Alongside her desire for more control however was the conflicting awareness that it was her father who provided a degree of security and stability in her live. We call this acquisition of competing notions growing up.

Other children with different personalities would have built different inner concepts of themselves from similar circumstances and learned different strategies as a result. Some would have become more self sufficient. Perhaps they would have become more physical, more robust and noisy with their demands, and more philosophical in dealing with their disappointments than Diana. Her Water element nature and belief in her own lack of worth inhibited her from overt and direct strategies for getting her way from the adults around her. She acquired the more subtle manipulations of little-girl charm and emotional blackmail, telling her father for instance that if he loved her he would not send her away to school. She acquired the habit of exaggerating the truth to make people think better of her or to avoid responsibility for her bad behaviour or mistakes. Her displeasure when she failed to achieve her ends would be apparent in petulance and an unflattering pout.

At home Diana did learn to compete vigorously with her siblings for a place in the family pecking order, and for attention from her father when he was in the house. Even still deep waters can be moved to storms. The Spencer household was described later as a turbulent environment, one in which there was constant infighting as there usually is in a large family. Faced by any perceived aggressor form outside however, the family united against the common enemy. From this environment Diana assumed that forceful behaviour when she was challenged by her peer group was usual, if not necessary, and that families stuck together when they had to. For a while, when she started at boarding school, Diana showed signs of being too confrontational with her new classmates when she felt aggrieved by their behaviour towards her. She soon discovered that bullying gained only resentment and unpopularity and so became quieter and learned better ways to gain appreciation.

While she slowly learned what did and did not work for her Diana acquired the early beginnings of something she would express much later in her life to devastating effect. If she believed she was unjustly treated Diana became angry and consumed by a need to right the wrong done to her. In her early life she exercised her grievances with pranks on her nannies. Later she was forced to curb her emotions and came to hate the feeling of being forced into situations she did not like. As an adult she would not be so restrained.

Now though she is coping quite well. Her inner frame of reference is represented by an effective repertoire of habitual reactions and behaviour suited to most situations. Her customary facial expressions, body posture and gestures are signs of her inner beliefs and unconsciously suited to prompting the responses she needs from others. The choices she makes and the language she uses are still driven by her deep needs but she has learned what will work to have them met.

Even her eating pattern has been influenced by the same unconscious mind set which underpins all her choices and provides her with relief from anxiety. She has always had what is described as a good appetite. At school she could always be relied upon to accept a dare which involved eating large amounts, perhaps in a forerunner of using eating as a way of achieving the feelings she wanted, in those cases acceptance and admiration. Almost certainly she experimented with vomiting up food after she had overeaten, behaviour which when it becomes compulsive is associated with bulimia nervosa. That her appetite for a long time has been for substantial amounts of high carbohydrate foods is significant. Her father even kept a note she sent him from school asking for *Big choc. cake, ginger biscuits, Twiglets.*

Carbohydrates in quantity tend to relieve feelings of anger, sadness and frustration although the penalties for such a diet are cravings for repeated doses of the sugary, starch-laden foods, depression if meals are not frequent enough, fluid retention in the short term and accumulations of body fat in the long. Diana is unaware that for a long time she has been using her food as a way of relieving her emotional symptoms or that her body is being adversely affected. What she is aware of is how much better she feels when she eats.

Fairly recently other influences have become evident, developing and defining parts of her inner self and providing her with more and better strategies with which to get what she needs and avoid her dark and painful emotions. With more knowledge she might have noticed a pattern developing but she does not. She does not realise that for several years natural aspects of her personality have been emerging to help her fulfil some of her needs and diminish her uncomfortable feelings, even offering other means of gaining pleasure and satisfaction.

From quite early on in her life Diana felt naturally drawn to those who were in need or suffering, she genuinely cared how they were feeling and wanted to help. Her beloved grandmother was a wonderful role model in this, being well known for her good works. Diana learned much from her but she had her own powerful natural impulse to assist. Her childhood recollections include how she comforted her little brother when family arguments upset him. Others recall how she shopped and tidied and chatted every week with an elderly lady as part of her school's 'good citizenship' program, and how she crawled on her hands and knees to interact with hyperactive children unconcerned about her clothes and the dusty floor. She had an easy instinct for connecting with touch and the right words and gave herself readily to caring work even then, and she received much in return.

From every unbidden exchange in which she gave affection and comfort, she received affection and comfort in return. She was tactile with a distinct need for direct human contact. Opportunities to offer caring touch became opportunities to accept caring touch she did not get elsewhere in her life. When adults praised her sensitivity to the needs of others and her ability to help them, she was validated as an individual and her need for acknowledgement and appreciation was fulfilled. Without thought, and quite automatically, these affirming experiences were added to her still developing inner reality and became reference points of self-esteem and evidence about how she could be happy and satisfied in the world. They were also a means for gaining control over her inner and outer worlds.

Now helping others makes Diana feel good. Significantly it enables her to avoid feeling bad and it has helped her develop notions of self worth to counter somewhat the darker aspects of her make-up. Helping is a natural outlet for her caring nature and an extension of her instinct for mothering.

Diana has been collecting families she could mother since she was very young. She had families of pets, families of stuffed toys and dolls and when her mother left home she mothered and cared and fussed around her brother and father and even her sisters. She used her sensitivity to other's feelings to offer comfort and caring to family, staff and anyone else who came into her orbit. She honed her talents without realising they were in any way unusually developed for a girl of her age. She was just being herself. In return she received more of what she needed. Her father was more aware she was around, and he appreciated the love she gave him and offered more affection in return. Her self-appointed mothering gave her a role that imposed some stability in her life. She tidied and cleaned and took care of her clothes despite having paid staff available to take care of these things. Tidying gave her a sense of control. Later she even referred to remaining chaste as "staying tidy".

During the past couple of years since she left school, her unconscious preference for mothering roles has resulted in work as a domestic cleaner for well to do families and even for her elder sister. She has been a nanny and baby sat and now teaches in a kindergarten.

Her most recent family consists of the group of girl friends who share her apartment, and for whom, according to the sign on her bedroom door, she is the self-declared "Chief Chick". She is the landlady. She mothers them. She makes the rules, organises the rotas for cleaning and washing up. She always has a duster in her hand, is always tidying up.

The past year in her London apartment has been the happiest time of her life. She has a place, and a distinct identity which very nearly fits her most optimistic vision of herself. She has a sense of control over her own life at last. She is accepted and appreciated by those around her, her "family", for her thoughtful caring ways. She enjoys the warm companionship of her few close and trusted friends who provide a level of emotional connection she has not experienced before. With them she can chatter about their boyfriends or talk seriously about the personal details of life and love, and what it will be like to be married with children, during make-do meals at home, or out to a friend's dinner party or a small restaurant.

She enjoys as well the frequent comings and goings of what seems like a tribe of well bred and fairly well heeled young men. They are part of the family: boys of her brother's ilk, Old Etonian and army officer types she has known or known of for years. She has met many of them often, during family skiing holidays in the famous resorts her peer group enjoy, or at society occasions such as house parties, dinners or shooting parties to which the young Diana was asked, sometimes just to make up the numbers. Now they often drop in to see her and her friends and share tea and company and occasional friendly dates. Diana irons shirts for them and offers tips on how to dress, mothering again.

In this family Diana is comfortable enough to come out of her shell and join in the boisterous fun and childish pranks, laughing more than she can remember laughing before. This is her way. Naturally reticent, wary and low in self-confidence, especially in new surroundings and amid groups of strangers, she can become bubbly and witty and fun to be with when she feels sufficiently at ease. And yet sometimes she needs peace and quiet, as if the excitement becomes too much and she needs solitude.

Ever since she can remember there have been times when she was desperate to be alone, to have time to take stock and to think and feel inside what was happening. She has always loved playing with her dolls by herself or sitting quietly reading. Time out with her little pets, stroking their furry warm bodies would calm her. At school, during the day she was boisterous and noisy, enjoying the skylarking with her classmates, but then she used to come down in the night and dance for hours alone in the assembly hall. At Althorp, the imposing Spencer family seat, she would find private places in which to practise in solitude, discovering solace and inner peace in the flowing ballet movements. Later she would describe how, "It always released tremendous tension in my head."

Now she enjoys being here alone in her own space. She tidies and dusts and reads, mostly romantic novels, and she enjoys watching television on her own or listening to classical music. Ballet and opera are favourites.

Crowded noisy pubs and discos make her feel uncomfortable, she doesn't know why. Most people seem to have a good time at them and she has tried, but she prefers it quieter and with fewer people so she can connect and talk, have a proper conversation about things which matter. In rowdier places she will be vibrant and bubbly for a while and then her vitality will just fizzle out like a candle being extinguished. Her senses seem to become overwhelmed and she will feel herself withdrawing and becoming detached, more observer than participant in events. She will begin to struggle and long to get away to be on her own. Maybe there is something wrong with her. When Diana was a child she often thought there might be. She felt different to everyone else then and still does. Later she would describe the feeling of alienation in her own words "I always felt very detached from everyone else. I knew I was going somewhere different, that I was in the wrong shell."

She uses her time alone to consider her life and what it might bring but Diana's thinking is not intellectual in the accepted sense. She has no patience with logic and linear reasoning, which might answer why she is not gifted academically. She believes what has become family lore that she is simply dim and now it is a constant confirmation of her low sense of self-worth. She always wanted her father to be proud of her and feels badly about her failure to achieve at school even now. During the concerted campaign she raised to be brought home from the Swiss finishing school she detested she even sent him a newspaper clipping describing academic failures who had developed qualities in later life and achieved unexpected success. In the future she will describe her time at school: "I wasn't any good at anything. I felt hopeless, a drop out." She ignores the awards she gained at sport and her facility for English, she disregards her interest in history and art, albeit she was unable to reproduce it in exams, and she discounts the recognition she received for her caring nature and ability to help others. As a child she had already acquired the habit of denigrating herself. It would affect her badly later in life.

Diana's style of thinking is more of a reverie, a kind of daydreaming during which she muses on people, events and ideas to discover how they make her feel and what her intuition tells her about them. She is seeking guidance, the inner guidance she has come to rely on. She is capable of intense focus on matters that are important to her but her lack of ability for what most people regard as useful thinking makes life difficult for her. Diana is seen as a romantic with little to offer in discussions of weighty matters. So she often stays quiet, holding back her contributions, partly because she now has a deep rooted sense that she has nothing worth offering anyway, partly because she has acquired a habit of acquiescing to the opinions of others she regards as more intelligent than herself, and partly because she is not very articulate.

Lucid, eloquent speaking has never been her style and it simply does not go with how her mind works. She is much more capable of expressing herself in writing. Even then what she writes will lack the linear character of logic and reasoning. She finds it hard to put things into the words in the way most people seem to. She expresses her ideas intuitively and in terms of feelings and personal issues. Sadly these are not given much weight by those who more easily offer their views. Highly sensitive to the possibility of being wounded Diana rarely speaks in what most people consider normal discourse, except in conversations with close friends she trusts will not hurt her with ridicule and hurtful words, because she has learned the result will be she ends up feeling unintelligent, unimportant and misunderstood as usual. When she was young even her quicker witted little brother discovered he was able to wound his sister with sharp retorts when he could not compete with her physical dominance in their sibling squabbles. But she has a good sense of humour and when she does speak about things she is interested in she is witty and funny. She uses clipped sentences and pithy one-liners, albeit often picked up from other people like her older sister whose sharper facility with words she admires.

All her life Diana has come across as shy and withdrawn to those who do not know her well or with whom she does not feel at ease. The adults around her when she was young describe her as quiet, unassuming, dependable and young for her age. She is assumed to be a dreamer without the ability to consider important matters and offer conclusions of consequence. This misunderstanding of her will soon cause considerable problems for those without her intuitive awareness of people and feelings.

Diana has always been very perceptive but lately her sensitivity to others has become a stronger and more accurate empathy. Her abilities are accentuated by her own experiences of what it feels like to be misunderstood and discounted. She just knows how people are feeling and senses what they need. In the past, as far back as her childhood she had the ability. There is a story of one Christmas when Diana was in her mid teens. She gave one of her Christmas presents to a grumpy and belligerent night watchman who intimidated most of those around him. She recognised his loneliness. After she met Prince Charles for the first time a couple of years ago, at an Althorp shooting party she described him as "...a sad man".

For some time now Diana's thoughts have been about how to help more people. Her caring for others is developing into a strong desire to help make the world a better place. She already has a sense of destiny, an indistinct feeling she has been placed in the world to do something special, but now that feeling is coming into clearer focus for her. Perhaps it is because her new contentment relieves her of the constant distraction of her darker, more limiting beliefs about herself, and she has the time for a bigger picture.

Perhaps it is because she comes from a noble family. Behind her are centuries of history and noblesse oblige. She has been brought up with a sense of responsibility to the less fortunate. The inclination to help and protect the disadvantaged has been instilled in her since she was a small child, reinforcing what was already a powerful part of her own nature. She has always been a carer and now is beginning to believe she will help many more people in future. She just doesn't know how yet.

Despite her happiness now Diana still feels unfulfilled. When she speaks of a destiny to help others and making the world better even her closest friends seem bewildered and she senses it. She recognises that even they do not fully understand her and it intensifies her conviction that she is different and increases her longing to be understood and to feel she truly belongs somewhere.

A modern psychologist would tell us that Diana is different and that few people are likely to be able to understand her very well, and certainly not to the degree she craves. Our expert would point out that she embodies perfectly normal personality traits in a combination which is shared by less than 3% of women and only about 1.5% of men. But we can tell her none of this today and so she remains with her sense of alienation still nagging at her.

We cannot tell her that she is normal. We cannot explain she has the typical psychological profile for someone moderately introverted with extremely well developed feelings, nor that her type is very perceptive about people and situations. People like Diana do experience their world inwardly and intensely and allows their emotions and intuition to guide them. Like them Diana naturally has a powerful sense of destiny and constantly evaluates herself and her every experience for how it fits into the bigger picture of life and what it can show her about how to help humanity and make the world a better place. She is genuinely caring and wants her life and work to mean something and to be of value. She tends to keep her conclusions and emotions inside and rarely shares them with others. She is an idealist with a strong sense of personal values.

Our oriental mystic could confirm for Diana that the powerful sense she has for what is just or not, is also a natural trait of the Water element she is, especially when it involves their children and home. We cannot tell her that either, but she will learn it soon enough.

A few of our expert's observations might not seem accurate. We could look at her and wonder where is the much vaunted need for her work to have meaning and value? She cleans other people's homes and cares for their children. The answer is that the degree to which these characteristics are expressed depends on other factors from Diana's upbringing and other natural characteristics she has. To Diana, the Water element who needs a family and home, nothing can have more meaning and value. A neuro-linguistic programming (NLP) expert would identify that of the three primary modes human beings use for interacting with the world Diana's most dominant is kinesthetic rather than visual or auditory. That is she would prefer to use touch in as many situations as she can rather than her eyes or ears to gain information about her environment.

Touch, that is to say hugging, holding and stroking rather than just a brief shaking of hands, is not an acceptable way to get to know someone in Britain or many other countries. Yet Diana is a physical individual and touch is her primary sense for connecting with those she meets in it and without it she is operating at a disadvantage. During the past few years her kinaesthetic awareness has developed. In the past her tactile nature has been expressed through contact, first with her pets then as a part of her caring for the elderly or disadvantaged. Dancing and riding when she was young developed her physicality more. At school her physical side was marked by proficiency in dance, swimming, diving, netball and tennis. Now she works with children and is admired for how happy she is to romp on the floor with them. Her family was unable to give her the loving touching she needed when she was young. Now she is often compensated, but she still feels a deep need for human contact.

That she is of a tactile nature might answer in part why some people see her as shy or experience her as withdrawn or aloof. They will notice she is not comfortable looking directly at them, especially if they themselves are visual dominant; or that she does not seem to be listening to them, especially if they happen to use speech most to communicate.

Diana is only just coming up to nineteen. The most distressing parts of her inner self have not gone away, they have just been made more comfortable by time and the acquiring of unconscious coping strategies. Mostly the problematic aspects of her make-up have been suppressed or side stepped. In some cases, especially as she has entered womanhood, newer facets of her personality have been added or emphasised. The many deep rooted needs her inner reality gives rise to are only partially fulfilled in her current circumstances. Despite experiencing more contentment than ever before she still feels different to everyone else and misunderstood. In her quiet moments of introspection she wants something more than her present life is offering. She longs to be part of something that will provide her with all the love, recognition and understanding she craves. She wants for once and all to be accepted and included totally and unconditionally.

The notion of marriage has been attracting her more and more lately. Her youngest sister Jane is already married and her big sister Sarah is attracting a lot of attention and will surely succumb soon to one or other of her titled and wealthy suitors. Diana has not been oblivious to the constant stream of handsome young men, quite a few of whom seem to really like her and she enjoys the attention they pay her and the way they make her feel noticed and special, feelings she has craved since childhood.

Except for hazy ideas of working with children and doing good works Diana has given little thought to a specific career. The assumption, natural amongst her group, has always been she will pass her time in pursuits which will bring in a small income until Mr Right came along. She will then marry and have children and support his career and be taken care of and, do more unspecified good works. Diana has been perfectly happy with this vision of her future because it fits so well with her instinctive Water element nature and lack of ambition. It fits too with the belief she has acquired that she can do nothing else.

Now, reflecting quietly alone and guided by her feelings and intuition, she concludes that she must have a home of her own with a husband and family to take care of. Marriage is her answer and her future.

Diana the emotions-driven Water element, the intuitive, feeling, home maker and carer is certain she knows the best future she can possibly have. If she operated by reasoning then her logic would be indisputable, to herself at least. She adores children, she longs for children of her own. She knows about looking after people, she has done it since a child. She feels their emotions, knows what to do to care for them. She knows she can care for a husband and family and be everything they need. She has proven she can look after a home and children. Marriage to a man she loves will provide everything she could possibly need. She has more certainty about this than anything else ever before.

The reasons for her certainty would not convince many others but she does convince herself, because her judgement is made through the filter of her own inner reality, her own construct of self-limiting beliefs and needs. No matter how much she might try to weigh pros and cons objectively they will only be able to provide her with an answer that is distorted by a perspective which craves affection, acknowledgement, caring and stability and sees herself as largely ineffective in directing her own destiny. So the perfect scenario she imagines is one in which she is chosen by someone who wants her to be his wife and mother to his children.

She is certain as well that she knows about love. Love is what she feels for the people she cares about. Love in marriage will be about caring for someone enough to give herself completely to them. Love is about being taken care of as well as taking care of someone. Diana has elevated the idea of love until it is seen as an almost spiritual experience which can be expressed through physical and emotional intimacy, marriage and family. She wants to feel what it is like to be truly loved and cared for. She has no doubts she will love the man she marries, and their children, and be loved in return.

Her notions of romantic love however have not been shaped by experience but have come mostly from reading about it. Diana's preferred genre is romantic fiction of the kind written by authors like Barbara Cartland who is a favourite and who, in a twist of irony, is mother to Diana's nemesis, now stepmother, Raine. To the emotions-driven but emotionally inexperienced and impressionable Diana tales of passion and idyllic love, with titles like *Kiss the Moonlight*, *The Love Pirate* and *Love in the Clouds* speak to strengthen her existing beliefs of how things could be, should be between a man and woman in love.

Gossiping with her more worldly friends has given her an earthier perspective. She has not yet experienced the sensual, sexual side of herself but her tactile nature and needs make her curious and she is drawn to the physical intimacy of marriage almost as much as she is to the emotional intimacy it will give her. Her desire to be touched and to touch with love will be met by her husband on that too she is clear.

Her clarity has no firm basis in anything at all except the untested beliefs which underpin her imagination. Her experiences of men up to now have been limited to the young chaps who visit her flat. A few clearly have romantic inclinations towards the well bred and increasingly good-looking Diana but for anything beyond simple friendship she is unapproachable. In any case she is not seriously attracted to any of them as a prospective husband. They are on another wavelength to the one she occupies most of the time. They rarely have time to talk and share their thoughts and feelings about the things she finds interesting, and they are always in a hurry. Diana cannot imagine them providing her with the idyllic peace filled home, the safe and secure environment she sees in her dreams of the future.

Not a very young man then, so who? Her father has been her most prominent male role model for most of her life. He was 12 years older than her mother when they married. From him Diana recognises qualities she wants in a husband and some she does not. Hugs and touch feature prominently in her list, and attention as well as generosity. Her stepfather who she admires and likes has also played a part in the making of her inner image of what her own husband should be like. The pages of her romantic fantasies and late night chats with girlfriends have played their parts in building her ideal vision of an older man, mature, strong, brave, thoughtful, caring, quiet, and imagines happy-ever-after. Perhaps it will be an ambassador or a successful businessman with social connections. She sees herself as provider of support and love to a man who will take care of her and be father to their children.

Her thoughts meander to who might be a candidate. Now she has ruled out those of similar age to herself there are not many she can think of. She knows Prince Andrew quite well from her childhood, but he is only a year older than she is, so too young, and anyway he has just joined the Navy so won't be around much. David, Viscount Linley, was also a childhood friend, but he is the same age. She is sure she has met plenty of eligible men at dinner and house parties, shoots and the like over the last couple of years but she has not got to know any of them at all. There never seems to be time to sit and talk properly and she was rather young and chubby so they probably would not be interested. Her face drops at the thought.

She remembers seeing Prince Charles at a shoot at Althorp when she was sixteen, when he looked sad. She blushes with embarrassment thinking about how she was on that occasion: "...podgy, no make-up, an unsmart lady but I made a lot of noise and he seemed to like that". He did smile at her at the dinner her father gave for him that weekend and asked Diana to show him the collection in the picture gallery. She smiles as she remembers how miffed Sarah was. Well big sister was flavour of the month then so it was probably a good thing she left them alone. Later he said Diana was jolly and amusing. She is thinner now and feels much more grown up.

Charles is definitely older than she is by about 12 years, the same difference as between her father and mother. He is very active. He rides, plays polo, shoots, fishes and flies aeroplanes and helicopters. They even call him "Action Man" in the papers sometimes she has noticed.

She met him again when she was invited to his thirtieth birthday party she recalls, but that was a year and a half ago. As her thoughts drift Diana remembers she saw Charles last February at the royal house party at Sandringham. She smiles at the memory of how grown up she felt. The incongruity in that thought, that she did not see herself as a grown up just four months ago and now she is considering marriage, passes her by. Instead she ponders on the invitation she has accepted to a weekend house party at the de Pass' home in Petworth next month. She chuckles to herself when she remembers their son Philip telling her that Prince Charles will be there and saying she was "a young blood" and that "she might like him".

Would he, could he really become interested in her? She glances at herself in a mirror. She is too fat. But men are attracted to her, she knows, so she can't be that ugly. And she can be fun and sparky if she knows the people.

Her idle reverie continues to explore the fantasy taking shape in her mind. Actually he could be perfect. What if she fell in love with him, wouldn't that be romantic? What if he fell in love with her? He needs taking care of she is certain of that from the few brief times she has seen him up close. She has no doubt she can take care of him. Make a home for him, somewhere for him to come back to after his busy days. He is quiet like she is and they both love classical music she seems to remember, opera especially. I hope he likes ballet. The daydream takes on momentum. We would make a good team, a good family. She just knows she could take care of him.

Would he want children? Diana considers... She is one of four, five if you count poor John; Charles is also one of four so he is used to a big family. Her eyebrows shoot up with the sudden realisation her son will become King. Wow! The silent word forms on her lips.

He is sophisticated and smart she knows from dinner that time. She is so dim, not smart at all. Her shoulders droop momentarily before she pushes the thought aside and with it the painful feelings which threaten to cascade in behind it.

Quickly her thoughts plunge on into new territory. Marriage to him would give her a chance to be of some use, not like now. How much more useful can a woman be than to be married to a king, well someone who will be King anyway. Maybe that is her destiny to help the future King of England. Her father would be pleased as well, he would have to be proud of her then.

If Charles did become interested it would have to be marriage and nothing but, her chin and bottom lip firm up in determination. She does not want to just be another conquest like her sister and all the others. She frowns. He is experienced in that department, but then she brightens she would love him so much he would not need anyone else, ever. She giggles as an adolescent preoccupation drifts into her mind, what would he be like in bed?

She would have to think hard though, about marrying him. They would not be able to get divorced, but that means she would never have to go through what her mother did. The example of her parents' marriage is not one she intends to repeat, she is determined about that. Anyway she would know if it was the right thing, she can rely on her intuition. She wonders what his birth sign is and how compatible they are and makes a mental note to look it up, and wipes her duster over the window sill again.

There she is then, Diana Spencer with a background more difficult than some young women but no more difficult than most, inexperienced, immature and normal. Out of the co-incidence of her innate personality, and attitudes she has acquired about herself during her childhood, has come a workable self-identity she now holds in her unconscious. Her self-identity is the person she believes herself to be, the one who now feels safest and most comfortable, most in control. She is the carer and wife-in-waiting. She is Diana the happy and mischievous, some would say shallow, young woman, the Sloane Ranger who laughs a lot and is enjoying her freedom.

Behind the mask of her self-identity is an entire raft of insecurities and unfulfilled needs hidden within walls of preferred thoughts supported by behaviour and choices that together have created for her the life she now feels so good about. She has created a home and a family of sorts to take care of and people around her, all of which fit with the person she is comfortable being. She has a quiet and controlled lifestyle with time for solitude and little to disturb her emotions. She has children to care for, albeit not her own.

Her self-identity does not stop her frailties from influencing her life and her body. Diana Spencer is tall and not very slim. She is by no means an Amazon but she could be taller. She rarely lifts her head, as if she is trying to disguise her height. Striking blue eyes therefore glimpse from under a fringe of fair hair, part demure, part puzzled. She does not realise that her stooped, eyes-down posture derives from her sense of low self-esteem, nor that the way she holds herself reinforces the feeling. She has a quality of vulnerability about her. She does not recognise the darker parts of her inner world, her wariness of people, her low self-worth, her need for validation from those she allows close. They are still parts of her make-up however, and they have a purpose to serve. They express themselves in her unconscious choices and actions.

Driven by the unrecognised aspects of her own inner self Diana has made choices which now mean she does not have to deal with too many people during her days, nor does she have to be the centre of attention except with the children she teaches. She has created a life in which she is able to avoid feelings she is uncomfortable with, feelings like guilt, criticism and rejection, because she does not take risks. She does not allow herself relationships which might challenge her beliefs and teach her who she really is and how fragile is her notion of what will make her happy.

Diana Spencer believes implicitly that a loving partner will take care of her, and that home and marriage will provide her with purpose and fulfilment and control of her future. So far she has avoided the possibility of disappointment by developing a distinct idea, a model of what her partner must be like. Up to now she has not met him. Her inner self has now brought that deficiency in her life to the forefront of her mind and her intentions. She wants to meet her ideal man and soon, and she believes she will. Her belief will soon be tested in the real world. She is unaware of a paradox in her thinking. Diana believes that marriage will give her control and certainty about her future, but she also believes that her husband will take care of her. The two ideas are not guaranteed to be compatible.

Diana Spencer is almost nineteen years of age but going on about fifteen in almost every respect except for the one which will change her life in a few weeks from now. She has the world at her feet. She is investing her imagination and emotions in visions of a perfect marriage and her daydreams are gravitating towards a prince who will be king. She is impatient and excited about a future she is certain will bring her happiness, and she has a mind-set which is about to carry her step by painful step into her worst nightmare.

PART TWO

LIFE TRAP

Until you make the unconscious conscious,
it will direct your life and you will call it fate.
C.G. Jung

Diana's first step towards disaster took place shortly after her nineteenth birthday in the seemingly innocuous setting of a barbecue party in the grounds of a country house in Petworth, West Sussex. Here there occurred a common misunderstanding, the sort of thing which happens to everyone at some time or another. Its repercussions however would bring a royal dynasty almost to its knees, touch the hearts of millions and cause the two souls involved immense pain in the years which followed.

On a bale of hay Diana and Prince Charles sat in polite and companionable conversation while the party flowed around them. Charles mentioned the death of his beloved uncle Lord Louis Mountbatten, the first anniversary of which would be the following month. Diana responded with her instinctive compassion. The interaction which followed started them on the path which would bring them to marriage and for them both the opposite of almost every expectation they had of that institution.

Of all the possible topics about which Prince Charles could have spoken he chose one which drew from Diana that part of her self-identity which excelled and in which she was most confident. Almost any other would have shown up the unbridgeable differences that existed between them. If he had spoken of fishing, or hunting, or organic farming or architecture she would have been hard pressed to hold his attention for more than a minute, but he did not. His subject was associated with bereavement and it was one she responded to with a genuine and compassionate sensitivity for his sorrow. Her desire to ease his distress was as instinctive to her as breathing. Her own experiences of loss added weight to her sentiments when she responded by telling him how she had seen his sadness when he walked up the aisle of Westminster Abbey at his uncle's funeral service, how tragic it had seemed to her.

She may have touched him gently with her hand while she touched him with her words. It would have been natural for her to do so. For Charles, Prince of the Realm, to have someone reach out to him, especially a young and pretty woman, was not common and he was deeply moved that she seemed to sense his deepest need and told him he should be with someone who could look after him. In that brief encounter there arose between them an immediate bond of empathy they both failed to understand entirely.

Their conversation continued through the evening and during it Charles saw a Diana who seemed older than her years, a young woman who was open and natural and easy to talk to, sensitive to his inner feelings and not afraid to express directly her concerns for him. What he could not know was that her apparent maturity and confidence were qualities isolated to that part of her make-up he had unwittingly engaged, the instinctive carer. They were not ones she was likely to be able to replicate in other situations.

Diana experienced a deep connection of a kind she had not had before with any man. She knew artifice and insincerity and Charles exhibited none of these when he talked with her. He was attentive to what she said and appreciated her comments, he acknowledged her and was easy to talk to. She felt validated by their conversation and sensed he was warmed by her genuine concern for him. What she was unconscious of, so occupied was she in responding to him, was the complexity of his personality and life beyond the topic they were sharing. She simply saw and reacted to the sad and lonely man she sat with then and his needs at that moment and was flattered by his animated response to her, if a little bewildered by its intensity.

There was between them as well that magic chemistry which facilitates the attraction of one human being to another, non-verbal communication. Without knowing it, Diana's demeanour, facial expression, tone of voice and choice of words made evident the wife-in-waiting part of her self-identity. Quite unconsciously she was sending subliminal signals to Charles' below his conscious radar that she was available and he was tuned in to receive them. We call it romance.

Prince Charles' impression that Diana might make a suitable wife was already taking shape by the time he left for Buckingham Palace the following day. He had formed an affection for her during their chat and just a few weeks later was hinting to close friends that he had found his future Queen. Diana was certainly attracted to Charles. The impression she gained of him during their deep discussion reinforced her daydream that he could be the future husband she had been waiting for.

Charles had experienced only one side of Diana's complex personality and make-up but it was a part he found very attractive because it met his own needs so well. His vision from then on was unconsciously filtered by what he wanted to see in her. She had seen only a small part of the complex character that was Prince Charles and hardly anything of the life she would be expected to share if they married. She was drawn instinctively to that in him which fit her own dreams and expectation. She blinded herself to signs that he was not the one and closed her ears to any doubts. Their instant mutual attraction was based on a co-incidence of partial personalities and a strong compatibility between their unconscious needs. It would be sustained by unsupported assumptions and their unspoken expectations. With objective analysis the signs of their incompatibility in the wider context should have been clear, but romance does not give itself to objective analysis and their particular road to torment was paved with the best of intentions on both sides

The few weeks which followed did not alter their first impressions but served to reinforce them. Charles asked Diana and her grandmother as chaperone, to accompany him to a performance of Verdi's Requiem at the Royal Albert Hall and then to supper at Buckingham Palace. Very soon afterwards, in early August, he invited her to share a day with him and his companions on the royal yacht *Britannia* during Cowes Week. At times, in conversations with close friends, he made the case for Diana to be his wife mentioning fondly the qualities he noticed in her, her warmth, her openness, how much she enjoyed country life and her family background. He invited her to join him at Balmoral for the annual highland games weekend at Braemar at the beginning of September.

Charles found Diana to be straightforward, warm-hearted and uncomplicated. When he considered her suitability as a future wife he would have been able to add to her catalogue of virtues that she was of a quiet and thoughtful disposition which seemed similar to his own. She was demure and compliant compared to other women he had considered marrying. Certainly she was young and lacked experience, but that was a good thing according to the advice he had from his late uncle Lord

Mountbatten. She could be taught more easily the role she would have to take on when they married.

She was as well the daughter of one of the oldest noble families in England. Her background had brought her into close proximity to the royal lifestyle so she would surely have some idea of what to expect. When he had seen her at shoots and house parties she was jolly and funny and those occasions would have reinforced his assumption that she was used to the country life he enjoyed so much himself. He knew of no tarnished past, no previous loves that would damage the monarchy or his own reputation, some discreet enquiries would confirm it. She seemed perfectly suited to be the companion, wife and consort he had been seeking for so long.

He could tell she genuinely cared for him by her obvious concern for his wellbeing whenever they were together and he was becoming fonder of her all the time. He did not love her yet, he knew what love was and had not expected to be able to replicate it immediately in his marriage anyway, but Diana seemed similar in some ways to his closest friend and the love of his life, Camilla Parker-Bowles. They were both warm and affectionate women who appeared to have the same sense of knowing when he needed a kind word or sympathy and they were both completely supportive of him. He felt sure his fondness for Diana would deepen into genuine love. He had not thought to be so lucky that he would find someone suitable and for whom he had genuine feelings. His hopes seemed to have been answered.

His friends, family and advisors agreed with his assessment, or at least most of them said they did and he made it clear he did not welcome the very few contrary opinions which were offered. Pressured by a weight of duty and years of expectation that had begun to distress him, even the press were demanding to know when he would marry, Charles saw his path ahead clearly enough to start upon it by paying even more attention to Diana.

In her turn Diana had built, from unlikely sources, a mental image of an ideal husband and if the past few weeks were anything to go by its flesh and blood counterpart was appearing in the form of Prince Charles. The scenario she had so carelessly fantasised for them now seemed possible, even likely. She was sure he needed her. She was in love with him. He obviously felt a strong attraction to her. She wanted to be married to him so they could love and take care of each other and share the idyllic home and children for which she yearned. She was clear about herself and looked forward to the future which seemed to be opening before her. It just remained for her to show she was perfect for him.

Less than four months had passed since the two of them had sat together at Petworth and spoken at such length. In that time Diana had been invited by Charles to social occasions where she could meet his friends and some of his family. At the dinner parties, weekend house parties, hunts and shoots she was invited, to the teenage Diana behaved impeccably. She did not make any serious gaffs and impressed almost all of his friends and family. She was seen as sweet natured and utterly smitten by Charles, in love, happy in his company and game for anything his rural lifestyle offered. She seemed to enjoy the trappings of his royal life with enthusiasm and without pretension and had that refreshing "good-egg" eagerness to be part of everything so typical of archetypal well bred English schoolgirl types. Below the surface however things were not as jolly as they seemed and it was during this early period of their relationship that the ground was set for many future problems. It is difficult to imagine there could have been any other outcome.

In the complex workings of the mind every event can take on significance beyond its apparent importance at the time. Events and experiences are seen through a filter of self perception and compared unconsciously to past situations stored in the mind. It is part of the process by which we produce responses and reactions without needing to think about every choice we make and everything we do. If the essential qualities of a new experience match closely enough something from our early life which provided us with a significant conclusion about ourselves, it awakens those conclusions and the emotions connected with them, so we will react appropriately. If the new event is similar to ones which gave us pleasure before, we anticipate more pleasure and respond accordingly. If a situation resonates to past events which made us feel uncomfortable and unhappy, we feel the echoes of our past unpleasant emotions and respond to the new circumstances in whatever way we can to avoid a repeat of our distress. Diana was about to feel the echoes of her oldest doubts and fears.

In the context of a romance this unconscious comparison of new experiences with old plays out as a weighing of good points against bad. In our awareness we experience the resulting thoughts and feelings adding weight to one side or the other as we try to answer the question "is this the person for me?"

Charles' courtship of Diana, for courtship it surely was by now, was already confusing her and she did not respond well to uncertainty. It brought echoes of past insecurities and vulnerabilities – she needed certainty. The nineteen year old, very young Diana, whose make-up did not contain a solid base of confidence or a facility for self-validation, needed a great deal of reassurance from Charles to counter her doubts. She felt unable to seek it. In the early days she was intimidated by his position and the situations in which she was a newcomer amongst his familiar friends. In any case she and Charles did not have as much contact as she would have liked. Her perception that they spent a lot of time apart for a couple supposedly in love and for whom marriage was at least on the cards added weight to her emerging concerns about what importance she might have to the man she loved.

When Diana and Charles were together, protocol and the need for decorum demanded it was in the company of others and in circumstances far removed from the peaceful, private surroundings which suited her personality best. She was reassured by her friends, whose advice ranged over all matters pertaining to royal etiquette, dress code, fashion, social decorum and how to conduct a romance and it was romantic and exotic and exciting to be invited into his life, but she confessed herself "terrified" at times and "intimidated" by the situations she was having to deal with.

Diana had never wanted materially. Her family homes were impressive even by aristocratic standards and she had visited Sandringham occasionally as a child, so by the time she was nineteen she had some experience of the lavish surroundings Prince Charles took for granted. In these new circumstances however she often felt out of her depth, especially in the royal households of Balmoral and Sandringham. Her preference for a relaxed and familiar environment she could control was challenged by the customs associated with being in grand houses. She enjoyed the opportunities to share weekends and evenings with Charles but would have been grateful when she could return to her London apartment to take stock and dream of the lovely home she would make for her husband.

Charles' friends were strangers to her, considerably older and of an outlook suited more to the deep thinking Prince of Wales, lover of country pursuits, than the young emotional Diana recently of South Kensington. They were mostly landed gentry with backgrounds in politics and business and connections with the monarchy and British establishment, these were all well bred movers and shakers. Diana's introverted nature meant that she was made anxious by having to meet groups of people she did not know. Her young age and low self-esteem meant she did not enjoy spending time with anyone who did not share her interests. Her sense of low self-worth meant she was uncomfortable with those who were worldlier than she. They made her feel immature and un-smart, but she wanted to make a good impression on them and her aristocratic upbringing enabled her to deal with most situations well enough.

She enjoyed conversations with some of the ladies, several of whom seemed happy to discuss the kind of topics she enjoyed and from them she was able to learn a lot about Charles and what he liked. She would have discovered he was in tune with her in those things which mattered most to her. His friends were well aware how much delight he took in children and that he longed for a family of his own. They knew he wanted a peaceful and rural family life away from the intrusion of the press and as a respite from his duties. Diana gained some reassurance from their conversations, but later professed herself suspicious about how much they seemed to know of matters she and Charles discussed together in private.

The people who were strangers to Diana were to Charles friends, with whom he shared great affection and trust. Diana found it difficult to accept their easy familiarity with the man she wanted to herself so they could talk and share precious time quietly together but she kept her frustration inside. In hindsight it is possible to see how the situation she was in began to play on her emotions and raise in her the relentless self doubt and frailties she harboured deep inside.

The self-identity with which Diana was most comfortable, the caring wife-in-waiting, had only recently been established and did not fit into these new surroundings. While Charles was attracted to the caring, concerned side of her nature, her style of connecting, by offering and expecting to discuss personal matters was not suited to conversations with the men and women the Prince called his friends. Her catalogue of unconscious coping strategies and the behavioral patterns that usually gained her the responses she needed to feel comfortable in the environments she was used to, did not always work here. Conduct shaped so she could fit in with the youthful peer group which surrounded her at Coleherne Court, or the other teachers and kids at the kindergarten, seemed gauche and immature in these circumstances.

Unconsciously Diana settled into being that of herself which was as close as she could manage to what made her feel most secure. She was ingénue, enthusiastic tomboy and devoted girlfriend with marriage on her mind. In the early days and especially when Charles was in attendance to give her reassurance, her relaxed persona was genuine and endearing. Later, as her inner resources were stretched, it was a facade behind which she struggled to remain calm.

Her naturally sensitive and introspective nature recognised she was uncomfortable in these surroundings with these people but she did not have the knowledge with which to examine what she felt and come to any conclusions other than ones she had made when she was much younger. There started to open up in Diana the well of self-doubt and self-criticism she had only recently been able to cover up. Her consequent need to be acknowledged and appreciated and her craving for approval were not adequately fulfilled by the behaviour of the unsuspecting Prince Charles or his friends. She began to turn her disturbing feelings away from herself by projecting judgements onto those she saw as the cause of her distress. It is something we all tend to do to avoid facing our own self-doubts. We cope with them by finding flaws in those we blame for our discomfort. Had Diana been more self-knowing and confident she would have looked to what made her feel the way she did rather than make the judgements she now made.

Diana accepted that she should address Charles as "sir" because of his position but his friends seemed to enjoy a familiarity with him she did not and it troubled her sense of self-worth. She judged their attention towards him as fawning, sycophantic and not good for him, but she was unable to recognise the incongruities within her observations. Diana, who for most of her nineteen years had longed for admiration and appreciation and sought the validation of others, saw flattery and pretension in the behaviour of friends Charles had trusted for years when they listened to his opinions and praised him. She was convinced she knew what was best for the 32 year old Prince although she had known him for only a few months.

Implicit in her judgements, besides reducing her esteem for her rivals in order to unconsciously bolster her own self-worth, was a subtle diminishing of the regard she held for Prince Charles. Unknowingly she had begun to slowly change her view of him as a sad and lonely man to someone who needed her to protect him from being badly treated because he was unable to take care of himself. She questioned also what she saw as his friends' over friendly attitude towards herself and she was suspicious of their motives. Given how sensitive she was to the demeanour of those around her there may have been some accuracy in her observations, but Diana's personality and make-up gave them a significance which caused her considerable discomfort when she fretted over them later on her own.

One particular issue gave Diana more concern than all the others. She was already suspicious about the exact nature of the friendship between Charles and Camilla Parker-Bowles from the few social occasions they had all attended together. Camilla was remarkably free with helpful advice about how to handle the Prince and she seemed to have made a special mission out of befriending Diana who was rapidly gaining the impression Camilla knew a good deal more about Diana's private conversations and times with Charles than was comfortable. When Diana asked him about his past girlfriends Charles admitted they were mostly married woman he considered it "safe" to be with. She probably wondered how safe Camilla was. That she and Charles were able to discuss such a sensitive issue speaks well of their relationship then, but it seems Diana did not wonder about the attitude to marriage which was implied by Charles' response. We all tend to blind ourselves to what we do not want to see, perhaps Diana did then. Her misgivings about Camilla also inferred unconscious suspicions about Charles and a further subtle erosion of her trust in him.

When Diana and Charles were able to spend time together they basked in mutual affection. He was attentive and caring, all she wanted from him, all she needed from him to validate her position in his life. He fished, he rode his horses, they picnicked and they laughed. It was "wonderful" and the reassurance she gained temporarily pushed her doubts to the back of her mind. Diana needed these experiences to confirm his feelings for her and hers for him. She extracted comfort from their all too brief and infrequent times together and with it maintained the dream of how perfect it would be when they were married.

Even more stress was added to Diana's life by increasing press attention. Journalists sense stories like sharks sense blood in the water; very little is needed to attract them to a scene which might offer good feeding. Whispers that Prince Charles might be casting his romantic eye towards Lady Diana Spencer had already reached them and they set off in pursuit of evidence and the weighty pay packet that would go with it.

Tabloid photographers had almost recorded a confirmed sighting at Balmoral when they managed to sneak close enough for a photograph while Charles was fishing the River Dee with his new girlfriend in attendance. Diana spotted them and they were foiled by the clever way she handled the situation, managing only indistinct pictures of a girl unidentifiable in an all-concealing scarf and flat cap. The incident gained her Charles' approval and added another small piece of evidence to their beliefs that they were suited to each other. She sensed his frustration with the intrusion and sympathised, but her quick witted evasion did not gain her much time. Soon packs of newshounds and photographers identified her as the Prince's new love interest and were laying siege to her flat and the kindergarten where she worked. They followed her whenever she emerged and pestered her with tape recorders and cameras for quotes and photographs. They phoned at all times of the day and night hoping for something new that would provide the next headline and increased circulation figures. They spoke to her friends, flat mates and neighbours and almost certainly, unless they acted quite out of character, offered money for stories.

However cynical their campaign, these were very shrewd and experienced hacks. Their instincts told them that if Charles was serious about this young woman, her lineage and background indicated she could well be the future Queen and that was a very important and valuable story. They redoubled their efforts to get the confirmation they needed and over the next few months, as Charles' courtship of her progressed, Diana suffered. Her naturally introverted and introspective nature and the stress she was already under from her new social life, made it essential that she find time and space for peace and solitude so she could take everything in and reflect. With her apartment besieged and her detested stepmother Raine now in residence at her family home Althorp she had nowhere to properly stop and contemplate what was happening. Her emotional and physical discomfort increased as a result.

To one of Diana's disposition the initial novelty and excitement of press interest soon became a heavy burden. This was another situation she was completely unprepared for and her mixed emotions were difficult to deal with. Since childhood she had always longed for attention and wanted to be acknowledged for some special achievement or quality. The clamour for stories and pictures was seductive, after all Prince Charles was courting her, no one else. She was also nervous. She had her sister's experience of a couple of years before to warn what happened when a royal girlfriend spoke to the media about her relationship with Charles. An indiscreet comment in a magazine interview had resulted in Sarah being quickly sidelined, her own romance with Charles at an end.

Diana found the desperate antics of the press infuriating at times and farcical at others, but she learned quickly. Aided and abetted by her trusted friends she went to extraordinary lengths to avoid the tenacious pack by swapping cars, jumping on and off buses, dashing through shops and dropping suitcases from her window on makeshift ropes lest her weekends with Charles became public knowledge. At times it must have seemed like St. Trinian's meets the Keystone Cops as one bizarre incident followed another. When she was caught in the open and they snapped and scribbled and filmed around her, she treated them politely, with a disarming good humour and shy grace that softened even their hard hearts a little, but gave nothing away in response to their barrages of questions. Not an indiscreet remark, not a single hint to whet their appetites. Her silence however did not stop Fleet Street's finest from speculating.

Without help from any other quarter but her equally inexperienced friends Diana was poised in public and distressed in private while she suffered lies, innuendo and intrusions in the newspapers, until the situation became so bad the Palace was forced to act. Diana was not an accredited member of the royal family and the machinery which surrounded and protected them from the press would not normally have become involved unless she was, but a particularly scurrilous story, alleging Diana had spent a night with Charles on the royal train, called into question the reputations of Diana and Prince Charles and persuaded the Queen to authorise her press secretary to demand its retraction. Diana's mother wrote to *The Times* to berate Fleet Street's editors for harassing her daughter and a contingent of Members of Parliament tabled a motion in the House of Commons "deploring" her treatment by the media. Their efforts did little to slow down the media juggernaut which rather than following Charles' and Diana's developing romance was now pushing it along.

An attempt was made to relieve the pressure she was under when a press photo call was negotiated in exchange for some breathing space. Diana feeling manipulated posed unhappily with two borrowed children. She was devastated when she saw the resulting, now infamous, pictures in the following day's papers. The sun shone brightly from behind her, straight through the fine fabric of the skirt she was wearing, making it almost transparent. The expert photographers must have known precisely what they were doing. Diana felt betrayed. She took little consolation from Charles' amused reaction to the photos and his comment that her legs were even more spectacular than he had thought, though he wondered why she had to show them to everyone. It was an early upset in the love-hate relationship she would have with the press in the coming years when her media profile would become critical to how Diana's life would unfold.

Determined media attention can be unnerving to even the most experienced celebrity. Diana, calm and modest during her jousts with the press pack, gave way to her intense and confused emotions in private. Each new experience resulted in laughter or tears, anger or anxiety as she railed, cried, or giggled over the stories that appeared in print each day. When she gave voice to her thoughts about this period in her life she would say, "The whole thing got out of control" and "I couldn't cope." But she did cope. She acquired that most necessary of all celebrity trappings, a public face behind which she could hide her private thoughts and she discovered the press has its uses.

The press supplies a product familiar to unwary celebrities who have fallen under its influence. It was probably at this time that Diana tasted it for the first time. Her self-esteem was low, her energy was depleted by strain and her emotions were in turmoil. Her deeply ingrained need for encouragement and appreciation was unsatisfied by anything she received from Prince Charles. Black ink on white paper, lauding her virtues and demanding if and when Charles would make Lady Di his bride, offered an antidote to her distress. No matter she will have scorned the idea aloud, it became exciting to look through the newspapers each day for signs that she was understood, or seen to be attractive or valued. She found she experienced a tangible lift in mood and energy when her search uncovered a good story, as it invariably did in those early days. The buzz was magnified by the realisation that millions of people all over the country would discover nice things about her. The chemicals of the mind are as powerful as caffeine or cocaine and just as addictive. Diana acquired a craving for good press which was to increase and last as long as her craving for reassurance and that would be a very long time.

Charles was under pressure as well, from the media, which represented their view of the public's great desire to see Charles and Diana married; from his own conscience which required that he consider all the implications of his proposed marriage before asking Diana to wed and from his father the Duke of Edinburgh. Charles knew there was an entire range of constitutional, social and practical considerations to be weighed against his own desire to be happily settled and he was still unsure that Diana was suitable. The decision for him was monumental and could not be taken lightly from any viewpoint. It took him time to get the advice he needed and to consider. He wanted to be sure he was doing the right thing by his country and his family as well as by himself and Diana. In the end however it was his father's strongly worded advice that Charles be mindful of the effect it would have on Diana's reputation if he should delay too long, that finally made up his mind to commit to the marriage if she would have him.

During his deliberations the strain on Diana was more than Charles could have imagined. He was of a different background and personality. He was also a busy man. He had a full calendar of royal duties which sometimes took him abroad, he had his career in the armed forces and he enjoyed social engagements to which Diana was not invited. He was away from her a good deal of the time. Without contact to reassure her, she fretted about when she would see him again and what he was doing. When they were able to spend some time together it was easier and they sustained the connection they had formed at their first encounter. Diana was still as attentive and caring and now sympathetic of his workload. He was convinced by her obvious desire to be with him and devoted his attention to her. She was convinced by his consideration and kindness and concern for her wellbeing.

When they were apart however Diana's deep rooted self-doubts emerged and her mind struggled to make sense of a situation for which she had no practiced response. Her safe haven at Coleherne Court still filled her with laughter, but tears were in evidence as well now and it was no longer the place of freedom and fun it had been. She was fast losing all the control she had achieved over her life. She had committed her dreams for the future to the relationship with Charles, the outcome of which was still not certain. In her confusion her self-belief plummeted and her still adolescent imagination and intense emotions began working feverishly as she reviewed over and again the times they had spent together, seeking signs that would bring her some comfort.

Far from finding reassurance she succeeded only in reinforcing her doubts and in reducing her confidence further. About whether Charles' feelings for her were genuine, he was not acting the way she expected he would. He was not always available to talk when she needed him and he didn't seem to miss her as much as she missed him. Did he have to be away so often? Then there were his lady friends from the past, women who were much more sophisticated than she was. He was not very sympathetic about the constant harassment she was getting from the press. He seemed more concerned because Camilla had a few reporters outside her house.

What was Camilla to him? Diana's suspicion had grown and the relationship between Charles and Camilla was becoming the main issue that eroded her self-confidence. In September 1980 the gossip columnist of the *Daily Mail* had written that Diana had been approved as a future wife for Charles by his friend Camilla. Diana's sensitivity about her possible rival became a state of hyper-vigilance for any small sign that should concern her. The possibility that Charles might prefer Camilla raised the spectre of rejection in Diana's mind. Her distrust of other friends of his had increased. When she was with them she was on guard for the slightest indication, a less than direct gaze, a laugh not quite genuine, a tone of voice perhaps superior or condescending, which might confirm her sense that they thought her not good enough. Of course she found such signs, anyone would have, and she did not have the solid core of self-assurance required to dismiss them as the normal background noise of powerful egos fuelled by good wine and good living. Instead they touched deeply to her ingrained negative beliefs about herself and echoed past painful emotions she associated with her lack of worth.

She worried as well about her suitability for the role she would be expected to play in Charles' life if they were married. She knew she could do wife, mother and home but she was not so sure about the rest. She was not sure what the rest involved but was afraid to ask lest she seemed dim or ungrateful and no-one seemed to think it necessary to tell her. Perhaps they did not think it was worth it.

Diana's doubts were natural perhaps for any inexperienced teenage girl contemplating marriage to a man 13 years her senior, let alone one being wooed by a future king. To one of her emotional sensitivity and poor self-esteem they were agonisingly painful. Awake late into the night, agitated, heart lurching with each dismaying thought, nerves on edge, muscles tense, her digestion disturbed she tried to identify what it was she was sure of. Always she came down on the certainty that she would make a perfect wife and homemaker for Charles and their children and rationalised that it would be fine if they were married and she could take care of him all the time in the ways she wanted and assumed he expected. She was desperate for him to ask her so she could start creating a home where she had some control and knew what to do. Her comforting conclusions inexorably led her deeper into the trap she was creating for herself.

On 6 February 1981 at Windsor Castle Prince Charles asked Diana to marry him and later professed himself surprised that she gave her answer so quickly. He was delighted that, after a nervous giggle, she said "yes please". Both sets of parents expressed themselves pleased. Diana and Charles were extremely happy and probably relieved that the decision was made. Diana's brother commented on how blissfully happy, "ecstatic", his sister was when he saw her a while later. Prince Charles, in conversations and correspondence, told his closest friends how lucky he felt and how nice it was to be able to share things with someone who loved him and how amazed he was that she agreed to have him. Clearly neither of them saw any way of going back now, nor any need for it.

The engagement did not provide the release from doubt Diana might have hoped. In her nineteen years she had lived in three homes and been sent away to three different boarding schools, each move had stirred the deep sense of insecurity she felt about her world. Now she was on the move again. On the evening of the 23 February, the day before her engagement was due to be officially announced, she was moved from her own apartment with its memories of laughter and being free and in control of her life, the happiest place she had known, to Clarence House. A few days later, after the announcement was made and the happy couple had posed before the world's press, Diana moved again to an apartment made available for her use at Buckingham Palace. Here she would stay for just five months, arranging what she needed for the wedding. She found the environment disturbing with its inhospitable, overly grand rooms, its formal servants and its stuffy courtiers who seemed unapproachable compared to the more informal staff she had been used to in her childhood homes. Protocol and pecking priorities were the order of the day here and it was not her style.

A series of incidents, each fairly small but significant in the perception Diana was building in her mind further magnified her concerns. During a ten day secluded holiday with her mother and stepfather in Australia, shortly after Charles had asked her to marry him, she received only one phone call from him and that had come after she had tried unsuccessfully to reach him. Flowers she received from him when she returned to the country did not contain a personal message. She had seen him on only one occasion, briefly, before official duties again took him away from her to Wales. The police bodyguard who had escorted her to Clarence House when she left Coleherne Court blithely informed her she should make the most of her freedom that evening because it would be her last. There had been no-one to greet her at Clarence House except the staff. On her bed she had found a note from Camilla, written two days before the engagement was announced, asking her to lunch. Charles left her again on an official tour which lasted well over a month to Australia, New Zealand, Venezuela and the USA.

Camilla seemed very interested in how often Diana might hunt when she moved into Highgrove the country home she would share with Charles. The teenager's concerns about how she was regarded by her future husband and her suspicions about Camilla upset Diana's equilibrium even more. Her emotions, always shifting in response to what was happening to her, always the touchstone for what she should do, began to fluctuate more rapidly than ever.

Preparing for the wedding and her future made Diana feel as if she had more control of events and at times she was able to be confident and assured. She was living the dream and preparing for the role she wanted most, wife and mother to a man she loved and she was doing it in grand style. She had the attention and admiration of her mother and sisters and the envy of her friends who visited her at Buckingham Palace and helped her with her arrangements. She was building up the wardrobe of clothes she would need with the assistance of fashion experts from *Vogue* magazine who guided her towards top designers for the wedding dress and formal clothes she would need afterwards. From jean bedecked tomboy who often wore billowing frocks and borrowed smart clothes from friends for dinner parties and country house weekends, she now had to become a Princess with clothes suited to every public occasion, sometimes changing outfits several times a day. The downside to all this female fun was that Diana's self-image took on a greater significance for her than at any time in her past.

The press invariably commented on what she was wearing and how she looked in their articles, their reports were naturally accompanied by photographs. Prince Charles, on putting his arm around her on one occasion jokingly referred to her chubby figure and he had been less than complimentary about the black dress with the plunging neckline she wore to their first official function together. The resulting tiff had not helped her self-confidence. A roundabout of fittings and photo sessions brought her perception of herself into stark focus and her naturally low self-esteem made her worry what people thought about her and whether she was good enough. She wanted to be perfect for her future husband and everyone who now had new expectations of her where they once had few.

During the five months leading up to the wedding Diana lost five inches from around her waist. Her dance teacher had given her private lessons at the palace, she dieted and she discovered bulimia nervosa. Her figure became thin and angular to the point where it caused comment in the press and concern to her friends. Her mood and emotions began to fluctuate wildly to the extent they were alarming Prince Charles and his staff. The dance classes would have toned up her muscles as her body slimmed down and would have helped ease the stress she was feeling. The shift in her diet would not have been so helpful. Altering an eating pattern based on a spontaneous grazing of foods mostly rich in sugar and starches would have been likely to cause mood swings and emotional disturbances, like coming off a drug. Withdrawal from these feel-good foods will have allowed her negative thoughts and feelings to push into an awareness already troubled by the suspicions and doubts which had developed in the months preceding the engagement. The bulimia had more pernicious effects to add and they would affect her for years to come.

Her time at Buckingham Palace before the wedding was difficult for Diana. She found the atmosphere there emotionally cold and remote and it did little to help her regain any equilibrium, still rocked as she was by the changes her life had undergone in the past few months. She needed solitude to be able to reflect and assimilate her feeling but could only benefit from it in a safe environment where she was in control and where she was relaxed and happy. At Buckingham Palace she felt her control on her life slipping inexorably away. She had few opportunities to step back and reflect and she was desperate for reassurance. Her friends were not always available and her increasingly erratic emotions and intense need for his time and attention were making it difficult for Charles to respond as she wanted.

Diana began to feel uncomfortable with the team of secretaries, private, assistant and unofficial, Charles had provided to help her acclimatise. Domestic staff had been a feature of Diana's life since childhood but the environments at her family homes, Park House, then Althorp, had been much more informal than Buckingham Palace. At age nineteen she was not skillful at directing servants or office personnel and in any case they were not her employees but her husband's. But they were all supportive and wanted very much to help their employer's wife-to-be. Needing validation and assurance as always Diana reached out, in the way she automatically did with everyone, to connect with the staff on a personal level, showing warmth and genuine concern for their wellbeing while being apologetic for the work she caused them. She successfully drew them into the informal associations she preferred and away from the more staid ways they were used to. When, however, she asked them about her future husband's relationship with Camilla they, not surprisingly, were evasive which fuelled her fears even more. When she went against their advice and opened a parcel sent for Charles and found inside a bracelet clearly intended as a gift from him to Camilla Diana was distraught. An angry exchange with Charles did not dissuade him from his decision to deliver the gift personally and Diana's trust in her fiancée suffered another blow. She also realised where the true loyalties of his staff lay and began to be suspicious of their motives as well. They in turn were bewildered at her behaviour and found it difficult to strike a tone in their dealings with her that would please her. In the royal setting, where a bottom lip which wanted to quiver with emotion was reason to make the upper even stiffer, it was unnerving to everyone. Certainly none of those around Charles at the time had the personality or make-up to understand her distress or her needs

Diana was under enormous stress, from the demands of her new position and from her own demands on herself. She was increasingly affected by self-doubt and her suspicions about the people around her now ranged from Charles and his friends and courtiers to those closer to her. She once quipped, only half ironically, that she supposed the pianist who played at her dance lessons in Buckingham Palace would "now go direct to Fleet Street." She found Charles' insistence that Camilla would not be a part of his life after he and Diana were married difficult to believe and she was becoming indignant at Charles for his behaviour towards her.

Diana's sense of what was right and just was being challenged by Charles' standpoint. Her reaction was typical of the personality type she was when they are under duress and their personal values are confronted. She became very critical of those around her and began finding fault in small things. Her innately caring nature gave way to a bossy manner which ignored others' feelings and she felt an obsessive need to eat and exercise. A simple word or small gesture from Charles could placate her in an instant, inwardly and outwardly, but the respite did not last in face of an onslaught of new situations and renewed doubts. Naturally good natured and inclined to avoid conflict, her own behaviour upset Diana as much as it did those around her. When she recalled it in private she was ashamed of herself and racked with guilt, at the same time as she was angry at Charles and his staff. With her feelings out of control and her world becoming chaotic Diana found what seemed like a solution in bulimia.

She was in any case feeling a familiar desire to overeat as a response to her stress. She had been well known amongst her peers from her early teens for gorging large helpings of food and found that doing so made her feel comforted. Bulimia made some sort of sense as a way to lose her chubbiness.

That she should get rid of any food she ate by vomiting it up before it could add to her weight seemed a logical thing to do. Unhappily the reasoning does not follow the experience.

Bulimia involves compulsive over-eating followed by vomiting, sometimes several times a day. During episodes sufferers experience feelings of well-being and a sense of being in control, they feel better for a while then worse than before because self-disgust and shame eventually overcomes any benefit. Their outward disposition belies their inward distress as they vehemently deny to themselves and others that what they are doing is problematic and maintain a cheerful face in public. Over the long term depletion in minerals and effects on body and brain chemistry can cause the very symptoms a sufferer is trying to avoid: depression and mood swings. In the months before the wedding Diana experienced a switch back ride of alternating euphoria, excitement, confidence, anger, fear, guilt and self loathing when the bulimia exerted its influence on her as she tried to deal with a confusion of personal and public situations.

People noticed her vulnerable and emotional state during her occasional public appearances with her fiancée. Like Charles they put her outbursts of tears and panic stricken look when faced with packs of photographers and crowds of admirers, as natural to someone her age with the stress she was under. They assumed she would be all right in time.

Diana was doing the best she knew how to live up to the expectations of everyone including Charles, their two families, friends, the media and the public. She believed she should have been the happiest person in the world, accumulating wonderful memories of a special time. Mostly she blamed herself for the fact she was not.

Charles was bewildered at the changes in his fiancée. From the pretty, compliant, lovable and caring young woman, supporting him and ready to stand beside him, she had become thin and pale, someone whose moods and emotions he could not predict and whose behaviour bordered on hysterical. Sometimes she was the jolly and confident Diana whose company he enjoyed, sometimes withdrawn and sullen, sometimes shouting with rage. He was concerned about her but had no idea what to do. He was having doubts about his decision to marry her, but he was committed and saw no way of going back. His doubts were alleviated somewhat by Diana's performance during an ITN interview with journalists Angela Rippon and Andrew Gardner when Diana acquitted herself perfectly. He was convinced she would be able to adapt to life as his wife. Diana had her own doubts and shortly before the wedding day even spoke about pulling out. For them both the words "Sorry I can't do this" were pushed back and swamped by duty, the expectations of others and fear of failure. Instead they clutched at the first in a series of emotional lifelines and trusted it would all be all right when they were married. It was not to be.

Diana moved again the day before the wedding, back to Clarence House to await the momentous day. She later described feeling deathly calm and like "the lamb to the slaughter" who could do nothing about her fate. Charles was also calm and thoughtful that evening, set on his duty. Realising the importance of the marriage to himself, his family and the nation, he also felt concern about the ordeal Diana was about to face and his future with her as his wife.

On 29 July 1981 Charles, Prince of Wales and Lady Diana Spencer were married before an estimated three quarters of a billion television viewers worldwide, an audience of over a million around St. Paul's Cathedral and an intimate congregation of 2,700 which included sovereigns, heads of state, governors-general, friends and family. Diana later described it as "the most emotionally confusing" day of her life. The wedding went off almost perfectly. Diana did not trip over her dress or make any of the errors she dreaded might occur apart from a small mistake with her vows when repeating her husband's string of names. The couple was happy. The public were ecstatic, if millions of people can simultaneously experience the same emotion. The press was satisfied. The day was a triumph and by the end of it Diana was radiant and certain again of the love she felt for Charles. Those who should know about such things told Diana and her husband that the media frenzy which had accompanied the wedding and its preliminaries would quiet down soon afterwards. Diana looked forward to being able to settle into the tranquil life she longed for with the man she loved. Before that was possible, however, she had some more moving to do.

Two weeks honeymoon on board the royal yacht *Britannia* combined official receptions at their various ports of call with informal moments of fun, accompanied by more than 200 officers and men. The cruise was followed by six weeks at Balmoral until the end of September. There were high points when Charles and Diana were able to share time and leisure together without distractions and lows when Diana saw more evidence of her husband's strong feelings for the woman she believed was her rival for his affections. Her bulimia continued as did her mood swings and erratic behaviour; one moment she was loving and warm towards her new husband, the next in tears and despair. The sympathy and concern Charles felt for his young wife began to wane as her inconsistency continued after the marriage. In large part though he was optimistic and happy enough to enjoy reading, painting and attempting to share his interests with Diana during the prolonged period away from his hectic life. She struggled with the deep topics he enjoyed discussing and the oppressive feelings she always experienced at Balmoral, but she was contented by his attention. Their holiday was followed by another move, to Buckingham Palace for several months while the redecorations at Highgrove and their London apartment were completed.

Quickly Diana became pregnant and acute morning sickness was adding to the problems caused by her continuing bulimia. Outwardly the newlyweds seemed happy and devoted to each other. Behind the scenes Diana's swings in mood and personality continued to baffle and upset her husband who was unable to respond supportively when she embarrassed him in front of his family, friends or staff.

The pregnancy was not easy. Diana's morning sickness did not abate. Her emotions swung violently back and forth driven now by pre-natal hormone shifts alongside the worries which had been her persistent companions since she was engaged. Her anxiety was made worse by new trials that brought the frailest parts of her make-up out for severe examination in the most difficult of arenas. Diana was now expected to undertake royal duties in public. Her first as Charles' wife was in Wales where she gave a short speech, partly in Welsh. For the introverted twenty year old it was a nightmare situation made worse by low self-esteem and her pregnancy. The very prospect of being faced by a large crowd, then having to speak in public, made her rigid with fear and nausea. It was surprising she was able to cope at all. Her sense of duty and obligation to her husband made her carry on. Her natural grace and caring personality carried her through triumphantly as she held the hands of pensioners and allowed children to touch her. Her pale and waif-like beauty elicited sympathy and adulation from the public who were unaware of her pregnancy, her struggles to cope with the crowds and her bulimia.

The experience exhausted Diana but enchanted the press and public. They were blissfully unaware that her turbulent emotions and nausea had constantly threatened to overcome her and had embarrassed her husband and his staff, who clearly did not realise that what was normal and commonplace for other members of the royal family was exceptionally difficult for Diana. Where she hoped for praise they offered what they probably thought of as constructive feedback by pointing out what she might have done better. Diana experienced it as nit picking criticism when what she needed most was unconstrained encouragement and support. Her self-confidence and her esteem for Charles took more blows which were repeated throughout the following months during other engagements.

Something Diana failed to notice while she was in Wales and during subsequent engagements was the emergence of a new phenomenon. Rather than diminishing, public admiration of her and therefore press attention to her, was increasing. Great stress tends to produce self-absorption and Diana's natural tendency for introspection accelerated her withdrawal into herself. She became increasingly disinterested in events which did not directly affect her own situation. Her sense of alienation from Charles and the royal world she inhabited grew. It was perhaps just as well she was not aware of the demand for her to appear more often in public. The thought of doing so terrified her and she was completely drained by the actual events.

Instead Diana's attention was consumed by her pregnancy and her turbulent inner state. Sometime in the future Diana would refer to bulimia as a condition which resulted in a compulsion to "dissolve like a Disprin and disappear". Now, in the darkness which began to consume her mind, this sense of intense anguish and desperation, rooted in childhood conclusions she was unwanted and uncared for, was given substance by the thought that her life was no longer worth living and that she would only have peace if she ended it. In one desperate attempt to draw Charles' attention to her plight, she threatened to commit suicide then threw herself down the stairs at Sandringham. The incident did not make him change his plans to go riding but it did reinforce Diana's sense of worthlessness and failure, increased her sense of guilt and further eroded her esteem for Charles. His regard for her was going through a similar change. The sense that his affection was becoming indifference was painful to her and fuelled behaviour which provoked him to react. Any response was better than none.

More threats and other episodes of self-harming followed but none caused serious enough injury to dissuade Charles from his belief she was doing anything more than seeking attention like a spoilt child. He misunderstood the intense emotions and despair that would have been necessary to make Diana act on the impulses provided by her desperation and confusion. Her actions were not those of a spoilt child but were childlike cries of pain. There is a considerable difference between the feeling of not wanting to be alive and actually doing something about it, no matter how inefficient the method chosen might seem in rational or cynical hindsight. For Diana the intensity of her emotions must have been frightening. She misunderstood her husband's lack of sympathy. By this time it is doubtful anyone would have been able to consistently give Diana enough attention and love to balance the weight of self-destructive thoughts and feelings she had accumulated. Various therapists and counsellors tried to assist her during the months which followed. Diana was not open to their efforts; significantly none of them seem to have considered her at serious risk or Diana's story would have taken a different turn.

Her own opinion, that she simply needed her husband's unqualified support and more time to get used to her role, was mistaken. Her logic was childlike and naive because it had as its source her childhood experiences of not feeling she was loved and appreciated enough. Consequently she believed that more love and appreciation would be a solution. With hindsight what was required was a complete self-evaluation from which she could have realised that her demands on Charles for his assurance went beyond what was possible for any man to give. For months he had been sympathetic, attentive, concerned and caring, but whatever he did was not sufficient, nor would it be until she was able to value herself enough to believe what she was receiving from him was genuine.

Diana's problems and their solution lay within her own perception of herself. To accept that and embark upon the necessary inner changes with the help of therapists, would at that time have required that she confront past issues and mistakes that were far too painful to contemplate. Instead she continued to confuse herself and those around her with her changeable moods and behavior. At times she became inconsolable in her despair, sitting with her head bowed, not communicating for hours. When her time with Charles was not violated by distractions from outside, from friends and duties, she gave him and herself a glimpse of the sweet natured and loving Diana everyone delighted in.

In place of the lasting solution Diana was unable to grasp, the prospect of their first baby was a new lifeline for Diana and her husband to clutch at. Perhaps a child would make the difference that would erase her jealousy of Camilla and give her full confidence in her husband's commitment to the marriage? They both longed for children. For Diana motherhood was a significant part of the self-identity which was rapidly crumbling about her but had not yet been completely destroyed.

Diana's caring side was rarely expressed in the marriage now. The differences between Charles and herself had become more obvious during their honeymoon and sojourn at Balmoral. They simply did not share the same emotional, spiritual or intellectual terrain and it was becoming clear he did not need her in many of the ways she expected he would. Since the marriage Charles had been gravitating back to the reading, riding and rural pursuits he loved when he had time, interests Diana did not share with anything like the same enthusiasm. So far Diana's experience of being his wife was not matching the idyll she had envisioned and she could not ignore the fact that Charles was unhappy as well. Perhaps he would realise her values as mother to his children. A child might bring them back together. The irony of the situation might have struck her about this time if she had reflected on the similarities between her parent's marriage and her own. The age gap, her disenchantment with married life and their hopes that their newborn would save them, it was all a little too familiar.

In February 1982, four months before her baby was due, a significant event seemed to support the idea that she and Charles could salvage their marriage. They were enjoying an interlude of peace and closeness in a private home on a secluded island in the Bahamas, sharing cooking duties and relaxing in the sun and surf with the Romseys, a couple who were long time friends. Even though Diana was unable to take great pleasure in her husband's tendency to spend much of his time reading and painting, it was in Charles' words "a second honeymoon". Their pleasure was marred by news that photographs of the pregnant Diana in a bikini had been published in British tabloids. The public's interest in Diana had apparently been interpreted by disreputable members of the press pack as carte blanche to now pursue her in virtually any situation and in particular to their island retreat. Charles and Diana shared a sense of outrage. She saw in the incident and the holiday, signs that her husband really did care for her. The episode also pressed home just how limited her life was becoming and what little real freedom she enjoyed.

When they returned home however, Diana was again distracted by the now familiar circumstances that dragged her back into her own private misery and more dark thoughts and despair. The way pregnancy can make expectant mothers forgetful and unable to concentrate may have had some effect but the result was to intensify the problems she already faced from other, longer standing causes. She seemed not to notice even the Falkland campaign which lasted from 2 April until the week before her baby was born. As the due date approached Diana was almost certainly concerned about her baby's health despite being assured by doctors it was doing well, not least because it is natural for first time mothers to worry about such things, but also because she was aware of what had happened with her poor baby brother John who was born deformed and did not survive. The press was following the progress of Diana's pregnancy with obsessive interest. The intense and widespread anticipation of the important birth of a new Prince of the Realm added pressure she found difficult to bear. It did not help that her husband's time was taken up by his armed forces role during the conflict in the South Atlantic.

Five weeks before her baby was born Diana moved again, into Kensington Palace to await the birth. Neither the apartment there nor Highgrove House were ever to become the idyllic family home she had envisioned.

On 21 June 1982 after a difficult birth, the long awaited baby was born, a son, healthy and perfectly formed who was named William. It is impossible to underestimate the impact he had when he emerged into Diana's life. Never mind the satisfaction of her husband or the pleasure of the royal family, her father, sisters and brother, or the country at large, here was a scrap of life for which she was responsible. It offered unconditional trust and absorbed every ounce of love she lavished upon it and called for more. William's birth provided validation for her identity and place in the world and over the next two years he would enable her to recover sufficient self-belief to start rebuilding her life.

It was not to be an easy journey back.

Soon after the birth post-natal depression battled with the joyous aspects of motherhood to take her back into the darkness of her depression. The outcome was in the balance for many months. Diana was still bulimic, still alarmingly thin and her physical frailty was exacerbated by exhaustion after the birth. Her emotional state was equally frail. She still harboured deep suspicions about her husband and Camilla and by now believed the household staff and his friends were colluding to deceive her about their relationship. The press was printing spiteful gossip about her in one story after another alluding to her state of mind, health, damaging influence over her husband, sacking of staff and discarding of his friends. Diana was called "the mouse that roared". Some interpretations of the facts might have given an impression of truth to the tales presumably sourced within the circle close to her.

On the other side of the balance was the absolute delight in their new son she shared with her husband who seemed to be at home more and was loving and attentive. As mother she rightfully had the dominant role and Charles appreciated her for the gift she had produced and was happy to take on the subordinate duties of nappy changing house-husband. There were elements here of the life she had envisaged and the self-identity behind it. Camilla could not compete with this. Things could still work out all right after all. She began to feel more confident and able to cope better than she had for a long time.

Research suggests that new mothers undergo changes to their brains which increase their motivation and promote behaviour that helps them protect and care for their baby. Diana's natural Water element instinct for caring and mothering would have magnified the phenomenon. Whatever the reason she now developed a new assertiveness and strength of will that led those around her to hope she was at last recovering from the dark chapter of her life. William's presence in her life pulled Diana from self-absorption and directed her towards caring for her son and then others again. She debated with Charles about the names her son should have and won. She confronted a journalist she believed had misrepresented her in a story. Three months after the birth she sought support from her husband for the idea that she should attend the funeral of Princess Grace of Monaco who had been sympathetic and helpful when Diana was starting her royal career. When the support was not forthcoming she appealed directly to the Queen and was given permission to go.

Six months later Diana accompanied Charles on a triumphant official tour of Australia and New Zealand. Their six weeks away required every ounce of energy and self-confidence she could muster to overcome her fear of performing in public, the jet lag, the heat and the attention of a crowd whose adulation of Diana bordered on hysteria, but she was brilliant. Her natural grace and gentle lack of formality endeared her completely to the crowd who, in true antipodean fashion, were not backward in expressing their preference for meeting and greeting Diana rather than her husband. They even groaned when Charles emerged from a car for an official walkabout because it wasn't their Princess. Diana was in turns elated, exhausted, amazed and frightened.

The essential support Diana and Charles gave each other on the tour was acknowledged later by them both in communications to friends. She acknowledged how he had pulled her out of her shell, how his experience had helped her and how his presence had reassured her. Charles wrote of his concerns for Diana and how she had helped him and kept him going when he felt gloomy. Brief periods spent in private away from the frenzy on their base, a sheep station in New South Wales, prompted Charles to declare how "extremely happy" they were and "the great joy was that we were totally alone together." The presence of William gave the couple a mutual focus for their attention and the antics of the nine month old little boy delighted them both. Nothing could have suited Diana more and reconciliation must have seemed possible at that time despite the fact that Charles later admitted he was jealous of the attention given to his wife.

For Diana the tour underscored her new strength of will and purpose. She had been triumphant on one of the most difficult tours anyone could recall and had, by her presence and abilities, excited unprecedented levels of public interest in the British monarchy. She had exhibited strength of character, stamina and a natural deftness of touch, literally, for the work which was part of her role as her husband's consort. To her introverted and self-doubting personality public appearances were situations during which Diana risked rejection, by people and press. The numbers who turned out and the media coverage confirmed she was accepted. Where her heightened sensitivity previously meant she felt as if she might be overwhelmed by the sheer weight of sensations and emotions she experienced when meeting large numbers of people, she now began to feel less anxious. A few weeks after returning to Britain to rapturous acclaim the couple embarked on another tour to Canada with similar results. Diana's reward for her efforts was a new level of self-respect and the beginnings of the ability to appreciate herself and validate her own accomplishments as a mother, royal figure and partner to the Prince, her husband. The natural process we all experience in our lives at last seemed to be reshaping Diana's self-identity into a form that might offer her happiness and health.

Back in England and again in the environment she must have found oppressive and reminiscent of her past distress she was comfortable enough with herself to start making contact with old friends whose acquaintance she had neglected during her unhappiest times. It was difficult. Diana had changed from the jolly nineteen year old they had known before. Now she was going on twenty two, was Princess of Wales, wife of the heir to the throne and mother to the second in line. She was more worldly and confident in many ways and had been through experiences none of them could imagine or therefore understand. She was also scarred emotionally by her two years of marriage and unhappy with the restrictions placed on her by her position.

There was barely a moment when Diana was not under scrutiny and inwardly she chafed against its various manifestations: the constant media attention to her public and private lives, the attentive staff who surrounded her and the constant presence of her bodyguard. Ever perceptive, she noticed that people looked at her and treated her differently now; where she had once enjoyed easy familiarity she now experienced deference, where there had been closeness and connection there was now distance. Diana felt alienated from the majority of people by her position and experiences they were unable to comprehend. Her thoughts and feelings began to echo again with past impressions of herself she would have preferred to avoid.

Baby William, constant delight that he was, also added to the inexperienced Diana's self doubts, as a first baby will with any new mother who has a lot to learn. Her relationship with Charles was better than for a long time but his role still took him away a great deal. He in turn was jealous of the attention she now commanded from the press and public. It was especially clear when he appeared with her and Diana was aware of his increasing discomfort and bitterness. One member of his own staff described the situation as like working with two pop stars. Notwithstanding the divisions between the pair they were happy enough for Diana to become pregnant again early in 1984. Diana later described the time, "We were very, very close to each other the six weeks before Harry was born, the closest we've ever, ever been and ever will be."

Diana's second pregnancy was made difficult by repeats of the morning sickness and mood swings she had suffered when carrying William, but not to the same extent. She was able to fulfil her round of public engagements in the UK which affirmed her popularity and continued to validate her and her informal approach to royal duties. Her turbulent relationship with Charles continued during the pregnancy. Diana had not resolved her suspicions about Camilla and Charles' friends remained a source of anguish that ate away at Diana's respect for herself and her affection for Charles. Charles lost touch with friends and resented her impact on the life he had known. They alternately argued and shared periods of calm and mutual fondness during which William was the adhesive which held them together. Together they managed a fairly stable married alliance but they were not able to restore the bond they had shared at the beginning, or to alter the basic fact that their outlooks and interests were incompatible.

Prince Henry was born on 15 September 1984. Charles apparently expressed disappointment his new son was not the girl he had longed for and that he had red hair. Diana felt criticised and experienced again the echoes of her own sense of rejection by her parents who had longed for her to be a boy. She was to say later that at that moment "Something inside me died". She knew then her marriage was probably irrecoverable, but it did not stop her clinging to the wreckage for some time. By his own admission Charles also accepted that his marriage to Diana irretrievably broke down not long after.

Within a year or so of Harry's birth Charles resumed his loving relationship with Camilla and Diana is said to have been comforted by her police bodyguard, the dependable and fatherly Sergeant Barry Mannakee. Later Diana said she had an intimate relationship at age 24 or 25 with someone who worked within her environment. She had talked with him about living together and was "like a little girl in front of him...desperate for praise..." and "...he was chucked out." Barry Mannakee was moved from royal protection duties early in 1986 allegedly for his improper association with Princess Diana.

When Diana resumed her official duties after Harry's birth, both with Charles and on her own, she was even more accomplished than before and more confident. Familiarity through repetition had made her public appearances easier to perform, even enjoyable. She was the epitome of the smiling caring Fairytale Princess. Her maturing beauty and unceremonious approach gained approval and admiration from the public and the media which could not produce enough photographs and stories about Diana to satisfy people's appetite. Diana still felt constrained by unwritten rules which seemed to mean the royal family must remain remote and unreachable. Diana's informal style was regarded with disapproval by her husband and courtiers, but it provided her with validation which balanced the feelings of inadequacy produced by her marriage.

With her confidence renewed Diana began socialising with friends whose ages were closer to her own twenty five years. She enjoyed lunches, dinners and cinema with girlfriends and some of the young men she had known for years. She met her friends when she and Charles were on skiing holidays and attended house parties and discos with them. In hindsight it seems she was going through a chapter during which she tried to recapture the happy times at Coleherne Court.

Perhaps she was also influenced by the reaction of Charles and other members of the royal family to her friend Sarah Ferguson who had become part of the royal scene through her father who was Prince Charles' polo manager. In 1985 Sarah met and was soon being courted by Prince Andrew so was consequently at many of the same functions and family gatherings as Diana. Sarah was seen as a breath of fresh air. Compared to the complex and often unhappy Diana, Fergie was straightforward, enthusiastic and full of fun and laughter. She seemed to fit easily into royal situations Diana found oppressive.

Inevitably the press pack sensed stories in Diana's new private life. Rumours of problems in her marriage were already circulating and she was being tracked and followed whenever they could find her. Pictures and gossip about her activities and her friends, especially the young men, began to appear in the tabloids alongside the accounts of her official duties.

In the autumn of 1986 Diana fell in love and started a prolonged affair with James Hewitt, a Captain in the Household Cavalry. He had agreed to teach her to ride again so she could recover the confidence she had lost as a child falling from her horse. With her new lover she shared closeness and happy times, often in the homely surroundings of his mother's cottage in Devon. Diana later said she had loved and adored him. Their relationship was clearly one within which she felt wanted and loved and enjoyed shared times of intimacy and domesticity, all of which she needed to feel her life was worthwhile. Her public role was becoming easier and more satisfying. Her sense of purpose was being restored and it seemed she might be drawing closer to a life which would fit her personality and make-up and fulfil to some extent the self-identity constructed five years earlier.

Unfortunately it did not satisfy that side of her which needed to have influence over her own future, nor did it resolve the pain and sense of injustice she felt whenever she was reminded of her husband's deep affection for Camilla. Perhaps it was because she was aware that her own affairs did not match the deep and abiding love Charles experienced with his mistress, a love she believed would be hers. Whatever the case, it remained a source of anguish and produced bitter arguments between her and Charles when they were together which was becoming less often. When they appeared together in public they maintained the facade of a happily married couple eager to do their royal duty and Diana was seen to be a star performer in the royal show. Away from the cameras and microphones their relationship was becoming more and more spiteful.

Throughout 1986 and into 1987 Diana's press profile was higher than ever with applause for her public role and censure for silly behaviour and a number of mischievous pranks in which she was often abetted by "Fergie". There were tales of them dressing up as policewomen in order to gate crash Prince Andrew's stag party, boisterous behaviour during a photo call at Klosters and prodding a friend in the buttocks with umbrellas at Ascot races. Diana danced beautifully on stage with ballet star Wayne Sleep at the Royal Gala Performance and was caught on camera giggling at an officer's Sandhurst passing out parade. She was being portrayed as frivolous and undignified. At the same time articles were appearing in tabloids and serious news media openly calling into question the state of her marriage. The story was of constitutional significance to the nation given Charles' and William's positions in the line of accession. It was of personal significance to Diana given she was wife to the one and mother of the other.

Her press coverage had been of concern to Diana since the early days of her engagement and she was constantly aware of it. Now it became even more important. People around her had noticed how avidly she seemed to scan the papers and presumed she was obsessed by her own image or seeking to identify herself through her portrayal in the stories she found. The latter was closer to the truth but still far from what was actually happening. The accomplishment she had achieved in her royal role so far had been hard won and was a source of self-esteem and validation and not insignificant pleasure when she read glowing praise. It fitted too her need for purpose in her life. Charles had helped her learn her duties to an extent but ever since her first engagement in Wales it was clear she was eclipsing him. Increasingly he was expressing his displeasure in sharp remarks and she responded in kind. He and the royal courtiers had always tried to shape her to a traditional style similar to that of other members of the royal family and when she diverged from their influence they tended to become critical. Diana's perceptive side knew that her natural, caring, tactile style was touching chords in the public who came to see her. She resented the absence of unqualified support and understanding for something which was self-evident to her.

Since she was a child Diana had always devolved validation of herself to others, first to her parents, especially her father, then her siblings and teachers and most recently to Charles. James Hewitt was important to her sense of self as an attractive woman and for that part of her caring self in a personal relationship. Her sons were important to her self-identity as a mother. The media however was now more than ever her touchstone for her sense of self-worth on a bigger scale and the place she could look for support and to see if she was understood. Critical stories, no matter that they were often highly embellished or even fabricated, hurt her fragile feelings and caused her darker perceptions of herself to take on more substance.

In August 1987, while on holiday in Majorca at the Marivent Palace home of King Juan Carlos, Diana, a few weeks past her twenty-sixth birthday, reviewed her position. She had not enjoyed the superficiality of the frivolous social life she had been trying to fit into over the past year or so. It went contrary to her natural introversion and preference for close connections with just a few people and time to sit quietly and reflect. Her idea of heaven, as she sometimes stated, was beans on toast, on her own, in front of the television but she also needed people. She was now trying hard to create a life which would have a semblance of normality. She had her lover to replace the emotional desolation of her marriage. A celebrity tennis club gave her opportunities for more exercise and meeting people she hoped would have similar backgrounds and interests, no matter that she did not really enjoy tennis and preferred solitary pursuits like swimming.

Her newly appointed personal protection officer, Inspector Ken Wharfe, was on hand to lend his unsuspecting ear to Diana's summing of her situation. From Diana's own lips he heard the story of her disastrous marriage. He would have made a very poor bodyguard if he had not already noticed. Wharfe had been looking after the safety of the young Princes for a year before his appointment to the senior role on Diana's protection team. He had seen and heard vicious spats between Charles and Diana, had met James Hewitt and accompanied Diana to their trysts and nights away in Devon. He had spoken with his colleagues and household staff at Highgrove and Kensington. Wharfe knew what was happening but not the extent of his principal's unhappiness. Now he heard of her fears for her boys and how trapped she felt in her loveless marriage and of her anger at Camilla. During their conversation, as they sat in the Spanish sunshine, Diana declared it was time for her to spread her wings. Such a statement implies self-belief and that she felt she had "wings" to be clipped, it certainly speaks of optimism. Diana felt her life and role in the royal "firm" were not under her control and inhibited her, perhaps she also sensed she had been limiting herself and was now becoming ready for bigger challenges.

Back home again in the less invigorating climate of the UK a joint trip, to south Wales, to offer solace to those affected by severe flooding was arranged as an opportunity for Diana and Charles to show a united front. It was successful in a Public Relations context but in terms of their personal relationship it was disastrous. Diana attempts at conversation were bluntly rejected by her husband and they virtually ignored each other throughout the trip. Speculation about their marriage was rife in the media and gossip about Diana's possible amorous liaisons was touted in the press. Despite her bold declaration in Spain there was no appreciable difference to Diana's activities, or any change in her unhappy state in the following weeks.

The connection Charles and Diana had made seven years before had not strengthened or deepened over time as they might have hoped. Even with William and Harry providing motivation which might have kept them together, their trust and affection had been damaged beyond repair. For Diana, respect for Charles had been eroded by the impatience and criticism which had met her efforts to fulfil her duties and fit into his life and corroded by her rage at the way he had rejected her and turned again to Camilla. With sufficient knowledge and objectivity Diana might have considered the intensity of her anger at Charles and Camilla and realised its origins went far deeper than his rejection and her jealousy of the woman he loved.

The bond which forms when two people express their genuine attraction through shared intimacy is immensely powerful. It is founded in changes to their biochemistry and psychological states which are difficult to dissolve, even when the relationship fails for practical reasons. Diana's love for Charles was her first. Her commitment was absolute. The bond she made with him and the changes which occurred within her were consequently very profound. Charles by comparison already had a very strong bond to Camilla and while his intention was to step away from their relationship his connection to her would not have simply disappeared. He is not likely to have been available to replace his bond with Camilla with one for Diana for whom he felt great affection, despite his belief that he would come to love her. Diana would have sensed this.

Perhaps Charles' uncle Lord Mountbatten was right when he advised his nephew to choose someone to be his wife who had not loved before, suggesting that if Charles was her first love he would be her last. The intention was to help Charles make a marriage that would last a lifetime. It answers instead the question of why Diana was so obsessive about her husband's relationship with Camilla and so filled with rage and indignation even when reason said the marriage was doomed and she had taken lovers of her own. Such bonds overcome reason and whenever Diana considered the possibility of parting from Charles she would have felt grief similar to that probably felt by Charles when he tried to part from Camilla.

Diana was angry and confused. She was desperate to turn the tide of speculation about the marriage away from herself. Her make-up made it difficult for her to receive adverse comment without experiencing it as personal criticism. Inwardly she felt guilty about her past behaviour and to close friends even admitted she had been difficult to deal with when times were very black. She genuinely believed however, that the blame for her shambles of a marriage should be laid at Charles's door and especially at Camilla's. Heroes do not give up and he should have stuck by her, would have stuck by her if it had not been for that woman. Now, despite all her excellent public work she was being castigated for a situation in her private life which was not her fault.

During the autumn while in Scotland, and later again in October during a walk on her favorite Dorset beach, Diana again contemplated her life and tried to work out what she could do to make it more satisfying. She resolved to change, to accept the fact that she was not in the same position as other women her age. She decided to apply herself more to her public role which she found so fulfilling but did not quite know what to do differently. Her role was defined by her husband's office and ultimately by the Queen. Other people held the reigns to Diana's official life and any opportunity to do more in public was guided by their whims. Nothing she could think of doing would bring control into her own hands and it was a sense of control she needed, feeling helpless was very distressing. Diana entered the New Year more confused and lost than ever.

A turning point came in March 1988 when Diana and Charles were on holiday with friends at their favorite skiing resort Klosters. Diana was in their chalet with flu when an avalanche caught her husband's party out on the slopes. A close friend, Major Hugh Lindsay was killed and another, Patti Palmer-Tomkinson was badly injured. In the chaos of practical and emotional concerns which arose during the forty eight hours that followed Diana acquitted herself well and contributed greatly to helping those others affected by the tragedy. Reflecting afterwards on what had occurred Diana was able to acknowledge to herself the calmness, strength and abilities she had exhibited as she dealt with the crisis. Later still she took stock of herself for the fourth time in nine months and this time emerged sufficiently shaken to act where she had not previously.

At the time of the accident she saw the immediate effect the tragedy had on all those who were present that day. In the aftermath she experienced close hand the impact on Hugh Lindsay's pregnant wife Sarah as she tried to come to terms with the sudden loss of her husband. She stayed for a few days with Diana and her sister Jane at Highgrove. Diana comforted her as best she could. Anyone would have been moved by the young widow's grief and confusion but Diana, as sensitive and intuitive as she was, empathised especially closely with her situation. It would have been surprising indeed if Diana had not then gone on to think about how things might have been if it was Charles who had been killed, as it so nearly was. Such speculation would have made Diana see her life in a completely new and alarming light.

It must have come home to her as never before that just then her husband was the keystone to her entire future. If Diana became a widow, what then for her place in her son's lives? In William's life if he was heir, what place for her in the world then? Diana's deliberations on matters such as these were not a reasoned weighing of possibilities but more a gut instinct based on her emotions and the prospects for her in the current climate of her life would have been frightening. She was being portrayed as a useful and attractive adjunct to her almost estranged husband with an unfortunate propensity for spending a good deal of money on clothes and holidays. Perhaps other thoughts reinforced her apprehension, what if her affair with James Hewitt was made public? Diana's response was to make an inner vow to transform her life once and for all, to change what had to be changed so she would remain where she needed to be with her children, even if that meant staying within the cage she found so distressing. She still had no idea how to proceed, but it is perhaps when you most need help that it comes to you.

Carolyn Bartholomew, with whom Diana had shared the Coleherne Court apartment, had long been a friend. She was alarmed at the effect bulimia was having on Diana and, in a curt phone call, explained her concerns and issued an ultimatum. Diana had one hour to call a doctor and get some help or Carolyn would make the public aware of her secret illness. In the circumstances Diana was forced to comply. She was guided to top psychiatrist and expert on eating disorders Maurice Lipsedge.

During their first consultation at Kensington Palace the doctor impressed Diana with his knowledge of the condition by asking how many times she had tried to commit suicide and about her childhood and her relationships with her husband. Lipsedge recommended books which explained the condition and showed Diana she was not alone with the problem and was not peculiar. His treatment improved her general health and view of herself and made her aware that the stress of being with her husband at Highgrove or in the oppressive atmospheres she experienced at Windsor, Balmoral or Sandringham triggered an increase in her bulimic episodes. Her six months of work with Dr Lipsedge gave momentum to Diana's stalled journey back to wellness and was the start of her self-discovery. Her bulimic tendencies were not completely resolved but the improvement in her health was clear.

There is no quick fix however when it comes to the complexities of the human condition. Diana's efforts, now driven by new energy and new purpose, to make a more serious commitment to her work were not supported by her husband and the courtiers who held sway over her schedule and even her travel arrangements. She was not resilient enough to deal with their rejection and as Christmas 1988 approached, with the prospect of the traditional royal festivities, Diana began to feel the familiar sensations of stress and echoes of her old self-doubts. Whichever way she looked at it she was trapped in a broken marriage and her life was a mess, with no hope of it becoming better.

After eight unhappy years Diana's carefully constructed self-identity had finally fallen apart as surely as if a sudden disaster had smashed it asunder. The hopes she had nurtured were broken and had not been replaced by anything remotely desirable. Only fragments of her teenage dream remained. They provided her with no solid foundation for future happiness. Her sons gave her the opportunity for motherhood but even that could be ruined by her husband if he chose to make things difficult. Very soon William would be going away to boarding school and her influence on him would be reduced. It was utterly terrifying to think she might not be able to take care of her boys and protect them.

Diana had become expert at her public role so that she could fulfil her duty to her husband and his family, with the expectation she would be appreciated for what she contributed. Instead of appreciation she received suspicion from a husband who was challenged by her success and disapproval from courtiers and other members of the family for her style. She was becoming increasingly dissatisfied with how she had to present herself as the forever smiling Fairytale Princess in her public role. Her instinct told her she should be offering more care and comfort, more contact, to the sick and distressed she met during many of her engagements. But her job was controlled by the royal machine which already frowned on her ways, so her caring side was diminished by her circumstances. Diana's sense of who she was and what she could become, what she needed to do to cope, were gone and she had lost sight of any future that would offer happiness and love.

Her marriage was not as it was supposed to be, as she had imagined it would be. There was no loving husband to care for and who was caring for her. There was no peaceful home filled with laughter and love. Thoughts of what Charles and Camilla had done to her caused Diana's rage to boil but she had no answer to the predicament she was in. At times she felt consumed by her emotions. Anger, fear and despair conflicted with compassion when she worked and love when she was with her boys. Her muscles were tense and painful all the time and her heart seemed to lurch whenever she paused to consider her situation. She could feel herself wanting to eat and be sick just to take the feelings away. Thoughts of suicide crowded into her mind. She was stuck in a dead end with no way back or forward.

What Diana did not recognise was her own contribution to the circumstances she was in. She blamed Charles and Camilla for her situation but failed, through lack of knowledge, to realize she had helped to build the gilded cage she now occupied. Her trap was the natural manifestation of those darker aspects of her own inner world that she had tried so hard to suppress and avoid. Deep down the teenage Diana had accepted her own low self-worth and by the path she had chosen she was now treated as having little value. She had submitted to the belief that she could not influence her life and that her husband would take care of her; through her marriage to Prince Charles she now had little control over what happened to her and while he was the source of everything she had, it could not make her happy. Diana's capacity for compassion and her gift for caring for the weak and disadvantaged had been shared with the multitudes who came to look at her and touch her yet it gave her no fulfilment. She had not believed she deserved love, not really and she had chosen a man who said at the outset he did not love her and was now unavailable to do so. She had assumed her destiny would come through her marriage and it had, but it was not a destiny which fulfilled her. Diana's prison was constructed within her own mind long before it ever became reality. She would discover that it was in her mind she must look for her means of escape.

When she spoke of her distress with a friend, it turned out to be her first step to finding her freedom and her first step towards a transformation the world would watch with wonder. The friend in whom Diana confided was a client of mine who told Diana about my work. Within days I was asked whether I would be prepared to see the Princess. I confirmed I would be happy to. The royal way is to make sure an invitation will be accepted before offering it, to avoid the possibility of being refused. I was asked for my date of birth and car registration number. Presumably these were all that was required for security checks which would gain or deny me access to the most famous woman in the world. A telephone call from Diana's dresser followed shortly afterwards and, at 4.15 p.m. on Wednesday 14 December 1988, I found myself driving towards the gates of Kensington Palace.

PART THREE

TRANSFORMATION

I believe intensely
– much I am unsure of
but this I believe with all my heart –
in the long run we shape our lives,
and we shape ourselves,
and the process never ends until we die
and the choices we make
are ultimately our own responsibility.

Eleanor Roosevelt

1989

The Greatest discovery of my generation
is that human beings can alter their lives
by altering their attitude of mind…If
you can change your mind, you can change your life.
William James

According to Shakepeare "all the world's a stage" and as the curtain rose on the year 1989 Her Royal Highness Diana, Princess of Wales stepped onto the boards of a global theatre to take the starring role in a drama being played out before a worldwide audience of millions. Act One had ended with Diana full of hope and expectation. The curtain came down on Act Two with her lost and in despair, her dreams shattered. Act Three was about to begin.

Diana co-starred alongside her husband Charles, his mother the Queen and innumerable bit part players, some more significant than others. Their script was improvised, each responding to the lines uttered by other characters. Stage direction was provided by the world's media and various individuals and groups with vested interests in what was a quintessentially British tragedy.

✦ ✦ ✦

The members of the royal family of the House of Windsor are threads woven into the very fabric of the British Establishment and society. Head of the family is Her Majesty the Queen. At the start of 1989, as now, she had two main jobs: one was to perform the duties of Sovereign as required by the historical traditions of the nation and its unwritten constitution; the second was to ensure the continuity of her royal lineage.

As Sovereign, her role and influence were those permitted by the people, her subjects and largely they were directed by the government of the day. She was not expected to have a personal agenda and if she did, it was unlikely to be tolerated. Then, like now, powerful critics in the media and within the Establishment were arguing against the idea of an unelected Head of State with 'subjects'. The Queen's role: to play her part wisely and sympathetically and with astute awareness that if her monarchy failed to perform as expected, the result could be the end of an institution that had endured for centuries. This, for Her Majesty, is unthinkable.

That January, Elizabeth II was sixty two years of age. She had played the part of Queen for thirty five years almost without fault, as an exemplary professional. She understood her throne was balanced on a proverbial fence from which she must not descend to favour any particular side of opinion in matters regarded as important to those who would criticise. Her personal accomplishment in this first aspect of her job was seen by the great majority as an unequivocal success, one for which she was respected, even loved. She had provided decades of stability to a system which changes its government every few years and offered to those with the real power a great wealth of experience and wisdom acquired since she was crowned at the age of twenty seven.

What of the Queen's other responsibility, to ensure that her family, the Windsor dynasty, would continue to provide sovereigns to the nation for as long as possible? How successful she might be at this second task hung in the balance, not least because of Diana's entry into her family seven years previously.

✦ ✦ ✦

Next in line to the throne was Prince Charles, the Queen's first son and Diana's husband. He carried out all the engagements required of him with quiet professionalism promoting British interests and representing the Queen, the Head of State, at home and abroad. But he was not content. He had areas of interest close to his heart and caused consternation in the corridors of power by voicing in public strong opinions they would prefer he kept to himself. Charles' personality was not given to keeping his opinions to himself and it is perhaps unsurprising that he was often said to be "meddling" in matters that were none of his business.

A thoughtful and intelligent man who cared much for ordinary people and their wellbeing, Charles wanted to help improve lives and to use his position to create a better world. He preferred to play his part where he felt it would be most effective, behind the scenes where important decisions are made in government and commerce. He knew he could make a difference by influencing what was happening to the fabric of people's lives, to their surroundings, to the buildings in which they lived and to the food which sustained them. He had a strong feeling for the state of the natural world and was deeply concerned about the environment. He thought about the future and his own potential to do good in it.

His sense of destiny however was conflicted. The Prince's desire to influence matters which concerned him had already caused him to extend the duties expected of him to include issues he chose to champion. He saw his role to be one in which he made known his beliefs and unease about important matters such as the environment, religion, health, agriculture, architecture and the management of the countryside. Not surprisingly, his views delighted those he supported and angered those he criticised. Charles had been raised as the future King and in public, modern-day kings are supposed to be neutral in all things. As a result of Charles' interventions, questions were being asked about whether he would make a good king or not. Inevitably, the opinions of those who argued the monarchy was an institution which had passed its use-by date were bolstered by his outspokenness.

His public style and his media profile also seemed to work against Charles. Stiff, formal and fussy was how he came across in speech and manner. He seemed to combine aristocratic detachment with New Age dottiness, overlaid with a garnish of indecisive. It did not lend itself to a powerful popular image. Such were the times. No matter the genuine substance of the man, no matter how heartfelt his intentions and the wisdom of his views, if they were to convince the decision makers of the world they must first convince the public, the consumers. For that he needed to be presented in a media friendly package that would command the sympathetic attention of ordinary people. Charles made too easy a target for ridicule and criticism by the media, which controlled what the public saw and heard.

Frustrated by his inability to get his messages across effectively and conflicted by his role, Charles needed answers to his problems. He was not greatly appreciated by the people, nor as loved as he would like to have been, despite arguing for what he believed would improve their lives and the world in which they lived. As Prince of Wales and heir to the British throne he had a voice in the great debates of the nation and the world and was respected for his opinions by those who knew him. As King he would have to keep his views to himself in public and become a cipher and figurehead for the opinions of others. He was not sure how easily he would be able to endure the constraints the position would place on him.

Charles did not believe his mother understood him or appreciated his work as much as he would have liked. He thought she was probably disappointed with him. Certainly he believed his father was. His belief that he disappointed them made Charles unhappy and frustrated. He knew it had implications for his future as monarch. Perhaps he also felt guilty for bringing Diana into the family? He knew his wife's behaviour had upset his mother at times and was beginning to cause her concern for the future of the family. Charles now found himself in a constant state of nervous tension when he was with his wife and when they were with the family at Sandringham, Windsor or Balmoral.

Official engagements and public appearances were always a trial for Charles, especially when he felt he was being asked to give a performance. However, the situation had become worse in the last few years. The sheer numbers who turned up when he was with Diana and the noise and hysteria she seemed to generate for doing not very much at all except look pretty, baffled and disturbed him.

His marriage to Diana was supposed to have helped Charles and the family. She was supposed to support him in his work and provide him with the home he longed for, a place to relax away from the demands of his duties, a place of mutual affection where she would have his children and he would talk to her about his ideas and vision for the future. She was supposed to help him with his aspirations as Prince of Wales and, in due course, with his role as King. Sadly the marriage had done none of these, quite the contrary. Yet she had seemed so right for the job.

When the Prince and his Princess worked together people said what a good team they made. The press however was starting to comment as much on what might be happening behind the scenes as it was on what the royal couple offered on the public stage. Journalists, with many sources amongst those who surround the royal family, were asking if the marriage was in trouble. Of course the question was largely rhetorical. They already had a good idea what the answer was but dared not publish it except as rumour at that time.

Those within the Buckingham Palace press office, whose job it was to ensure good stories providing the most desirable view of the monarchy were published prominently while damaging ones were suppressed whenever possible, were increasingly worried about how much journalists actually knew and what their editors might print next. Everyone has secrets they wish to keep private but the royal family's privacy, it seemed, was being eroded more and more with each passing year.

As much as Prince Charles despised the horse trading that went on between his press office and the media, he knew he had to rely on the media to get his messages across. He was determined for the sake of his family, his future and the monarchy to show a united front with his wife. But it was difficult; his relationship with Diana was deteriorating daily and, to make matters worse, Diana's solo engagements were attracting more attention than his own. Quite simply, Diana was more popular than Charles, more popular than any other member of the royal family if truth be told. He felt she was diverting attention from his important causes to what he believed were her less important issues. The situation undermined both the fragile esteem in which Charles was held by his audience and the confidence he had in himself.

Charles could not understand why Diana always seemed so angry with him. He had tried hard to help her since they were married. He could not have done more. If she was so unhappy why could she not just find a place for herself as he had to do, a place within the family firm doing what she wanted to do? She must have known there could be no going back, no divorce. They were stuck with each other come what may. When they were alone together their disappointment spilled out into uncontrolled and spiteful wounding words. It was becoming worse and neither of them seemed to be able to stop themselves. She was making his life unbearable and his work more difficult than ever.

They tried to stay as far apart as possible in those days, avoiding spending time together unless doing so would attract unfavourable press comment, or unless they needed to be there for their boys. In private sometimes, Diana still acted with him as if she were a teenager again. She was nervous and timid, until she was angered by something, some perceived slight or neglect he was unaware of. Anything, any situation or word which brought Camilla to her mind would set his wife off into a rage and nothing he could say or do would stop her vicious taunts, or her harsh reminders that she, Diana, was his wife and mother to their children. He felt deep sadness and a sense of loss for the happiness which had seemed possible but had not been realised. Thank God for Camilla. What would he have done without her?

✦ ✦ ✦

When Diana married into the royal family at the age of nineteen she had such high hopes for her future in the most important family in the land. They seemed so solid, so stable and together, so supportive of each other. Diana assumed they would be loving and caring and supportive to her as well but her expectations were not fulfilled. Despite her every effort to date no one had said "well done," no one had put their arm around her and showed they cared about what she had gone through to please them and the public. No one had ever shown they gave a second thought about what she was feeling. Despite all the people who flocked to her official engagements when she appeared on her own or with Charles, despite all the press coverage she had gained, the royal family still acted as if she was a strange creature amongst them all. When she was with them Diana felt just like she did as a child, different, lonely and helpless.

Diana was trapped; of that she was certain. There was nowhere she could go and nothing she could do about her situation. Prince Charles and ultimately the Queen had complete control over Diana's official agenda. All her engagements were authorised by them. Every detail was prescribed by the courtiers, the "men in grey", who acted for the monarch and her son. Her life had been taken over by this family, this establishment and there was no escape. She was not like other women; divorce was out of the question for her and, in any case, she must stay with her sons. How could she leave them, even if she were able to, with this family? She had talked, in her anger, about running away with her children, but that was silly talk. Where could she have disappeared to with the heirs to the throne? Anyway she wanted more children and still fantasised that a marriage of the kind she had expected with Charles might still be possible. Sometimes she even imagined it might be possible with Charles; other times her every emotion rebelled at the idea. But who would have her now the world's media followed her every step?

Such was Diana's confused and frightened state of mind.

Early in the New Year Diana's dresser phoned me one evening to request another appointment. After we'd made the arrangements and hung up, I poured myself a glass of wine and settled back into my armchair to think about the last time I'd seen the Princess. During that first massage session I'd been convinced and had convinced her, that most of her physical and emotional problems were connected and rooted in the beliefs she held about herself and the world she inhabited. Clearly, from the fact that she had arranged to see me again, she had accepted the possibility of what I had told her. That the solution to what was ailing her could be found there, in her mind, amongst whatever damaging ideas she had accumulated there.

Her health was to be the focus of the work we would do together. That was the commitment I made to my clients. I would help them improve their health. But it would not be health the way most people think of it. My concept of health involved working with the mind and the body in a process that transforms both; if successful it would mean she could create an entirely different future to the one she now envisaged. I wondered if Diana would be able to deal with what she would have to do to become comfortable in her skin and comfortable in her life.

By that January I'd spent more than ten years immersed in the tidal wave of New Age teaching that was sweeping through London and around the world. It was a fascinating and energising time. What I'd learned already had undoubtedly saved my own life and brought me success in my career and not a little satisfaction. It had also brought me to Diana's door.

For over a decade I'd been a course junkie, attending classes in all manner of massage, mysticism and psychotherapeutic technique. I'd undertaken procedures lasting months at a time aimed at personal transformation and health improvement. For years I'd studied Japanese tea ceremony and martial arts. I'd walked on hot coals and meditated and visualised. On my journey I met human teachers, spirit guides and totem animals and learned from them all. I read books, discussed new paradigms in private and spoke about my ideas in public. I was like a sponge soaking up information and applying it to my life and my work until it was difficult to distinguish between them.

Everyone has a gift given by God or fate, whatever you will. It had taken me twenty seven years and many false starts before I finally discovered my own gift for massage and hands-on bodywork. Now, twelve years later, bodywork had become the core of my work as a successful therapist helping famous, wealthy and influential clients all over London with their health and appearance. It was an exciting and rewarding time of my life. Early in my career I'd learned that tightness and restriction in muscles can mirror limiting thoughts and beliefs acquired through life and held in the mind.

You only have to look at the defeated posture or angry, bitter expressions that for some people have become permanent, to recognise that mind sets beget muscle patterns. Massage techniques which release these constricted muscle patterns can also release their associated thoughts and feelings into the mind to be experienced again. I also came to understand that the condition of muscles, their tone and elasticity and ability to operate well, can be linked to the state of health of other systems and processes in the body. That knowledge left me with a dilemma; what should I do when I recognised that behind my client's muscle and joint problems, behind the pain they wanted me to resolve, were issues with mind or body that no amount of probing and kneading could mend? In those situations massage alone was not a long term solution.

Most massage therapists accept that they can only do their best with the medium in which they work. After that all they can do is to offer advice and insight, then leave the rest to the client. I took another view. I wasn't prepared to leave my clients trying to deal with these underlying situations on their own even if they did understand what was happening, especially if my work had opened the door onto them. With my background I had the tools to help clients resolve much of what was behind their physical problems. I saw it as part of my job. Now, a dozen years and a seeming lifetime later, my work as a massage therapist had developed into an approach to health based on working with the relationships between every aspect of the body and the mind. I had a method which went further than massage therapy alone and I had invited Diana to accept my help. By making another appointment Diana showed she had heeded her wake-up call and was ready to find out what I might be able to offer her.

There would have been wake-up calls before. I knew that. Calls she had ignored. Quiet, insistent calls, prompting her to recognise that all was not well in her world and her body, calls disguised as pain and distress which had become louder and more persistent over time. It was sad that she had to get as low as she was now before answering those calls, but such is the way we all operate; we are often reluctant to face the obvious, reluctant to change what we are familiar with, even when it is hurting us.

Finding out what she was dealing with would not present much of a problem. There really is nowhere to hide when you've got most of your clothes off and are lying on your back on a massage table. Whatever masks Diana normally presented to other people in her daily life, there were none she could wear with me. Years later I would learn about mirror neurons and parts of the brain which enable one person to empathise with another through an awareness of their thoughts and feelings. At that time I simply didn't question my ability to recognise her emotions while I worked on her body. I took it for granted that while I worked on Diana, I would be unconsciously absorbing and translating the flickers of facial expression, changes in muscle tone, shifts in breathing and pupil reactions and that they would be presented into my own mind as insights, then into my hands as intuitive massage moves.

I suspected Diana was also good at picking up the wealth of non-verbal cues people give out all the time to tell those around them how they are feeling and what they are likely to do. I wondered why Diana did not feel sympathy for Charles similar to that she obviously felt for the sick and dying? I would have had to be a hermit not to have noticed the stories in the newspapers suggesting her marriage was in trouble. I did know that if I worked with her for any length of time and got to know her well, the empathy I felt while working with her would probably diminish and become lost in the background noise of the other feedback and information I received from her during massage sessions.

Massage techniques would enable me to make her body more comfortable whatever else I did. They would also help me understand, through her muscle tone, quality and balance, what was going on in the relationships between her mind and body. Massage would help me identify the best way into her inner process and find the keys she could use to help herself. That was how it had to be, I couldn't do it for her. She had to make the journey herself. All I could do was to show her the path and walk along it with her for a while as a kind of guide. Anyway, with each of my clients I tried to teach them how to take care of themselves, in case I was run-over by the proverbial bus, or they chose not to see me again. The next time I saw Diana might be the last and I wanted to leave her with as much as possible.

Frankly I didn't expect to see her just once more. I didn't realise it at the time but I had developed a way of working that was different from most therapists. I had relatively few clients, all wealthy enough to see me as often as they wanted. They were scattered all around London. They all came to me by personal recommendation and we usually ended up working together every week, sometimes more frequently, for years.

I took it for granted that the techniques I used were effective enough to make a client want to work with me for a long time. Of course, some chose not to and there was the occasional one I felt unable to help, so I gave as much advice as I could before we parted company. Nor did every one of my clients need the kind of work Diana did. Some didn't want to know what lay beneath the problems they asked for my help with, so I just worked on their bodies and advised on diet and exercise to help them look good and be as fit and comfortable as possible. But that would not be enough for Diana. She required an approach that would transform who she was and how she operated in the world. As I had told her at our first session, if she worked with me she would change and her body and her life would alter as a result. The trick would be for her to make the best changes possible.

We would need to address some major issues quickly. Diana's feelings of despair and thoughts of suicide had to be top of our list. The bulimia would be having major effects on her general health and ability to respond to what I would be asking her to do, so that would have to be addressed quickly. The intensity of her emotions, particularly her anger, was also likely to inhibit her from seeing herself and her situation in the positive way I wanted her to.

There could be no plan however. At this early stage it would be all about crisis management and awakening her to her potential for transforming her own health and life. I felt if I could produce some rapid results, she might be motivated to continue with the longer commitment which would be necessary for the deeper work of reorganising what was underpinning her difficulties. Then we'd have to identify the particular beliefs Diana had which were causing her problems. That could be done by taking notice of the signs they produced. Muscle problems, negative emotions, actions and reactions, digestive problems, vocabulary, body language were among the many indicators Diana already exhibited.

After that it would be a matter of skill and perseverance. The techniques available for self-transformation were numerous and varied. What would work for Diana, what I would need to teach her, would depend on what she responded to best and I wouldn't find that out until I started working on her.

Of course it might not be her time. There is a natural process which brings about opportunities for personal transformation to no discernible timetable. It can be felt inwardly, as intuition, a sense of something about to happen, a moment of clarity that an anticipated action is perfectly suited to the situation. Diana was the only one who could tell whether she noticed these signs. As for me, she seemed ready enough and I would help her all I could.

✦ ✦ ✦

Diana started that January with her official diary full of engagements. True to her vow the previous year she had accepted a busy schedule of charity events and visits to tidied up hospital and schools, with their usual smell of fresh paint and their pristine lavatories, immaculately organised to the time table of her visit. She anticipated singing choirs, dancing children and curtseying women with eager, shining eyes and excited looks. She anticipated earnest mayors and local officials, all dressed in their best to impress her and the ranks of photographers. She anticipated the proud managers, matrons and factory workers. She anticipated the old, the young, the babies, the sick, the dying, the grieving and the sad.

In her public role Diana was now very polished. She slipped quickly from her private worries and stresses to cloak herself, for as long as required, in an aura that projected calm assurance and genuine caring with smiling charm and grace. She had discovered a capacity for connecting instantly with anyone and making them feel at ease. In exchange she was uplifted by how the public responded to her with warmth and gratitude, although she found it difficult to accept their admiration. She was being presented by the media as the Fairytale Princess, her relationship with Charles was being portrayed as troubled but not greatly so. Diana knew both impressions were far from accurate.

High points in her year to come would be when she could actually hold those who needed comforting, not just shake their hands. Instinctively she wanted to reach out and touch them and speak with them properly about their troubles and let them know she understood because she had felt the same. She began to realise she was becoming more and more aware of what people were feeling as soon as she was close enough to look into their eyes or touch them. It was almost uncanny. The way they changed when she connected with them was amazing and wonderful. She wished she could do more of this work. She wondered why Charles could not understand how important it was not just to meet and talk to people, but to really connect with them. It was so obvious to her that to help people you had to be able to reach out and really touch them.

The low points she knew would be when she was working with Charles; the ceremonies she must attend as wife to the heir; and holiday times with her husband and other members of the royal family at Balmoral and

Sandringham. The events when she would be on display and have to dig deep to be the smiling marionette everyone wanted her to be.

✦ ✦ ✦

On 18 January I drove up to the gates of Kensington Palace once more. Having reviewed the situation I was clear on what I wanted to do but even so, I found myself wondering what I would discover this time.

Every treatment started with the massage which conveyed, without words, "I care about you – I know about you – I am here to help you." At that stage I intended to use simple techniques to relax the tensions in her body and remake the connection of trust, all the while waiting to be guided by what I found, by what came forward to be dealt with.

I wanted to establish a basic massage routine as a norm, a systematic structure to the work Diana could identify every time from then on – face up, left leg, right leg, right arm, left arm, shoulders, neck – turn over – right leg, left leg, upper back, lower back, entire back and neck – start with sweeping movements to spread the oil, move on to whatever was needed to reduce tightness and tension and bring balance. There should be no surprises, no sudden changes to what she expected.

It was important that Diana be able to slip into the relaxed and therefore responsive state we needed as quickly as possible. The routine itself, regardless of any other techniques employed, would become a physical cue, a signal to her body and mind to let go of any tension and resistance, a conditioned response to save us time.

At this session she was in a much more positive state than before. There was more tone and more energy apparent in her muscles. Her facial expressions and her language, both body and verbal, all indicated she was more engaged with life and more hopeful. I took a brief inventory of her emotions by slipping into a receptive state and allowing myself to feel anger, fear, grief and despair in succession, searching, as I briefly touched each emotion within myself, for any response, any kind of resonance, from within her. I recognised the presence of most of them but not at anything like the intensity I had been struck with before. She was still at a low ebb however, still harbouring thoughts of giving up.

I decided to address the issue quickly and head on. She needed to see her life as worth living and to make that possible I needed her to make a major adjustment to the way she saw herself and her situation and I needed it to happen quickly.

From my perspective I accepted that Diana no longer had the certainty and clarity about her future that strong effective personal beliefs could have provided. Whether she had ever had such beliefs and what they might have been were irrelevant. She'd arrived this far alive and relatively unscathed physically, which meant at some time she had a workable self-identity, with a reasonably effective set of beliefs and attitudes behind it. But something had smashed through her carefully constructed inner reality, shattered all the most positive and enabling ideas she held about herself and had gone on to reinforce the most negative and disabling aspects of her inner self. The only expectation Diana was left with was that her life, for as far ahead as she could see, was going to be painful and bitter. If she was to heal herself I needed to help her believe her future was something she could look forward to. She soon gave me my opportunity.

'You know,' I murmured as I worked, 'everyone has an inner plan, a hidden future-vision of how they must be and what they must do if they are to survive and cope with life. It's not a plan you'll be aware of. When you think, consciously, about your future you can only bring a tiny fraction of what's really in your mind. Your inner future-vision is made up from everything you've come to believe about yourself, good and bad, from all your experiences since you were born, some would say from before you were born. Your mind and body work together to bring that vision about, the good and the bad, automatically and without you having to consider it. If some of the beliefs you've acquired conflict with others, or are not workable in the world you are actually bumping into, it causes problems, in your body in your thoughts and feelings and in your life.'

'Look at what's happening to you. You've created what most people regard as a fantastic fairytale life. For that to have happened you must have believed it was possible for you to marry a Prince and you must have believed it was possible for you to become a Princess, those things couldn't have happened unless you were able to accept they could. But it clearly hasn't worked out as you expected. Somewhere along the line other beliefs, beliefs you didn't know you had, have become involved and the result is your body is in pain, you are hurting inside and your life has become almost unbearable.' She nodded.

'Maybe part of your deeper belief is that marriage inevitably leads to what you are experiencing. Maybe what you believe about marriage isn't possible in the world your husband lives in. Maybe it's not possible with anyone. Maybe deep down you believe something about yourself which means you expect more from your husband than he can give. Whatever your hidden beliefs are they've resulted in you becoming very angry and your anger is causing the pain you get between your shoulder blades here. You're frightened and your fear is casing the tension in your shoulders and neck here and here. It's really important you make sure your beliefs are what you want to live by, because your health and your future depend on them.'

'I don't have a future,' she said bitterly 'I'm stuck with this bloody family.'

'Well that proves my point about your beliefs. The fact is they are stuck with you until you decide otherwise. You can always change any situation. It just depends on what you are prepared to do about it and that means what you believe you can do.'

'There's nothing I can do.'

'What you mean is you can't imagine what you could do because you don't have beliefs that offer you any other possibility than what you are seeing now. Think about it. Yes you can accept what you've believed up to now and stay as you are which will probably not make you happy and will almost certainly mean your health will suffer and your body will become more and more uncomfortable over the coming years. You can do what you've been thinking about and opt out for good, leave it all behind. If you're dead you won't have to feel the way you do. Or you can leave the marriage and start again, what's to stop you? Why does it have to be different for you than for all the millions of others who have separated because they made a mistake? Or, if you can imagine a future with Charles, you could talk to him, communicate, find out if you can see a future together and what you would each have to do to make it work. I'm sure you can come up with more options if you try.'

The massage continued in silence for a while as I left her to ponder what I'd said and dealt with the tensions that had come into her muscles. After a while, when I felt her relaxed, I spoke again.

'I have a suggestion for you. If you feel comfortable with it I'd like you to make what's called an affirmation. That's a statement which declares to yourself a reality you would like to live with, something you want to believe in. We get our beliefs about ourselves and the world in two ways mostly. The first is from single significant events which cause us to feel intense emotions and change the way we see ourselves. The second is from repetitions of events or messages from which we get ideas about who and what we are. The second type is the most common; people repeatedly telling you that you are no good at anything and treating you as if you are useless builds a certainty in you that you are no good at anything and that you are useless. You can even do it to yourself by believing what you've been told by other people and repeating their negative messages to yourself all the time, inside your head and when you talk about yourself to others.'

'The affirmation I suggest you make is "From this moment on I choose to be alive." Did you get that? "From this moment on I choose to be alive." You can say it out loud now if you are OK with that and it will be very powerful to say it with me as a witness. Alternatively you can think about it and if you're happy to try it you can write the words down, or say them aloud, or do both, when you are alone later. The important thing is you don't just think it. You have to make it real by speaking the words aloud or writing them down. If you want, if it feels right, you can repeat it or write it out a few times, ten will be fine and do that every night for a week or so. But it is such a powerful statement to make you will probably find you only need to do it the once for it to be set in your mind and start to work. Do you understand?'

I could see she was thoughtful but she responded firmly 'Yes, I understand.'

'Something else, don't tell anyone about any affirmation you make. Everyone has their own beliefs and even your best friend, no matter how much they care about you, could offer an opinion that will affect how your mind accepts the messages you want to place there.'

She didn't make the affirmation aloud to me then. Not surprising really. It was a very powerful phrase, a hair up on the back of the neck affirmation for anyone with deep feelings of despair considering whether they want to stay in the world. I never asked her if she ever spoke the phrase aloud or wrote it down as I suggested. The process Diana was now starting was hers to follow. It wasn't for me to push her to do anything which didn't fit with what she was able to imagine for herself. All I could do was offer her more information and guidance, information about herself and her body and mind and guidance about how they worked, so that what she could imagine was not limited by what she had been able to pick up by accident during her life to that point. If the affirmation was right for her it would already have touched deep chords within her the moment I said it. Indeed just my saying it might even have been enough to plant the seed I wanted to offer her mind.

I reviewed the conversation later that evening. My reasoning had been simple enough. I had picked up Diana's beliefs, that she had no future to look forward to and behind it that she had no control over her life and they seemed to me to be based on a situation I'd been thinking about for a while and which seemed to fit her. Unless you accept some New-Age thinking which proposes that before we are born we sit in the world of Spirit and ponder what experiences we need to have in life to bring us closer to perfection, then choose the parents and a life situation to be born to as a means to having those learning experiences, the simple fact is we are all born without our own volition and at someone else's whim.

This situation could be experienced by some as the ultimate loss of control. If their life is difficult early on, and there is a growing sense that they have neither power nor influence over events, it could lead to feelings of not wanting to be alive and thoughts of suicide, feelings I was aware of in Diana. If this scenario was true for her the affirmation I suggested would affect her deeply and powerfully. The statement might not be an easy one for her to make but once integrated into her set of personal beliefs, the notion of choosing to be alive meant she would have to accept responsibility her own life and future. It made blaming anyone else for her predicaments, parents in the past or anyone else in years to come, pointless. It would prompt her to take control of what happened in her own life from then on. She would no longer be able to see herself as helpless.

I pondered for a while on the power inherent in the words we use in our communications with other human beings and the responsibility which goes with that power. I remembered a group who had come to London a few years before. They called themselves immortalists and gave themselves the name The Eternal Flame. Their credo was quite seductive and based on some ideas which later gained a degree of acceptance in parts of the scientific community who would soon be investigating whether we have death genes which stop us living forever and "immortality" genes which stop our cells dying. The science of epigenetics would suggest that some features of our genetic code can be triggered or suppressed by how we think and feel about ourselves. It seems we do have a degree of control over whether a disease, to which we might be predisposed genetically, actually develops. Or as the immortalists put it, we have the power to choose not to die. And they offered the proposition that anyone could live forever by making the simple but very powerful affirmation before witnesses "I am immortal and I will live in this physical body forever."

It was fascinating to watch the effect on people who stepped up and made the statement before audiences of hundreds. The sheer joy they experienced and their change in posture and energy was amazing. Unfortunately the immediate effects did not last long and I soon began to hear stories of nervous breakdowns, marriages ending, physical ailments and emotional reactions in those who had made the affirmation. My girlfriend at the time and I tried an experiment. We sat together one evening and witnessed each other make the affirmation. We both spent the following day flat out with flu like symptoms and unable to move because we felt so depressed.

I realised something then I have never forgotten. An affirmation can indeed introduce a new, very powerful concept of self into the mind, but if that idea goes counter to a deeply held belief that already exists, then the resulting conflict between the two can cause serious disruption in the body and mind. It was like an induced Post Traumatic Stress Disorder, in which the traumatic event was an idea. An idea that encoded a few minute brain cells with a new message then released them to connect with the rest of the mind, until the entire basis of what had been assumed until then was altered. It was the butterfly effect; only this time it was not the fluttering of a butterfly's wings that caused a hurricane on the planet, but the flickering of barely discernible electro-chemical synapses in the brain which caused a storm of changed perceptions and physical reactions within individual people. The way I explained it to myself was that if someone has lived for decades assuming that someday they will die, a powerful affirmation to the contrary will collide against their original belief with unfortunate results.

Words once spoken cannot be unsaid. I had reframed Diana's belief that she was helpless by showing her, that it was the royal family who were stuck with her until she decided different and I had given her a powerful affirmation that could change for the better the entire perspective she had on her life. I wondered if the affirmation might set up an inner conflict. I concluded that on balance the phrase would do no harm and might produce immense benefits for her. Whether she used it as I suggested or not the idea, the thought-seed, had been sown. As long as it fell on fertile ground in her imagination, as long as it met her aspiration for herself and was nurtured, as I would try to make sure it was, it would grow and spread throughout her mind and reshape many of the limiting attitudes she had about herself and the world. The results would be seen over time in changes to thoughts feelings and behaviour as well as in her body.

During our sessions in the weeks which followed, I nurtured the seeds that had been sown by using massage to keep Diana's body and mind open and receptive and by challenging her gently whenever she spoke her limiting beliefs aloud.

'What do you know about elemental typology?' I asked one day as I worked.

'Nothing, what's that?'

'It's a system which enables you to recognise how people prefer to operate in the world by looking at the face and body shape. It's based on the Eastern concept of the four elements which make up the world, Fire, Water, Air and Earth. You are Water with Air.'

'How do you know?'

'Well your body and face shape are softer and more rounded than other types and your eyes are blue so you have a lot of Water. That means you rely a great deal on your emotions to tell you what to do. Family, home and children are the most important things in the world to you. You're tall so that means you have some Air characteristics as well. Air will give you a sense of duty, a feeling for tradition and the ability to think and reason.'

'Ha! That's a laugh. I'm as dim as they come. Everyone knows that.'

'I think it's more likely that you haven't found what it is you want to think and reason about. When you do you'll find you can work things out well enough, although your emotions will always have the final say in what you decide to do.'

There were to be similar conversations many times throughout the coming years as I offered my client a new view of herself and her life through my eyes and experience. I can't remember a single occasion when we spoke in detail about any topic. My observations were intended to be brief and striking reframes of her negative beliefs and thoughts, signposts pointed out to her from which she could make her own map to the person she wanted to become. If the seeds of positive self-belief I had already sown were taking hold, the person she chose to be would enjoy life a lot more than the one lying on my massage table.

Some seeds take a long time to grow and produce noticeable results. Others grow quickly and produce rapid changes in the mind, body and life. It wasn't long before Diana began experiencing some of the effects of the sowing we had done.

✦ ✦ ✦

At the beginning of February Diana accompanied Charles to the 40th birthday party of Camilla's sister Annabel. There she confronted the woman she had come to blame for her plight when she sought out Camilla and Charles who had left the main party for a private conversation with another guest. According to Diana's version of events, while the others retreated and left them she invited Camilla to sit and talk. Despite feeling intimidated by her rival, Diana was then able to have a brief, calm conversation during which she told Camilla in essence "I do know what is going on. Don't treat me like an idiot." Another version from a friend of the Princess has Diana more timidly asking Camilla "What am I doing wrong? What is wrong with me?" and asking why Charles preferred to be with another woman. Whatever the actual conversation it marked a new level of self-belief for Diana and sufficient confidence that she felt entitled and able to confront the woman she believed had taken her husband.

Later the same month Diana made a blockbusting solo trip to New York City. Her itinerary included a visit to the Harlem Paediatric AIDS Unit. During her flight back to Heathrow, Diana chatted with a tabloid journalist who had managed to obtain a seat on the same Concorde. The following day front page banner headlines heralded a two page story about Diana's experience meeting children suffering from HIV+AIDS. According to her chief of staff, Patrick Jephson, the informal interview was Diana's first step to what became frequent unofficial press briefings she gave during the years which followed.

✦ ✦ ✦

The blueprint for our work over the coming years was set in those early weeks of 1989. The massage routine was established quickly and by the time I started work on her left calf I invariably found Diana had relaxed and was ready to learn more. Sometimes I just had to hold her feet and stand quietly for a few seconds to feel her relax. I was already working to make this a quicker cue to the receptive state I was looking for.

A constant in my work was to help Diana really believe things would get better. One of the changes I wanted to get her to make was to be more positive in what she said outwardly in conversation and inwardly to herself. I knew there was little to be gained from challenging her every time I heard her use words like "must," or "can't" or "shouldn't" in self-limiting ways. It would be too confrontational and hardly conducive to the relaxation and peace of mind she expected from my ministrations. Instead I employed another approach, not as obvious as the affirmation I had given her but effective nonetheless.

I rarely spoke before she had slipped into the relaxed, receptive state except in our initial greetings but then I deliberately chose phrases which would prompt her into a positive frame of mind and anticipation of something good coming from our session. Experience had shown me that an earnest "So how are things today?" usually invites people to go through a mental catalogue of all their problems to find the one they feel worst about. Saying instead, "Tell me something good that happened for you this week," would usually prompt Diana into a review of the week's high points from which she would choose something good to tell me about.

Conditioned responses can quite easily be established by mistake. If every time I saw her she found herself thinking about her problems it would have been a good way to make her dread my visits. I wanted Diana to look forward to the time we spent together knowing I was focussed on finding solutions for her. Getting her to say aloud something good about herself and to hear herself saying it, was an important part in the process of changing the negative aspects of her perception of herself to ones which were ever more positive. By listening, I became both a witness to the fact that there were good things in her life, things to enjoy and look forward to and a cue to start thinking nice thoughts.

Invariably the positive things she chose to tell me about were how wonderful her boys were, or experiences she had with sick or disabled people during her work. In contrast the tension and stiffness of her muscles showed me she was under almost continuous strain and dealing with intense emotions. So I worked to reduce the tightness and restore flexibility knowing it would make her feel more comfortable. I didn't ask what was troubling her. Sometimes I had an idea from stories I had seen in the papers, sometimes I just knew what the emotions were, but I preferred to wait for her to offer personal information when she was ready. In the meantime there was plenty to work with and always massage to help her become open to positive thoughts and feelings about herself

At the end of February I appreciated receiving a brief note from Diana in the flowing scrawl I came to recognise well. Written on purple bordered Kensington Palace note paper bearing the motif of a crown over the letters C and D entwined, it was dated *February: 20th 1989* and was signed *Yours sincerely, Diana.* The note thanked me for a visit I had made the day before, a Sunday and mentioned "several distractions from a certain young man!"

The certain young man was Prince William, then six, who pestered his mother for her attention even while she was smothered in oil on my table. Not every visit I made was marked by intense and meaningful transformation work!

The transformation in Diana when her sons were with her was a delight to see and she seemed to me to have found a perfect balance between effusive love and firm guidance in important matters such as the social niceties. Every occasion when I visited her and found the young Princes there as well Diana ensured that they greeted "Mr Twigg" politely before being sent off to wait until we had finished our work. They didn't always stay sent-off though and her note marked one such occasion.

✦ ✦ ✦

Despite the uneasy state of her marriage and the new ideas beginning to take root in her mind, Diana continued to perform on the public stage with aplomb. In March she joined her husband on a successful joint tour of the Gulf States and perfectly executed what was later called a "charm offensive". Photos of her in unguarded moments however showed the unhappiness hiding just below the surface poise.

In the UK she continued her round of royal duties. Journalists and cameramen captured her every official move and tried ever harder to catch her private ones. In early April it was reported Diana had four wisdom teeth removed during a minor operation but was soon back on duty fulfilling her role as the smiling, caring Princess.

In May she gave what her private secretary Patrick Jephson described as her "first real breakthrough" speech in a "firm and steady voice with just the right amount of girlish hesitancy". Previously Diana was so lacking in confidence and obviously uncomfortable with public speaking that she was hesitant and halting.

The newspapers described her six minute presentation at the 25th anniversary event for Turning Point, the charity for drug and alcohol abuse, as "important" and "poised and polished". Other stories offered continued speculation about the state of her marriage. On balance Diana enjoyed good press and continued to eclipse her husband. In private she and Charles were in a state of uneasy truce living virtually separate lives and coming together only to be with the boys or when duty demanded.

✦ ✦ ✦

'Are you still being sick?' I offered the question as a way of gauging whether Diana was ready to work on another serious issue.

'Yes, mostly when I'm under a lot of stress. Then it becomes quite rampant.'

'Do you want to get more control over it?' I didn't need to ask what was causing the stress. It was not relevant to the changes I wanted to propose and would only prompt her to review painful experiences.

'Yes I'd like that. It does take over a bit.'

'There's a process I'd like to suggest if you feel like trying it.'

'OK.'

I worked her muscles a while longer to let the idea sink in. Then started 'When I've come across the problem before with clients there have been two main reasons for it. The first is that it seems like a good way to stay slim. When they hear how it messes up the body and mind they realise it's not such a good way of staying in shape after all.'

Diana nodded her agreement. Unknown to me she'd heard this before and had read books about it.

I went on. 'The second reason people do it is because it makes them feel better. It helps them cope with what's happening in their lives. They do it to have some control over things when they feel helpless.'

Another nod.

'What I want to do is to show you how to find another way of coping so you won't have to be sick to feel in control. Is that OK with you?'

A nod.

'Tell me something. Do you think you are the same person all the time?' Diana looked quizzically at me. 'Think about it a minute. Are you the same when you are in public as when you are with your boys, or with your husband?'

Diana grimaced, 'No. In public I am doing a job. With the boys I'm their mother. Charles often makes me feel like a useless little child.'

I didn't want to pursue the conversation into territory that would make Diana remember anything negative so I chose the more positive option.

'When you're with the boys do you do the same things as when you are in public?'

'No with the boys I have to be their mother and love them, give them hugs and teach them how to do things. In public I'm dealing with grown-ups and sick people, I have to handle them and be caring in a different way.'

'Do you have to think about it every time?'

'No it just comes naturally.'

'So in different situations you automatically change to become who you need to be and to do what you need to do? In other words you have a different part of you to deal with, to cope with, every situation? And you do it automatically?'

A nod as recognition started to dawn.

'Good. We're all the same. The problem is some of the parts we use to cope, some of what are called our sub-personalities, are built in our minds when we're under stress and don't have the time or information we really need to build something that works better long term. I think that's what is happening with your throwing up. You have a part of you which is trying to help you cope with feeling stressed and helpless by making sure you can do something about it. It works for you in the short term but it is actually causing you harm in the long.'

A nod from Diana.

'OK! Now this is what is called an inner-dialogue process. Close your eyes and listen to what I say.' I stopped working on her muscles and placed my hand on her foot – the cue for relax and be receptive. 'Ready?'

She nodded.

'Just go into your mind and say inwardly, not out loud, just inside your own mind "I want to talk to that part of myself which make me be sick" and let me know when you get a response. It might be an inner voice you hear or some other reaction. Just tell me if you get a reaction inside.' I half expected it to take a few attempts before there was a response from her inner self. A lot of people feel embarrassed when being guided through a process that requires them to talk to themselves, or they are distracted by trying to work out what is happening. Diana had no such problems. Perhaps it was because she had become used to giving herself a good talking and now she recognised something similar.

'I have it. A voice telling me it's there.'

'Great. Just inwardly thank that part of you for coming forward.' I paused for a moment while I searched for the right words, then went on

'Now tell that part of you that they haven't done anything wrong and thank it for what it's been doing for you.' I paused again. 'Have you done that?'

A nod from Diana.

'Good. Tell me can you see, in your mind's eye, what that part of you looks like?'

'Yes. It's a little girl.'

'How old about?'

'Seven or eight.'

'How does she feel?'

'Frightened. Lonely.'

'Ask her if she needs anything to feel better.'

'She needs a hug.'

'Would you like to give her a hug?'

'Yes.'

'Go ahead.'

A tear rolled from the corner of Diana's eye as she made a loving connection with the fragile part of her inner self.

'Will you ask that part of you why she helps you by making you be sick?'

'She says she wants to stop feeling bad.'

'Ask if she realises that what she helps you do is actually going to hurt your body and make you unwell if you keep doing it?'

'She says yes.'

'Ask her if she will help you do something else instead, something else that will stop her feeling bad but help you be better?'

'She says yes.'

'Ask her what she needs.'

'More hugs. She needs to know someone notices how bad she feels and is taking care of her.'

'OK. I have a suggestion. When you are under stress, in a situation when she would usually make you feel as if you want to go and be sick, how about she waits for five minutes after she feels that way so you have the chance to do something else?'

'What else?'

'Well make sure she gets the hugs she needs to feel better for one thing, so she knows she's not on her own and the chance to choose whether you stay in the situation for another.'

'She says that sounds OK but she isn't convinced.'

'All right, ask her to sit quietly for a minute, tell her you won't go away...is she doing that?'

'Yes.'

'Now I want you to ask inwardly to talk to that part of you which is the wise carer, the part which knows everything about you there is to know and loves you for yourself.'

Diana made no objection to my description of a sub-personality common to us all but with which most of us have no contact. 'Are they there?'

A firm nod. 'Yes.'

'Ask that wise part of yourself if she will look after the little girl and hug her whenever she feels bad.'

'She says yes.'

'Ask her if she will tell you what to do instead when the little girl makes you feel as if you should be sick.'

'Yes.'

'Is the little girl part of you happy with that arrangement?'

'Yes. She's very happy.'

'Ask the wise part of you to hug her.'

'She's already doing it.'

The inner negotiations continued for a while longer and ended with a strategy agreed by all parties. Recognisable signs, emotions and tensions in muscles, would make Diana aware very quickly when she was under stress and needed to do something about it. She would get ideas about what to do but would also retain the ability to use a bulimia session in extremis and as a last resort to deal with how she felt.

During the following weeks I worked to alter Diana's perception of her body and show her how it was involved in everything she felt and everything she experienced. I wanted her to become more engaged with what her body could tell her about herself and how it could help her resolve her problems. I suggested a healthy diet, food combining based on the Hay system, which would help her digestion work more efficiently. It would enable her to achieve her most *appropriate* body shape, appropriate in the context of her basic physique and the type and amount of exercise she did, not one that she fantasised to meet anyone else's ideals or one that was distorted by poor eating habits.

A few months later, while I worked and we chatted Diana said, 'I threw up again yesterday. The first time in ages.'

'Good!' I said, 'At least you know you can still do it if you need to. If it gets to be a problem just go back to the things we worked with before, check in with those parts of you that agreed to help you. I'll just see if there's anything I can work on here in your muscles now.'

I expressed no surprise which she might have interpreted as condemnation. No criticism to reduce her still developing confidence. No drama – we might have been discussing the weather. Indeed I felt no unease. As far as I was concerned, this was a normal and healthy event in the process of transformation we had undertaken. Bulimia had become like an old friend she no longer needed all the time, but there was no harm in it visiting occasionally. To the best of my knowledge that's how it remained for the rest of her life, an infrequent visitor.

✦ ✦ ✦

A few years later, in a speech on eating disorders, Diana would speak from the heart and no little experience of her own bulimia. She would describe the illness of an eating disorder, for those who suffered from it, as a "shameful friend" and "a "refuge from having to face the more painful issues at the centre of their lives" and "a way of 'coping'".

✦ ✦ ✦

Media commentary on the state of Diana's marriage continued alongside stories of her public successes. Private sources were already telling journalists about the parlous state of the royal couple's relationship and some articles intimated Diana had accepted the situation and might even take a lover.

An article by Lesley Garner in *The Daily Telegraph* on 17 June 1989 was fairly typical of the view held at that time. She wrote:

"If ever The Princess of Wales was just a frivolous Sloane (Ranger), she has surely changed beyond all recognition...."

On 25 July Diana opened the new Landmark AIDS Centre in London and was photographed without gloves firmly shaking the hand of Jonathan Grimshaw the Director of the Centre and an AIDS sufferer. She had made the same gesture with an AIDS patient in April 1987 when opening a specialist HIV+AIDS unit at the Middlesex Hospital. On both occasions the press commented on how much her actions meant for AIDS awareness and how much they would do to de-stigmatise the disease.

It was widely felt at the time that no other member of the royal family would have agreed to such a powerful way of improving people's knowledge of AIDS and dispelling some of the misconceptions associated with it. This time however Diana was more able to accept the praise and her sense of self-worth and her belief in her own informal and personal approach to her duties, were boosted along with her confidence.

✦ ✦ ✦

On my first visit to Diana after the handshake, while I was working on her, I murmured, 'Nice job with the AIDS Centre.'

'Oh you saw that?'

'Yes. Do you realise how difficult most people would find it to do something like that? It's not easy overcoming the natural impulse to pull back from what the majority feel repulsed by. To do it in public with the media all around you must have been even harder.'

Diana looked at me closely and frowned, 'I hadn't really thought about it that way.'

'When I was working in the health farm years ago, I hadn't been doing massage for long. One day I was waiting for my next body. It was like a production line in a factory, we had about nine massages a day one after the other, anyway this guy came in. American, long robe down to the floor, came up to my cubicle and I went through the usual routine, said "Hi" and introduced myself, told him how I wanted him on the table for his massage.'

'He got undressed and took his left leg off. I was stunned. It took me completely by surprise. No one from the office had told me, no one had warned me. I'd been doing simple basic body-work and sports massage for a few months, never seen an amputation up close. Then he asked me to massage the stump. It was a seminal moment for me and one I'll never forget. I found a level of caring and compassion I never realised I had right there. Didn't bat an eyelid to show what was going on in my head. Worked the stump, worked the rest of him. Then went and asked the girls in the office to let me know in future. It was all about acceptance, total unconditional acceptance of people and never rejecting. I never knew I was capable of that until then. Do you feel something like that when you're able to connect with people others would feel uncomfortable with?'

She nodded vigorously. 'Yes, yes I do.'

At every opportunity which presented itself, I validated Diana's most positive traits and invited her to see her achievements for what they were, rare and something to be proud of.

By the latter part of the summer of 1989, about nine months after we started working together, I realised Diana's intense and destructive emotions were holding her back from achieving more positive changes.

'I want to focus on reducing the tightness and pain you get in your back, between your shoulder blades. In my understanding, partly based on Chinese medicine, that's an area which is related to anger and I know you've got a lot of that in you.'

Diana nodded, listening intently now.

'Anger when it's projected outwards at situations or other people, is associated with your liver; when it's kept inside and directed at yourself, it's associated with your gall bladder. The gall bladder is related to feelings of depression, self-criticism and inability to see a meaningful future.' I watched her eyebrows lift in surprised recognition and filed a mental note before I continued.

'So these muscles, the emotion of anger, your liver and gall bladder are all involved together, not in any medical way but if you allow the situation to continue for another ten or twenty years and it's been going on a long time already, it could become a distinct health problem. If these muscles remain tight and tense and keep becoming inflamed like they have they will permanently shorten and start affecting the alignment of your spine. The impact on your gall bladder or liver could make it difficult for you to digest some foods or absorb some essential nutrients and there could be a knock on affect to other organs in your digestion or systems in your body or mind.'

I went on to suggest that in order for her to respond to any situation with anger, even anger at herself, she needed to have a certain view point which might not be as accurate or as reasonable as she believed it to be. If she could alter her viewpoint, the result could be to change the intensity of the anger she felt or it could result in her feeling a different emotion altogether. In effect, by challenging her own way of seeing things, Diana could learn to experience anger more appropriately, in context and make the emotion more useful so it didn't disable her from effective communications or cause her to do something she might regret. I could see in her expression and her nodded agreement that a lot of what I was saying was touching chords in her.

'With the amount of anger you're experiencing all the time you won't be able to see behind it to be able to decide if it's reasonable to be angry. Even if it is reasonable, you won't be able to communicate properly why you're angry, to yourself or anyone else, the emotion will take over. You'll be flipped into an old pattern of reaction which will almost certainly echo old childhood situations and childlike reactions and not be appropriate to your present adult situation. I want to see if we can adjust the intensity of anger you feel, so you have a chance to consider whether it's appropriate and how you want to express your feelings. When you do become angry I want it to be in a way that won't be so damaging to your body. OK?'

A nod.

'Good. Emotions are part of us. They have a purpose like every other part of us. They help us to deal with our lives better but they can make our lives wonderful, or more painful if we don't learn to manage them. Emotions are real stuff, natural brain and body chemicals which, if generated very often, become stronger and more persistent until they just won't go away. That's why some emotions can get to the stage where they are out of proportion or quite inappropriate to the events which trigger them, because we produce a lot of that particular emotion-chemical. What we produce doesn't have time to disperse before something makes us feel angry again and then we produce more and because the chemicals are always there in our body and brain we feel that emotion more easily than others. It's like a catch 22. The more you practise feeling an emotion, the stronger it becomes and the less likely you'll be able to feel other, more positive emotions, instead. Personally I think love, compassion and tolerance are better emotions to practise than say anger, jealousy or fear but that's my opinion. The emotion that's most persistent for you at the moment is anger. What I'm going to suggest should alter your experience of it.'

After months of increasingly firm but still general bodywork Diana was ripe for the deep tissue massage I wanted to use in the process I had in mind. I described the very deep work in which I would use my elbows and knuckles to stretch the fascia surrounding her muscles, the thin layer of connective tissue which keeps muscles separated and allows them to work independently of those around them and which forms the tendons which attach the muscles to adjacent bones.

I explained that releasing habitual tension in the muscles could result in her having flashbacks to events which had produced the feelings which were now locked into the tissue or to her feeling the emotions, either as we worked or afterwards, usually within forty eight hours. Another feature of the process would be to directly address her liver and gall bladder function so I asked Diana if she would agree to me using remote muscle-testing to put together the strategy she would need.

'Somewhere within your body and mind is all the information about everything that's ever happened to you and muscle-testing is a way of accessing it and getting answers that will help you. I prefer tuning in to you from a distance so I can find out what you need,' I said, somewhat mysteriously. The truth was I could only speculate on how the remote connection worked. It did however, and I used it, when I had permission, both to project healing and to test for strategies like the one I was putting together now, Diana was happy to agree albeit she seemed a little perplexed.

Muscle testing is a technique which makes use of the way our muscles can become weak, or "turned off", when we are challenged by anything that's negative for us and are strengthened, or "turned on", by foods, people, supplements or environments which enable us or are good for us. Sceptics have a good time with this one since the differences are often very slight and very dependent on the conditions under which the test is carried out. They can be felt however and are quite common. Think how you feel when your spirits drop and you feel uncomfortable after just a few seconds in an environment that overwhelms you, like in some supermarkets, or when confronted by someone who is very angry with you. Perhaps, like many other alternative health systems muscle testing relies strongly on the intuition of the person doing the testing and the cooperation of the one being tested, hence my request. I wanted Diana to consciously agree to the process, which would make the connection easier for me. It was also an opportunity to introduce her to the more mysterious workings of the body and mind.

I wasn't very good at direct muscle testing on other people. I was better at a distance when I was alone and relaxed. Then I could tune in to my client, my intuition would kick in and I would be able to test for what they needed by checking my own muscle integrity using *opponens pollicis longus*, a convenient muscle in the hand at the base of the thumb.

After giving Diana some coaching on how to receive the deep massage work, by focussing on the point of contact and using breathing techniques to release any pain without tensing and resisting, I started work. Fascia sculpting techniques can be painful especially if it is applied too fast, so I made the moves very, very slow. I tried to use my thumbs as much as possible when I pushed deep through the layers of elastic and pliable muscle to the knots, scars and strings I wanted to soften or stretch. My hands were also able to feel shiatsu points as they popped open, a bonus but not the point of the treatment. When I sensed Diana instinctively tensing as I approached a particularly painful block of tissue or tight cord of tendon I waited, backing off ever so slightly while I projected energy, call it ki, or qi, or prana, what you will, until the block opened up and I could move through it. I sometimes waited more than a minute. My elbows and knuckles weren't as sensitive as my hands but sometimes I had to use them to drive through large muscles. There was no talking now, except for the occasional "breathe" or "let go here". We were both completely focussed and in a state similar to that which can be achieved in meditation.

Later, 'It's important you understand something. There could be times during this process when you suddenly find yourself releasing your anger uncontrollably. You need to find ways of releasing your anger without dumping it on people who don't deserve it. Either that or get used to apologising.'

'How can I do that?'

'Well for a start keep moving. Long walks, exercise more, hard exercise not gentle, work at it, drink lots of water, eat lightly to support your liver and gall bladder functions. If you feel your anger building up and have the chance get yourself outside, just let it out. When I was doing this, I used to go for a drive in the countryside or by the sea and scream at the top of my voice. Hell on the vocal chords, because not many people really open their lungs and let rip very often, but it feels good. If you are worried about anything, call me.'

A week later I provided her with a combination of herbal tinctures and mineral supplements with instructions about how to use them between deep massage treatments to release the reservoir of intense rage within her.

✦ ✦ ✦

In mid September, Diana attended her brother's wedding at Althorp. During the church rehearsal, reacting to her mother being ignored by Raine Spencer, now the new matriarch of the Spencer family home, Diana exploded with anger. Years of pent up rage poured out at the woman who 13 years earlier had replaced Diana's mother and stolen from the little girl her father's attention when she needed it most. As Diana later recalled "I've never known so much anger."

During the same month, prompted by Cardinal Basil Hume and without the protocol and formality which usually accompanied such trips, Diana began making private unpublicised visits in secret to homeless centres and hospices. The genuinely caring part of her self-identity had been suppressed during the past few years. She had been distracted by fruitless attempts to be the person she thought Charles, the royal family and the press wanted her to be and by her need to fit into the dutiful public role they expected of her. Now her true self was quietly emerging again and she began to seek more contact with the people she felt most connection to in her public role, the sick, the disadvantaged and the dying. Without realising it yet she was responding to her true calling.

✦ ✦ ✦

Just two weeks after we began the new phase of work I found Diana waiting for me as I arrived for our appointment.

'You were right about the anger.' The words tumbled out instantly, breathlessly.

She then told me that intense feelings of anger had been surfacing during the week since my last visit. She had been irritable and short-tempered with everyone around her and finally she had "really let rip" at someone. The scepticism she had felt when I first described what might happen had vanished and she became more eager to learn. She spoke about events during her life that had made her angry. I was pleased she was at last being relieved of a burden she'd suffered since childhood but I felt sorry for whoever had been in her way when the lid came off.

We chatted a while about how releasing tensions and restriction from the body's physical structure could open the mind and release memories and emotions. I mentioned that it wasn't just anger which could be freed. Any restricting emotions like fear, grief or jealousy could be released to give way to feelings like love or forgiveness which tend to make the body structure more open and mobile.

'Try this,' I said, 'make an angry face.'

Diana scowled a scary look, her eyes hooded down, her chin thrust forward and as I expected her shoulders moved slightly forward and her fists clenched slightly.

'Notice which muscles you are using. All right relax a minute, did you feel any emotions?'

'Yes of course. I felt angry.'

'Why of course? I said make an angry face, not get angry. Now smile as if you had just seen your boys.'

She relaxed instantly. Her shoulders dropped back and her head came up. Her face opened into a smile so bright it was like sunlight coming into the room.

'How do you feel?'

'Really happy.'

'Emotions affect your muscles for sure, that's why we're incorporating some deep work to help release those which are restricting you, but it's a feedback system. If you experience an emotion all the time your muscles take up habitual patterns that reflect the way you usually feel. After a while, because your muscles are in that pattern you will find yourself feeling the emotion even when there's no reason to. It's as if your body starts telling your mind what to feel, like you just experienced. You can practise feeling the way you want by using the facial expressions and posture that go with the emotions you prefer.'

On another occasion Diana asked, 'What do you think of astrology?'

'It can be great, a useful tool for understanding yourself and other people. My personal preference is for astrology that offers guidance about how to be rather than predictions about what's supposed to happen. I don't believe our lives are predestined, maybe predisposed to a range of possibilities but not written out in some cosmic plan.'

'The world around you and especially the people in it respond to what you project from within you, because of how you are. You're in the process of altering what you are showing to the world by examining what you believe, think and feel and starting to change what hasn't worked for you. As you change you'll find the experiences you have will change as well. You'll find yourself choosing to do things you never believed you could. People you thought would be with you forever, will move on out of your life. Others will come into your life quite naturally, as if by chance. Opportunities will open up as your attitude towards yourself enables you to see possibilities you were blind to before. Personal change is an inner process that influences the outer worlds of your body and your life. I haven't ever come across an astrologer who was able to predict what's happened to me and my life, but I have met several who have helped me make good decisions by pointing out things I needed to know about myself.'

Every visit was an opportunity for me to nurture the newly sown seeds of self-belief and scatter new ideas which supported in Diana the conviction she could transform herself and her situation.

✦ ✦ ✦

By early autumn Diana's relationship with James Hewitt had cooled. He accepted a posting to Germany and was soon busy with training and exercises before he finally left the UK. Later he described Diana's anger and feeling of rejection. Their three years together had been a source of comfort and support to her, an acknowledgement that though she was rejected by her husband she was still a desirable woman who could be worthy of a man's love. The affair had fed that part of her personality which needed a close personal relationship. Around the time that James Hewitt began to withdraw from her life, Diana started spending time with James Gilbey, a friend from her past.

In early November Diana joined Charles on a tour to the Far East. In Indonesia, during a visit to the inspiring Sitanala Leprosy Hospital in Jakarta, she was photographed gently holding and touching leprosy patients. Diana described it as "trying to show in a simple action that they are not reviled, nor are we repulsed."

✦ ✦ ✦

'What do you think of acupuncture?' Diana dropped the abrupt question into our conversation one day.

'It's great if you are one of those people who respond to it. I don't think everyone responds to it the same but if you do, it can be very beneficial. Some of the work I do with you affects the energy flow and systems that acupuncture works on as well. Try it and see. Find out if it works for you.' I didn't ask what her interest was nor did I ask if she had tried it. If she wanted to tell me, she would, In the meantime I respected her commitment to the journey she had undertaken and had no doubt that whatever she did would in one way or another bring her to where she wanted to be.

After I finished the last massage for that year, I gave her a Christmas present, a book, *The Tao of Pooh* and a large bottle of my own favourite Badedas bubble bath, the latter to recall the occasion when I'd commented after seeing the familiar green bottle in her bathroom. Harking back to her char lady days, she brightly reminded me, 'You don't have to clean the bath after using it.'

◆ ◆ ◆

As the curtain started coming down on 1989, Diana was in better physical and mental shape than at the year's beginning but she was still far from strong. The inner seeds of her new self-belief and confidence were still pushing into her sub-conscious and needed careful nurturing if they were to bring their best influences to bear on her way of seeing herself. Her world was one which challenged every new and positive insight with situations which pushed her back towards the dark frailties within her.

In public Diana had given superb performances every day whether officially on display or not. She had helped maintain the impression that her place with Charles and within the royal family was secure and permanent even though she resented doing so. The fairytale myth was sustained for the people, albeit slightly tarnished by the assumption that Diana was conceding to the historical compromise of accepting her lot and making the most of it.

In private Diana's relationship with Charles, when they were together, was marked by loud arguments during which they traded cruel remarks and bitter silences during which they exchanged hurtful rejection. Diana's resentment of Camilla was as strong as ever and matched by her antagonism towards Charles. Increasingly, Diana's anger was spreading to encompass the royal family, not as individuals but as a collection of people who had not offered her help when she needed it. Her self-worth had increased sufficiently for her believe she deserved better from her husband and his family and her innate sense of what was just was giving rise to indignation at the way she was still being treated. She saw no irony in her having sought consolation in other relationships during the past four years. She would not have chosen to if the promises she was given had been fulfilled.

During the year, Diana's developing desire for self-understanding and search for more knowledge about New Age ideas was marked by a growing collection of books on alternative medicine and psychology to add to those on bulimia, suggested by Maurice Lipsedge the previous year. She engaged a new astrologer, Debbie Frank, whose style incorporated astrology and counselling. Oonagh Toffolo, a trained nurse and devout Catholic, was asked to provide Chinese acupuncture and to share prayer and meditation.

Diana's royal Christmases at Sandringham usually provoked a prolonged bout of bulimia. The strain that year was relieved by an impromptu visit to the home where she had spent her first years as a little girl. Park House was by then the Leonard Cheshire home for the disabled. Diana spoke about it in a telephone conversation with her friend James Gilbey that New Year's Eve.

> DIANA: There was really something strange; I was leaning over the fence yesterday, looking into Park House and I thought: 'Oh, what shall I do?' And I thought: 'Well, my friend would say go in and do it,' I thought: 'No, 'cause I am a bit shy,' and there were hundreds of people in there. So I thought: 'Bugger that.' So I walked round to the front door and walked straight in.
>
> GILBEY: Did you?
>
> DIANA: It was just so exciting.
>
> GILBEY: How long were you there for?
>
> DIANA: An hour and a half.
>
> GILBEY: Were you?
>
> DIANA: Mmm hmm. And they were so sweet. They wanted their photographs taken with me and they kept hugging me. They were very ill some of them. Some no legs and all sorts of things.

Unknown to Diana and James their conversation was being recorded and a transcript would appear years later in the newspapers at a most difficult time for the Princess. During their conversation, Diana's obvious distaste for Charles comes across but with it came the first inclination of a plan that would enable Diana's flight from the trap of her marriage.

> DIANA: He makes my life real, real, torture I've decided. But the distancing will be because I go out – and I hate the word – "conquer the world" – I don't mean that, I mean I'll go out and do my bit in the way I know how and I'll leave him (Charles) behind. That's what I see happening.

If Diana was ever a bird trapped in a gilded cage her prophetic words would be the sound of her wings, the wings she longed to spread, beating against the bars. In truth however they were the sound of a Phoenix about to take flight.

The conundrum for Diana, ever since she realised her marriage was not what she wanted or expected, was her inability to see a future that gave her the possibility of happiness and fulfilment. The vision she had of herself and her future when she was aged nineteen had finally been shattered a year ago, and its traumatic destruction left a void which has been a source of torment ever since. Indeed during most of her marriage, through the good times and bad, the gradual crumbling of that vision cast a shadow over her every thought about what would become of her.

Now a new vision was emerging. It was one built on the ashes of the old and it was not complete. It did not answer all her questions nor fulfil all her dreams but it was a start. And it provided an antidote to her feeling of helplessness, that most corrosive of feelings which wore away constantly at Diana's health and heart.

The sense that her life was controlled by others she did not trust and who did not care for her, distressed her beyond measure. It was in her make-up to do anything to avoid such feelings even, in the past, to the point where she had been seriously contemplating ending her life. Now she saw that she could act decisively and change the situation herself. She did not know what the outcome of her actions would be. She was not made to weigh the pros and cons with fine judgements. Rather she relied upon her intuition and her emotions which were telling her what she should do.

Media coverage of Diana's role through 1989 had started out offering the public more of the Fairytale Princess, beautiful, smiling and superficial. By the end of the year their portrayal included images and stories of a serious, mature and caring woman who brought genuine compassion and courage to the work of helping people who were afflicted with diseases most saw as hideous. No fairytale can attach to HIV+AIDS and leprosy except in the most cynical of minds.

In the past, Diana had viewed her media coverage wryly, as a bag of mixed blessings. Now she saw herself being acknowledged for work she knew was genuine and heartfelt, a true representation of herself and she was able to acknowledge the truth of it. Diana was accepting that she had a rare ability – and an even rarer opportunity – to make a difference in the world as she had always believed she would. She was accepting that she was very good at what she did and enjoyed it when she could do it the way she wanted to. She was accepting that her media profile was a tool she could use to restore her life to some semblance of what she wanted and she was ready to fight for it.

Her awakening to a new sense of self-worth had enabled Diana to see the possibility that people might accept her for being who she was, a truly caring woman with a gift for loving the most damaged and distressed in society. It almost certainly did not enter her mind that she would be reprising a role for which she gained acknowledgement and affection as a child and was now contemplating it on a stage far larger than she had then. It was an intuitive leap which perfectly suited her personality, her self-image and her circumstances.

Diana's senior personal protection officer Ken Wharfe recalled Diana's strength and determination at that time in his memoirs. He described her as believing she could do anything, including leaving her husband and establishing a rival court. In December 1989 *Vanity Fair* magazine marked her transformation by calling her "dedicated Di" and reported that some people were talking about her "as a saint."

As the year drew to its close, it dawned on Diana that she might develop a presence in the world which would have to be taken seriously; a presence that could not be treated lightly by her husband or his family; a presence that somehow might provide a way out of her unhappy marriage. It could enable her to remain the main influence in her children's lives and be a force for good in the world. She recognised that the way to do it was through her public role, doing what she did best, what gave her most satisfaction. Diana was no longer suicidal; she was waking up to the fact she did have a life which could become worth living, she did have a choice and she did have a future worth looking forward to.

"I mean I'll go out and do my bit in the way I know how and I'll leave him behind.
That's what I see happening."

1990

Whatever you can do, or dream you can,
begin it. Boldness has genius, power and magic in it.
Begin it now.

Goethe

However simple the idea may have seemed it was not easy for Her Royal Highness the Princess of Wales to present herself to the media in the way she wanted. Her opportunities consisted of the usual annual royal ceremonies and family events throughout the year; official duties to be undertaken solo or with her husband; abroad and at home; and engagements associated with her own charities or other organisations which sought the Princess' high profile presence in the expectation of gaining media attention and a cash bonanza to support their good works.

The latter were offered, usually months in advance, by invitations sent to her office. Here they were checked against fixed dates in the diary and the engagements of other greater and lesser members of the royal family, lest there be an embarrassing clash. The practicality and suitability of the remaining opportunities were assessed by her staff who then presented their proposals to Diana as options from which to make a final choice. Accompanying the resulting shortlists were briefings, produced by a staff member, who shaped their recommendations to gently direct Diana to the choice they believed would be best for her. What they thought would be best for her was deduced by their perception of her intentions and mood, and their own desire not to precipitate any disasters for which they could be blamed. All the engagements Diana finally chose would then be checked again against her husband's diary to ensure there would be no conflict that might spoil the impact of any major speech or appearance he was due to make.

Prince Charles' diary took precedence. Diana's small dedicated staff operated as a minor addition to the much larger organisation which ran her husband's working life. Diana's role was seen as merely an accessory to the

Prince's more serious work. In the words of Patrick Jephson her equerry "it was an addition that was loftily tolerated, despite its perceived irrelevance to the main work of the organisation." At periodic meetings, to plan their joint engagements, Diana's needs and involvement were often overlooked by those she came to call "the men in grey suits".

There were, as well, other men in grey to be appeased. These were the courtiers who administered the monarchy's official affairs for the Queen under the umbrella of a Buckingham Palace conglomerate, of which Prince Charles' organisation, and those of all the other royals, were mere satellites. There was a royal pecking order when it came to who did what in public.

Buckingham Palace's grey men reflected the Queen's view. They saw no possibility of any formal change in the status of Princess Diana's marriage to Prince Charles so they were effectively stuck with her, but they recognised her public relations value. She had not put a foot wrong in her official capacity and she attracted an enormous amount of good will to the family. They were content to see her make the most of her public duties as long as they did not damage the image of the larger royal "firm" or its members.

By the beginning of January 1990 Diana was a very accomplished performer on the public stage. She knew what the royal machine expected, she knew what her charities wanted from her, and she knew what would please the press and what would not. She also knew how to connect with the public. Most important of all she knew what she wanted to do and that was to express more the genuine concern and care she felt for people who were sick, dying or disadvantaged.

In fulfilling her aspiration Diana faced another difficulty associated with the royal system which gave her access to the public and the media. She did not employ her own staff. It was paid for from her husband's budget and this fact alone called into question where its ultimate loyalty lay. Her efforts to raise her media profile might meet resistance from her husband. Diana would require a staff she felt comfortable with and which she could ensure would give its full commitment to her efforts. Diana since childhood had been guarded in her attitude towards those around her lest they by some word, or act or non-specific dissonance in attitude or demeanour, hurt her fragile sense of self-worth. Since entering the royal family and in response to her troubles in the marriage she was wary of her staff as well. In the early part of 1990 Diana set about making sure the people around her were those in whom she had most confidence and with whom she felt most comfortable. In particular she let go of her senior member of staff Anne

Beckwith-Smith and replaced her with Patrick Jephson, her equerry during the preceding two years and a man less inclined than his predecessor to seek to maintain a united front with the Prince's staff in all matters.

Never adept at dealing with staff and inclined to set a tone in her relationships with them which could be misconstrued, Diana was not good at handling situations which required her to replace individual members of her household or administrative team. Since childhood she had never found it easy to accept responsibility for her own mistakes or shortcomings. Her make-up made it difficult for her to share her intuitive and emotions driven decision-making processes. Her behaviour, as she gradually became uncomfortable with a member of her staff, and then finally came to the decision to replace them, was often seen as arbitrary or underhand.

Such was the case now as Diana reorganised the team she would rely on to help her reach her new goal. As these changes occurred around them her remaining members of staff became concerned for their own positions, a situation which was not helped by Diana's reticence about sharing her new plan with them. Indeed it was not a plan at all really, it was more an intuitive response to circumstances. Not surprisingly Diana's staff struggled to understand what she wanted to achieve from the pressure she began applying to them to secure for her more public appearances. Indeed some judged her behaviour and increasing interest in how many official engagements had been undertaken by each member of the royal family, as signs of a rapidly inflating ego. Patrick Jephson saw "guile and gamesmanship" and a lack of scruples in Diana's activities to "attract attention" and "to signal an independence from her marriage."

Diana's instinct told her there were two main rivals to her achieving the powerful public and media profiles she wanted. Her husband was one. Diana realised that increasing the media response to her own activities might encroach on the attention given to Charles' work. She was prepared to risk it given her animosity towards Charles, and her determination to show him what she was really capable of. She was nervous that it might cause more conflict between them, but she had been dealing with that for years and now felt able to handle another source of dispute.

The other rival she identified was the Duchess of York. Diana's relationship with Fergie had blown hot and cold since she had entered the royal domain. Diana recalled how Fergie had been welcomed by the family as a breath of fresh air. The newcomer had even been offered to Diana by Charles as an example she might like to emulate. The efforts Diana made to be more light-hearted and boisterous had resulted in her being criticised in the media, and by the men in grey, for un-royal and undignified behaviour.

The press had also embraced the presence of the feisty new member of the royal family ever since she became engaged to Andrew, seeing in her a wonderful source of stories good and bad which would sell newspapers. Now Fergie's picture vied with Diana's on magazines and newspapers and currently she was attracting extra attention because she had a baby, one year old Beatrice, and another due. Babies made good pictures and Diana's boys, now seven and five were no longer as newsworthy as a gurgling infant. Diana did not want Fergie to outshine her on the public stage as she had on the private.

Diana would have found no inconsistency between her official duty and her personal determination to create an unassailable media profile and public presence. She wanted to be taken seriously by Charles and the royal establishment. She wanted to be appreciated by them for her true worth and by the public for her place in their lives. Her desire to heighten her profile was perfectly compatible with her duties to the Queen and the country if not to her husband to whom she now felt no obligation.

Not so compatible was Diana's desire to alter the media coverage that continued to support two false notions. First was the charade of her marriage. From her appearances in public it seemed she had cheerfully accepted a working arrangement, in private she knew this to be false. She was still filled with anger and indignation at the way she had been treated. Diana was desperate to be out of the situation and resented having to add substance to the lie being presented to the world, but she could see no way to correct the misconception. Her instinct however told her she was on the right track by deciding to improve her profile in comparison to Charles'.

The second pretence was that of the "Fairytale Princess". Diana's improving sense of herself meant she saw this as a shallow representation of who she really was. It was a myth, and one she could influence, unlike that of her marriage, by being true to her instincts and by showing her genuine caring nature and ability to comfort the sick and distressed when performing her royal duties.

Having lived for nine years with unremitting pressure from the press, Diana's new intention to make the media fit her own agenda immediately reduced her stress to more manageable proportions. Diana was at last ready to exercise more control over her life.

Her year started quietly with a brief, post-Christmas visit to a health farm followed by one of her frequent visits to marriage guidance seminars held by the charity Relate. She was happy to be photographed supporting the charity of which she was patron, but managed to keep her participation in the therapy sessions and role playing private.

✦ ✦ ✦

I started 1990 in my usual way, on my own, quietly contemplating what each of my clients might need when we started work again after the holidays. Twelve months with Diana had given me more insight into her make-up and I had a better idea how I might help her move forward.

She shared very little about what was happening in her life and it was clear to me I wouldn't be able to absorb her in the nuts and bolts of the process we were engaged in.

She simply wasn't inclined to know the details. She followed the instructions I gave her or listened to what I said without much comment, without debate. Later I came to recognise Diana's way was to take in information and ponder it at leisure so she could make up her own mind about whether it was of value to her or not. At that time it meant I couldn't take the methodical and systematic approach with her I would have preferred in order to make the transformational process faster and more effective. Without answers to direct questions about what was happening to her, and how she felt or what she thought as a result, I had to employ a more spontaneous and organic approach.

Powerful new ideas, strong, good ideas had been sown in Diana's mind already. These would influence her thoughts, feelings and choices and bring about beneficial changes to her health and life, as long as they were nurtured and not displaced by less useful ones. The new ideas would require supporting with frequent validation and evidence of their truth, until they were strong enough to be self sustaining. Strongly held beliefs and ideas prompt their counterparts in thoughts, feelings and behaviour thereby reinforcing themselves. If I could help Diana believe she was strong and capable, then she would think, feel and act strong and capable, and thereby prove repeatedly to herself that she was strong and capable. During our sessions I was already sensitive to signs in her body, speech and demeanour when she felt less than strong and capable, and responded with techniques of massage and quiet suggestions which were gradually helping to alter her negative expressions and ideas into more positive ones.

The trouble was I didn't really know what Diana wanted to believe about herself, nor what she wanted her future to be like. So far I had been working with the generic idea that everyone wants to be happy, healthy, fulfilled and to have more influence over their own life. With Diana I was more aware of what she didn't want. She didn't want to be frightened, so I could help her see her courage, something she wasn't aware she had. She didn't want to be unhappy, so I could support in her the feelings of contentment, satisfaction and joyfulness. She didn't want to be helpless and I had already gone a long way to showing her she was not. I could continue to help her see she had more control than she imagined over situations. If we were to get better results more rapidly, however, I needed to introduce another new idea, something more all-encompassing and far reaching than the piecemeal adjustments to her inner self I had offered so far.

During our first session in the New Year I began the usual relaxing massage and then turned our quiet conversation back to the notion of her inner future-vision. It was a topic I'd touched on in a previous treatment when we had reframed her belief that she was stuck with the royal family. This time I explained that we all construct a future-vision from everything we believe about ourselves, and all we have experienced. I described it as the hidden driving force behind all our choices and decisions, and the process which binds our body and mind together. Something which, starting the moment we are born, we acquire spontaneously and without volition, not realising the power it has until we find things going badly in our life or we experience illness in our body. I offered Diana the chance to start creating a future-vision that would bring her the life and health she wanted.

With her eyes closed and her body relaxed I guided her through a visualisation process that took her into a meditative state. There I suggested she see herself, in her mind's eye, as she would like to be in her ideal future, in as much detail as she was able to create.

'It's important you don't visualise any particular person with you or see yourself in any specific place. Just see yourself as you want to be. See yourself in colour, looking how you want to be, standing how you want to be standing, moving how you want to be moving. This is about how you are when your life is the way you want it to be. So see the person you will be when you have everything you want in your life, not what has to be in your life to make you the way you want to be. When you have a clear image of how you will be, allow yourself to step into the person you have created and feel how you feel when you are as strong and as capable as you will be. Experience what your body feels like, sense what your emotions are like, look with the eyes and the wisdom you have when you are the way you want to be. Experience the emotions you want to be having. What are you doing? What is around you? What kind of person is with you? In your mind become the person you want to be.'

'Remember the world spontaneously responds to what comes from within you. When you are ready inside you will change and so will your world. The people who can be with you as you become who you want to be will be there. Those who can't will not come into your life or will have moved on quite naturally.'

'The poet Rumi spoke about love by saying something like "Your task is not to seek for love, but to seek and find all the barriers within yourself that stop you experiencing love." This is the same thing. Your chosen future-vision will start to come about spontaneously. If there is anything within you that is stopping that future happening you will notice it, and have the chance to change it. Life is just feedback. If you are not the way you want to be, or your life is not how you want it to be, think about what you are believing for your life to be the way it is, or your body to be how it is. That will tell you something about what's in your future-vision that you might need to alter.'

After I concluded the visualisation process I continued the massage in silence to allow Diana to consider the experience. I knew her well enough by then to recognise the state of reverie she slipped into when she was processing her thoughts and feelings about something important.

Before I finished the session I added some more information. 'Your future-vision cannot be fixed and rigid. Ever since you were born it's been changing and adapting, responding to your experiences as you grew older. What you've just created will also need to be changed as you meet new situations, or take on new ideas of how you want to be. It can be altered whenever you want by just going inside your mind and clarifying what you want. The key is to make your vision the best you can imagine at all times, and to keep looking for new information which will improve it. One thing you can try is to think about women role models who have attributes and qualities you would like to have. You're in the perfect position to make contact with and meet powerful women, heroines from all over the world. When you meet someone you admire, or read about someone, notice what they do, how they stand, how they move, what their face looks like and the words they use, then mentally try them on for size to see if you can make the words or the face fit. If you meet them ask them how they do the things you admire, get detail, find out what their mind is doing to enable them to be the way they are, then try out their thoughts and feelings for yourself.'

What I was describing, without telling Diana where it came from, was an adaptation of the technique of "modeling" from neuro-linguistic programming. During the months which followed, I fed Diana with examples and concepts I thought would help her clarify her future-vision of herself. I also validated qualities I noticed her exhibiting in her work so she would come to recognise and accept them at a conscious level and reinforce them in her vision-self as a result.

If Diana had shared with me what she visualised on that day I might have recognised a problem I only noticed much later, a paradox in her projection of how she wanted to be. Diana was an emotions-driven, caring, family orientated Water element and I anticipated she would have seen herself enjoying a perfect home, family and partner. Despite my warning that she should not visualise any particular people with her, I doubted she would have been able to imagine herself in the future without her sons William and Harry. Doing so was not likely to cause any problems. I also thought it likely she would see herself enjoying an idyllic and relatively normal family life and home, without Charles, again not a problem. But I did not know enough about her personality to realise what else she was likely to have included in her vision. It would be months before I did notice, in the problems she was experiencing, what their source might be.

Diana had a very strong sense of destiny and a need to make the world a better place, and almost certainly her future-vision would have seen her engaged in work that fulfilled that desire. To reconcile into a living reality her deep need for a normal family life alongside a profound sense that she could improve the world, would require immense changes to occur within and around her, to her perception of herself, to her self-belief and to her circumstances. As it transpired over the years ahead, she suffered much to hold onto these two conflicting aspects of her future self.

In personal transformation terms Diana was seeking to climb the equivalent of Mount Everest. The success or otherwise of her quest would rely on how much courage she would find to carry on when she wanted to give up, and how much support she could attract. There would be many obstacles for her to overcome before she reached her goal.

✦ ✦ ✦

During the years since Diana had entered public life she had come to view the media as her primary source of validation and acknowledgement. In the absence of support from anywhere else, what was said about her, and particularly what was written about her, was her gauge of how she was perceived by the public. She sometimes resented the way camera wielding journalists infringed on her private life. She was angered when loudly clicking cameras and flickering flashbulbs intruded on special moments when she was comforting a sick child or old person who could be distressed by the media's attention. Her main frustration however lay in her inability to control it. If she could only ensure they took their photos when she wanted them to and wrote or said what she would like then she would feel better about them. In general though Diana accepted the media presence in her life and now her intention to use it more to her own advantage felt good.

In her mind it was a simple equation, she would set about increasing the amount of work she did and show her true nature when doing it and the press would have to write the supportive stories she wanted them to. Thus people would understand her better and her popularity would increase. It was risky strategy. Diana knew the press could be fickle and it hurt her when even a journalist she thought was friendly towards her would write a supportive piece one day and a critical piece the next. But she was beginning to believe she had the ability to turn almost anyone in her favour if she could speak to them face to face. She had started to chat to journalists the previous year and intended to carry on doing so with the expectation that she could persuade them to support her.

The news media however was never likely to be directed by anyone, not even Princess Diana. They fiercely protect their right to publish what they believe is important, or what they can get away with, depending on their perception of their role in the society to which they offer their product. As far as the press was concerned if someone signals they want more media attention and are prepared to offer information, as Diana was beginning to do, they would be happy to oblige. The actual content of what they published, the angle they put on their stories, was for them to decide.

✦ ✦ ✦

As the year progressed and she travelled the country in her official role, Diana's media strategy began to emerge alongside a developing vision of life without Charles' influence. Her police bodyguard Ken Wharfe would later write: "by early 1990 Diana talked of nothing but escape." How she interpreted the notion of escape at that time, how she was seeing herself free, was not so clear.

Diana was wife to the immediate heir to the throne and mother to two young boys who were second and third in line. Her sons were still only seven and five and Diana would not want to do anything to jeapardise their happiness or their future. It was easy enough to imagine a future without Charles in her home, but less easy to see what their relationship might be. With divorce still a seeming impossibility, and her sons to consider, it would have been difficult for Diana to see herself entirely free of the royal family, but it was a dream she could hold out for. Realistically the best thing Diana could do for her children, and herself at that time, was to make sure she was in the strongest possible position within the royal family. It seemed that might mean remaining married to Charles, at least for the foreseeable future. In the meantime Diana would continue to push firmly at the limitations which had been imposed on her professional role.

Patrick Jephson, Diana's assistant private secretary, later described the subtle messages that were implied by the reorganisation of her office. To the other Palaces it said "the Princess could no longer be counted on to acquiesce when it came to conforming to conventional ways of doing royal business." To her charities and admirers the message implied by Jephson's appointment was "her (the Princess's) office had a new face and in many ways a new philosophy."

In the early skirmishes of her move towards the recognition she sought Diana found she had a degree of influence within the royal system she might not have expected. Whether because of her popularity, the positive attention she attracted to the royal family or the simple fact that the men in grey did not want to upset her for some other reason, there was no discernible reaction to Diana's modest flexing of her muscles.

In March Diana and Charles made an official visit to Nigeria and the Cameroons in West Africa. In temperatures sometimes approaching 45°C they performed the usual round of engagements associated with such a tour. BBC journalist Elizabeth Blunt described how the press pack followed Diana to every engagement and reported what she did and what she wore on every stop she made at children's hospitals and women's projects and the like. Charles' efforts on the other hand, although just as worthy, were virtually ignored and received little coverage.

Blunt writes of the contrast between Diana's tactile style at a leprosy centre in Northern Nigeria and Charles' obvious reluctance to emulate his wife. Another description tells how clear it was that Diana was bored at an official banquet but "her eyes kept drifting sideways to where the royal press corps was sitting – old friends and familiars, who accompanied her every day of her life. She gave them conspiratorial looks, flirted with their cameras. Then at one point she turned and spotted me, crouched on the floor over my tape recorder, recording the mind-numbing official speeches. She looked straight at me and gave me a sudden utterly ravishing smile. For just a moment I had her full, dazzling attention; more than a moment, I would have been her slave for life."

Following the Africa tour Diana escaped with her sons, and other members of the Spencer family for a holiday on the Caribbean island of Necker. Prince Charles was not invited and chose to spend the time in the Scottish Highlands. Press reaction to the separate arrangements highlighted a developing theme in the criticism which was to be directed at Charles around this time. "Another Holiday Apart!" screamed the tabloids as they collectively lambasted Charles for seeing his boys for only two days in the preceding two months.

◆ ◆ ◆

One of the ways I had an inkling of what was happening to Diana in her daily life, and how she was reacting, was through the state of her muscles. I could track good times and bad by the amount and location of the tension I discovered during treatments. Invariably I found a consistent area of tension in her shoulders and neck.

'These muscles here,' I prodded her shoulders with my thumb, 'and here,' I prodded her neck, 'are associated with stress and anxiety, which could also be affecting your stomach and kidneys. I want to just check another area that might confirm that.'

I rearranged her towels and then worked deeply into the areas around the crests of her hip bones, and between her hip bones and rib cage. I found, as I suspected I would, that the muscles, the iliopsoas groups, which connected the front of spine to her hip bones and upper thigh bones on each side, were tight and dense despite all her swimming and dancing. Over the weeks which followed I worked deeply into these muscles and those of her shoulders to release their tension and discomfort. My intention as usual went beyond the physical. The muscles were, in my perception, associated with fear and I expected her to feel less anxiety as a result of the work.

I also expected her to be able to stand straighter and taller. 'Remember your body tells your mind how to feel as well as vice versa. Look after your body. Help it to be the way that shows you and the world what you want to believe about yourself. If your body feels strong and flexible you will feel strong and flexible.'

On another occasion Diana and I were chatting about her work in hospices and discussing the process of dying. 'I can't understand why Charles doesn't realise the importance of personal contact when we go out and meet people,' she said referring to her instinct to touch and hold people who were in difficulty.

'If you lined up a hundred people and asked them who thought the same as you did what do you think the answer would be?' I responded.

'Well some would agree and some wouldn't I suppose.'

'Right, but some would think you should hold and touch people more and longer, some would think just a light touch would be enough, others wouldn't see any need to touch people at all and just wouldn't understand why you would need to in order to help them. There's an entire spectrum of possibilities and only a few would be the same as yours.'

'One of the things most people do a lot is to assume that others see the world they same way they do. Then they get surprised and hurt when they find not everyone shares their viewpoint even to the point where they judge other people as wrong for not doing so. We're all different. I think the best way is to assume other people are as right as me, they have their truth, I have mine. Then I can try their truth on for size and see if I can make the two fit together. It saves a lot of heartache. Religions are like that. Why believe in one when you can believe the important parts of a lot of them without rejecting any or judging anyone?'

✦ ✦ ✦

In early May Charles and Diana were entrusted with the first official visit by any members of the British royal family to a Warsaw Pact country when they toured Hungary. When they were met by the newly elected interim President Goncz, Diana found it quite natural to stand listening to the arrival speeches holding the hand of the President's wife. During the four day trip the royal couple performed their roles perfectly. The press commented on their consummately professional performance in Budapest, and in response to seeing the couple so seemingly at ease with each other, speculated on the possibility there were renewed romantic feelings between them despite the rumours to the contrary.

Patrick Jephson, who accompanied the couple, wrote later: "you would have to be very close to the action – and very cynical – to understand the guerrilla warfare that was being waged below the surface."

Diana had shown she could still play the game when it was required of her. In the process she further enhanced her reputation as an asset to the country and an important member of the royal firm, albeit one who should be handled carefully, as Prince Phillip once observed.

The Hungary trip was to be the last public occasion on which Diana gave any indication she was comfortable in her husband's company.

✦ ✦ ✦

I was enjoying my work with Diana. Her body was responsive and she let go of its tensions quickly and easily, although their continued recurrence indicated she was very stressed by her lifestyle. I hoped in time her perspective would change so that she didn't become stressed by whatever she was being affected by. I suspected it was her marriage. I'd seen the odd story in the press, but it wasn't for me to ask or necessary for me to know. I trusted the process I had initiated would bring about whatever changes were required, in her and in her circumstances, to resolve the problems she had. Unless of course she had seen herself knotted like a pretzel with tension in her future-vision, in which case I was wasting my time. Most sessions provided me with opportunities to offer her insights and new ideas about how she might like to become and validation for what she had achieved.

'Think back to this time two years ago. Were you the same person then as you are now?' I said one day, trying to make the point that everything is changing all the time.

'Oh no. I'm a lot different to how I was then.'

'And in another two years you'll be different again. You are changing. Everyone is. The difference between you and other people is that by looking at your innermost beliefs and ideas you are directing your changes so you are becoming how you want to be. Most people just react to situations by habit, and only when they have to do they change and do something different. Problem is that it usually takes a lot of unhappiness or illness to force them to change and do something different. It's a good trick to learn, to change before you are forced to. It doesn't take much to notice the signs that tell you it's a good idea to look at what you're doing and maybe change something. Your health and your life are the signs. That's why we feel pain, to tell us we're doing something that's harming us, it doesn't matter if it's physical pains or emotional ones.'

✦ ✦ ✦

By June 1990 Diana was beginning to receive the kind of media coverage she wanted. By contrast Charles' press was less than flattering. Diana was lauded for her good works, her 'star quality' and patience with her husband who was described as "selfish" and distant.

An example of how the media portrayed them was the situation which developed when Prince Charles broke his arm while playing polo.

It was 28 June and Charles' arm was initially strapped in the expectation that the double fracture would heal naturally if kept immobile. On 1 July he was discharged from the Cirencester hospital, where initial treatment had been provided, so he could recover at home. The Prince remained at Highgrove in considerable pain for days afterwards until he eventually sought the opinion of another specialist who recommended surgery. During the ensuing prolonged debate about whether Charles needed an operation to pin the fractures, he spent much of his time, still in pain, at Highgrove and Balmoral. Diana undertook some of the public appearances Charles had been forced to pull out of. Charles' friends visited him to offer sympathy and support. Predictably these friends included Camilla Parker-Bowles. Meanwhile, the Princess was not encouraged to visit Charles at Highgrove, or to accompany him when he subsequently spent time with friends in Majorca and France.

On 2 September Charles' arm was finally operated on in an NHS hospital, the Queen's Medical Centre Nottingham, where a small suite of disused rooms was reopened and prepared for him so members of his staff could set up a temporary office. It was inconceivable that Diana would not make highly publicised visits to Charles while he was recovering in a public hospital. The media would have had a field day speculating why. Diana duly travelled from London to Nottingham to see him. When Diana was not there Charles was visited by his friends.

On 10 September, eight days after his operation and while still undergoing a course of intensive and very painful physiotherapy Charles accompanied Diana and Harry when they went with Prince William to Ludgrove School in Berkshire, to help him settle in for his first term as a boarder.

Press coverage during this period variously criticised Charles for his reckless participation in a dangerous sport, and admired him for his stoicism in the face of painful injury. When he was abroad and suffering continuous pain from his injury he was photographed unshaven and looking depressed. One news story had the Prince romantically linked to a former girlfriend while he was away recuperating. The story was retracted a few months later. Other stories erroneously had him enjoying a candle lit supper with Camilla in his private suite in the Nottingham hospital, and complained he did not look cheerful enough when he left to go home.

The press reported that Diana had apparently confronted Camilla in a hospital at which, in fact, their paths did not cross. Diana was also supposed to have sat by his bedside for hours offering concern and sympathy. It was duly noted and reported to the public that after his accident Charles was absent from his public duties for four months, and that Charles and Diana spent thirty nine days apart after they had appeared together to settle William into his new school.

Charles was criticised for neglecting the public who would become his people when he was King; being a distant father to his children; and for rejecting his wife while enjoying the close friendship of Camilla. For Diana there was sympathy for the deteriorating marriage and the opinion that, since divorce was impossible, she had reached an accommodation with Charles to continue the marriage for form's sake.

Media coverage of the events following Charles' accident rippled on for months. A Sunday paper, reporting on a concert at Buckingham Palace to celebrate the Queen Mother's ninetieth birthday on 4 August, commented that Charles had completely ignored his wife. Diana received pity and plaudits, while Charles received few of either. Diana did not actively seek the sympathetic coverage she received, although she would have been very well aware of the opportunities to do so and knew it would further her own agenda

Diana's protection officer, Ken Wharfe, later recalled how Diana posed for photographs with Charles when he had left the hospital in Cirencester to return with his wife to Highgrove. Press photos had captured her smiles but also, through no contrivance of hers, captured Charles' more sombre expressions. Wharfe's recollection of the events which followed immediately afterwards took years to reach the media. Within minutes of the couple's arrival at Highgrove Diana departed for Kensington Palace, accompanied by Wharfe, and in genuine distress because she was not being allowed to care for her husband as she wanted to. During the car journey back to London Diana declared that the incident was the last straw from which the marriage could not recover and according to Wharfe, she expressed the view that "she was simply no longer prepared to try to make anything of her marriage."

Later, in the Nottingham hospital, after Charles' surgery, the couple had little to talk about and by then not much sympathy for each other. Unable to leave the hospital too soon lest there be adverse comment in the press, Diana wandered the hospital corridors and spontaneously dropped in on patients to offer them her comfort and support, something which was second nature to her now. These much appreciated personal gestures, which included subsequent notes of sympathy and a visit to one family's home, were intended to be private. The press were informed about Diana's kindness, not by her but by one of the families involved.

Not all publicity Diana received was automatically sympathetic or positive. In October she made a solo visit to Washington DC in the United States. There to support fundraising for London City Ballet she would have encountered a significant amount of bad press if it had not been for the speedy reactions of her new assistant private secretary Patrick Jephson. Emerging stories of royal "Viking raids", which diverted the money of charitable Americans away from local needy causes, and Princesses rejecting all good things American by insisting British food and furnishings be brought over for the Royal Gala dinner, were likely to damage Diana's reputation as a royal big hitter.

As events unfolded before Diana's departure to the States, and Jephson struggled to rescue the event, he noticed Diana's attitude to the trip change from enthusiastic to apprehensive. He rightly attributed her changing mood to concerns about the bad publicity. Jephson had recognised Diana's drive for a higher media profile but was unaware that there was a purpose behind her activities beyond ego inflation. From Diana's viewpoint, bad publicity in Washington would not only undermine her reputation for performing successful royal engagements, but it would damage her wider plan to establish a media profile of such strength that she could not be criticised by anyone.

Happily for her the necessary negotiations allowed the event to be a success and Diana triumphed in American again. Guests who doubted they could attend the function discovered they were able to do so, and the White House found it was possible after all for the Princess to meet President and Mrs Bush. Diana's visit, and reputation, was further enhanced by a visit with Mrs Bush to "Grandma's House". The home for underprivileged children likely to die from HIV+AIDS had been assured of a substantial donation from the backers of the previous night's gala. Diana's self initiated plan was still on track as she flew back from America certain of good press coverage and in the knowledge she had performed her duty by her country, the royal family, her charity and AIDS awareness. She had also brought comfort to dying children who had met a real life Princess and she had served her own cause in the process.

✦ ✦ ✦

Her husband was not fairing as well. Since his accident the previous June, Prince Charles, already inclined to melancholic moods at the turn his marriage had taken, became more withdrawn and depressed. This was possibly because of the pain he was in but more likely because he saw the approaching demise of his ability to play polo, the game which in his perception kept him sane. For four months Charles virtually hid himself away from all but his closest friends, in a variety of locations far from London. Late in October, the Prince emerged from his convalescence and self imposed exile, and returned to Highgrove, only to be rebuked by *The News of the World* for nipping off "for a chat with former love Camilla Parker Bowles". The story suggested the couple had chatted from late one night until the early hours of the following day.

Not surprising then that on 31 October, when the Prince returned for his first royal engagement after his accident, he did not endear himself to the waiting media. Asked by a TV camera man how he was feeling, the irritable Charles was abrupt to the point of rudeness and replied "What an original question. If you really want to know, I'm barely alive."

✦ ✦ ✦

In August Iraqi forces had invaded Kuwait. Diana was aware that a war involving British forces was imminent. In October President Bush himself, over cups of coffee in the White House, had asked her about the British attitude to war in the Middle East. Her answer was suitably oblique and did not commit the British Government to anything. She said "I think it's all very worrying" much to the relief of Patrick Jephson and the British Ambassador who were also present. And it was very worrying for Diana. She knew James Hewitt was commander of a tank squadron in Germany and liable to be called into the action. In November, after a long period of silence following his departure from the UK, Diana contacted Hewitt to ask if he would be going to the Gulf. Hewitt confirmed his regiment had been selected and Diana arranged to see him before he left for the war zone. A few weeks before the year's end Hewitt and Diana were passionately reunited at Highgrove and found their emotional attachment for each other to be as strong as ever.

When Diana gave herself to a relationship it was no insignificant event for her and she was unable to disengage easily from her attachments and the emotions she associated with them. This was as true of her bond with her husband as it was of that with James Hewitt. No doubt there was as well a romantic aspect to the situation of her soldier lover about to risk his life in war against a tyrant, but Diana's love and concern for Hewitt were genuine enough.

By now Diana's office team was dialled in to her desire for more and better publicity opportunities even if they did not realise the true reason behind it. A proposal that Diana should visit British troops deployed in the Gulf was put forward by Patrick Jephson. It coincided with a similar suggestion from Prince Charles' staff. In December it was Charles who visited the troops in the hot and dusty desert and acquitted himself well, reprising his action-man persona and joking about his polo injury. Diana was sent to cold and damp Germany to visit their families. By then, completely committed to her new strategy, she was disappointed she had not been given the opportunity to show what she could do to raise troop morale in the desert.

In mid November Diana accompanied Charles to Japan as official representatives of the Queen at the enthroning of Emperor Akihito. The visit was described as "brilliant" and Diana was "back on top" and "radiant". A message however was clearly sent to those whose job it is to notice the subtle signals given out by royals on official visits. While Diana was radiant in those situations which required it, there were no shared glances or fleeting moments of connection with her husband, nothing to keep alive the idea they had a working arrangement. While not openly sabotaging the visit Diana made it clear she was not going to continue pretending she was happy in her marriage to Charles.

✦ ✦ ✦

'I'd love to go to Japan,' I said when I saw Diana on her return. 'I spent two years learning the Japanese tea ceremony. The whole purpose of it is to create a brief period of time when the tea master and guest can experience a Zen state, a feeling of insight about themselves and their place in the universe and the nature of all things. The Japanese use all kinds of art forms, calligraphy, sculpture, painting, martial arts, tea to achieve the state and the art they produce when they achieve it reflects the mindful state they were in. I stopped learning when I realised it was really a lifetime study. In any case I recognised I was already achieving the same state sometimes when I gave a massage. It becomes like tai chi or chi gung, moving meditation.'

'There's a story I like that tells of a tea master who set his pupil the task of cleaning the garden around the tea house in readiness for a ceremony. There's a lot of discipline and correct form in the tea ceremonies and the garden has traditional features designed to help the guest achieve a peaceful state of mind before the ceremony. Anyway the pupil scrubbed and cleaned and washed until every part of the garden was tidy and every stone on the wandering path gleamed. Then he went to call his teacher to inspect the result.'

'Tea master comes out, looks around, says "Hmph!" and goes away. The pupil is mortified, he's done something wrong but doesn't know what and his teacher is unhappy. So the pupil stands there for a while looking around and then it comes to him. He walks up to a cherry tree in blossom and bangs his hand against the trunk. A few petals of cherry blossom fall onto the stones of the path. He gets his teacher again. Teacher comes to look, smiles and says "perfect."'

'The message is that there is always imperfection in everything so celebrate your imperfections and do not try to be perfect.'

'What do you think about reincarnation?' Diana dropped the question into our conversation one day.

'If you mean do I think we come back for many lifetimes and experience karma as each life is affected by the one which went before? I don't have any idea whether that's the case or not. I've studied a bit but can't find any evidence that convinces me one way or the other. So I think the best thing to do is to try to live this life as if you might have to come back and deal with what you're doing now. As far as karma is concerned I think we're living it every day. The way we are inside brings us into contact with experiences and people. The way we deal with them has repercussions, good or bad, that we have to deal with, sometimes for the remainder of our lives. To me it's just another reason to decide how you want to be.'

From Diana's growing heap of books beside her bed I recognised a common pattern I'd seen before and experienced for myself. She was undergoing a spiritual awakening in which she was opening up to new ideas about her place in a picture bigger than the small environment of her life.

✦ ✦ ✦

During 1990 several factors seemed to have caused a distinct shift in Diana's tactics. Her husband's temporary withdrawal from his public duties and generally poor press; Diana's own successes and consequent improvement of her media profile; the seeming acquiescence of Buckingham Palace to her strategy all had raised her confidence to new levels. Add that she was almost certain her marriage was irretrievable – although such a conviction could never be a 100% certainty for one of her make-up – and that she was now determined to "escape", whatever that might mean, and Diana was already taking a tougher approach to her plan than she had been at the year's beginning. From a vague notion to "go out, and do my bit in the way I know how" and to "leave him behind" Diana was now teetering on the verge of an open attack on her husband's position.

The press had continued their preoccupation with the state of the marriage through the year and there had even been suggestions Diana and Charles might both have other partners. There were increasing references to Charles' friendship with Camilla and Diana's instincts, and possibly friendly members of the press pack, were telling her they knew the truth about her husband's mistress. Diana was not aware that at least one tabloid had been holding back from publishing a story about her own relationship with James Hewitt. She continued to be frustrated that high as her media profile had become it still seemed to trivialise her by focussing as much on her clothes and appearance as it did on her accomplishments. There was irony in the fact that one of the few critical pieces written about her had been about the £100,000 she was supposed to have spent on clothes during the year.

With more measured consideration Diana might have realised that part of her appeal for the press was her attractiveness and her charisma when compared to Charles. A significant part of her media success was due to her appearance and her seeming lack of gravity. Diana's intuition told her however she should continue to push for an even higher profile, and create more media coverage for "serious Diana" to increase her standing in the public eye – to show her true self.

✦ ✦ ✦

Rebuilding her media profile was not the only reconstruction Diana had been engaged in during the year. Her improving self-image showed in Diana's commitment to her health and appearance. A new, short, some would say masculine, hair style had changed Diana's look immediately. Two years of massage therapy had altered her perception of her body. Serious swimming, dance and occasionally tennis had been Diana's spontaneous fitness regime for years, and the exercise helped her deal with stress. In 1990 Diana engaged a personal trainer, Carolan Brown, to help her improve her body further. Diana, the previously bulimic depressive with low self esteem was developing a powerful body image to go with her new self-confidence.

Two years of body-mind therapy had brought about a similar renaissance in her self-esteem and sense of self-belief. Had Diana taken inventory of her inner-self she would have realised that many changes were also occurring within her. Matching the outer projection of strength and purpose was a developing inner power. Although she continued to dread any feeling of helplessness she had self-belief sufficient enough to enable her to be influencing aspects of her life she previously believed were out of her control, most notably in her public role. Diana remained angry and filled with indignation about the way she had been treated by Charles and the royal family, but the edge to her rage had gone and she was now more detached, more resigned to what had passed, and able to look forward to what she might become. She was frustrated by much of the media coverage, which continued to show her more as a fashion plate than a woman with value and abilities, and her marriage as a satisfactory working arrangement to which she had acquiesced, but she now had a course of action she felt would alter the situation.

On Boxing Day 1990, a few days after making a brief farewell from Diana in London, James Hewitt deployed to his regiment in the Gulf. Their all too brief interlude renewed Diana's feelings for her lover, and when he left she was distressed by another parting from him, and deeply concerned for his safety in the war zone.

✦ ✦ ✦

1990 was drawing to a close. As far as my work with Diana was concerned it had been a good year I thought. I'd seen signs of self-discovery and new awakenings to her potential. Judging by her occasional questions and books she was accumulating I thought she might have friends and other professionals such as astrologers to guide her. That would have been natural. During the early stages of personal transformation people often reach out to try all sorts of things. I was happy about the ideas I'd put in place and was content that she would learn something worthwhile from everyone she met.

'Last time you did that I ached for a week,' Diana complained as I stepped back from running my fist across the top of her shoulder.

'Well I guess you needed it then,' I trotted out the mantra of all massage therapists. If it hurts then you must have needed it. I followed it swiftly with another favourite adage. 'Things sometimes have to get worse before they can get better.' I grinned. Had I known what was about to happen I might have kept my mouth shut.

For Christmas I gave Diana a pack of Rider-Waite tarot cards and a book to show her how to use them. I'd chosen cards which would give her insights into herself and I hoped she would use them for that rather than to try to work out what was going to happen for her in the future, although the two things can be one and the same. Earlier in the year I'd given her a copy of *Frogs into Princes*, not without my tongue firmly stuck in my cheek I have to say. This classic book describes some good neuro-linguistic programming techniques that can be used for self-transformation. I wanted to try to underpin what we were doing with some information that validated it.

Diana's note of thanks for my Christmas gift was on paper with a simple motif of the letter D topped by a crown over KENSINGTON PALACE. C for

Charles was a thing of the past. The note dated 23 December told me how thrilled Diana was with my present and was signed *With my love, Diana.*

✦ ✦ ✦

Two years before Diana's perception of herself and her life had brought her to the edge of despair and self-destruction, now she believed herself capable of making her life work, even if she didn't yet know precisely how it could. In the near future she would need all the strength and courage she could muster to sustain that belief.

Earlier in the year, amateur radio enthusiast, Cyril Reenan had offered to sell *The Sun* newspaper a tape recording of Diana's New Year's Eve telephone conversation with James Gilbey. Diana's voice was quickly verified and Gilbey was identified as the James to whom she was speaking. The "Squidgy" tape, as it came to be called because of the many times Gilbey called Diana by that pet name, contained many interesting snippets which gave insight into her opinions about her marriage and other members of the royal family, including Fergie, Prince Charles and The Queen Mother. It also seemed to indicate that Diana was in an extra-marital affair with James Gilbey, and might even have had a liaison with James Hewitt. Executives of *The Sun* placed the tape safely away with their collection of material stored for publication when suitable opportunities arose.

By the time 1990 drew to its final close Diana was aware that journalists had approached her close friend James Gilbey. They were working hard to authenticate the Squidgy tape. Stuart Higgins, an editor at the paper later confirmed; "Diana certainly knew the contents and had seen a transcription, but I cannot say how." As far as Diana was concerned the existence of the tape changed her position instantly and completely.

In Diana's mind exposure of the tape in the press would undoubtedly ruin everything she had been working so hard to create during the past year. She had not been entirely successful in her plan, and coverage leaned more towards the state of her marriage than to showing Diana as she wanted to be seen. The media profile she was so carefully trying to cultivate would be damaged beyond repair by the tape's revelations. That she had taken a lover, especially if the public was not confronted with Charles' infidelity first, was bad enough, but there was clearly a sexual content to the tape and she had mentioned her fear of becoming pregnant. Diana feared both the personal humiliation, and the effect on her sons, if it was all made public.

Her views on her marriage, and other members of the royal family, would result in their disapproval which would surely be replaced by anger. Diana was once again pitched back into feelings of panic and self-doubt familiar from her childhood when she was faced with the possibility of disapproval and rejection which, she believed, would surely result if the tape was made public.

Dreadful thoughts of the consequences which would follow publication of the tape filled her. She could be marginalised from the family so effectively that she might even lose the contact with her children who made her life worthwhile. Their welfare, and the certainty that she must be in a position from which she could be the main influence in their lives, was the key reason she had set out at the beginning of the year to strengthen her position. The thought was terrifying and she could not think what to do.

Diana's new found inner strength was still fragile when compared to the darker, more negative aspects established in the preceding twenty seven years. Throughout 1990 she had frequently found herself responding to stressful situations by slipping back into her habitual ways of feeling sorry for herself and blaming others for what was happening. Now feelings of guilt flooded back and she felt familiar dread when she considered telling Charles and the Queen about what might surface in the press at any time. Diana could not face their accusatory looks and anger, had never been able to accept blame unless forced. No she could not tell them. She felt her hard won control slipping away, and feelings of helplessness began to release in her the well-known sensations she associated with wanting to eat and be sick, just to take away the dark emotions that threatened to overwhelm her. Diana could not think what to do and where to turn for help and her despair gave rise to the thought that it might just be too much to bear.

With no one in whom she could confide and with her lover at war and unable to provide comfort, Diana was frequently tearful during the end of year holidays and screamed at Charles so much that their staff feared she might be suicidal.

"Things sometimes have to get worse before they can get better."

1991

Strong reasons make strong actions.

William Shakespeare

It is difficult to imagine the panic and terror which must have enveloped Diana during the early days of 1991 as she imagined the repercussions which could follow publication of the Squidgy tape. What a comical name it was for something with the potential to shatter so many lives. Diana had met and overcome many challenges in her life up to then but this one was of a magnitude beyond anything else. She had reached depths of despair and fought back. Now she was grasping at the opportunities life had given her. Her plans of the previous year were proof positive of a strength and determination to make her life work. She had weakened the hold of debilitating thoughts and emotions and her eating disorder, to place herself on the brink of a new path which could bring her, she knew not how, to the life she wanted as mother, carer and public influence for good. Now everything was threatened by one of dozens of similar telephone conversations, plucked from the air and offered to the world to expose her private life and most intimate thoughts.

When the tape's contents were revealed, and there was little doubt in Diana's mind they would be made public at some time, it would be the first serious attack on her character and it would be devastating. It seemed so unfair, all her indignation about the situation she was in, through no fault of her own, through the deception of her husband and the lack of help from his family, emerged full force. Why were the newspapers not telling people about Charles and Camilla? There had been hints and innuendo, but nothing specific, nothing definite had been written. The state of their marriage was being questioned constantly, Charles' role as a father was being criticised regularly, so it was completely unjust that she should be the one who would be blamed for everything, as she knew she would be when the conversation on the tape was revealed.

Diana's concerns were as much for her sons as for herself, although in her mind the two were inextricably linked. Everything she did, everything she imagined, was shaped in part with her boys and her own future with them, in mind. She was sure the tape, especially the sexual content of it, would have a devastating effect on them. Certainly William, only eight and at boarding school without her, would have a hard time when the story, in all the lurid detail Diana's mind imagined, hit the tabloids. And there was nothing she could do to protect him and no one she could talk to.

Certainly she had friends and she did speak to them about her need to escape, but she kept a great deal back. She could not face their accusatory looks and words. Diana always found it difficult to own her mistakes or accept responsibility for her errors. The thought that people would think her a fool, or wicked, or worst of all a bad mother, was unbearable. She had other professional people around her, already helping her, and she believed they had her best interests at heart, but she could not trust anyone with this story. The temptation was always there, she knew, for anyone who came within her orbit to see her as a commodity with immense value in an open and demanding market.

She was more certain that Patrick (Jephson) and Ken (Wharfe) would keep the story to themselves but what could they offer her in the way of help or even advice? Diana sensed that both of them thought she should stop making a fuss and settle down to a very nice life of fame, fortune and discreet infidelity, while letting her husband do the same. Neither of them understood her, no one understood her. She could not imagine trading her emotional needs and dreams for a marriage of convenience with someone who did not love her, or remaining in a family which treated her with such disdain. Others, who were more cynical, might be able to, but she knew it was out of the question for her, not in the cause of duty, or the good of the country or even for a quiet life. How could life be quiet if she was being eaten away from the inside with regret for what might have been?

No. Her bodyguard and chief-of-staff did not know her or what was important to her at all. They accompanied her and observed her as she worked, but they did not actually have to do what she did, nor were their lives as wrapped up with the royal family as hers. They could leave any time they wanted. Diana knew she made their lives difficult sometimes but they seemed to expect her to be able to put her emotions aside and do the job without it affecting her, but then she would not be the person she was, would not be able to reach out to the hurt and sick and see them respond.

She could sense their reactions to her when she was struggling, these men who guarded her and her working life.

Ken was kindly and obviously concerned for her. His fatherly advice was meant well and he seemed to know her sometimes when he advised her to listen to her own instincts, but he could be overbearing and there was nothing he could do to help her with this problem. She felt it when Patrick became irritated and frustrated with her, when she was drained by the strains of her work and not behaving as well as he thought she should. He barely showed any sign that he recognised how difficult her life was. He did not know how she was affected by the ever present shadows cast into her mind by trying to keep up the pretence of her marriage. Neither did he know what she was dealing with now and she must keep it from him, after all she could not be sure where his final loyalty lay, with her or with the family.

Alone, scared, confused and unable to think clearly, Diana felt familiar sensations of the helplessness she had dreaded all her life, She searched frantically in her mind for some action, anything she could do to avoid the overwhelming emotions and doubts which threatened to swamp her. Her new confidence and the new plan to make her life work had emerged less than a year ago. Beneath there still remained nearly three decades of self-doubt to be overcome and she had not yet developed the resilience to absorb the emotional impact of this new threat. Diana was being tipped back towards her previous patterns of coping.

Wary of everyone and carrying a huge burden of doubt, guilt and fear Diana stumbled into the New Year. James Hewitt had left for the Middle East and Diana immediately started writing to him, sometimes several letters a day. She had done similar, writing incessant pleas to her parents, when she was a teenager and had been sent to the finishing school she despised in Switzerland. Her letters to Hewitt over the coming weeks would graphically portray the emotional conflict which was playing out in her mind. Amidst the endearments and entreaties to take care, she told her lover how she was trying to understand herself and how she had given Charles an ultimatum that something had to be done about their marriage. According to Hewitt, Diana's determination to be free to enjoy a normal, quiet family life led him to dare hope they might be together sometime. Diana wrote repeatedly that she believed her life would change dramatically that July. She also described her belief that people would understand her better if only the truth about Charles and Camilla was to come out.

In January 1991, while Diana's inner conflict raged, it's very bloody counterpart in the Persian Gulf escalated when coalition forces started their air assault on the Iraqi invasion force in Kuwait. Lacking clarity about what to do and acting on an intuition which had no clear answers for her, Diana instructed her staff to clear her diary of most of her engagements and entered a kind of limbo state for the duration of the Gulf conflict. Pulling back to spend most of her time alone in Kensington Palace she followed every step of the war. Hungry for any news of Hewitt's tank squadron Diana scanned the papers, listened in to the constant news on the radio and watched non-stop reports on the television. She prayed in church and visited Hewitt's mother in Devon. Her concern for her lover matched that felt by wives and husbands of armed forces personnel in the war zone.

The conflict in the Gulf gave Diana a focus for her turbulent emotions and time. There was little chance of a major story about the tape being published while all the headlines were about the war. As a consequence Diana had time during which a solution to her personal crisis might emerge. Buoyed as well by 'mother's strength', her boys were still the major concern in her life and Harry was at home and sometimes watched the events in Kuwait with her, Diana worked the problem. Perhaps it was during this time she came up with what seemed a perfect solution to her dilemma. Later evidence would suggest so. Thrown back onto the most basic of survival reactions Diana's thoughts went, as they often had in times of crisis the past, from fight to the possibility of flight and James Hewitt offered an opportunity for an escape which might work.

Casting about for a solution, Diana inevitably revisited past ideas from when she had been at low ebb. During their early years together Diana and Hewitt had shared the romantic idea that they might set up home together. In a letter written in August 1989 Diana had expressed her love to James: *I just long for the days when finally we will be together for always, as that is how it should be.* At the time the constraints on Diana's freedom had not enabled them to do more than share a fantasy. They looked at details of houses they might live in and endlessly made plans for a future which did not transpire. Now, with their affair likely to be made public at any moment, the idea of them building a life together made perfect sense again. Diana could leave Charles and the royal family behind and set up home with James.

Such a move would take care of all the other problems the tape might produce, her feelings about Charles and her criticism of other members of the royal family, everything. William and Harry knew James well, they had been with Diana on occasions when she visited James at his mother's home in Devon. The revelation of a long standing relationship which resulted in the lovers sharing their lives would be so romantic and far less sordid than the casual affair the tabloids would almost certainly portray otherwise. Comparable even to Charles and Camilla's long standing romance perhaps. But first James had to survive a war.

While Diana's mind worked furiously and she lost sleep trying to follow her lover's fortunes and now her new dreams, in the Persian Gulf, Patrick Jephson was becoming frustrated by her lack of cooperation. It was his job to organise her professional agenda. During the preceding year he had recognised her objective to create a higher media profile and more independence from her husband's side of the organisation. Since then Jephson had been working hard to make Diana's intention possible against increasing resistance from those less supportive of her. Now Diana seemed to have abandoned all sense of her intention and her public duty to follow a war hundreds of miles away just when there was a fight in progress on their doorstep.

Jephson realised Diana was worried for James Hewitt but failed to understand why she should seem so preoccupied with his welfare. He was most concerned about the forces arraigned against Diana within the royal establishment gaining strength while she prevaricated. As Jephson would put it later "She had allowed herself to become obsessed with the Gulf War" and "Every attempt to make her do something unconnected with the war...drew her violent opposition." He would go on to describe how, in his opinion, Diana lost a perfect opportunity to set aside any other ambitions she might have and place herself in service to the Crown, something he believed she should do to ensure her future. He did not recognise that his well meaning agenda and therefore much of his hard work, went contrary to fundamental aspects of Diana's personality and her deepest desires. Nor did he know about the real conflict in Diana's mind and its ultimate cause, the Squidgy tape. Jephson's impatient exhortations, that life must go on and Diana ought to consider accepting some of the invitations she did not want to even discuss, caused a temporary rift in their working relationship and "agonies of doubt" for him about his job.

✦ ✦ ✦

Following the Christmas and New Year holidays and a little more rich food, wine and caffeine than usual, it took a while for my brain to get back up to speed. Eventually my thoughts went to my clients and I reviewed how things stood with Diana. The way I had to work, without much verbal input from her, was frustrating me a little. I was pleased enough with our progress but it was like coaching an athlete who didn't believe they were world class and wouldn't tell me why.

Up to then I'd helped Diana remove some serious obstacles to her self-belief so she could see her own potential better. I'd helped her establish a goal, a personal best, to strive for with the visualisation process and I'd worked to give her the confidence to reach for it. Every session, during the massages, I was quietly keeping her pointed towards her goal with inspirational stories and ideas. But I could have used more direct dialogue. Her own words would have enabled me to challenge some of the self-defeating language I was sure she was using to herself and in her every day conversations with others. If she would only speak more openly I would be able to reframe her negative attitudes better and point out evidence that she was getting closer to her goal. But then I wasn't a psychotherapist, if I had been we probably wouldn't have achieved all we had. It was clear to me that Diana would have found it difficult to put herself under the level of scrutiny which would have resulted from conventional psychological therapy. On balance I thought my body-mind focussed holistic massage was as much as she could accept at that time. It didn't involve pushing her to revisit painful memories of her past, or even to acknowledge she was involved in any sort of psychotherapeutic process. The latter reason was something I'd come across before with other clients.

I could tell a lot about Diana, as I could have with an athlete, from the state of her muscles and her overall demeanour. What was beginning to concern me was the persistence of the muscle tension that showed how much constant stress she was under. After two years working with anyone else I would have expected to be able to make much more impact on the muscles associated with fear and anxiety. With Diana the tension just kept coming back. Her structure was changing, the core body muscles were improving, but every time I turned up to work on her the reactive muscles in her shoulders, neck and mid-back were like piano wire again.

From the newspaper stories I saw nearly every day I was aware of the amount of press scrutiny Diana was under all the time. Just the thought of experiencing the level of media attention she did was enough to give me a very unpleasant feeling in my gut. I also knew that Diana was having some problems with her marriage, but I had hoped our inner work would have kicked in to help her see her situation in a way that would reduce the stress her marriage put her under. As I pondered the situation I supposed I was being too ambitious for her to expect so rapid a change. Clearly Diana had some way to go before she became more comfortable. The answer from my viewpoint was to continue with the work, massage and sharing ideas, making gentle adjustments to mind and body which would eventually result in thoughts and actions that would take her in the right direction on her path. The eventual outcome would be changes to her circumstances which would spontaneously bring about the vision she now had for herself. My concerns about the level of physical and emotional stress she was under however, redoubled at our first session that year.

'Crikey this feels like you've been fighting grizzly bears all over Christmas,' I muttered as I gently stretched the muscles of her neck then began to strip them between my thumb and fingers. When I talked to Diana it was as an equal rather than with any acknowledgement of her status as a princess of the realm. She never gave any indication that she expected me to be formal with her at any time, although I did drop the occasional ma'am into our chat to keep us both aware of our places in the relationship.

Diana grimaced. 'Things are a bit tense just now,' she said.

'You're telling me.'

Clearly that was all I was going to get from her right then and anything else from me would probably have seemed insensitive. The condition of her muscles indicated she was in no state to listen to inspirational chat or to start a new process right then. I concentrated instead on creating the most peaceful and caring environment I could. By using the most soothing techniques of massage and by making a mirror for her of my own even breathing and state of relaxation, I tried to guide her to some sense of calm. The same approach was the best way I could help her for the next few weeks.

✦ ✦ ✦

During February, while Diana struggled to deal with her alarm about the possible imminent exposure of her taped conversation with James Gilbey, she was wrong footed by a quite a different tabloid story about a different James, James Hewitt. Gossip columnist Nigel Dempster revealed the

Princess's concerns for her "good friend" Hewitt, who was serving in the Gulf and went on to mention how the erstwhile riding instructor had joined Diana for picnics or tea "while Prince Charles was away."

The world did not shift on its axis and no great fall-out hit Diana from this unexpected revelation. The innuendo in the story was clear, although it went short of naming Hewitt as Diana's lover. The additional threat of exposure stunned her for a short while, but she was not hauled before the Queen or her husband to explain. In fact no one seemed to take much notice. Perhaps because her relationship with Hewitt was known about within the family; perhaps because it was to all intents and purposes condoned, even encouraged; perhaps because Diana was seen to be on the back foot in terms of competing for media coverage, whatever the reason she was not called to account and the rest of the press made no great deal of the story. Diana's need to find a way out of her situation however became even more urgent. The tape mentioned that she had clothed Hewitt from head to foot at her own expense and that would be enough to confirm in the minds of many that he too had been her lover.

On 28 February the Gulf conflict ended with the liberation of Kuwait and James Hewitt immediately contacted Diana to tell her he was unhurt. Much relieved Diana started to make plans to return to her duties while she anticipated his homecoming.

◆ ◆ ◆

As I expected I wasn't able to tune into Diana's emotions every time I worked on her by early 1991, although I still felt them emanate from her at times during a massage. Instead of feeling her raw emotions, I experienced a new level of connection, a kind of unconscious tuning in and awareness of her mood and thoughts. It was not unexpected and I was used to the phenomenon with other clients and had come to trust it implicitly. The experience manifested itself in my just "knowing" what was uppermost in her mind and being prompted unconsciously to offer insights and use massage techniques, which were perfectly suited to her situation. I knew what she was experiencing and during the past few weeks had been aware of increased levels of fear and anger. A story I'd seen in the *Daily Mail*, about her and a guy called Hewitt gave me some insight into the constant pressure she was under. Shortly after the Gulf conflict ended however, I recognised a change in her and decided it was time offer some more information to add momentum to Diana's growing self-understanding.

'I think you'll find this interesting,' I told her at the end of the session we'd just finished. I produced some sheets of paper from my case. 'This is a questionnaire which will help you identify your personality and character type. It's just a series of pairs of statements marked A and B. All you have to do is tick the one from each pair which you feel is most like you. It's called a Keirsey Temperament Sorter.'

'Would you like to try it? I'll pick it up next time I see you and let you know what it means when I've had a chance to check it.' I handed her the sheets.

'OK I'll let you have it when I see you next week.'

A couple of weeks later I handed back her questionnaire and a print out describing the personality type which had been indicated by its analysis. 'You're an INFP,' I declared, 'which is interesting because we're very similar, I'm an INFJ.'

Diana was scanning the pages. 'That's me,' she said. 'That's me.'

'Fascinating isn't it? I remember how I felt when I saw my personality described in black and white. I'd been wondering for ages why I felt so uncomfortable at parties and night clubs for instance. When I found out I was an Introvert like you and what that means when we're around people for too long without a break, I realised I wasn't as strange as I thought. Mind you we're both quite rare. Only about two or three percent of the population is like you.'

We huddled over the pages of notes I'd taken from *Please Understand Me* the book by David Keirsey and Marilyn Bates.

'Look, look it says "they care deeply – indeed passionately – about a few special persons of causes" and here "this type is idealistic. At times this characteristic leaves them feeling isolated." It really is me,' she said pointing at the pages.

'The Princess of mythology,' I paraphrased, '"to understand INFPs their cause must be understood...willing to make unusual sacrifices for someone or something they believe in." Do you recognise that?'

'Yes, yes I do.'

I'd never seen Diana so animated.

We pored over the pages picking out characteristics "often have a subtle tragic motif running through their lives" and "fierce in protection of home and family."

'That's the same as your Water element, remember?'

'That's certainly true,' Diana nodded, completely engrossed now.

'Look here,' she pointed, '"a deep commitment to their pledges" and here "prefer having decisions made for them – until their value system is violated. Then dig their heels in" and "excel in fields that deal with possibilities for people."'

'I've got to go,' I said, 'I've added the title of the book I took those notes from if you're interested.' Diana didn't answer, her gaze and her attention were still on the pages before her. When I left the room both Diana and I had a great deal more insight about what drove her than when I had entered.

✦ ✦ ✦

Knowing her personality type and being able to recognise as natural and valuable the very characteristics she felt had set her apart from others all her life, energised Diana. She was inspired to greater efforts to be true to her nature and the clearer vision she now had of herself.

At that time Diana believed she was facing imminent humiliation and private and public disaster. Yet when faced with the threat, although she buckled precariously on occasions, she did not crumble. She did not become disabled by depression, as she had earlier in her life and she did not return to the rampant bulimia she would have used to cope in the past. Instead she sought a solution. Even in the depths of her distress she was "finally trying to understand herself." She was no longer the perennial victim. The seeds within her mind, some sown two years previously, were bearing their fruit of new self-belief. As the year progressed Diana displayed more signs of her inner strength, although the uninitiated would have been hard pressed to see them and they went largely unrecognised by herself.

Diana's vision of a worthwhile future re-emerged, refreshed and given better shape by her soul searching during the conflict and she formed an iron resolve to pursue the path she had been on at the end of the previous year. If she was to be in her strongest possible position she would have to make the royal establishment wary of challenging her. For that to happen, the real Diana must be appreciated and supported by the public. It was essential therefore that Diana be seen as the most important person in her sons' lives and that she undertake work which demonstrated to ordinary people how much she cared about each of them. It made even greater sense now to press for a presence on the public stage more independent of the traditional royal role. This time however she could act with a better notion of the outcome she wanted to achieve. The idea of a life with her lover, apart from Charles, was a real possibility in her mind. Her plan would be more likely to succeed she felt if she was backed by public sympathy, as long as the Squidgy tape did not come out too soon to undermine her efforts. She would fight for her place and do it her way.

During March Diana pressed on with her plans, urging her staff to arrange more engagements during which she could show the people and the media her caring side and informal style. During the year Diana's patronages increased from 60 to over 100.

Disaster loomed constantly in the background. The tape was still out there and its harmful revelations would be in a league far higher than anything in the Hewitt piece published earlier in the year. Diana remained under great strain but continued with her work and her plan.

Another story connecting Diana with James Hewitt appeared in March in the Sunday tabloid *The News of the World*. An ex-girlfriend of Hewitt's claimed her relationship with James had been ruined by his infatuation with the Princess and that she had encouraged his obsession by sending letters and gifts to him while he was in the Gulf. Again there was no direct assertion that Diana had committed adultery with Hewitt. Press reaction warned that Diana could not afford to be the subject of false rumours. At the Palace she noticed the same reaction as before. Her world continued to turn without faltering. The message Diana received was clear enough, it was business as usual and she was free to push ahead with her plans.

Her campaign still relied on maintaining her place as the most prominent royal in the media spotlight. Diana had always kept track of what the papers were saying about the Duchess of York and, more recently, the Princess had been pressing her staff to make sure her own profile eclipsed that of "the redhead", as she called her sister-in-law on occasion.

Diana's relationship with Sarah was complex. Their personalities were very different so they had little in common on which to base a genuine friendship. What they did have in common was a situation which made their lives very difficult for similar reasons. Diana and Fergie had both married into the royal household and their husbands were sons of the Queen. Neither of the two women wanted to remain with their husbands. Both wanted a different life than they were able to foresee in their current circumstances, but they did not know how to change things. Both Diana and her sister-in-law were constrained by their position within the royal family and by issues associated with having royal children.

The connection between the two royal wives could more rightly be called a convenient alliance founded on shared needs. The coincidences of their individual circumstances gave them a basis for collaboration and a sharing of mutual support. Their marriages were failing and they were both struggling to see their individual ways forward. It was natural for Diana and Fergie to see each other as an occasional ally with a common purpose and for them to encourage and help each other when the going got tough. "You egg each other on" the Queen is said to have observed to Diana at one time. The two young royal wives did find support from each other in a situation few others would appreciate. Chatting about their dilemma helped them both to explore the implications of separation and divorce. On a practical level they were able to pool information about the royal family, their husband's situations and the organisation that held sway over so much of their lives. The two women also shared a fascination with astrology. Both of them found readings useful when they needed the reassurance that came from believing they knew what was likely to happen in their rarefied royal world. The Duchess in particular was happy to share every prediction, no matter how bizarre, with the Princess.

Make no mistake, however, theirs was not a friendship. Fundamentally, it was a rivalry and Diana knew it. Sarah's presence in the royal family was more inconvenient than beneficial. In the past Diana had been compared unfavourably with the newcomer but when she tried to emulate Fergie's cheerful personality and ebullient behaviour the results had been disastrous. Diana's press coverage and her reputation within the royal organisation had suffered as result. Diana was also well aware of her sister-in-law's propensity for risky behaviour and was savvy enough to know it was only a matter of time before disaster struck the Duchess. Stories about the two women had often seen them linked with each other in the past, now some commentators were calling attention to what seemed like similar problems in their royal marriages. Diana's inclination was therefore to distance herself from the Duchess in public and making sure she was seen as more serious about her work than Fergie.

Diana was astute enough to know that the Duchess was not really a rival for press coverage, but the plan, such as it was, called for Diana to dominate the media with a serious profile. She noticed Fergie was occasionally featured supporting causes which overlapped Diana's area of expertise and interest. The seriously sick and dying were Diana's territory and she now increased her efforts to make that clear, especially since she expected her own position to deteriorate rapidly at any time when the Squidgy tape came out.

From her viewpoint Diana was engaged in a fight to ensure her future and while she was sometimes stressed beyond words by her situation, she was determined to win through. Diana consequently increased the pressure on her staff to come up with engagements which would make sure the Princess eclipsed the Duchess in the press. If she saw stories about Fergie which supplanted her in the newspapers Diana pressed her private secretary, Patrick Jephson to solicit her charities and other organisations for opportunities to make unscheduled visits which would capture the headlines and show Diana as the hardworking and caring person she was. It was a ruthless strategy, not fully understood by those involved in carrying it out, or those who observed it.

Jephson resented being asked to "tout for business." Diana's demands put him and his small staff under considerable pressure and made it difficult for him to maintain the relationship he had built with Prince Charles' side of the organisation in which he worked. The extra work involved often came at inconvenient times such as holidays, when Diana would ask her private secretary to help her escape from Balmoral or Sandringham by arranging private day trips at short notice to a hospice or hospital or to visit the homeless. Already sceptical of her motives, Jephson was suspicious and cynical when stories of Diana's apparently secret visits and work as a volunteer sometimes found their way into the newspapers.

Diana's actions seemed to Jephson to be distasteful, misplaced and self defeating. He thought he understood her desire for more autonomy and saw it as his job to make it happen as best he could, but believed her apparent obsession with Fergie to be unnecessary and simply a part of Diana's self-aggrandising. It is difficult to gain any other impression than that Jephson often saw Diana as immature, manipulative and unnecessarily petulant, but of course he did not know the real reasons behind her behaviour. He was unaware of the Squidgy tape and the devastation Diana feared would result from it. He did not have the necessary information or insight into Diana's psychological make-up, which would have enabled him to understand her properly and realise the pressure she was really under. And he did not know of her instinctive strategy to garner public support and sympathy through an unassailable media profile. Instead he seems to have assumed that some minor failing of his, or some irrational perception of hers, were the causes of Diana's increasingly frequent outbursts of irritation. He also believed that animosity from Prince Charles' side of the organisation was certain to result in a backlash which would ruin the Princess's plans for a more independent role.

The results of Diana's activities did indeed not go unnoticed on her husband's side of the organisation. They were annoyed when their carefully crafted plans to show off the Prince and his role were undermined by his wife's less serious engagements, especially when her appearances seemed to be scheduled at the last moment. It looked to them as if Diana was deliberately undermining their employer's role, which at times it has to be said she was. They did make attempts to outmanoeuvre the Princess but she was too adroit to suffer any serious blow to her image. Diana's media instinct meant she knew precisely how to keep the advantage with frequent appearances. Charles' side was struggling to deal with Diana's constantly moving target. As one Palace aide described their view at the time "We wanted her to stay with some things, we were concerned that she was not getting in-depth experience. But Diana didn't want that. We tried to impose that, but she needed a flash of publicity that she could give and then move on."

What her opponents misunderstood was something fundamental in Diana's make-up, something that was also a source of frustration for some of her friends and allies. Diana's personality was based on the absolute certainty that individuals were more important than organisations, be they the monarchy, or a country or government. If an organisation had no one within it, or associated with it, to whom she could offer caring, support and affection, she saw no great purpose in it. Diana could not give her affection to an organisation. She could not touch the monarchy nor hug the Government. She could not care for the abstract or impersonal, it was simply against her nature. That is not to say she felt animosity, she did not. She felt nothing. Emotional connection to anything other than a person or people did not make sense to her.

Diana's focus then, in her public and private lives, was to give everything possible to single individuals. In her public role it was up to others to interpret those actions as support for a wider agenda. Her style was to travel the country and more latterly the world, connecting in her genuinely caring, informal and tactile way, with individuals who suffered from dread diseases or disadvantage. This was her way of bringing attention to the organisations whose objectives were to address the particular cause. When speaking on behalf of charities involved with AIDS, leprosy or eating disorders, she did not exhort people to support the organisation but to understand the individuals who suffered and act towards them in a similar way to herself.

This style of "flash" publicity was based on a completely different philosophy to that most people would have applied in their support of worthy causes. Diana had no master plan to help any organisation, no great strategy for helping them hit their financial targets, she just turned up and did what her instincts told her to do. The cameras and journalists followed and people recognised something different and special in her way and the money was offered.

Diana did have serious campaigns she was committed to, most notably AIDS and she supported them for years because they were important to her. More important however was that she could see the people involved believed in her and the people they helped needed the caring she brought to them. The men in grey had never acknowledged Diana as a serious player since she married Charles. She had always been treated as an accessory to her husband's more important work. The impression she gained from them, one she rejected, was that they would have liked her to be more like her husband and the rest of the royal family. Given her success perhaps they should have tried to understand her better. As it stood, by early 1991 Diana was head and shoulders above any other member of the royal family in terms of attracting attention to worthy causes and important social issues.

Despite the constant threat hanging over her from the Squidgy tape Diana was gaining confidence again. She found that through her staff she could influence what was happening and her scheme was working quite well. Her activities were not being seriously challenged by her husband's side, although she knew they were unhappy. In her mind she was working with a definite plan based on her intuition and she had the sense she was controlling matters.

A few weeks after the end of hostilities in the Gulf Hewitt returned to England and was reunited briefly and passionately with Diana. According to Hewitt's later recollection Diana continued to talk about them having a future together. In her letters to him while he was in the Gulf she had expressed her determination to change her situation once and for all that summer, during which she would pass her thirtieth birthday and tenth wedding anniversary. Her time frame was undermined because the marriage of the Duke and Duchess of York was also faltering and it was inconceivable the Palace would allow two failed royal marriages to be declared at the same time.

When Hewitt saw her on his brief visit to the UK at that time Diana prophesied she would someday live by the sea in Devon and asked "Are you prepared to wait for me?" Hewitt confirmed he would and left again to return to his unit in Germany for a further six months of his tour. During that time most of their telephone conversations were dominated by discussions about more newspaper stories alluding to a relationship between them and how difficult it would be for them to see each other, let alone be together permanently. On his return from Germany to the UK Hewitt claims he continued to speak to Diana on the telephone and visited her for lunch once or twice in Kensington Palace, but their relationship could not progress while Diana was still entangled with Prince Charles and the royal family. Ultimately it just petered out.

The recollections of Diana's bodyguard Ken Wharfe differ markedly from Hewitt's. His account has Diana telling him unequivocally while Hewitt was still in the Gulf that she felt her lover was getting "too serious". Wharfe's version has Diana suspicious of Hewitt's motives and so unconvinced by his protestations of love that shortly after he returned to the UK from Germany Diana told him in a phone conversation they should "cool it" and that, to all intents and purposes, was the abrupt end of the relationship.

Part of the truth lies in the letters Diana sent to Hewitt while he was at war. Since they formed a major part of the verifiable evidence for Hewitt's later book about his affair with Diana, it seems likely his version of events was correct from his viewpoint. Wharfe had no apparent reason to tell a bald faced lie either. More likely is that Diana was spreading false information to her bodyguard who despite his goodwill and concern for Diana was still a serving police officer employed by the state to protect the daughter-in-law of the head-of-state; deception was becoming second nature to Diana by April 1991.

In the bigger picture James Hewitt became a side issue for Diana during that April. She remained focussed on her strategy of developing a bridgehead of public affection which would forestall any attack on her position when the Squidgy tape came out. Regardless of the uncertain situation with James her media profile was still Diana's best way to assert her strength and confront any attempt to diminish her influence over her children or push her into a future not of her choosing.

At Easter Diana braved the arduous chore of being with other members of the royal family and was photographed with her sons attending a royal family church service at Windsor. On 9 April Diana and her sons were photographed skiing at Lech in Austria without Charles, prompting the press to criticise him once again for being an absent father. Writing in the *Daily Mirror*, tabloid journalist James Whittaker produced a typical slating piece and wrote "Sadly, his (Charles') absences from the family scene have become a habit." Another trip without Charles to Thorpe Park amusement centre the same month produced the same result. On 12 April Diana gave a speech about the effect of AIDS especially on children and suggested a hug was good therapy. Of course she demonstrated how as often as possible by hugging her sons in public.

So it continued. Almost everything Diana did on the public stage strengthened her image at the expense of her husband's personal and professional reputation. That the image was primarily of the doting mother to the two Princes however meant the identity Diana sought was not emerging entirely as she would have liked. Following the stories about her connection with James Hewitt, most of the coverage at that time was examining the state of the royal couple's marriage rather than the importance of Diana's work and her way of performing it. What was clear was that the press was placing the majority of the blame for royal couple's marital problems at Charles' door. Perversely the press insisted on telling readers about a "glimpse of the old magic" and "a united front" when Charles and Diana made a successful official tour of Brazil at the end of the month.

After ten years without respite in the eye of a media storm Diana wore her public persona as the smiling, caring and tactile Princess easily. It was completely genuine and remained largely unaffected by her private concerns, although her personal agenda meant she was always aware of the value of every move she made and every word she uttered. Like a costume to be worn when she needed to connect with the sick, the dying or the distressed Diana enveloped herself in that part of her persona which gave her work purpose and showed her as she wanted to be seen. When she stepped from the stage and re-entered her private world however, Diana's problems always waited to confront her. By May 1991 she had already suffered an enormous amount of strain trying to press her plan forward and avoid disaster. The obstinacy of the press in failing to recognise and report what she needed them to was frustrating. Stories of problems in the marriage competed with others suggesting that a spark of romance still remained, or that the royal couple had come to an accommodation and were content with the status quo. Diana's plan was not going according to plan and she felt instinctively that time was running out.

From Diana's perspective that May she remained in a precarious position. Her connection with James Hewitt had been made in the press. The Squidgy tape, when it was revealed, would help crystalise suspicions which already abounded, that she and Hewitt were lovers. Diana would be condemned for having committed adultery while married to the heir to the throne with not just one lover, but probably two. The tape would also make it clear that the marriage, still being represented as a workable arrangement, was a sham in which she seemed complicit. Similarly she would be seen to have condoned the impression that she was content enough to remain within the royal family. Diana's private sentiments on the tape did not match her behaviour in public where she was still largely acting the dutiful role of wife and royal princess. Significantly there had been no exposure of Charles' relationship with Camilla, which in Diana's mind was the reason for the debacle of her marriage and the cause of most of her pain in the past ten years. The thought that she might be blamed for all the events the tape would reveal, while Charles and Camilla might not, filled her with anger and fear. The possibility that she might, as a result, be marginalised and see her boys slipping from her control, petrified Diana. She must have the public on her side.

For months Diana had been discussing her dilemma with friends, one of which was Dr James Colthurst. James was an old acquaintance of Diana's from 1979 when they had met while skiing. In October 1986 they had renewed their friendship when Diana, responding to her friend's personal request, had opened a new radiology scanner at St. Thomas's hospital where he was working as a registrar. Since then they had kept in touch. Over the intervening years the doctor had come to realise how unhappy Diana was and, like other mutual friends such as Carolyn Bartholomew, he was concerned for her health and wellbeing, which seemed to be deteriorating. A conversation he had with Carolyn about the long term affects of bulimia had resulted in Diana being given the ultimatum which led her to seek help from Maurice Lipsedge in 1988.

On one occasion, during 1990, Colthurst was shocked when Diana said she felt like standing in the middle of Kensington High Street and screaming out loud to tell everyone what was happening to her. "At that stage she wanted to shout her outrage from the rooftops" he recalled later. Even if he had been aware of the process of transformation which was occurring within Diana then, Colthurst would have needed more experience than he had to help Diana work with her emotions in an effective way. Instead, utterly alarmed by Diana's outbursts of rage at her situation and aware that amongst Diana's fears was that she would be labelled insane and thereby lose control over her children, he began to help her.

If Diana had learned more of the details about the process of transformation she was involved in, she might have wondered at the coincidences occurring in her life. She had renewed her friendship with James Colthurst in 1986 and had enjoyed occasional lunches with him since. His concerns for her had either taken five years to develop into active assistance, or there was now something different about Diana which made her open to receiving his assistance and invited him to offer it. The role Colthurst played in bringing about Diana's plan for herself was essential and unique. It is doubtful she would have had anyone else within her circle who was in the position to provide the help Colthurst now gave. Such is the way when the inner self is altered and the persona within projects outwards in demeanour and expression, new messages about who they are becoming. Diana had created a new vision of the future she wanted. The people around her were already beginning to respond, automatically and unconsciously, to accommodate who she had chosen to be.

Over the months that followed Colthurst's newly awakened concerns Diana's shared her problems with him and sought his advice. She asked him to draft a statement for James Hewitt to read to the press in March that year when her connection to the army officer was made public. At the time she did not tell Colthurst that she and Hewitt were lovers. Neither did she tell him about the Squidgy tape which had been hanging over her like an ominous shadow for nearly fifteen months by then. Had the doctor been seriously concerned for Diana's mental health it is certain he would have insisted she get professional help. Instead he correctly identified that her anger was caused by the situation she was in and discussed with her various ways she might exercise some control over her circumstances. For Diana, being able to act rather than wait for things to happen, was always attractive. Confronting Charles yet again was an option swiftly dismissed as pointless; the relationship had deteriorated too far. Seeking medical help for her emotional symptoms was raised as a possibility and rejected because they saw no way that counselling could change the circumstances which constrained the Princess. Favourite was for Diana to reveal her story to the public and of all the options possible, a series of articles, a book, a TV interview, the book idea was the one she preferred most.

As the idea took root and developed Diana realised that a book could get her out of the deadlock once and for all. She could expose the sham of her marriage and tell the world about her husband's affair with Camilla. People would recognise her for her true qualities and see that Charles was to blame for what had gone wrong with their marriage. Even when the Squidgy tape came out she would be vindicated and people's sympathy would make sure she was treated properly and not lose her sons. As the idea developed in her mind Diana saw the book as a way of presenting her story the way she wanted it told. All she needed was someone to write it.

Diana was aware of all the journalists who were sensitive to her situation even if they did not seem to know what was actually happening to her. Amongst them was Andrew Morton, a royal correspondent and experienced freelancer whose articles showed considerable insight into Diana's position. Morton had already published a generally sympathetic book called *Diana's Diary: An Intimate Portrait of the Princess of Wales* and Diana knew he had already embarked on writing a full scale biography about her.

As coincidence would have it, Diana and Morton shared a connection through one Dr James Colthurst. The journalist had covered the hospital event in 1986 for *The Daily Mail* and had discovered, when he interviewed Colthurst, that the doctor had known Diana for years. Morton tried to cultivate the well placed friend of Diana as an inside source for royal stories but failed. Nevertheless the two men became friends who played squash together on the hospital courts and enjoyed "large lunches in a nearby Italian restaurant."

That March, Diana had told Colthurst about the imminent and very sudden departure of Christopher Airy, joint private secretary to Charles and Diana. When the story duly appeared in *The Sunday Times*, written by Andrew Morton, Diana realised he might be the man to write her book and her friend Colthurst might be the man to make it happen. A piece by Morton for *The Sun* newspaper, insinuating that a close relationship had existed between Charles and Camilla for months, possibly years, gave Diana more evidence that the journalist could do the job.

At about the same time, the now anticipated departure of Christopher Airy gave Diana another opportunity to demonstrate her intention to act more independently of her husband's part of the office. A few weeks after Airy left his post Diana appointed Patrick Jephson as her own personal secretary. He was relieved. His relationship with the Princess, following his strongly worded advice to her during the Gulf conflict, had soured and he suspected the delay in his selection for the vacant post was because Diana was trying to arrange employment for James Hewitt. Jephson's appointment confirmed he was back in favour and he immediately rearranged the office accommodation so Diana's small staff was physically separated from Charles' much larger contingent but still adjacent to it.

For some time Diana's staff had been referring to themselves as the A Team at her suggestion. She boosted their morale with occasional A Team lunches at one or other of London's top restaurants. The B Team was her husband's. The physical division of the two teams simply made real a situation that had already developed but not been acknowledged. Prince Charles' organisation was now split into two distinct factions at odds with one another. The move did result in occasional attempts to have Diana's small staff moved out of the shared offices at St. James' Palace. Later he would write "... from time to time the host organism would try to expel us" explaining how he resisted the attempts to make Diana's staff retreat to Kensington Palace because it would place the Princess outside the "great debates that were soon to ensue...about the future of the Waleses."

Jephson's strategy also owed something to his own agenda for Diana. Describing the royal family as a "federation of semi-independent households" he was worried about reaction of the other members to Diana's activities as she attempted to pull away from her husband's organisation to set up her own independent situation. Jephson was seeking a way to keep Diana securely within the main organisation while letting her feel she was independent. Remaining close to the action where he would likely be more aware of rumours and plots was essential to his plan. He did not know Diana was considering a book which would tell her true story and he still did not know about the Squidgy tape.

✦ ✦ ✦

I was quite glad really that Diana had not picked up on my suggestion that she and the children should wear Groucho Marx masks and chomp false cigars at the photographers' scrum in Lech. We'd been talking about how difficult it was for her with the boys – William was just coming up to nine and Harry was only six, when they were constantly being pressured for photographs, even when they were on holiday.

'Well you don't have to cooperate every time do you?' was my response. Then I made the Groucho Marx suggestion. The way she looked at me said "You just do not understand."

'What's the worst that can happen?' I asked with a wry grin. 'They can't shoot you for it.' As usual I was making a serious point even while being humorous. 'A lot of people stop themselves taking risks because of fear about what they imagine will happen. Try imagining the worst you can think of and then ask yourself if you can face it. You'll get further than if you don't do anything because you're scared of what might happen.'

Throughout the months of late spring and early summer the media conflict between Diana and Charles continued to escalate and Diana went from being seen as a nuisance, to being regarded as serious threat to Charles' position and perhaps the monarchy itself. With the proverbial bit between her teeth Diana was becoming impatient. The knowledge that her story would soon be told gave her the confidence to assert herself more overtly, even recklessly. In the office she instigated a clash with her husband's side when she ignored Patrick Jephson's warnings about a conflict between her diary and her husband's. Diana had agreed to make a speech at a combined National AIDS Trust and National Children's Bureau conference. The date conflicted with her husband's major speech on the standard of English in schools. Diana went ahead and not surprisingly grabbed the headlines. Not only was Charles trumped but his office was criticised for its inept scheduling.

The conflict around the offices at St. James' and Buckingham Palace was also apparent within the pages of the nation's various newspapers. Andrew Morton in *The Sunday Times* described Prince Charles as a danger to the future of the monarchy and as a man who was unfeeling, hypocritical and self-indulgent; The *Daily Mail's* gossip columnist wrote about Diana's petulance and ingratitude for refusing to let Prince Charles give her a special ball to celebrate her thirtieth birthday; after a briefing from Diana, through James Colthurst, Andrew Morton responded with a piece in *The Sunday Times* which gave her reason for rejecting her husband's offer, that it would be a meaningless gesture and nothing more than an opportunity for Charles to be with Camilla in public. Written while she was still considering whether to collaborate with Morton on a book, this story gave Diana all the proof she would need that she could take control of how her story would be presented to the world. She asked Colthurst to approach Morton with the idea for a book which would tell her story and explain any action she might decide to take subsequently.

Andrew Morton, for all his inside sources and fine instincts was completely surprised when he heard about the real state of Diana's marriage from Colthurst. Even he had expressed in print the view that the couple, although leading separate private lives, had acquiesced to a convenient public arrangement for the sake of the children and the monarchy. He quickly came to terms with the revelations and agreed to write Diana's story.

From there the book project proceeded apace. Recognising the need for secrecy and realising he could not meet the Princess in person to interview her, Morton arranged with Colthurst and Diana that they would make audio tapes containing Diana's response to the journalist's questions. The first "interview" was taped at Kensington Palace that May and their sessions continued throughout the summer and autumn.

In the context of Diana's self-transformation her choice to collaborate on a book which enabled her to review her entire life and have a witness, in Colthurst, to her story, was significant. During the months of remembering and talking and taping Diana was reinforcing her reasons for needing to move on. She was recognising important influences from her past in the light of her developing interest in psychology. She was able to recognise the progress she had made from the pitiful state she was in a few years before and she was refining as a result, the future-vision she had established in her mind. The feeling that she was actively participating in altering her life was also profoundly important for the woman who had for so long been seeing herself as a pawn in everyone else's game but her own.

As the book took shape Diana was able to hold draft pages in her hands and make changes or suggestions. Inevitably Diana's perspective was represented in the end product, which blamed her husband for the failing marriage and identified his relationship with Camilla as the problem which caused the end of the fairytale. Diana unsurprisingly made sure she was shown in the best light possible while allowing issues such as her bulimia and self harming to be revealed. It had already been decided that Diana must have plausible deniability when she was asked, as she inevitably would be, whether she had met Morton or provided information for his book. As a result it was written as a biography which enabled Diana to allow the inclusion of contentious material without giving the media direct quotes from her own lips. Diana was only too aware of the distinction between what Diana was supposed to have done and what Diana actually said she did, when it came to media coverage and the possible repercussions.

Despite the feeling of freeing herself which came from telling her story at last, Diana would live the next year under a burden of immense stress. She was afraid what the outcome might be when the book was published and she still dreaded what might happen with the Squidgy tape, the existence of which she had kept from Morton. With remarkable inner strength Diana carried on and continued to fulfil her royal duties as usual.

I was using deep massage most of the time now in my sessions with Diana but I wasn't really trying to alter the connective tissue. What I wanted was to get her engaged in being focussed on her body and out of her head. If I used lighter techniques I could see that she often drifted into a reverie state during which her thoughts and emotions caused her body to tense, far better to keep her occupied releasing tension for an hour.

'What other people think of you is none of your business,' I pontificated when Diana complained about criticism in the press. 'It's much more important what you think of yourself. Anyone looking at you and judging you will do so through the filter of their own beliefs about how people should behave. There will always be people who don't approve of what you do or how you do it. What you believe about yourself is much more important. Knowing who you are and being true to yourself is the only way to be genuinely happy and to help your body be healthy.'

'Anyway what people think can't hurt you. It's what they do as a result of what they think that you need to take notice of.'

On another occasion when Diana muttered "after all I've done for that family" I responded by suggesting there was a gift in every situation if she cared to look. From her marriage and being in the royal family she had two wonderful sons and the opportunity to discover an amazing ability to transform people's lives throughout the world. I was really pressing her hard to stop thinking in clichés she'd been used to for years and to start seeing the positives in situations.

Another time, now knowing she was a personality type who relied heavily on her intuition, I spoke about the way her instincts would be linked to her future-vision. 'Rely on your instincts,' I said, 'but only when you have your vision of how you want to be completely clear and firm in your mind. Your intuition can only come up with an insight or idea out of all the information you've accumulated over the years and the future you envisage from it. If it's bad information and the future-vision your mind and body are creating is a bad one, then your instincts will be bad too. Good instincts come from good information and a good future-vision.'

What was now being dubbed The War of the Wales's became increasingly bitter from early June after Prince William was accidentally hit on the head with a golf club while at school. He was taken to the Royal Berkshire Hospital and both Diana and Charles rushed, separately to their son's side. They followed when William was transferred to the Great Ormond Street Hospital for surgery. After taking advice and understanding from Diana's demeanour that he was not needed or wanted, Charles proceeded to fulfil his engagements with a visit to the opera and an overnight trip by train to Yorkshire. Diana kept vigil until William was sufficiently recovered from his surgery for her to feel it was safe to leave him. During her stay in the hospital she visited and comforted other children and their families, with whom she could empathise even more closely as a result of her own son's misfortune. Over subsequent years she re-emphasised her work for the head injuries charity Headway. Press coverage for several days after the accident branded Charles as callous and unfeeling and portrayed Diana as a saintly and caring mother.

The accident to William prompted a seminal change in Diana's attitude to her husband. Notwithstanding that, according to her bodyguard Ken Wharfe, "Diana made it clear she did not want him (Charles) around". Diana saw Charles' insistence on carrying out his engagements while his son was hurt as symptomatic of all she abhorred about him and her own situation in the royal family. When Charles later blamed Diana's overreaction to the accident for his bad press and she had to tell the Queen in person that her grandson's surgery was not the trivial matter she had understood it to be from Prince Charles, Diana realised there could be no going back to any life in which he was involved. As a Water element, for whom her children's safety was paramount, Diana could not imagine spending any more of her life with a man with such different priorities to her own. She renewed her determination to force the issue of their marriage through the book with Andrew Morton.

Despite winning so many public and private skirmishes, that summer Diana was feeling "as if the lid was being put down on her" according to Morton's later recollection. A significant reason was the renewed efforts Charles' side of the office was making to curb her growing media status. More worrying for her was the whispering campaign suggesting she was mentally unstable. Friends had told her she was being referred to as the "mad cow" at dinner parties and later reported she was very worried about being seen as potty and that she had approached the Queen and Prince Phillip for help only to be told the problems were all in her mind and she should get psychiatric help. The campaign, which had been going on for years originated, she believed, with Charles' friends. It dated from as far back as her early years with the Prince when she had been so badly troubled by bulimia, depression and self-doubt. Ever since she had been concerned that her mental state might be used as an excuse to marginalise her, even commit her into an institution and wrest the children from her control.

Through his sessions taping material for the Morton book, Dr James Colthurst was aware of Diana's bulimia, self-harming and suicide attempts. He knew of the various psychiatrists and psychotherapists who had been called in to help her during the early part of her marriage, none of whom seemed to have thought her insane or insisted she be treated as anything other than one of the many "worried well". Aware of Dr Maurice Lipsedge's treatment of Diana, Colthurst had no evidence the the eminent psychiatrist believed any different to his colleagues from earlier years. Colthurst had frequent opportunities over several months to observe Diana and listen to her talk about herself and her life and to advise if he had become aware of anything which gave him concern. He did not and it can be assumed from all this that Diana was not mad as some were suggesting at that time and others would continue to assert in the years to come.

The War of the Wales's was being fought on Diana's territory, in the press and she needed to keep it there, her master stroke would be the book when it was published. The attempts to damage her media profile by influencing her public role and attacking her personal reputation, simply added venom to Diana's efforts to bring her situation before the public. The forces opposing her had made yet another serious error of judgement through simple ignorance. Diana's INFP personality credentials included an idealistic sense of justice. She was convinced of the rightness of her case against her husband and the royal organisation behind him. Diana's make-up also included features of the Water element for whom family was a paramount consideration. Suggestions that she might be mentally ill were a direct threat to Diana's position as mother and primary guardian of her sons' future and wellbeing. To attack such a one, whose entire outlook is based on the absolute certainty that their rightful place is beside their children, is to provoke a reaction that does not bear considering. They will lie, cheat, steal and act with a cunning you would not expect. If the men in grey and the family they served thought they had seen everything Diana could produce to challenge them they were much mistaken that summer of 1991.

The Morton book was under way and Diana was impatient to see it become a reality. The suggestions of mental instability and her sense of injustice, made it essential that she not be blamed for what occurred as a result. As long as she could maintain she had nothing to do with the book she would be held blameless. But the book must provoke Charles into a reaction so that he would bring an end to her situation by his own hand. The moral strength of her position and her unassailable standing in the public eye would ensure she could resist whatever inevitable backlash occurred.

Throughout that summer and autumn the Duchess of York and Diana were discussing their options and the thorny question of separation and divorce. Sarah continually pressed the idea that the two royal wives should jump ship together. Diana, aware that to make such a pre-emptive move could result in her losing her children and, already having the Morton book project behind her, was prepared to stay. Diana knew that Fergie had been tempting fate since 1990 having been linked with other men while her husband was away on duty in the navy. Diana did not want to be too closely associated with the Duchess when her marriage fell apart, as Diana was sure it would. She preferred to be on the sidelines to see what she could learn when it happened.

1 July 1991 was Diana's thirtieth and a landmark, birthday. Diana could truthfully say that only one year, her nineteenth, had been truly happy.

Otherwise she had experienced brief moments of happiness amongst a lot of sadness and pain. Her vision of the future at that time would certainly have included more children, but not with Charles, and Diana's biological clock was ticking inexorably. She felt even more pressure to make something happen. She had refused Charles' offer of a grand celebration as hypocritical and her husband felt insulted. A brief spatter of sniping in the press marked the occasion. The shots were fired by journalists but the ammunition was clearly provided to the journalist by allies of the warring factions. The hostilities were accompanied by news of a national opinion poll which voted Diana the most popular member of the royal family. She attended a lunch at the Savoy in aid of the Rainbow House children's hospice appeal and celebrated her birthday quietly at Kensington Palace.

At 5.19 p.m. on the day after her birthday Diana sent a message to Morton and Colthurst making it clear she was impatient for the book to come out and indicating her suspicion that Camilla was the source of a news story about the rejection of the birthday ball.

The viciousness of the exchange in the newspapers made everyone take a step back for a breather. A number of journalists wrote conciliatory pieces even backtracking on the couples' respective links to James Hewitt and Camilla Parker-Bowles, describing them as nothing more than friendships. Andrew Morton's article in *The Sunday Times*, under the headline TRUCE told of moves by various friends of the royal couple, including Sir Jimmy Saville, to mediate in what was now a full blown battle. Another intermediary during 1991 was the urbane Oliver Hoare who, with his wife Diane, had been friends of Charles and Diana for years. His sympathetic attempts did not succeed in helping Diana understand her husband better as they were intended to do. Instead they prepared the grounds for an attraction between Hoare and Diana which would emerge later.

As part of the attempt to calm the impression given by their conflict, Diana and Charles appeared in public together at the Royal Albert Hall, for a gala performance of Verdi's Requiem, but beneath their veneer of civilised behaviour a primitive fight for survival was raging. Diana saw the threat posed by the Squidgy tape as potentially terminal for any chance she might have of a happy future. Her response was the Morton book and her escalation of hostilities against her husband in the media. Charles saw his life's work and future being threatened by overt acts of sabotage and was fighting back.

Now committed to her course Diana also had to fight her own darker thoughts and feelings to maintain the momentum of her plans. No longer disabled by constant crippling lack of certainty, she was still subject to severe emotional reactions and feelings of self-doubt when she felt attacked or unappreciated, which was often. She still felt misunderstood and her lifelong tendency to take criticism at a deeply personal level still emerged when she was feeling low. In the main those around her did not understand her and were frustrated or baffled by her mood swings and by what seemed to them strange decisions, although her choices made perfect sense to Diana's instincts.

Diana's bodyguard, Ken Wharfe, recalled comforting a tearful Diana after an interview with the Queen. The Princess had been told in unequivocal terms by her mother-in-law that she thought Diana was misguided in her close involvement with HIV+AIDS, which at the time was a contentious issue generally seen as a "gay plague" visited on people who did not deserve much sympathy. "The Queen does not approve of what I am doing with AIDS, Ken," she told him at the time, then added with complete certainty that her own way was best. "That bloody family after all I've done for them." Diana, with her people orientated make-up, could not understand or accept a perspective different to her own. Where others could foresee her focus on AIDS might damage many people's perception of the monarchy, Diana could not see how caring about individuals who were suffering from such a terrible condition could harm an institution there to serve the people.

For Diana a few tears shed were like healing balm and she soon recovered her strength of purpose. Despite being aware of the Queen's concerns Diana continued her involvement with the disease and ensured it received considerable media coverage. On 17 July she visited the AIDS unit at Middlesex Hospital with Barbara Bush, wife of then President Bush. What was already a high profile engagement attracted even more media attention when Diana spontaneously hugged a weeping AIDS sufferer.

A month later Diana defied royal protocol and by definition the Queen, again. She left Balmoral without asking the Queen's permission and drove through the night with her bodyguard to be in London for the passing away from AIDS of her friend Adrian Ward-Jackson. During the preceding four months Diana had quietly and without any media fanfare supported, then actively assisted, the efforts of a mutual friend, Angela Serota, as she took care of Adrian while he succumbed to his disease. Her experiences with these two very special and spiritually aware people, one of whom was facing his own death, had a profound effect on Diana during a time when she was consumed with fears and worries of her own.

Just prior to her unsanctioned dash to London Diana had spent part of the summer holiday with Charles and her sons on board the luxury yacht *Alexander*, owned by millionaire John Latsis. The palace press briefing indicated the romantic cruise might be a sign of a possible reconciliation between Diana and her husband. While this was extremely unlikely given the open warfare of the previous months, the news media chose to sell to the public stories of the "love cruise" as a "second honeymoon" during which the "two lovebirds" were "closer than for ages". In fact it was anything but a "love boat". Most of those accompanying the Prince and Princess were Charles' friends and people of whom Diana was deeply suspicious. Diana had invited Graham Smith, her former protection officer who was very ill with cancer and who had to retire a few months after the trip. During the holiday Charles maintained contact with Camilla and Diana stayed in touch with Morton and Colthurst, who by then had been recruited to help her with her speeches.

Interesting to consider is why the palace briefing would try to represent the cruise as a sign that Diana and Charles were happy in each other's company. Possibly it was just a cynical exercise, a habit those in the organisation simply could not bring themselves to break in favour of the truth. Quite likely as well it was an indication that Diana was succeeding with her strategy and that those high in the Buckingham Palace organisation saw Diana as both an asset they did not want to lose and a threat they did not want to confront. The issue of a separation had not been resolved and divorce was still thought to be entirely out of the question. Diana's popularity by then would have made the men in grey very wary of being seen to attack her and hopeful that they could keep her on side and within the royal fold. Unfortunately it seems they did not inform Diana that she was wanted. Perhaps their reticence was because Prince Charles was unlikely to hold the same opinion. As a result Diana's indignation about the continuous false reporting of her situation with Charles was reinforced, along with her determination to alter her circumstances.

Diana's impression of how she was regarded by the royal family and the palace establishment had been formed by their reactions to incidents such as her determination to be on hand at the death of Adrian Ward-Jackson. The royal way, so different to Diana's own, was to make just a token visit. Diana had to resist pressure to do the same in order to remain in London for the four days it took her friend to pass on 23 August. Six days later she broke royal protocol again by attending Adrian's funeral. The men in grey simply could not understand that Diana put people before protocol and organisations no matter how august those organisations might be and now was inclined to put herself and her sons before the needs of the monarchy.

✦ ✦ ✦

'What do you think of the monarchy Stephen?' Diana dropped the question on me early in another session.

She knew by now I wasn't going to tell her anything but my own truth when she asked me a question. I didn't worry about whether she might be upset by what I said. I was a free agent. I could walk away whenever I wanted to. I respected the fact that Diana could stop seeing me anytime by just failing to make another appointment.

'I presume you mean the monarchy as an institution rather than your in-laws,' I said.

Diana nodded.

'Well I think the monarchy is like a lot of big organisations – government, businesses, local authorities you name it – they're too impersonal. It seems to me they're missing something very important. I believe people need to know that someone cares about them as an individual and will do what it takes to help them if they get in trouble. I don't think big organisations do that and for every person we see on the news who couldn't be helped because it was too expensive, or because we don't want to upset some government or other, there are thousands thinking "what if that was me?"'

Not surprisingly Diana the INFP, the carer whose entire ethos was built on caring for the individual, nodded in agreement with me, the INFJ. Then again maybe she was agreeing for a more personal reason I didn't know about.

I didn't know anything about a journalist who contacted me around this time either. Andrew Morton had been given my contact details by someone who knew of my work with Diana and he wanted to talk to me. This was odd because in the two and a half years I'd been visiting Kensington Palace I hadn't had a sniff of a journalist. No one knew I was working with the Princess, except the client who had introduced me to her. Morton's pitch was that he was writing a sympathetic biography to tell Diana's story and concerned friends were contributing because it might help the Princess. He understood I was playing an important part in her life. Could he interview me for the book?

Intrigued I mentioned the contact to Diana the next time I saw her and told her about the book. 'Don't touch it with a barge pole,' was her crisp advice before we continued with her session. We never spoke of it again. Nevertheless I contacted Morton to find out what he had in mind.

I had several conscious reasons for doing so. First I didn't want anyone writing about what I was doing without my input to make sure what they said was accurate. Second I was not averse to news of my ideas getting out to a wider public if it gave me an opportunity to talk about them and being associated with the most famous woman in the world couldn't hurt, could it? I believed implicitly in my methods and wanted more people to benefit from what I had learned. Third I was still working with very little knowledge of what Diana's life was like outside the room in which I saw her. I was interested to hear there were friends of Diana's who were worried enough about her to talk to a journalist apparently against Diana's wishes.

There was a less tangible reason for contacting Andrew. It felt right. Somehow, even when Diana said "don't touch it" it seemed OK to go ahead.

✦ ✦ ✦

During that August Diana continued to provide material for the book when she was able. Morton, needing to verify much of what Diana was telling him for legal reasons, pressed her for evidence of the assertions she made about a relationship between Charles and Camilla. Diana looked in her husband's briefcase and found a bundle of letters and postcards he had received from his lover and passed them to the journalist. The passionate letters went beyond being Morton's proof. For Diana they took her assumptions and suspicions, her imagined scenarios and hurtful thoughts, into the realm of real substance, words of love and caring written on real paper from another woman to her husband. The letters also showed that people who had represented themselves to Diana as concerned and caring friends, were in fact complicit in the deception played on her. These "friends" knew about her husband's lover, some had provided Charles with opportunities to be with Camilla and had misled Diana actively or by their silence. Diana's suspicions had been correct all along and were not the manifestation of paranoia or delusions.

For his part Andrew Morton was becoming aware of the seriousness of the project he had agreed to. His "TRUCE" article of a few weeks before had attracted the close attention of palace officials. Morton had included details which they believed could only have come from a very well connected inside source with access to Kensington Palace and they were determined to discover who it was. Morton was warned that the police had been asked to find the mole. A few months later his office was burgled, a camera was stolen and files were disturbed. It was fortunate that Diana and her co-conspirators had decided to use scrambler phones and shredders. Perhaps surprising is that no one seems to have suspected James Colthurst of being the mole. He was a frequent visitor to Kensington Palace ferrying notes and tapes between Diana and Morton. The palace gate log would have shown how often Colthurst visited. Maybe it was thought that Diana was involved in another affair, which is just what many close to Charles hoped she would do as part of a long term accommodation to her situation.

At the end of that September Diana undertook a five-day solo visit to Pakistan. The trip was a great success and the ambassador gave Diana rave reviews afterwards, although it is uncertain whether he mentioned the occasion when the exhausted Diana seemed on the verge of rebelling and derailing the entire trip. A fortuitous thunderstorm, a grounded aeroplane and a cancelled official dinner gave her the space to recover herself and she completed the tour successfully.

The tour was an important event from several viewpoints. It had been a long time in the planning and Diana had made considerable efforts to be prepared for it. Under the auspices of the Foreign Office Diana was representing the Queen. Had the news articles about her links with James Hewitt been of consequence to the Government or the Queen, Diana would undoubtedly have not been given permission to go. That she was entrusted with such an important mission, in such a politically sensitive part of the world, speaks to the idea that Diana was seen by the larger Buckingham Palace organization, and the Government, as an asset more than a threat and that they saw a continuing place for her within the royal family.

While Diana's relationships with Prince Charles had been deteriorating rapidly she had been careful, apart from her recent assertiveness around the AIDS issue and her friend Adrian Ward-Jackson, to maintain good relationships with the Queen. Diana saw her mother-in-law fairly often for private chats and took the young Princes William and Harry to visit. Perhaps Diana was not stopped from making the trip for fear of how it might seem to the media, but that is unlikely. Patrick Jephson records that "For the next four years...the Foreign Office never lacked enthusiasm for entrusting her with similar overseas missions." What is likely is that Prince Charles noticed Diana's developing contact with the Government and her support from the Queen which was implied by her tour. How that made him feel about his own position is not recorded. What is known is that Prince Charles gave his views on many matters to respective governments and felt his talents were underused by them. As a result of Diana's success Charles once again became the target of more critical press coverage, which contrasted his wife's hard work with what was portrayed as the Prince's relaxed and affluent lifestyle.

When the Pakistan trip ended Diana reinstated a practice which had been dropped by her husband several years previously, after some unguarded, and he assumed off the record, remarks had found their way into print. She held a press reception and cheerfully bantered with the journalists and cameramen who had accompanied the tour. Later she would find an opportunity to offer her private thoughts to selected news hounds.

During October Diana continued the collaboration with her book and maintained her media assault. Her unabated dedication to the AIDS issue was evident when she attended a conference by the National AIDS Trust and visited AIDS sufferers at Milestone House. In November she attended a charity function for World AIDS Day at Her Majesty's Theatre. In between times, on 21 October she made a well received speech about road safety and two days later went with her husband and sons on a well publicised six day trip to Canada. She probably greeted an article by journalist Penny Junor that October with mixed feelings. Junor wrote about the new Diana, "the complete woman" for whom 1991 was "the greatest year of her life", but went on to say that Diana and her husband spent more time together than tabloid reports suggested.

✦ ✦ ✦

The interview I finally gave Andrew Morton was not a topic of conversation at any of the sessions I had with Diana afterwards. I'd been extremely careful to talk about my work in general terms and to offer opinions from a broad context. I told the truth in understatement when I said I thought she was a courageous woman dealing with problems anyone could have, in exceptionally difficult circumstances which put her under a great deal of strain. I didn't get any information of value from Morton except the awareness that there were people around Diana who were very worried for her wellbeing and her future.

That Christmas I gave Diana some essential oils and a copy of the *I Ching* with three Chinese coins. The *I Ching* is a very old classic Chinese text and system of divination. Three coins are tossed to identify one of sixty four hexagrams, each of which is identified with a particular insight. When the coins are tossed as instructed, with a question in mind, the *I Ching* reveals the insight which helps to identify the best way forward. My reason for giving the gift to Diana was because the text spoke of how an ideal person, a man of knowledge, would see the problem and deal with it from a highly developed level of spiritual attainment. Like the tarot the year before I hoped Diana would recognise traits she could include in her future-vision while she gained insight into the difficulties she faced.

Diana's thank you note was on red bordered note paper with D and crown motif. Dated 20 December it mentioned her collection of books *My reading department has grown rapidly & is impressive even to the intellectual!* The note ended *Thank you, Stephen, too for your wisdom, kindness & support. With much love From Diana x.*

1991 was winding down after an exhausting and stressful year for the Princess. The Squidgy tape still hung over her life, but she had her Morton book to look forward to and to be concerned about. She had fought a good fight during the year to create a better media profile, as evidenced by her AIDS coverage and the Pakistan trip. Being voted "the most elegant and stylish woman of the year" by *Hello* magazine, would have been seen with a slightly jaundiced eye.

By that December Diana was committed to her book and there was no going back. A note, dated 1 December to James Colthurst, thanked him for his support and told him "Obviously we are preparing for the volcano to erupt & I do feel better equipped to deal with whatever comes our way!" The "we" was not intended to denote any royal persona but to acknowledge the team work which had helped her bring the project about. Even hearing from Patrick Jephson, that the Palace was aware of the book and suspected her involvement, did not deter her. She was fully committed and sure she was doing the right thing.

If she reflected on how she was able to be so strong and so prepared, Diana might have recognised the continuing effects of the self-transformation process she had started three years earlier. Underlying her ability to challenge her detractors, deal with her stress and perform her many arduous official engagements with aplomb, was a new vision of herself which was continuing to develop. Regular bodywork, in the form of massage, complemented by personal training directed by Carolan Brown, were helping her body translate that vision and express it in a new physical presence and energy which were subtly prompting different responses from the people around her. Acupuncture and prayer with Oonagh Toffalo and astrological counselling from Debbie Frank and more recently from Felix Lyle, added to the process which was bringing about the changes within her and to her outer expression of them.

Four months with Angela Serota and Adrian Ward-Jackson had given momentum to the spiritual awakening which almost always accompanies personal transformation. Diana already had a sense of the unseen connections between events and of another level of cause and effect beyond the obvious, through personal experiences of déjà vu and precognition since she was young. She was very interested in systems of divination, especially astrology. Her bedside pile of books now included the *I Ching* and Khalil Gibran's book *The Prophet*, a gift from Adrian Ward-Jackson, alongside volumes on astrology, tarot, psychology and religion. Had she understood the metaphysics of personal development she would not have been surprised at the co-incidence between her new beliefs and thoughts and the events occurring around her. She did not need to understand for it to happen.

Some of those around Diana, the men in grey and Charles' friends, responded to her new found determination by acting more emphatically against her. Others, like James Colthurst and Andrew Morton, were attracted into Diana's life, apparently by chance, to stand beside her and support her efforts. James Hewitt drifted almost unnoticed to the periphery of her life. Whatever Patrick Jephson thought of the Princess and her motives, he found himself committed to a role in which he was Diana's agent for change in the palace organisation. Ken Wharfe sensed the changes and years later wrote about Diana during that time: "She had become adept not merely at surviving, but at flourishing in the world in which she found herself."

The process Diana was engaged in was driven by her new but still developing vision of how she wanted to be. Unsurprisingly her vision, through lack of experience and simple error, would have contained unclear or even unsuitable elements. Diana's journey to her ideal future self would, as a result, not be an easy one. One problem was indicated by her conversations around this time. She was trying to work out whether she should stay within the royal family or leave it. Better would have been to see herself standing strong and capable regardless of whether she was in the family or outside of it. Diana's confusion about whether she would, or even could, divorce Charles would have been answered by the same vision of herself standing strong in the world as her own person. By trying to imagine the answers to complex questions Diana was creating difficulties she might not have had to face. The other problem, projecting a life in which she was independent and in control, alongside an equal desire to be taken care of by a husband within a normal family home, was creating paradoxes that would only be resolved by working through difficult moments during the coming years. The process of self-transformation would bring about what she wanted, but only when it had confronted her with her own uncertainties and the obstacles in her way.

A great deal had occurred during the year; infighting with the men in grey; the Hewitt revelations; confronting her husband and ignoring royal protocol. Despite it all Diana demonstrated her inner resolve and underlined her role as mother to Princes William and Harry by attending the Christmas Day Service with the royal family at Sandringham. She did not remain with them for the entire holiday. Acting on a suggestion by James Colthurst Diana had Patrick Jephson arrange an impromptu visit to comfort the homeless.

In her annual Christmas speech that December the Queen spoke of carrying on in her role "for some years to come". Whether motivated by a desire to bring some stability to the contrary impression given by the troubled marriages of her two oldest sons, or by something else, the implication was clear, the Queen was not going to agree to the suggestion being proposed that she step down in favour of Prince Charles. The message would not have been lost on Charles who could not now be expecting to become King in any near future. It would not have been lost either on Diana who, if nothing changed in her marital status, was the future Queen. No doubt Diana breathed a sigh of relief.

1992

You cannot consistently perform
in a manner
which is inconsistent
with the way you see yourself.
Zig Ziglar

There were optimistic souls in the palace at the start of 1992, who believed it might still be possible for Prince Charles and Diana to fulfil public duties together, remain married and live entirely separate private lives. The needs of the monarchy and the heir to the throne required it, they would have argued, obligations to the Church and duty demanded it of them. It was a forlorn hope as the optimists would have realised had they known Diana better. They would have completely given up any such fantasy if they had been aware of what she had instigated.

Diana was motivated by her emotions and her sense of what was just – her intuition told her what to do. When she loved she did so deeply and intensely. She was willing to make sacrifices for those she loved, and she expected love and sacrifice in return. Diana had loved Charles, and had struggled and endured years of unhappiness and despair trying to be what she thought he wanted her to be. She had not received his love. The sacrifices she made had not even been recognised – she had seen no similar sacrifice on his part. Now her vision of the future, like her heart, held no place for Charles. She wanted to move on and leave him behind, regardless of the needs of the monarchy, the heir, the Church or duty, but she was aware that moving on would be fraught with difficulties.

Driven equally by her sense of injustice; anger at Charles and his family; and fear for her future, Diana had taken the first step to ensuring her husband would not be a part of her future by arranging for her story to be told in Andrew Morton's book, *Diana: Her True Story*. At the end of the previous year Diana had written to James Colthurst to say she was prepared for the volcano which would erupt into her life in September. Even when she wrote the note she knew there was another volcano which could, at any time, spew its contents over the future she was seeking to create. Diana was certain the Squidgy tape would irreparably damage what was central to the vision she had of her future, her place with her sons. By January 1992 the tape had been hanging over her like an evil shadow for a year, threatening untold harm. Perhaps she was beginning to think it would never be revealed, although her instinct told her it would be. She could not take the chance that it would remain secret. Her book was her only hope of circumventing the mayhem the tape was almost certain to create.

In Diana's mind there was only one force which could protect her from the anger and retaliation of those who held duty, the monarchy, her husband's status and tradition above all else, public opinion. Her book would reveal to everyone the sham her marriage had been for years, and the sacrifices she had made to fulfil the role for which she was admired and appreciated by so many ordinary people. Her book would show that any blame for the end of the fairytale, and her search for love outside her marriage, lay with her husband, a man who had always loved someone else and had broken his promises to his young bride. The book would be her appeal to the public for understanding and support, and Diana believed in her heart her plea would be heeded. How could it not?

Her part in the book's creation was done. Publication of her story, and exposure of the reality of her life, was set for September, not to meet her needs but as a commercial decision – September being the traditional month to release best sellers. It was a race. The Squidgy tape could be revealed at any time, depending on the whims of newspaper editors and owners. Diana gambled her hopes and dreams on the book and getting it out first; she dreaded the tape emerging before the book's publication. She knew that either of these two cataclysmic events would change her life irrevocably, but in very different ways, and Diana had no control over which would win. Once again, as she had many times before in her life, Diana felt helpless in the face of events controlled by others, all she could do was continue to prepare.

Driven by fear of the Squidgy tape, Diana had purposely set out to create a media profile of such consequence that she would gain the support and sympathy of a nation, and ensure her standing was strong enough to withstand any attack that might challenge her future with her boys. There were signs in the press coverage of the previous year, and people's responses to her at her engagements, that she was achieving her aim. At the beginning of 1992 Diana curbed her fears and doubts and pushed ahead with her campaign. A visit to Rome to visit her inspiration, Mother Teresa of Calcutta, who was recovering from a heart condition, boosted Diana's morale and sense of purpose.

Without the inner transformational work Diana had already undertaken, she might well have been overwhelmed and paralysed by the panic and anxiety she felt when she considered what might happen later in the year. Although paradoxically, it has to be said, without that transformational work, she would not have had such a powerful vision of herself, and neither the self-esteem or courage to pursue it, so she probably would not be facing the challenges which confronted her. Had Diana remained as fragile as she was three years earlier, she almost certainly would not have embarked on the strategy to raise her media profile, nor would she have chosen to confront her situation once and for all by having the book written. Now she did have the courage and, as Patrick Jephson recorded in his memoir, Diana embarked on a program of engagements that for the remainder of the year "put her in the royal spotlight as never before".

Her focus on public work helped Diana in two ways. First her feelings of caring and compassion for others pushed her own uncomfortable emotions into the background. Second she was adding to the reservoir of public recognition and affection she hoped would translate into sympathy and support when the time came for her to need it. As January progressed Diana became completely focussed on how every situation would be perceived by the media and how everything she did or said might help or hinder her.

Concern about the marital problems of the Queen's two oldest sons was occupying the men in grey at Buckingham Palace at that time. Late in January 1992 The Duke and Duchess of York, Andrew and Sarah, visited the Queen at Sandringham to formally discuss their wish to separate. The Queen persuaded them to take time to reflect, during a two month "cooling off" period. The couple's estrangement was caused substantially by a situation very similar to that in which Diana found herself. During her marriage, Sarah too had become disillusioned with life in the royal family, and she also resented the constant criticism she received from the royal establishment and, in the Duchess's case, from the press. Like Diana she had turned to other men for comfort. Early in January, the *Daily Mail* revealed evidence of her indiscretion. A maid had found "compromising" photographs of the Duchess and her close friend Steve Wyatt taken while they were on holiday in Morocco.

Even while Diana discussed the situation with her ally they heard alarming stories about the reaction of the men in grey. A careless briefing by the Queen's press secretary led the BBC to tell the world that "the knives are out" for the Duchess of York at Buckingham Palace. Seen by some as a warning to Diana, as much as a comment on Fergie, the Princess must have thanked her stars for the decisions she had made.

Although her circumstances were strikingly similar to Sarah's there were significant differences. Diana had a very different media and public profile, largely because she had actively set out to cultivate good press. Diana was therefore viewed much more sympathetically than her sister-in-law. The Princess's extra marital activities had yet to be revealed, and her forthcoming book gave her some reassurance that she would be able to weather the storm, if her story was published in time. Nevertheless Diana must have been concerned in the weeks which followed the revelations of the Duchess's behaviour. Competing newspapers had a tendency to use lurid headlines to vie for market share and circulation figures. There was a chance Sarah's story would flush out the Squidgy tape before the Morton book could minimise its impact.

From January 1992 the palace, aware of rumours about a new royal book by Andrew Morton, was working hard to find out more. Supposedly a blockbuster which would raise the veil on Diana's unhappy marriage, the book was said to present undeniable evidence that she had been treated badly by Charles and the rest of the royal family. Diana was suspected of being involved. When the Princess was asked by courtiers if she knew anything about the project, she was able to say quite truthfully that she had never met Morton. Earlier that January – Morton's own records show it was the fourth – Diana had sought assurances that her part in the book would be kept quiet. By using James Colthurt as his go between, Morton had kept himself from direct contact with the Princess, and the book was written in a way which implied it was based on interviews with her friends and acquaintances. Diana was thus assured that, with careful use of language, she could maintain the impression she was not involved. Nevertheless the journey to the book's publication was not going to be a smooth ride for Diana.

In late February Diana was deeply disturbed by serialisation in *The Sun* tabloid of a book entitled *Diana: The Princess Nobody Knows*, by Lady Colin Campbell. The book described problems with the Wales's marriage and blamed Diana, suggesting she had been seeing other men. Diana contacted

Morton through her go-between James Colturst, only to be informed it would take another, bigger story to knock the Campbell book out of the headlines. In response she let Morton know about the Duke and Duchess of York's visit to the Queen, and of their impending separation. The front page story Morton wrote for the *Daily Mail* did the trick. No doubt in Diana's actions Patrick Jephson would have seen an example of the "brutal pragmatism" he had recognised in the Princess by then.

For Morton and his publishers, the Campbell book, and news of Fergie's impending departure from the royal scene, meant bringing forward publication of *Diana: Her True Story* to 16 June. Morton's project was in danger of losing its commercial value if other events or another book overtook it and stole its thunder. The same would be true if Diana left Charles before publication. Well aware that the Duchess of York had been pressing Diana to "jump ship" with her, Morton was worried the Princess might succumb if the pressure became too great.

✦ ✦ ✦

Fear comes in shades and subtle tones from mild anxiety to mind numbing, body paralysing terror. Imagine standing on a precipice, toes over the crumbling edge, looking down at the ground hundreds of feet below. The rational part of your brain, that which can usually direct your limbs at will, knows you can step backwards to complete safety at any time. But there's a primitive part of your brain which reacts to extreme danger differently. In the face of such a threat it overrides the more subtle processes of the mind and body and reacts, violently and irrationally. It causes the mouth to go dry and the breath to catch high in the chest and it causes the gut to tighten. The limbs that could take you to safety freeze in unresponsive immobility. Your sense of balance escapes you and you start to feel yourself falling. Such was the level of fear I recognised in Diana during our first session in 1992. Whatever precipice she was standing on in her mind I knew it was terrifying her, but I also recognised the effort she was making to control her fear.

Immediately, and without thought, I set about bringing her back from the precipice. Love is an unspoken, unacknowledged component of every healer's work whether they are a doctor or an alternative therapist. That's the way it is. Love, formed from caring, compassion, the desire to relieve pain and distress, to help reduce suffering, to restore, heals. Self love heals the self. Love given unconditionally by one human being to another is an offer of healing. Love is an antidote to fear. Every move I made during that massage spoke of love and caring for the human being before me.

I kept my hands soft, reducing the impact which hard palms or sharp knuckles would have made. Diana needed to be soothed not challenged. She was facing enough challenges. Working on her feet I held them longer than usual in my warm hands. I brought her attention to fixed joints and tense muscles with gentle rocking movements until she let go. I held my hands, one on her abdomen and one on her chest, until her breathing became even and deep. As I moved around the table I rested my hand on her shoulder and brushed hair from her forehead with light, even intimate touches. Her hands were clenched with tension, so I worked on them to make them open and soft. Massage to hands and arms for mechanical effect is carried out quite rapidly and efficiently with finger tips used to manipulate and work the joints and fine muscles. I worked slowly and held each of her hands in mine, her palm to mine, for long minutes, offering a more personal and comforting contact while my other hand swept over and encompassed her arm and shoulder. To the larger areas of her back and legs I applied, expansive and lighter than usual sweeping movements. Barely a word passed between us. None were necessary. Skin offers a direct connection, through the nervous system, to the mind – caring touch communicates that the fear is manageable. Joints, and the configuration of the muscles which direct them via the brain, offer opportunities to tell the mind that the terror is not in control.

I went to my next client more tired than usual by the treatment I'd given, and concerned about Diana's situation. Most of my sessions with her for the next few months would be similar.

By mid-February Diana was clearly showing the strain she was under. With increasing frequency she gave the press obvious signals of her dissatisfaction with her marriage. On a joint tour with Prince Charles to India, Diana was photographed sitting thoughtfully and sadly alone at the Taj Mahal, perhaps the greatest monument to love ever built. At a polo match in Jaipur a few days later, when Diana presented the winner's cup to Prince Charles, she humiliated him before the world's media by turning her head at the last minute so his kiss, aimed at her cheek, ended in mid-air. The press had a field day with stories which illustrated the gulf between the couple and lampooned the Prince for his lack of kissing skills.

Significantly, they missed one of the most important messages of the Taj Mahal visit. Before the tour to India even began *The Sun* newspaper ran a story pointing out that the couple's itineraries meant Diana would be at the monument alone. The piece reminded the public that during a previous visit in 1980 Prince Charles, in line with tradition, had promised he would return with the woman he loved. Plans for Diana's solo visit that February could have been altered to enable Charles to accompany his wife. Instead it was allowed to go ahead as planned and resulted in photographs being published alongside stories of Diana in "wistful solitude," and the "royal wish that did not come true." According to the memoirs written by bodyguard Ken Wharfe, it was the Prince who insisted he would not go with Diana, but instead would attend a business function scheduled for him in Delhi, 200 miles from the Taj Mahal. While Charles later said his decision was mistaken, and a wiser man would have accompanied his wife, Wharfe tells us he is certain the Prince had no intention of acting the hypocrite by going with her. Hypocrisy it would have been, but a more likely reason for his decision is that Charles intended to signal to the two women in his life, the Princess and Camilla, where his love really lay. The polo air-kiss was Diana's retaliation.

Whatever the truth, it was apparent to all who were there, that the India tour of 1992 marked a new low in the relationship between Diana and her husband, and a new high in the level of stress placed on everyone associated with the royal couple. Jephson tells of "new depths of animosity behind the scenes" and of Diana's luckless team of staff experiencing "her wintry side under the blazing Indian sun." It is doubtful her team would have been comforted by knowing that irritability, and nit-picking attention to small details, are common to Diana's INFP personality type when they too are under great stress.

The India tour made it clear to both sides that they were involved in open warfare and that a legal separation was inevitable. Back in the UK Jephson was informed by Richard Aylard, private secretary to the Prince, that they were consulting with Lord Goodman, the eminent and ferocious Law Lord. Jephson advised Diana of the development and he was instructed to seek out a lawyer who would be able to represent her interests. Another escalation of the War of the Wales' was thus accomplished, although the spats in India, and the arming of both sides with legal experts, were as nothing compared to the devastation that would be wrought when the approaching Morton missile struck. For the time being however it sat on its launch pad with the countdown ticking.

In March Diana embarked on a solo trip to Hungary in support of the English National Ballet. Amongst her engagements was another emotional visit to the world renowned Peto institute, which helps children suffering from cerebral palsy. Back in London Diana gave a speech on the prevalence of AIDS in women to a lunch time meeting of the Thirty Club at Claridges. Afterwards she answered questions from her audience, but was seen to be extremely nervous. It would not have been difficult to understand why Diana shook as visibly as she did that day. Her audience, later described as "a hard-boiled crowd", consisted of wealthy and influential movers and shakers in the media industry. With rumours of the Morton book rife by then, it was unnerving for the Princess to put herself in a position where she would meet, and be questioned, by the likes of Conrad Black, owner of *The Telegraph*, and Lord Rothermere, owner of *The Mail*.

The strain she was under was even more apparent from the content of a conversation she had during the lunch with film producer and acquaintance David Putnam. He recalls Diana suddenly telling him about the unhappy state of her marriage, and confiding that she had "allowed a book to be written", describing it as "the daftest thing I have ever done", and something that "will cause all kind of trouble". Clearly, and unsurprisingly, Diana was struggling with the enormity of her decision, as the book's publication date drew closer. She may have faltered but she did not step back. After the book was in the public domain, Putnam confirmed that Diana was well aware what she was doing when she took the calculated risk by making her story public, and is quoted as saying "I never heard one word of regret".

Her determination was apparent in a short note to her father that March. Diana explained her reasons for cooperating with the book, that it would provide the chance for her "own self" to emerge, and to ensure against her being drowned by "the system" – "it is very important to me". Diana's father did not survive to see his daughter's story made public. After many years of bad health he died suddenly on 29 March, while his daughter was skiing with her husband and her boys in Lech, Austria. Diana had initially resisted her husband's presence on the holiday, but had realised he should be there with their sons.

When news of her father's death came Diana was badly shocked. She vented her distress in the animosity she showed towards her husband. Diana declared her intention to return to England immediately, and alone: she did not want her husband's sympathy or support when he had been unprepared to offer it in the past. Yet even in such a crisis the royal machinations continued. Everyone, including Diana, was aware of the likely press reaction if she were to leave Charles at the ski resort and rush to be with the grieving Spencer family. Diana spoke with passion and venom when she asked her bodyguard Ken Wharfe, "why should I help save his face?"

When Diana's position was reported to the Prince's private secretary, Richard Aylard, the courtier seemed to blanch visibly. In the end Wharfe persuaded Diana that her father, an Earl and former equerry to the Queen, and to her father before her, would not have wanted to be the cause of a media circus.

Even so, in the days which followed, as she struggled to come to terms with her grief, Diana imagined she saw Charles' public relations interests being imposed on her father's funeral arrangements. Her suspicions were almost certainly true to some extent, and Diana was in no frame of mind to be able to view sympathetically the reasons which could have existed for what she now found offensive. Everyone in the royal family, Diana included, was well aware that every royal occasion was examined by the press for signs which could be interpreted. Every verbal nuance, every expression was captured in words and pictures, and mulled over for its significance to developing stories, and new insights, about the state of play in Britain's foremost family. The Palace always sought to give signals which would convey the messages they believed to be in the best interests of their employers and the monarchy, their motives were not always as simple and cold blooded as a desire to generate good press. The men in grey assumed the press scrutiny would continue even during the funeral of Diana's much loved father. Her grief, and the distress of her two young sons, would have been immeasurably increased if the arrangements gave rise to more press stories of the rift in the royal marriage. Largely the Palace succeeded in maintaining the impression of a family united around the grieving Princess. Diana was unaware of anything other than that her husband wanted to avoid being seen in a bad light, such was her animosity towards him. "He's going to turn my father's funeral into a charade" was Diana's tearful refrain to Ken Wharfe throughout a painful and difficult day.

With the loss of her father another supportive male presence was removed from Diana's life. Within her make-up was a powerful need for reassurance, which could be provided by paternal figures, but there were few available to her. Her husband, twelve years her senior, and her father-in-law, remote and disinclined to emotions, were non-starters. Ken Wharfe and Patrick Jephson were helpful and often thoughtful employees in whom she sometimes confided, but they were not privy to all her difficulties.

Diana's personality required the purpose in life afforded by a loving relationship. She needed as well, the appreciation and support which could only be provided by a lover, especially at this time of trials and self-doubt. Her husband had never played such a role for her, and James Hewitt and James Gilbey had moved on. Her future-vision included an idyll of partner, home and family. The Morton book was to be a step in freeing herself from the royal constraints which kept her from all she wanted in her life. How much of all this was in her conscious mind, and how much remained hidden in her unconscious, we cannot know. What is known is that during the early part of 1992 the 30 year old Diana reached out to Oliver Hoare, and started a relationship with him which would last until 1995.

Oliver Hoare was in his mid-forties, an expert on Islamic art and Sufi mysticism, and a personal friend of the late ballet dancer Rudolph Nureyev. Hoare had been the protégé of an Iranian princess and had lived in her home in Tehran; he had also lived in Paris where he was sometimes found playing guitar in Parisian cafes. An Old Etonian who moved easily in royal circles, he was described as having a "hint of the bohemian". The Prince and Princess of Wales became friends with Oliver and his wife Diane after meeting at Windsor Castle, during Ascot week in June 1985. Even then Diana, already struggling in her marriage, had found the handsome and cultured man with the colourful past, attractive.

During 1991 Oliver tried to help his royal friends with their faltering relationship. His sympathetic understanding became a source of support to Diana, who often visited Hoare's Belgravia art gallery, and telephoned him for advice. With the Squidgy tape looming, and her book about to be revealed, Diana sought the attention and guidance of the worldly Hoare more and more frequently until he became indispensible to her. Her need translated itself in her mind as deep and intense love. Following a pattern which she had established with Prince Charles and James Hewitt, one she did not recognise and therefore could not challenge, Diana invested all her romantic notions in Oliver Hoare. Over the coming months she would come to invest in him all her visions of her future. To begin with, she started to learn more about the interests of the new man in her life.

✦ ✦ ✦

In early March I received a note from Diana. Written on a cream coloured card with red border and motif of D topped by a crown, it was dated *March; 9th 1992. Dearest Stephen* she wrote *Thank you so much for coming to my rescue tonight* and went on to say how much it had meant to her that I had answered her S.O.S and made a difference to her neck and shoulders with my 'magic' hands. She signed the card *With all my love and thanks always, from, Diana.*

I didn't realise it at the time but she was fully aware of my conversations with Andrew Morton by then.

'Stephen, what do you know about Sufism?' Once again she dropped a question into the mind I was attempting to make a still pool of concentration.

I didn't stop working as I pondered and started to answer. I knew my hands would communicate anything I needed to pay attention to. 'Well it's a mystical branch of Islam, so like all mystical traditions it's involved with bringing a greater awareness of Spirit, God or Life Force into your everyday life. I don't know much about its spiritual practises or techniques, whether they use meditation for example, but one sect, the Dervishes use dancing, spinning around, to bring on a state of euphoria and altered consciousness. To me it seems as if there's a similarity with practises in other mystical systems which use the body to bring about a sense of connection between the earth, the physical world, and spirit, or the esoteric dimensions of reality. Did I see your eyes glaze over then?'

'No!' She snorted.

'Sorry, thought I was boring you.'

'No you never do that. Carry on.'

'OK, where was I?'

'Whirling Dervishes.'

'Oh yes – connection between the divine and the earthly. There's a card in the tarot based on that I think. The Magician – major arcana – one hand reaching up to heaven, the other down towards earth – making the connection between the two. Sufis also use stories to shift the rational mind away from habitual ways of thinking, to help a person achieve different perceptions of the self and the world, like with Zen koans, and Christian parables. There's a whole collection of Sufi stories by the Mullah Nasrudin, one of my clients used to tell them me.'

'The one I like is about the great King with his favourite horse. So enamoured of the horse is he that he calls all his wise men together and tells them he wants them to teach his horse to talk. If they don't they are no use to him, and not very wise, so he'll have them put to death. Of course the wise men don't know what to do and while they are arguing amongst themselves along comes Mullah Nasrudin, the wise Sufi.'

'When he hears the problem Nasrudin puts their minds at rest immediately "Don't worry" says he, "I'll sort it out" and off he goes to talk to the King.'

'When he returns they ask him what happened. "Well I agreed to teach the horse to talk," says Nasrudin. "But that's impossible," shout the wise men, "we'll all be killed."'

I paused to switch to Diana's other leg.

'"I told the king it would take me a year and that I wanted to live with the horse in the palace. Of course he couldn't expect the horse to learn to talk in just a year unless it had the best of everything so I suggested we have lots of servants to look after us while I taught him." The wise men look at Nasrudin with horror "You're mad" they shouted.'

'"Possibly says Nasrudin but during the year the horse might die, the King might die even I might die – anything might happen. In the meantime I'm going to be living in the palace with all the servants I want and the very best of everything available."'

We grinned at each other. I wondered if she got the message.

'There's a Sufi saying I like a lot,' I went on.'"Die before you die". It means if you can embrace the thought of dying, or anything you fear for that matter, it will not have a hold over you.' I moved on to work on Diana's arm.

In early May, just a few weeks before publication of *Diana: Her True Story*, the *Daily Express* newspaper, in the grand tradition of trying to undermine a rival's exclusive story by revealing its contents early, carried the first "spoiler". In a well informed article the Andrew Morton book was said to have been written with the cooperation of Diana and her family; officials, it was claimed, were concerned that Spencer family photographs were in the book; and Diana was reported to have "read the proofs and has the power to make amendments". To anyone who asked, Diana continued to deny having met Morton. During the remaining weeks of May *The Sunday Times* advertised the serialisation it was about to run, and more and more spoiler stories appeared in the newspaper's rival publications. Lord McGregor, chairman of the Press Complaints Commission, was put under increasing pressure by politicians and members of the public, to condemn the press speculation about the collapse of Diana's marriage to her husband the Prince of Wales. The pressure was mounting.

On 10 May Diana set out on a solo visit to Egypt. Already under great strain, she was further upset by the indignity of having her flight detoured to drop Charles off in Turkey, where he was to holiday with a party of friends which included Camilla Parker-Bowles. Stressed by the trying circumstances, and tired by the longer than necessary flight, Diana was dishevelled and in tears as the plane approached Cairo. In his recall of events Patrick Jephson tells how worried he was that the important trip would be ruined by what he described as "a bout of feminine weakness". In the event he was driven to admiration when Diana retired to the royal restroom, then re-emerged a short while later transformed from red eyed and distressed young woman, into power dressed Princess, ready for the arrival ceremony and demanding champagne. "Don't worry, I'm not going to let you down," she told him.

After their safe arrival, and when Diana had carried herself through the official arrival with "consummate professionalism, poise and devotion to duty", Jephson wrote, "I wondered if her opponents really understood the bloody-minded determination of the woman". Nevertheless Diana was still under extreme pressure. Throughout the visit constant rumours were emerging of a "big story" about to break back home. At one dinner in the British ambassador's residence, when an Egyptian guest quipped that his country could change their royal family every few years, Diana recklessly responded "In our country, we are stuck with ours."

The big story of the trip in the British newspapers featured sneak photos of Diana in a bathing suit. Quite conceivably the pictures could have upset Diana's Muslim hosts when they were published and shown on the BBC news. Taken with long range lenses, from a rooftop which overlooked Diana in the swimming pool at the Ambassador's residence, the pictures no doubt added further to Diana's frustration with her situation. Coming as they did shortly after the estranged Duchess of York had been criticised for an expensive Far East holiday; and Charles's excursion to Turkey was reported as his seventh or eighth holiday of the year; the swimsuit photos seemed to trivialise Diana's trip to Egypt, when in fact she was working hard. While there, Diana promoted British business interests, made a moving visit to a home for blind children, and met and charmed many important people including President Mubarak and his wife. True, she was also photographed alone at the Pyramids, and the Sphinx, in reprises of the Taj Mahal pictures, but she could hardly be blamed for what was written to accompany the photos. In all, the visit was another huge success which was rounded off by a reception for the travelling British press pack at which the Princess was "on top of her form."

An article by Ashley Walters in *The Sunday Times* of 17 May applauded Diana for her confidence in being able, despite all the recent stories about her marriage, to walk into a room full of tabloid hacks. Doubting whether Charles could have done the same, the journalist continued "the transformation in Diana has been quite remarkable...she is a very shrewd, sharp woman with amazing strength of character." Back in the UK, Diana showed more strength of character when she joined other members of the royal family at the kind of engagement she liked least, the Garter ceremony at Windsor Castle.

Diana had every reason to be buoyed up by her success. Despite the emphasis on stories of her swimming prowess in Egypt, Diana was generally being seen performing her duties abroad as an ambassador for Britain, and doing it very well. At home she was the epitome of the caring princess who reached out to the common man and woman, and could be moved to tears by their plight. While rumours were rife about her marriage and private life, nothing but praise was being offered in the press for her public role. Ironically, and in hindsight, the affection Diana engendered in the public seemed to have been unaffected by the possibility she had personal faults and weaknesses. It seemed the public could be more forgiving, more tolerant of flaws in those they admired than she believed. If she had recognised it at the time, perhaps Diana would have been able to face the next step of her journey with more confidence. Instead, just days before the serialisation of *Diana: Her True Story*, Diana's confidence fluctuated wildly.

For three years Diana had been fighting an increasingly bitter battle against strengthening opposition from parts of the establishment and the royal organisation. Diana's plan, her instinctive strategy, had been to use the media's obsession with her to gain the support of the public, in anticipation of the moment which was almost upon her. Without public sympathy she would surely be destroyed by the Squidgy tape or the book she had initiated. Until her story was revealed, Diana had no idea whether she had succeeded in her aim or not.

Barely two months after her father's sudden passing Diana was seeking the support of her closest friends as often as possible while waiting out the remaining few days before the book was due out. The battle she had waged with those who saw her behaviour as a threat to the monarchy, or to the succession, was as nothing to the struggle taking place in her mind. Whereas the battle around her was not of her choosing, the struggle within was one she had embraced. Diana was not accountable for how others saw her actions, nor for Charles' inability to understand what the public wanted from him. She was accountable to herself, for how she wanted to be and for what she wanted her life to be like, and for what she was prepared to do to achieve her vision of the future. Inwardly, old patterns of self-doubt, fear, helplessness and guilt once again asserted themselves in response to the threat she faced. Inwardly Diana fought to sustain and strengthen her newer perceptions of self-esteem, courage, confidence and the belief that she was capable of creating her future the way she wanted it to be. She swung violently between strength of purpose and panic, tears and stubborn determination. Her public work gave her respite from her private distress.

A week before serialisation of *Diana: Her True Story* was to begin, Diana met with the Queen to discuss the possibility of having her own home, staff and financial arrangements. The impression the Princess gained was that her mother-in-law knew of their problems and felt Diana and Charles should not be "artificially pushed together", if they were as unhappy as it seemed. Diana was encouraged, and felt her mother-in-law would not oppose a separation.

On 5 June, two days before serialisation, Diana gave a speech on drug abuse in London, at the premier of the film *Rush*.

On Sunday 7 June, Diana's already eventful life took yet another abrupt change of direction. *The Sunday Times* offered the world their first instalment of *Diana: Her True Story* and told of Diana's bulimia, Charles's relationship with Camilla, and Diana's suicide attempts. From that moment on Diana was on a rollercoaster ride of uncertain duration, and since there was no longer any remote possibility of going back, Diana began to look forward with renewed determination. A friend is quoted as saying: "She has strength and courage and I've never seen her so determined."

On 8 June Diana sat down with Charles and discussed the state of their marriage. Afterwards Diana phoned James Colthurst in a state of euphoria reminiscent to that her brother described when she had accepted Charles' offer of marriage. This time her reason for being "elated" and, as Colthurst later described, "out of control with excitement," was that the couple had accepted they were incompatible and Charles had agreed to a separation. That night, imagining she saw a light at the end of what had been a very long tunnel, Diana slept soundly for the first time in weeks without the aid of sleeping tablets.

During the days which followed Diana began to discover that seeing the light at the end of the tunnel was a lot different to walking out into the light. There were more than a few obstacles she had to overcome first, but she started towards the distant glow with renewed energy. She spoke with friends about finding a lawyer to represent her in any separation negotiations, and drew up a short list of five. Just the day after speaking to Charles, she called Patrick Jephson to tell him she and the Prince had "decided to separate." Jephson responded "good." Later he spoke to her on the phone again to say that if she suddenly disappeared with "Mr Perfect" he would be glad for her "so long as you send for me afterwards." Diana's laughing response was "No Patrick, we've got work to do."

Time and again Diana was almost overwhelmed with doubts and fears caused by the hysterical reaction to her story. Time and again she reached out to her friends for support and encouragement, and came back courageous and defiant to confront her detractors.

In the palace environment, Diana came under enormous pressure to denounce the book and those of her friends who had contributed to it. She refused repeatedly to put her name to any statement that would put the book's contents in doubt; maintained she had never met the author, and that her friends did what they thought was right. Of course, had she refuted the book, the tapes she had recorded for Andrew Morton at Kensington Palace would have been proof of her complicity in its creation. Nevertheless Diana showed tremendous resilience, and not a little artifice, in the face of direct questioning from the Queen's private secretary, Diana's brother-in-law, Sir Robert Fellowes, and from Patrick Jephson. The palace press briefing therefore stated categorically that Diana had not been involved with the book "in any way" and had not checked the text before publication, as some newspapers were insisting.

Sir Robert's assurances to Lord McGregor, Chairman of the Press Complaints Commission, led him to reproach the press for "dabbling their fingers in the stuff of other people's souls".

In the meantime *The Sunday Times*, Andrew Morton, and those friends of Diana's who were named contributors to the book, were coming under a great deal of criticism and scrutiny. *The Sunday Times* was ridiculed by its competitors and leading establishment figures, over what was being seen as a fabricated story. Similarly Morton was castigated for his invention, tabloid morals and questionable ethics. Diana's friends were being criticised by the press for their involvement in the author's false claims; and by other acquaintances who did not know about the book in advance, for betraying the Princess.

Diana's emphatic response, in support of her friends, her author and the editor and proprietors of *The Sunday Times*, was orchestrated by Andrew Morton himself. She agreed to be photographed with Carolyn Bartholomew, her friend and a major contributor to the book. The subsequent front-page picture of Diana, giving her friend a comforting and conspiratorial hug as she left her home after a brief visit, became the catalyst for mass outrage when it was correctly interpreted as the Princess's tacit admission of involvement in the book.

Senior establishment figures, and that echelon of the press which supported them, shouted their disgust. Newspapers which had railed against the treachery of Morton and *The Sunday Times*, were outraged. Lord McGregor believed he had been duped, and angrily called Sir Robert Fellowes while he was in Paris with the Queen. Sir Robert, realising Diana, and possibly Patrick Jephson, had misled him, offered his resignation to the Queen, who refused it. Diana received a stiff message from John Major, the Prime Minister, telling her he could not help her "if she tried to manipulate the press". Sir Robert Fellowes contacted Diana she was making his life "unbearable". Sadly, in the furore, none of the high and mighty of the land thought to consider anything except the effect the book might have on their own positions, the monarchy or the succession. Even when they were convinced it was, in fact, Diana's genuine perception of her life with Charles inside the royal family, they attacked her temerity for not keeping the family's secrets, instead of wondering whether she might be justified in her actions.

All that was in the first week. Another episode of *Diana: Her True Story* was due on 14 June and Diana was already stunned by the reaction. Despite her shock and her concerns she hoped to resolve matters about her future at a meeting on 15 June with Charles, the Queen and Prince Philip. Diana and Charles had already agreed they should separate and eventually divorce. It was only a matter of arguing their case with the Queen and Diana was sure she would soon be able to lead a more normal life.

On 12 June, three days before the family meeting, Prince Charles went alone to his mother to discuss his marriage and the possibility of separation and divorce. Diana was aware something was going on but did not know exactly what. A friend's diary recalled "chat going on behind closed doors" and of it being "very stressful at Kensington Palace".

On 15 June, at the start of Royal Ascot and after a week of frenzied press coverage and intense pressure, Diana met with Prince Charles, the Queen and Prince Philip at Windsor castle. The meeting shook Diana to her core. There was to be no separation. According to Diana's account, later noted in James Colthurst's diary, Charles did not speak up about the couple's meeting a week earlier, or mention that they had mutually agreed they should separate. Diana, well aware of the legal implications if she forced the issue, and in any case, determined that justice would only be served if Charles admitted fault, was only able to prompt her husband unsuccessfully with "tell them Charles what you want to say" and "we discussed all this on Monday".

James Colthurst's private diary makes it clear that the most distressing part of the meeting came when Diana was confronted by an "angry, raging and unpleasant" Prince Philip, who told Diana there was a tape of her discussing with a senior media executive the book's possible serialisation in the *Daily Mail* or *The Sunday Times*. When accused of bringing the family into disrepute, a tearful and shaken Diana denied having any such conversation, or any involvement with the book. The result of the meeting was that the Queen apparently gained the impression Diana was willing to remain by her husband, and Diana acquiesced to a six month "cooling off" period during which she would undertake her royal duties as usual.

Within hours of the exhausting confrontation Diana challenged her brother-in-law, Sir Robert Fellowes, about the supposed tape. Within a very short time Diana was assured that a tape did exist, but that it would not be used against her and she should forget all about it. Bluff or not, no tape ever came to light.

Diana may have agreed to business as usual for the time being, but it soon became clear the royal family was going to treat her very warily indeed from then on. Diana already had some idea of what it would be like to be shunned by the royal family. In March the formal announcement of Sarah's separation from Prince Andrew had been announced. Since then the "breath of fresh air" was treated like a foul smell which had to be extracted from the royal environment. If Diana needed any further convincing it came in the snubs and coldness displayed towards her, and Fergie's outright exclusion during that year's Royal Ascot.

On 16 June *Diana: Her True Story* was published in hardback and became an immediate best seller.

The summer continued with Diana trying to regroup and keep her future-vision on track, while she continued to fulfil her public role and fight innumerable skirmishes against her detractors.

Prince Philip wrote Diana a series of letters variously described by people who saw them as "warm and helpful", "stinging" and "wounding". Diana was not impressed by her father-in-law's appeals to her sense of duty, or his rebukes about her presumed role in the Morton book. As far as Diana was concerned she had been doing her duty with little thanks and even less recognition from her husband and the royal family for eleven years. She sought legal advice and the help of friends, to draft her reply to the Duke, and explained to him her position and expectations for the future.

While this exchange is significant, in that it highlights Diana's strength of purpose and her determination to react strongly to any treatment she felt to be unfair, it also speaks to the attitude of the Queen and her senior advisors. While Diana was obviously trying to escape from her marriage, a decision must have been made that she should be persuaded to stay, and pressed to repent. For whatever reason, the good of the children; the future of the monarchy; the threat to the Windsor succession; because of constitutional issues; because of Diana's popularity; because she might cause even more damage outside the family; or for all these reasons together, there was a clear attempt to bring the Princess to heel and keep her within the royal organisation. She had been persuaded to a prolonged cooling off period, she had been persuaded to carry on her public duties, for now the crisis was contained and there was breathing space and time to consider.

Prince Charles also seems to have agreed with the decision to try to keep Diana in the family. He instructed his friends not to speak to the press on his behalf. His biographer, Jonathan Dimbleby, confirms this. The journalist wrote later that Charles always believed his marriage could survive, and that the Prince had been hoping "Diana might learn to become his friend", and "for the sake of the children, and for the sake of the monarchy, they could live separate lives under the same roof and perform their duties together". Dimbleby also wrote that Charles' attitude changed abruptly when the Morton book came out in June 1992. It was a measure of the Prince's complete misunderstanding of Diana that he genuinely thought she would be able to ignore her deepest instincts and accept companionship in place of love. Even his own deep and powerful feelings for Camilla had not enabled him to appreciate what Diana understood by love. Her kind of love was all consuming, ever present, not something which could be fitted into a busy schedule. To her, love was the reason for everything which existed in a relationship. The foundation from which everything else derived, duty, shared pursuits and companionship included.

On 28 June *The Sunday Times* printed an article, "the Case for Charles", based on off the record comments from some of Charles' friends. While the piece did not add much that was new, it was mildly critical of Diana's difficult behaviour in the past, and suggested Charles was annoyed most by her refusal to admit her role in the Morton book. A piece in the *London Evening Standard* around this time portrayed the Princess as "an egomaniac convinced of her world importance"; "irrational and isolated" and "confused". The article went on "Prince Charles' friends are bitter and frustrated at the prospect of the royal family held to ransom by a spoilt and increasingly spiteful woman". The journalist Penny Junor wrote a long piece describing Diana as an explosive young woman teetering on the brink. Patrick Jephson, who was at the eye of the storm during those difficult days, is convinced that no one was authorised by the Queen to speak against Diana, and those who did were motivated by their own prejudices or perverted sense of loyalty to Prince Charles. While Jepshon may have been certain, Diana was less so. Whoever was behind them, the views being expressed increased her fear that her opponents meant to use her supposed mental instability as a reason to destroy her dreams.

At the end of June Diana was provided with an opportunity to answer her critics in the best way she knew, by performing important work sanctioned by the Queen and the Government. On 29 June Diana visited Belfast in a heat wave, and was greeted with an enormous amount of sympathy and admiration for her courage and fortitude. Belfast was still blighted by terrorism then and Diana walked amongst, and met, the inhabitants of some of the grimmest areas hit by "The Troubles". She appeared calm, poised and cheerful before the many thousands who came out to see the Princess whose personal troubles with the royal family had filled their daily papers for the past month.

The following day's news stories were ecstatic in their praise. "Diana Steals Ulster Hearts" and "The Bravest Walkabout of All" were examples of headlines which reminded everyone of the effect Diana could have when given the opportunity. Alongside the pro-Diana pieces was a smattering of stories which called into question the Princess's mental stability. To those initiated into the more arcane workings of public relations, or media warfare, these stories confirmed the existence of some who would like to see, if not the back of the Princess of Wales, then her downfall from her high position in the public's esteem.

Despite the claims of mental disorder the tide seemed to be turning in Diana's favour. Following serialisation of *Diana: Her True Story* she received thousands of letters of support and understanding from members of the public. Many of her correspondents suffered from eating disorders, and mentioned how Diana's example had helped them. In the weeks following publication of the book itself, the Eating Disorders Association reported an enormous increase in first time callers asking for help, a response which could only be attributed to Diana's courage in speaking out about her own problems with bulimia. The book was also a clear indication to Diana that she not only had friends who loved and cared about her, friends who were willing to stand by her, and take risks on her behalf, but that thousands of ordinary people understood and supported her.

When *Diana: Her True Story* finally came out I was as surprised as anyone at the furore it caused. I was also concerned for Diana. Every session, in the weeks leading up to the first part of the serialisation, and following it, showed she was under immense strain. I was amazed at how much stress she was dealing with. I found it difficult to equate the deeply traumatised Diana I worked with in our sessions, to the Princess who continued to perform in public almost every day, and was featured in news stories on the television and in the papers.

Shortly after the serialisation commenced in *The Sunday Times*, Andrew Morton contacted me to ask if I would contribute to an article which supported the book's contents. He explained that he and the newspaper were under pressure to verify their story. People were claiming it was fiction and that Diana's situation was in danger of being ignored. I agreed, with the proviso that I would only give my opinion of her circumstances and talk about matters that were already in the public domain.

The article written by Andrew duly appeared, the second part of the serialisation ran and my life turned upside down. For a week reporters and photographers loitered outside my flat in Little Venice from early in the morning until late at night. My telephone and door bell rang incessantly. I have no idea how I was tracked down or how my phone number became common knowledge. Under siege at the front entrance to the apartment block, I was still able to leave to see my clients by using a back door to the underground car park from where I was able to drive out past the waiting press pack. Every time I returned home I found slips of paper which had been pushed through the door, and voice mail messages, all offering money for my story. During that week I turned down or completely ignored offers totalling £300,000.

The palace was not amused at my public statements suggesting that Diana had been courageously dealing with very difficult problems for a long time. Or that I believed she deserved support, and warned there could be a tragedy if the situation she was in was not resolved quickly. I was requested to go to a meeting with Prince Charles' press secretary, Philip Mackie, at St. James's Palace. There I was told my services were no longer required. Quite who decided Diana no longer required my services was not made clear. I was not very surprised at the development. After all I had been described in the press as Diana's guru, her Svengali and as the Machiavelli in her life, and I knew there were some at the palace who were suspicious about my work with the Princess. Quite a few of my clients moved in the same circles as Diana and Charles, on both sides of the divide which separated them. Despite that, I don't think they knew I was working with her until the book came out, at least none of them ever tried to discuss her with me. Even when the cat was out of the bag and stories about me began to appear, my work with Diana didn't become a topic of conversation, except when one of my clients told me she heard about my "sacking" on the BBC World Service.

Life is feedback. That evening I returned home to consider what the feedback was telling me. At that time I was thinking of writing a book about my body-mind approach to health and was already in discussions with a literary agent. For some time I had been thinking about combining client work with teaching. I'd been working with Diana for three and a half years and no one in the press had given any indication they knew I existed. Now I was in the middle of a media maelstrom with no idea what effect it would have on my relationships with my wealthy but often media sensitive clientele. Any plans I wanted to make for the future required finance, and if it was to be a book, a media profile.

There was a lot of money sloshing around if the offers I'd turned down were anything to go by; *Diana: Her True Story* was already a best seller and its serialisation had scooped £250,000. I made a few enquiries and contracted to write a couple of articles explaining more about my work with Diana. I made sure I retained the copyright for the pieces, and the final say in what was printed, so I could control what appeared. I made it clear I would not reveal anything new, or any personal details about Diana which had not already become known, but would explain what I had been doing to help her deal with her situation.

Do not ever think you can control what appears in the press. During my Andy Warhol "15 minutes of fame" I gained a brief and very unpleasant insight into what Diana's life must have been like, on a much bigger scale, for eleven years. In my pitiful and naive attempts to tell people about the courageous work Diana had been engaged in, and to gather a little cash and kudos at the same time, I experienced duplicity, manoeuvring and downright lies designed to turn the simple and helpful ideas I wanted to put across into tabloid sensations. I do not know how Diana was able, on a daily basis for so long, to deal with what turned my stomach in just a few weeks. My admiration for her rose even higher than before. The letter I wrote to her at that time conveyed my admiration and appreciation for her courage, and my regrets for any embarrassment I had caused her.

Only one of my clients criticised what I had done and stopped seeing me. The friend of Diana's, who had introduced me to her, was very angry at what she described as my betrayal. In hindsight I realise she was not one of those who was aware that Diana instigated the book which led to my having what New Agers call "a growth experience", or "instant karma". Two clients down and very much wiser, I eventually slipped quietly back into my anonymous life.

✦ ✦ ✦

By mid-summer 1992, Diana's private secretary, Patrick Jephson, had firmly nailed his flag to the mast of Diana's beleaguered ship and was committed to travelling wherever her journey brought them. His loyalty was recognised by the Princess with more confidences shared, and later that year with a note, expressing her admiration and trust for the man who spearheaded her campaign for recognition. In the background Jephson had been preparing for the separation he knew was inevitable. Quietly he made plans and arrangements for Diana to pursue a strong role as an independent member of the royal family. Although he was concerned by her dramatically fluctuating levels of confidence, and the sense of isolation she described when with the royal family, Jephson believed the senior royal households were underestimating Diana's importance as mother to the future King, and as a much appreciated royal figure in her own right. Certainly he believed they "drastically miscalculated" what he called "her abilities as a fighter and survivor". In his memoir Jephson, the arch cynic, who in his frustration referred to Diana as childish or petulant, described her thus – "handled with honesty, respect and affection she would respond with co-operation, loyalty and appreciation". Sadly those who could have made all the difference to Diana's life up to then, would not have time to learn the lesson Jepshon and others had.

A round of meetings with charity officials at Kensington Palace, and some private visits to hospices, refuges for battered women and homeless shelters, helped Diana to restore some equilibrium before she went on holiday.

What possessed someone to suggest to the press that the family cruise, once again on the *Alexander* owned by John Latsis, was to be a "second honeymoon" is not known. In the circumstances, given the media feeding frenzy over *Diana: Her True Story*, it was most likely an odd sense of humour or an over indulgence on alcohol or addictive narcotics. Common sense clearly did not play a part, and Patrick Jephson disavowed responsibility in his later memoir. What possessed the newspapers to pick up the idea and run with it in their stories is even more baffling, but by August 1992 people were coming to believe that nothing was the way it seemed and anything could happen next. Had they been aware that Diana described the yacht not as a "love boat" but as a "floating hell", they might have altered their headlines.

While the cruise around the Greek islands was enjoyed by the young Princes, William and Harry, few of the adults aboard, some friends of

Charles' and some guests of Diana's, had as good a time. During the holiday bodyguards suddenly noticed that Diana had not been seen for two hours. Fearing the pressure might have caused her to do something extreme, like jump overboard, they searched for her. Ken Wharfe found her hiding in a lifeboat, under the tarpaulin, weeping inconsolably. Sitting there Diana gave voice to her anger at the humiliation she was feeling, knowing Charles was speaking on the telephone to Camilla every day and that all his friends knew, yet they continued to treat Diana with pity and thought she was mad. As her outburst continued, and she lambasted her husband for the "sham" being perpetrated, and for being "here with me because his mummy has ordered him to", Diana demanded Wharfe make arrangements for her to fly home immediately. In the end the loyal policeman was able to calm what he described later as her childishness and petulance, and Diana stayed for the remainder of the cruise. Sometimes the stress Diana was under just had to come out.

Back in the UK, on 17 August, Diana gave a speech on the dangers of drugs and their destructive effects on families to an international conference in Glasgow. When she returned to Balmoral for the annual royal holiday, more trials awaited her besides the cool reception she received from the family. While she was there the now infamous Fergie toe-sucking photos appeared in the newspapers, to illustrate lurid stories of holiday goings-on between the Duchess and her erstwhile financial advisor John Bryan. Diana watched in horrified fascination as her sister-in-law was ridiculed and roundly condemned. Wise enough to realise the scandal would affect Fergie's negotiations over the financial arrangements of her separation from Prince Andrew, Diana made a mental note to be extra cautious with her own love life. She was not surprised to be informed by the Duchess later that a source inside the palace had confirmed the photos had been a set up to discredit her.

The assumption that there were plots against her reputation was a fact of life for Diana by then. She regularly exercised extraordinary degrees of subterfuge and caution in her dealing with people to avoid a fate similar to Fergie's. Not surprisingly then, she began to suspect the Squidgy tape had all along been a conspiracy to damage her.

Her worst nightmare became a reality when the existence of the tape was revealed on ten pages in *The Sun* newspaper on 24 August.

Coyly the newspaper did not immediately name Diana and James Gilbey as the couple whose conversation was described, but the inference was clear and few doubted it was them. The palace offered the usual denial through a spokesman "on the evidence so far, there is no reason to take these tapes seriously", but the damage was done and continued through the rest of the week after Diana returned to Kensington Palace. Initially Diana suffered all the humiliation which might be expected from the cruel and abrupt exposure of her innermost thoughts and private life; and all the distress which could be caused by her worries for her children and her future.

The prolonged seepage, over many days, of juicy pieces from her conversation with James Gilbey, made the royal family, and the public, aware of her feelings towards her husband and the family she had married into. Everyone learned – first-hand – if they cared to call the telephone hotline set up by *The Sun* and listen to parts of the tape itself, that Diana hated her royal life. Diana, always sensitive to being blamed for wrongdoing, and already battered by the reaction to the Morton book, was shocked and badly knocked off balance for a time. Friends and staff describe her as swinging from devastated and in despair, to defiant and strong.

Eventually the storm died away and took with it forever the myth of the unsullied and innocent Diana. The "racy" conversation left few in any doubt that Diana and Gilbey had enjoyed an intimate relationship. The question of the exact nature of her friendship with Hewitt was again raised for discussion after Diana mentioned on the tape that she dressed him "from head to foot" at her own expense. Public sympathy for Diana, already primed by the revelations in *Diana: Her True Story*, was not diminished and soon she was back on track and looking to her future-vision once again. The Squidgy tape had not been the destructive force Diana feared on the contrary, it provided a necessary watershed moment without which Diana would have struggled even more to reach her goal of independence. The tape had killed off the Fairytale Princess, but it had replaced her with a more worldly and real person, a Princess still, but a woman who was bravely facing problems similar to thousands of ordinary people around her. Their sympathy and understanding was, if anything, increased by the tape.

It might have been different. *The Sun* did not reveal that part of the taped conversation in which Diana expressed to Gilbey her fears she might become pregnant. Diana was adamant that had it been published she would have "walked away" immediately. Instead she was able to say: "I've had two weeks bad publicity in eleven years…I'm not giving up."

✦ ✦ ✦

The Squidgy tape and my copy of *Diana: Her True Story* gave me an opportunity to review the work I'd done with the Princess. A great deal of the book was a revelation for me. There was so much she had not shared with me, like the fact she was working with other therapists and astrologers. *Good she's searching for information, help and advice. The process will automatically guide her to the people who will help her become how she wants to be.* When I read on I was gratified to see quotes and comments, which reflected the progress she had made. Friends spoke of her saying she had "opened up" and that "this is only the beginning". The chapter titles, in the form of direct quotes, powerfully confirmed her new perception of herself and her life. "I did my best" acknowledged she had let go of much of her tendency for self-blaming. "My life has changed its course" was a comment reflecting the new path she was on.

There was also a lot of information in the book about her childhood background, and her attitudes and beliefs which I might have been able to use to help her. The material about her marriage, and her relationship with Prince Charles, and attitude towards Camilla, enabled me to understand a lot more about the issues I had been working with, especially when I tied them in with what I knew about her personality type. The amount of anger and indignation she felt at her treatment was consistent with her personality type. Her devastating response matched her INFP and Water element make-up. Unaware that she had authorised every word I wondered if she would read the book. Seeing her story in print would give her a good deal of insight, I thought.

When I analysed the tape transcript I was even more pleased. Recorded two and a half years before, at the end of our first year of work, parts of her conversation highlighted progressive changes in Diana's outlook and beliefs. The inner dialogue work we had used, to give her a better coping strategy than bulimia when under stress, seemed to have worked. Diana mentioned suddenly being drawn to go into a home for the disabled. "There was really something strange; I was leaning over the fence yesterday, looking into Park House, and I thought: 'Oh, what shall I do?'...so I walked round to the front door and walked straight in."

I did wonder whether Diana saying she hadn't gone "jellybags" for a day, or whether the suggestion she might replace some undefined "urges" with anger as she had on a previous occasion, might be references to bulimic episodes. Using anger as a regular strategy for dealing with any situation was not going to be helpful, but the comment did tell me why I had been dealing with its effects so often. I was particularly pleased to read she had ended 1989 determined to "go out, and do my bit in the way I know how" albeit I was saddened that she foresaw "I leave him (Charles) behind". The frightened and confused Diana I had met a year before the tape was made would not have been able to formulate those ideas so firmly. In another comment she questioned for herself the notion "conquer the world". Nonetheless it spoke of her INFP drive, to make the world a better place, coming through even then. Recalling a conversation with the Bishop of Norwich, her caring skills were validated when he apparently asked her how she coped during her work with people who were ill or dying, and had told him: "anyone who suffers, I can smell them a mile away." I smiled to myself recognising the empathetic ability.

By the time I came to read the transcript and book, in mid-1992, I knew she was moving towards her future-vision. Her inner work had resulted in amazing changes since that telephone conversation with Gilbey. The book I held in my hands was just one demonstration. I'd had some amazing experiences of my own as a result of personal transformational work. It came as no surprise that Diana's life was also altering radically. *That's one powerful cookie* I thought. All in all I thought I'd done a pretty good job – pity it had come to an end.

✦ ✦ ✦

People were surprised that Diana was able to move on so quickly from such a difficult experience. They simply underestimated the inner strength she had been developing through three and a half years of personal development. And they did not know she had been expecting the tape for 20 months. Now it was finally revealed Diana was, in part, relieved, especially since her book came out first, and people were not spitting at her in the streets or calling for her to be locked in the Tower.

It was the time it took for the tape to reach the public domain that raised Diana's suspicion that its emergence was a considered attack on her reputation. News of the tape was first given in the *National Enquirer* in the USA on 20 August. By then it had been in the hands, and the safe, of the British newspaper *The Sun* for about two years. They were reluctant to publish it, but once the tape was out in the USA, publication in Britain became inevitable. *The Sun* published on 24 August, just two months after Diana's blockbuster story was shared with the world, and during a difficult week when she was on her annual holiday with the royal family. How the tape came to be revealed in the USA, and who gave the *National Enquirer* the story, is unclear. Editors of *The Sun* are reported to have said they would not have published even then, if the Queen's private secretary, Diana's brother-in-law, Robert Fellowes, had contacted them. He did not. The mystery could have many simple explanations, for Diana it further convinced her she was being watched, and was the subject of a dirty tricks campaign.

A week after its Squidgy tape stories appeared *The Sun* published an article which alleged Diana and James Hewitt had "enjoyed a 'physical relationship.'" Not to be outdone the *News of the World* published a story they too had been keeping under wraps for months. Based on information provided by Hewitt's valet, Lance-Corporal Malcolm Leete, the story linked Diana and Hewitt romantically, and while not definitively saying Diana had committed adultery, Leete confirmed she had lavished expensive gifts on the officer.

In the wake of revelations in *Diana: Her True Story* and the Squidgy tape, more tittle-tattle about Diana's love life was hurtful but not terminal to her plans for creating her own future. More worrying to her was the campaign of whispers and innuendo about her state of mind. Her antidote to that poison, and to the constant stream of pro-Charles stories then hitting the newsstands, was to make sure she remained in contact with the people and retained their support. Nevertheless, after a horrendous August, Diana was emotionally and physically exhausted. She had fought bravely but was in need of a great deal of reassurance. At the end of the summer holiday her second son, Harry, had joined his older brother at boarding school and Diana no longer had the solid foundation provided by her role as mother. She needed the support of someone who really cared about her and her future. Her need was part of her nature, reinforced by her background it became a craving.

Oliver Hoare occupied a significant place in Diana's new vision for herself. Intent as she was on bringing together the idyllic reality of a world changing role, and a normal home life in which she would be taken care of by a loving partner, Diana invested her dreams in Hoare, as she had in Prince Charles and Hewitt before him. So intense was her desire for his attention and support during the troubled times she was experiencing, she had taken to calling his mobile phone whenever she needed to hear his voice, which was often. Six or seven times a day was normal, twenty was not uncommon. Undoubtedly Diana was as jealous of Hoare's wife Diane as she had been of Camilla and of Hewitt's female friends. During that difficult September the Hoare household began to receive telephone calls during which the caller remained silent when the phone was picked up.

A busy working schedule for Diana throughout October included an AIDS conference and one joint appearance with Charles, at a service marking the 50th anniversary of the Battle of El Alamein. Light relief was provided when she took her sons to Buckmore Park in Kent for a spot of boy-toy go-karting. Foresight might have told her that this excursion for William 10, and Harry 8, was the harbinger of that phase in their lives when boys start seeking male role models, and more masculine pursuits.

In early November the Prince and Princess of Wales embarked on an official tour of South Korea. An optimistic press briefing resulted in one tabloid running a story with the headline "Charles and Diana Are Back Together." Almost at the last minute Diana bluntly refused to go, and insisted the trip should be called off, claiming it was a charade she wanted nothing to do with. Her views of the marriage and her husband were now common knowledge because of the Squidgy tape. *Diana: Her True Story* had put her case clearly. The trip would make her seem hypocritical. It took some blunt persuasion from Prince Charles and Patrick Jephson, and a little intervention from the Queen, to change her mind. It was not a happy trip. With virtually no communication between Diana and her husband, and their unhappiness on display throughout, the press dubbed them "The Glums". News headlines asked how much longer the marriage should continue.

During the tour the paperback version of *Diana: Her True Story* was released. It contained additional material describing Prince Philip's letters to Diana, and her response. The embellished tabloid reports gave Diana an opportunity to issue a press statement in support of the Queen and Prince Philip. "The suggestion that they have been anything other than sympathetic and supportive is untrue and particularly hurtful". While the statement did not reflect how Diana actually felt about Prince Philip's intervention, it signalled she could relieve them of press criticism and help them with their public image if she chose, and that she still expected their sympathy and support when it came to her own future.

Back in Britain the press had been speculating about the Korean debacle, and wondered whether it might have been the couple's final tour together. There was no positive response the palace press office could make to such enquiries. Headlines shouted "A Marriage In Name Only", and Diana was photographed with, but standing apart from, other members of the royal family at the Cenotaph during the annual Remembrance Day ceremony.

Diana's determination to assert the distance between herself and her husband was further demonstrated when she refused outright to be with him at the traditional annual Sandringham weekend which Prince Charles hosted for sixteen or so of his closest friends. Moreover, she declared her intention to take William and Harry to stay with their grandmother, the Queen, at Windsor. Charles spoke to his mother. Diana came under pressure to reconsider, for the boys' sakes, and for how it would appear when news leaked out to the press. A week of letters and telephone calls between Charles and Diana did not change her mind.

Contrary to traditional suspicions 13 Friday was an auspicious day for Diana as she embarked on a solo trip to Paris. "We'll show them!" she said to Patrick Jephson. "It's time I spread my wings" she insisted to Ken Wharfe, repeating the phrase she had used to him in 1988, at a time when she had no idea where she might fly to. Now she did know, and she intended to continue her journey no matter who tried to get in her way; "they cannot stop me" she declared.

The three day Paris tour was triumphant. *Paris-Match* carried the headline "Courage, Princess". Jephson described Diana's display as "flawless" revealing a professional "at the peak of her form" and reported that "no one, from the President...to the most cynical member of the press circus, was immune to her charm." The three days of the tour also saw the passing of a significant milestone, the end of the six-month cooling off period Diana had agreed with Charles, the Queen and Prince Philip.

Diana had kept her part of the deal, even if towards the end she had shown, with the Korean tour that she was not prepared to cooperate in any more joint engagements with her husband. The Paris trip was a powerful signal of what she could do on her own. She expected Charles and her in-laws to keep their end of the bargain and give her the independence she craved. Her stand over Charles' Sandringham house party had added weight to her message.

In London Diana gave a speech at a European drug conference. Speaking about how affection at home helps prevent drug addiction in the young, she suggested that addicts should be given understanding and a sense of belonging. Her words were even more poignant given the descriptions of her own childhood in *Diana: Her True Story*. Press headlines screamed about the "pain of a broken marriage" and the "pain of being unloved".

Friday 20 November was the first day of Charles' Sandringham weekend. It was also the day Diana was to take her sons to visit the Queen at one of her favourite royal residences, Windsor Castle, and the day a substantial part of that magnificent monument was gutted by fire. At about the same time, rumours began to emerge in the press concerning a tape recording of a telephone conversation between Charles and Camilla Parker-Bowles. What came to be called the Camillagate tape had been given to tabloid newspapers a few weeks earlier. Palace officials learned about its existence almost immediately. In the opinion of some of those in Fleet Street who had listened to the recording, its contents could put Charles' succession in doubt.

On 25 November 1992, Prince Charles finally instructed his office to commence the legal proceedings which would result in his formal separation from the Princess. Diana had her victory. Charles had initiated the separation. Exchanges between lawyers had been ongoing for several months already, after Charles' decision they were able to begin the tricky business of negotiating the precise terms of a formal document of separation.

In short order Diana's new solo life began to take shape. In the weeks which followed the Prince's historic decision, the couple's personal goods and chattels were collected together at their respective residences; Kensington Palace for Diana and Highgrove for Charles. The interior of each home was quickly altered to reflect the taste of their separated occupants, instead of the combined influences of the couple who had shared the dwellings for more than ten years. The domestic staffs of both houses were reorganised.

Visitors noticed a new and lighter atmosphere at Kensington Palace. Patrick Jephson later remarked on the overnight change in a home once oppressed by hushed voices and discernible tension. He noted "a great sense of team spirit" between house and office staff which brought their relations "to a point closer than I had ever known before."

✦ ✦ ✦

I answered the phone, 'This is Stephen Twigg.'

'Hello Stephen, this is Diana, how are you?' The familiar voice came over the line.

'I'm fine. This is a lovely surprise. How are you, how's things?'

'I'm OK. I was wondering if you would come and see me again.'

Without hesitation I replied, 'I'd love to.'

'Oh good, I'll get someone to call you and arrange it. Is that OK?'

'Sure. Do you need me to grovel and tell you again how sorry I am for any embarrassment?'

She laughed, 'No! I'll see you in a few days then?'

'All right, take care of yourself.' It was my usual exhortation when leaving a client. Everything I taught was about self-care.

I hung up the phone and considered the call. It would be good to help her some more. Nice that she had called me herself. That was not the usual way royals do things. Then I realised I didn't think of Diana as a "royal", not in the same way as I did the Queen or Prince Charles. Diana had a regal quality that was different and more natural, it came from inside. Well at least I hadn't caused her too much distress with my antics. That was good! In retrospect it's likely Diana knew all about my run ins with the press and my turning down so much money. She was also quite capable of realising I hadn't actually said anything that wasn't completely supportive of her.

I wondered what might be next on her agenda. *Probably have to read the papers to find out* I thought.

The last few weeks of the year were dominated by formal negotiations over the terms of the couple's separation. The first priority for both parents was to agree arrangements for their sons. The sharing of goods and chattels was discussed as were financial arrangements for Diana's life when she "went solo", as she called it. Not unexpectedly personal issues and highly charged emotions were aired on occasions, amid claims and counter claims, blame and recriminations. The lawyers had seen it all before and worked hard to keep things on track.

Soon however, it became clear that the Prince's negotiating team intended to use the proceedings to curb Diana's status and royal privileges, perhaps because of concerns about what she might do when free to act more independently. In the end their attempts to restrict the Princess's access to the royal flight and the royal train; to eject her staff from St. James's Palace;

and to reduce the level of protocol to which she would be entitled, were not supported by the Queen. It seemed that Buckingham Palace, unlike the Prince's office, still saw Diana as having a valuable part to play in the royal organisation. The only restriction made was that Diana would not officially represent the Queen abroad. Patrick Jephson later made the observation that it was impossible to define what 'represent' actually meant in that context. He believed the Queen intended to leave the issue open to interpretation.

On Wednesday 9 December Prime Minister John Major stood before the House of Commons and told the country, and the hushed Members of Parliament gathered there, that "with regret, the Prince and Princess of Wales have decided to separate." He went on to confirm that the decision "has no constitutional implications", the line of succession would be "unaffected" and there was "no reason the Princess of Wales should not be crowned Queen in due course."

In the week before the announcement Diana had visited her boys at Ludgrove school to tell them what was about to happen. The tears shed then, as she reassured them and told them how much they were loved by both their parents, reminded Diana of her childhood, when her own parents parted. She described the final, irrevocable announcement in Parliament as "very, very sad." Mixed with her sadness she felt relief.

On 15 December, at a function in support of the social care charity Turning Point, Diana spoke about the stress caused to families by Christmas, and took the opportunity to make clear her continuing commitment to charity work.

At that stage in Diana's fight to gain control over her life she had made a huge step forward. True, the matter of divorce was unresolved, for constitutional reasons above all others, but in any case it need not arise until two years had passed from the official separation date. On the day of the Prime Minister's announcement, Diana spoke to her friend, ballet dancer Wayne Sleep, and responded to his concern for her by saying "Don't worry...I'm strong. I'm going to fight this." Clearly she realised she still had some way to go before she could have the life she wanted. Formal separation would not be sufficient for Diana, whose hopes of freedom, and a fulfilling marriage, still outweighed every other consideration. Who or what she thought she might have to fight to achieve them was not so clear.

Given the events of 1992 many of those involved, especially her opponents, might have wondered where Diana was getting her strength from. Her history showed her to have been fragile and emotional, inclined to depression and bulimia and easily intimidated when confronted. Only four years previously, by her own admission in *Diana: Her True Story*, she had been full of self doubt and disabled by cripplingly low self confidence. Yet throughout the year they had all just endured it was clear that Diana had acquired more than enough strength of will, and resilience of spirit, to confront every move made to diminish her, and to confront them with skill and courage. The woman they saw before them that December had initiated a book which successfully gained her a huge ground swell of public sympathy, and had then ridden that wave of support to brush aside a challenge to her reputation that would easily have destroyed her a few years ago.

That Diana had not slipped back into depression, bulimia and suicidal thoughts was testament to the personal transformation she had made since 1988. Powerful new ideas and perceptions had, for four years, been cascading through her brain's neural network changing the very basis of her choices and reactions. The darker and more disabling parts of her make-up were giving way to new beliefs about herself and her place in the world. The results had been decisions and actions observers found unfathomable. Yet they were predictable when her personality was considered. Freed from the constraints imposed by low-self esteem and self-denigration, Diana's core values, to protect her children and to resist with her every fibre the injustices she felt had been perpetrated against her, had been released. Those values, fuelled by anger and indignation and by fear, had provided her with causes to fight for. Intrinsic to her personality was the ability to fight with unrelenting courage and tenacity. No wonder people were reeling with shock and disbelief by the end of that year.

✦ ✦ ✦

'You do realise what you've done, don't you?' I was holding Diana left arm over the crook of my own left elbow and trying to get the edge of my right hand under her left shoulder blade.

'What do you mean?' she mumbled into the pillow over which her head was lying.

'Well from what I've been reading everyone assumed there was no way you would be able to get out of your marriage once you were in it. A few years ago even you told me you were stuck. Now it seems you've begun to change centuries of tradition and the opinions of all sorts of experts by managing to get a legal separation from Charles. You're amazing. You impress the heck out of me.'

Earlier in the session, worried that I might have missed something important, I had discreetly checked for scars which might have been caused by the self-harming mentioned in *Diana: Her True Story*. I found only a few old lines and no more than would be expected from bramble scratches. I was glad to put my mind at rest.

Once again I wondered about the young woman I held in my hands. I simply didn't recognise the petulant, unstable and hysterical woman described in some of the press stories I'd seen. Yes she was angry sometimes, but she'd never lost control in my presence, and she had always treated me with great respect and courtesy, probably because I treated her like an adult, and so she responded as an adult. Warm, humorous and naturally gracious is how I would have described Diana, if asked.

I had one last message to get across to her. 'You've experienced some immense changes this past year,' I spoke quietly. 'You're excited and looking forward to your new life. But don't be surprised if you find yourself suddenly feeling a little deflated or melancholy. It's the way the mind works. It has checks and balances to slow us down and give us time to think. It's good to have doubts they help us clarify what we want. The best thing you can do is to take some time to look again at your future-vision of how you want to be, and make sure you have it as clear as possible. See yourself in the situation you want, looking out on the world you want to be enjoying. That will keep you on track. I have no doubt you'll create the life you want. Give it time to happen.'

As I drove away from Kensington Palace after our last session that year I was already considering how I might help her move forward.

In a speech at the London Guildhall, on 24 November, the Queen described 1992 as her *annus horribilus*. It was a fairly horrible year for a lot of people.

The Queen had been confronted with evidence that the monarchy, her Windsor dynasty, which ruled only with the popular support of the people, was not very popular at all. Her son and heir had been represented to the world as a cruel husband and bad father, a man whose betrayal of his beautiful, young and very popular wife, had led her to acts of desperation and despair. As a result he and other members of her family were held in low public regard, and many people were questioning the family's right to rule.

The Windsor Castle fire had been a personal tragedy for the Queen, and more, it had highlighted another major issue for dissatisfaction amongst her people; the public cost of the royal family. The uproar when it was suggested that the estimated £60 million for the Castle's repairs might be paid for by the taxpayer, had hastened negotiations which had been going on for months in connection with the Civil List. Six days after the fire the House of Commons was advised that henceforth the Queen and the Prince of Wales would pay tax on their incomes, and the Queen would reimburse the state for the annual cost of five members of her close family. Princess Diana's effect on the Queen's personal and professional circumstances, and her outlook as 1992 rolled to a close, had been profound.

Diana's impact on Prince Charles' life had been momentous. Her activities, and particularly the Morton book, had damaged him personally, and caused many to question his place in the line of succession. Nothing had yet been able to curb his wife's popularity or elevate his own. Having been forced into a separation, Charles was faced with a constitutional mess. Since divorce still seemed unlikely, the prospect remained of Diana, his estranged wife, becoming his Queen at some time in the future. It was not a prospect he relished. He had hoped Camilla would be by his side in some capacity when he became King, especially as she had shown great fortitude and patience during the past year. A sensitive and thoughtful man who was determined to do his duty, Charles had suffered agonies of unhappiness and a great deal of stress because of his marriage to Diana. He was no closer to understanding his wife after their eleven years together, and the probability was they would be bound together in desperate misery for the foreseeable future. At that time it would have been surprising if Charles was unaware of the Camillagate tape. If the rumours were true he was about to enter 1993 desperately unhappy and concerned about yet another monstrous crisis looming over him and his future.

The Establishment, that is the collection of high minded courtiers, politicians, landowners, media moguls and influential friends of the monarchy, the Queen and Prince Charles, had been outraged by Diana's behaviour. It is quite likely that through their eyes, the eyes of unquestioning loyalty to an institution and to duty, the primarily male eyes of cold logic and suspicion, the Princess's activities smacked of treason, and premeditated treason at that. Diana's emotional expectations, and her reactions when she had been let down, would never offer them sufficient explanation for what she had done, and how she had done it. From their viewpoint it could not have been intuition, driven by indignation, anger and a sense of justice, which had driven a young woman of questionable intellect to resist all their attempts to bring her into line. It was inconceivable that her campaign had unfolded by chance and was not deliberately orchestrated so as to damage the monarchy and Charles' succession. She was a Spencer, the member of an ancient noble family; a Princess with unprecedented public popularity; the future Queen and the mother to sons who were heirs to the throne. Surely she was up to something? For many Establishment figures the year ended with them wondering what they could do to help the Queen and Prince Charles resist the attack they were under.

For Diana, her trials and tribulations were best not considered any more that year. On 28 December, with her good friend Catherine Soames, the Princes William and Harry and a posse of bodyguards, Diana jetted off to the beautiful Caribbean island of Nevis, there to enjoy sun, sand and sea. An eighty strong press pack arrived within two days, some carrying ski clothing and equipment they had not been able to deposit anywhere, so hastily had they abandoned Fergie and her daughters Beatrice and Eugenie, whose holiday in Klosters they had been covering until news of Diana's unexpected break came through. The rest of Diana's holiday was marked by negotiations which almost equalled in intensity those held by her lawyers earlier in the year. Instead of royal privileges and parental access to children being at stake, it was the rights of a free press and photographers' access to the Princess and her sons which were traded. Ken Wharfe did sterling work on Diana's behalf. The result, wonderful pictures of a svelte, bikini clad Diana, considerable cash and kudos for the photographers, a happy press pack and a suntanned Princess.

1993

Even the rich are hungry for love,
for being cared for,
for being wanted,
for having someone to call their own
Mother Teresa

Twelve and a half years. More than four thousand five hundred days. Approximately fifty four thousand waking hours. All spent in a nightmare that had seemed at the start to be the perfect fairytale. On occasion, during those years, days and hours, Diana had believed she could go no further, bear no more. There had been times when she even thought she might take her own life.

By the start of 1993, Diana had endured an almost never-ending stream of life-altering trials of such magnitude the average person can barely imagine the impact of a single one of them, let alone their combined effect. Marriage to the future King had become an emotional wasteland. Intense first love had decayed into a desert devoid of the basic nourishment of love and appreciation she needed to thrive. Every day was filled with reminders of what might have been, should have been if only the promises made to her by her husband had been fulfilled. Diana's marriage had trapped her in an institution which had not evolved sufficiently in the centuries of its existence to be able to put individual happiness on a par with the concept of duty. As a consequence, two decent but disparate souls had been trapped by ideas and an ideology which constrained them as securely as steel bars and eventually set them against each other. As she struggled to come to terms with her situation, Diana had been subjected to continuous and intense examination, by individuals and organisations, which constantly evaluated her every action and reaction and even her appearance and declared them acceptable or not when measured by criteria she barely understood. Her husband, his family, staff, courtiers, public and above all else, because they commanded the eyes and ears of all the others, the journalists and their masters, scrutinised her to a degree beyond that which any person had ever endured and censured her when she did not fulfil their expectations.

No wilderness is completely devoid of sustenance however, and while she did not thrive as she might have done in different circumstances, Diana did manage to survive what her marriage had brought her. Out of necessity, she learned new skills and discovered qualities, for which she was loved by some and at least acknowledged by others. She found satisfaction and fulfilment in her unanticipated abilities and in motherhood. But there were some who found her too different from what they expected, too challenging to their own beliefs and they constantly lamented her inability to be what they required. So they rejected her but they could not let her go. Such lack of understanding and acceptance made Diana's life in this unforeseen situation very hard indeed. The voices which spoke against her were loud and given such importance that they were capable of making even those who cared for her turn their backs. Diana was in constant fear of losing what made her life bearable despite her efforts to please those who held sway over her.

Four years ago Diana began to emerge from her ordeal. Angry at the injustice of it, tired of living at the whim of others who did not understand her and whose motives went counter to her dreams for herself, she chose to challenge them with the very skills she had been forced to acquire. Motivated by a new vision of her future Diana started to take her own life, not to end it, but to begin it again; to grasp it and embrace it and to direct it to become what she wanted it to be. If Diana was surprised by her own achievements in such a short time she did not show it. Probably she did not recognise them. Her successes required her to overcome challenges so difficult that she was too preoccupied with what might happen next to consider what she was achieving.

In January 1993, Diana believed her formal separation from Prince Charles was a giant step away from the situation which had held her in thrall for so long and she felt she was standing on the threshold of a new life. It was good to look forward; too often her future had looked so bleak she felt only pain and despair when she considered it; now she felt excitement and anticipation even though she knew she still had a long way to go. At the end of 1992 she had said "I'm learning to be patient" and spoke of two or three years before she would be able to enjoy "the fun" she wanted her life to be.

The "fun" was to be the life she had envisaged when she was nineteen, a life filled with love, although Diana might not have been able to articulate it so simply. Love however, is what she still foresaw for herself, with a partner, children and a normal home. A home intended to be nothing more than a place of safety and caring and happiness and laughter. Love is what she envisaged when she saw herself continuing to help the sick and the dying and the most distressed of the world, for love is synonymous with caring, compassion and tolerance.

Diana was well aware she had more than the average person's ability to make a difference in the world. She had not wanted the media and public examination she attracted the moment she stepped forward to accept her husband's offer of marriage. The activities of the press and other media had been unpredictable and frightening for her. Over the years she had struggled to survive their attention. As time went by she had come to rely on it, then to harness and to control it, until eventually she had been able to use it to her own ends. By that January she believed she could make the media look in almost any direction she chose. She chose to show it the most damaged and hurt of the world and that part of herself which was able to give them the compassion and caring they deserved.

Such then was what Diana anticipated when she returned tanned and refreshed from Nevis that January. Ultimately, a lifetime of love shared through fulfilling partnership, home and children and valuable work which would make the world a better place. In the meantime, she would be content sharing love; with a man she adored but to whom she was not married, with her sons and, through worthwhile work, with anyone who was in need of her caring. She would share love her way, without the constant interference of her husband and the organisation of "grey men" which challenged her every notion of what "royalty" could and should be.

When, at the beginning of 1993, I reviewed the work I'd already done with Diana I was quite pleased but not entirely satisfied. I'd set out to help improve her health by using what I knew were life-changing methods. Her life had certainly changed and now she seemed set on a path I was convinced she could never have imagined, or embarked on, when we first met, a path which seemed to be leading her to becoming a very strong and powerful individual in the world she occupied.

I considered what had improved in her health. Physically she was stronger and more powerful. She was clearly integrating the bodywork she received on my massage table and in the pool and at the gym, which indicated to me that her mental state had improved as well. The improvements to her general muscle tone and strength could not have been achieved with the mind set she had when we first met. What troubled me though was the constant presence of tightness around her neck and shoulders and between her shoulder blades.

From my body-mind point of view I was dealing with issues related to the emotions of anger and fear but behind them I also recognised something I could only describe as lack of self-acceptance, or to be more specific, lack of self-love. In the context of her health it meant that despite all she had achieved in public life and all she had managed to change in her outlook and perceptions of herself, there were still major issues at work causing damaging emotions to affect her body. In turn that meant she must still be dealing with fundamental beliefs and attitudes which were limiting her body and her life, since emotions are born from personal beliefs.

The trouble for me was that I didn't know what those beliefs were precisely. I knew Diana was now operating with a new future-vision which would be pushing her from within to produce its outward expression. On the face of it she was doing well. All sorts of situations in her life had changed or were in the process of changing. I knew she would also be experiencing inner changes as well because the two go hand in hand. I had been trying to demonstrate to Diana that the inner changes precede the outer, that the way to improve health in body, mind and life, was to work the inner process with skill and awareness and allow the outer changes to provide feedback that would show whether she was going in the direction she wanted or needed to make some new inner adjustment. Months, no years ago, it had become clear that it was not in her make-up to engage in the work I had in mind. Her mind was completely given to her subjective, introspective processes of intuition and emotional responses. She was incapable of the objective, detached self-observation required to identify a particular emotion or thought as something unhelpful and to formulate a strategy to change it with techniques which needed to be learned and perfected. She did have an interest in psychology and alternative health, but her knowledge was superficial. Her interest in astrology and religions also seemed to indicate she was looking outside herself for answers to problems, rather than within, as if someone or something other than herself had to be persuaded, by prayer or some other exhortation to change her circumstances.

I'd been using massage to make her receptive while I quietly offered her mind a variety of new concepts and suggestions, on the assumption she would accept and incorporate into her inner mind, and thus into her body and life, those ideas which spoke to her new vision. It was an organic, subtle technique which I was comfortable did not infringe on her. I was not exhorting her to any particular belief or direction but offering her suggestions and alternatives from which to choose or even remain with those she had. The problem was it did not directly address any particular issue which might have been blocking an important change in self-perception. Diana's natural reticence, perhaps suspicion would be more accurate, meant she simply did not share the kind of information that would have enabled me to identify powerful, long held, limiting beliefs for which I could have offered more specific alternatives. I was concerned that my subtle approach would have little effect where she needed to make the greatest changes. I needed to find a way to help her shape her future-vision and its component beliefs, thoughts and feelings, more effectively if I wanted to help her achieve her goal.

My mind recoiled slightly. Her goal? Perhaps it was my goal for her. In which case there might be some truth in the Svengali and Machiavelli descriptions thrown at me by the press. An essential part of what I did was to remain neutral and unattached to the outcome of the processes I offered to my clients. With Diana I had observed all the difficulties she experienced in her well-publicised life with the same detachment I brought to my massage work on her body when I noticed the pain and discomfort evident there. Certainly I felt compassion and sympathy for her distress. I felt affection and admiration for what she had achieved as well but her life was not mine. Her body, her health, were not mine to take responsibility for. They were hers to own and to find out how to manage by the process of understanding them better and doing what she was capable of to improve them. My job was to show her what she was capable of.

As a consequence of my thoughts I approached my first session with Diana that year with a slightly different idea in mind to that with which I'd been operating before. I decided to be more active in offering Diana a context to her life and health that could ultimately transcend all the deep psychological constraints she was experiencing. I decided to offer her what can be described as a spiritual context, from which she could operate in every area of her life with a personal code and set of beliefs that could potentially override all her limiting beliefs and provide purpose and ultimately form, to whatever she wanted.

Spiritual awareness is something which comes spontaneously, as a matter of course, to many who are involved in self-transformation. Holism, after all, refers to the trilogy of body, mind and spirit. Usually I would have allowed the natural process and the passage of time to invite Diana to see herself in the context of a reality greater than her current perception of everyday life, one in which her presence and actions had purpose in a pattern of events where everything is interrelated and everything affects the whole. I was aware Diana was already showing an interest in spiritual concepts such as religions and energy based health systems and we'd chatted a little about karma and life after death. I decided to invite her into a wider exploration of herself on the basis that if she was not attracted to logic, science and reasoning she might find her next steps in faith and intuition. Certainly I thought her personality type and introspective nature might respond better to the notion of being a Spiritual Warrior rather than a body-mind mechanism.

'What was that?' Her question was a mumble but there was no doubting the incredulity in her voice.

I'd just concluded the massage, mostly comprised of deep tissue work, with an energy balancing and healing technique. Diana was face down on the table. I'd coached her beforehand by describing the situation I wanted to address. Even so she'd been surprised by the effects.

'This area here between your shoulder blades is associated with emotions of anger, fear and self-criticism,' I told her. I didn't mention her liver, kidneys and gall bladder. 'It also covers your heart chakra, the centre of loving connection with others and self. I'm going to use a healing technique to help the energy flow through that area which will mean you'll be able to give and receive more love.'

'That would be nice,' she'd said somewhat wistfully.

'And wash away the emotions which are limiting the love you can share,' I finished. 'All you have to do is feel yourself opening up through your chest area, as if there was a warm glow in your heart. The more you can allow that area to relax and be open, the more heart energy will flow from and to you. You can direct it to people or situations you want to extend love to; you can be open to love flowing from those people or events into and through you. It helps if you imagine it and if you see it as gold light or green flowing out and in.'

Even I was aware of the change in her when I used the simple laying-on-of hands technique, the sense of profound relaxation and balance where there had been discord and disturbance. So I wasn't surprised at the puzzlement she expressed. I didn't try to explain but ended the session by encouraging her to use the open heart visualisation as often as possible. Later, packing up my kit, I thought we might be onto something which would have some profound effects in time.

✦ ✦ ✦

Barely a week after Diana's return to Britain, following her Nevis holiday, a tape recording of a late night conversation between her husband and his mistress Camilla Parker-Bowles was made public. As with the Squidgy tape of Diana's conversation with James Gilbey, the content was abroad before being picked up by UK tabloids. Dating from about the same time, December 1989, the existence of the Camillagate tape, as it was dubbed, was first revealed that mid-January, by a magazine in Australia. Once in the public domain it was quickly featured on the front pages of more than 50 newspapers across the world. Two UK tabloids cautiously offered to the British public, snippets of what was a humorous but earthy, some would say crude, exchange of endearments between Charles and Camilla. *The Sun* opened a phone line and asked callers to say whether they wanted to see the full transcript. Sadly, but not unpredictably, the overwhelming response was YES! The complete text of the recording was duly published, after the couple had suffered a prolonged period of excruciating anticipation.

Exposure of the taped conversation affected many others besides the two people it featured. Diana, whose enjoyment of crude humour was well known, professed herself sickened by the more vulgar parts of the exchange. She already knew that people who purported to be her friends were complicit in deceiving her about her husband's relationship with Camilla. The contents of the tape fuelled her anger by providing more evidence that many had actually connived to assist him. Of course the Princess was vindicated too: the tape provided irrefutable evidence to support what had been implied in *Diana: Her True Story*, that her husband had committed adultery with Camilla and was to blame for the destruction of her marriage and her dreams. Diana's lawyers were delighted to have evidence to support a counter-claim in the event that adultery became an issue in any future proceedings between their client and her husband.

Those easily shocked by anatomically explicit humour, even when expressed in apparent privacy between loving adults, called into question whether Charles had the required character to be King when his time came. Those who had been ignoring all past references in the press to his association with Camilla, or who had believed the recent concerted campaign to pass their relationship off as "just good friends", also wondered loudly whether Charles should become monarch. The press published a wide spectrum of opinions. Figures from politics, the Church and the military all gave their views and advice to the heir to the throne. A tabloid poll declared the public's verdict, 68% thought Charles' reputation would be badly damaged and 42% thought Prince William should be the next king.

Charles' supporters were angry and upset and his palace team was demoralised by the turn of events. Some conspiracy theorists even thought they saw Diana's hand, or that of her supporters, on the peculiar emergence of the Camillagate tape. More likely is that both it and the Squidgy recordings, resulted from a systematic monitoring, by government agencies, of telephones used by members of the royal family and those close to them. Some disaffected, or even avaricious, operative had probably appropriated copies and ensured they reached the public domain. Whatever the truth Charles discovered what Diana had experienced a few months before, it was very unpleasant to have one's dirty washing laundered in public.

Ultimately, after the shock had worn off, Charles' response to the Camillagate recording was similar to Diana's reaction when she heard about the existence of the Squidgy tape, a determination to fight for his future. The Prince's entire forty four years had been spent preparing himself to become the next King. His birthright was undisputed but his right to be King by popular consent required that he embark on the same path his wife had two years before. He needed the sympathetic understanding and support of the British people. The battering his reputation and character had taken in the press during the past two years meant he was starting with a handicap. Diana had already gained the moral and tactical high ground through her own activities. Charles was going to have to compete with her for the media and public profile he needed. At that time it was assumed by many in his camp that Diana had set out to deliberately diminish her husband's image and standing. When the Prince's campaign began it seemed to observers at the time to be a systematic attempt by his palace organisation and his friends to attack Diana's royal status and her public role in order to elevate Charles'. If so, they soon found their task was not going to be easy.

A glowing feature article, by Anthony Holden in February's issue of *Vanity Fair*, followed the adoring tabloid coverage of Diana's Nevis holiday. The piece was echoed by much of Fleet Street. Under a front cover carrying a picture of the tiara adorned Princess and the headline "Di's Palace Coup", Holden waxed enthusiastically about how Diana had wrong footed her enemies to secure her new future. Holden's article was more telling than many because up until then his stance had tended to be critical of the Princess. Now he told how she was visibly reborn after her separation which he described as "a moment of triumph" for Diana and "a crushing defeat" for Prince Charles. The article, written around November the previous year, at the time of her spectacular Paris trip, looked forward to the Princess becoming "a heavyweight on the world stage" and commented on how her staff was "discreetly orchestrating" her move from minor to major player "in a drama whose plot gets thicker all the time."

When he read the article, Diana's private secretary Patrick Jephson, the spearhead of the Princess's media campaign and the person who was "discreetly orchestrating" her move, must have been delighted. The piece fitted perfectly with how he saw Diana's future and what he believed her intentions were at that time. He had an agenda which fulfilled his duty, as he saw it, to both the monarchy and the Princess. Jephson was determined to secure for Diana a lagely independent role, high in the palace organisation, serving the interests of the crown. Unfortunately he did not understand all that was driving Diana and he became seriously frustrated in his efforts to push her towards the goal he saw beckoning.

Diana's true motivation had been a source of misconceptions since her entry into the royal family and Jephson's lack of understanding was shared by most of those around her, friends and enemies alike. What she wanted was not what Patrick Jephson, or most other people, assumed she wanted. They saw Diana's desire for a high media profile as simple evidence of her craving for a lifestyle based on a powerful and influential role on the world stage. For Diana, the media presence was required in order to generate public support and sympathy. Her considerable efforts to attract positive media attention were born mainly out of her desire for a life in which humanitarian work co-existed with private happiness with a husband, home and family. Circumstances had dictated she invite and then pursue, the media attention and influence she now commanded, as a way to survive body blows which could have stopped her achieving what she sought. Her media and public presence was the means to an end, not the end result.

Unfortunately the paradox between the twin features of Diana's future-vision, public role and private happiness, was throwing up problems which, by the early part of 1993 were only too apparent.

Without the frantic drive for the safety of a high and sympathetic public profile and with time to consider what she must do to reach the dream she really sought, Diana became impatient and confused. On an inner level she was being driven by two desires she had yet to reconcile into a coherent and credible imagined future. As a result she was unclear about what to do to get what she wanted. In the absence of any conceptual resolution and in the presence of uncertainty, the conflict between her two aspirations could only be played out in the real world of actual events as she struggled to move forward. On the outer level, Diana's uncertainty manifested as mixed signals to those whose lives were linked to her own.

Patrick Jephson and his staff gained the impression that Diana intended to continue with her public work unabated, if not increased, after her separation. They therefore proceeded with arrangements to ensure Diana's media persona continued to rise in the eyes and estimation of the world. Jephson worked assiduously to create far reaching opportunities for long term involvements with a few significant projects backed by influential charities like the Red Cross and by the Government. At times the subject of his efforts enthusiastically embraced the path he paved for her because it represented one aspect of the future she sought. At other times, when her alternative, private agenda was dominant in her thinking, she prevaricated and even disrupted his plans, with what he later described as "capricious reactions" and "short sighted self indulgence where work was concerned".

Sadly it was his own lack of understanding which led to his inevitable disappointment and frustration. In his memoirs Jephson described how he was able to "use my growing knowledge of her mind" to direct and guide Diana. Unfortunately he only knew part of her mind and as a consequence was trying to direct her on a path which could not lead to where she actually wanted to be. Awareness of all of Diana's thoughts and aspirations would have confirmed what became obvious later. The further she travelled along the path of public duty and long term commitments to a world changing destiny, the more difficult it would be for her to achieve private happiness in a quiet home with a loving partner. Diana would have felt the contradiction instinctively even though she would not have understood its source. Not surprisingly she resisted committing to the long term plans Jephson and others offered her.

Diana's "self indulgence" during the early part of 1993 was to undertake the kind of introspective self examination that had always been her natural inclination. Within herself she would have felt, but not necessarily recognised, grieving for the loss of a twelve year marriage and a sense of rejection, despite the fact her life with Charles had been difficult and painful. She would have found elements of an almost bizarre impulse to go back to what was familiar, rather than have to face an uncertain future.

She would also have found some disquiet about her sons, those essential features to her vision of her future. Both boys were at boarding school and the separation agreement meant Diana must now share their holiday time equally with her husband, so she anticipated many occasions when she would be without them at Kensington Palace. But there was something else, she sometimes felt irritated when she saw her sons with Ken Wharfe. On holidays Ken swam and indulged in play-fights with the lads. Recently, on Nevis, the young princes seemed to show a more than usual inclination for cricket and meals with Ken and the bodyguards. It is unlikely that Diana would have recognised the natural impulse of boys of a certain age to start distancing themselves from their mother's warm but constricting embrace, or her own jealous reaction. She just felt disturbed and needed even more demonstrations of her sons' love.

Finally, when Diana sought the inner guidance she always relied on, she would have found something which spoke loudly to that part of herself which aspired to a home and life with a loving partner. She found her emotional attraction to Oliver Hoare stronger than ever.

Mirroring her previous commitments to Prince Charles and James Hewitt, Diana began investing her dreams for the future in the married art dealer who had captured her heart. Diana was almost thirty two years old, she had experienced only two significant relationships in her life and Oliver Hoare was her third. She was becoming obsessed by him. She imagined a future with him. She had even spoken aloud to friends of her dream to live with him in Italy. She sought the reassurance only his constant attention and support could give. The silent telephone calls to Hoare's home had not stopped since September 1992 and they continued throughout 1993.

The confusing variety of emotions and thoughts in Diana's mind at that time would have been adding to her uncertainty about what to do. Self-transformation is not a linear process. Despite her achievements in developing the self-esteem, strength of purpose and confidence needed to drive her work and public role, Diana had yet to develop those qualities in that part of herself which was expressed in a loving relationship with a partner. With men to whom she committed Diana remained attached to the idea that her life would be shaped and given purpose by their ability to mutually support each other. When Diana fell in love her impulses included a childlike need to give control over her future happiness to her partner. It was a model that was as bound to fail with Oliver Hoare as it had with Charles and Hewitt. If Diana had read her gift, Khalil Gibran's book *The Prophet*, she clearly did not subscribe to his description of marriage. He suggested two people should "Love one another, but make not a bond of love" and be like the pillars of the temple which stand apart and like "the oak tree and the cypress grow not in each other's shadow". Gibran's words speak of two individuals, standing strong, side by side, sharing their lives. Implicit in Diana's view was of two people leaning on each other, with her partner taking most of the weight.

During the early part of that year Diana was mentally unbalanced. She would remain so for some time. During 1992 she had been concerned about comments by her detractors alluding to her mental state. What they meant was some manifestation of a clearly defined mental disorder which could be diagnosed by medical professionals. The actual imbalance in Diana's mind was far less sinister. It was simply the natural conflict between the opposing aspirations of her private self and her public self; between her desire for a quiet personal life and home and a worthwhile, high profile role helping improve the world.

'Sad about the tape thing,' I said, mentioning the Camillagate issue when I visited her shortly after it appeared in the press. In the past I wouldn't have mentioned anything like that.

'Why sad? It's been a long time coming,' snorted Diana. 'Anyway it was sick, what they said.'

'Inventive perhaps,' I chuckled, 'but you know what it's like to experience that kind of press attack. I don't just mean the nasty comments I mean the thoughts behind them and the thoughts it makes other people have. Thoughts have energy and substance to them, especially when they're nasty thoughts held by a lot of people. You know that I'm sure. You can feel it when people don't like you can't you?'

'Certainly can. Anyway I thought you said what other people think of you is none of your business.'

'Yes that's true. That's why I'm asking you to do the heart energy stuff. If you're full of anger and fear, you'll feel other people's thoughts of anger and fear especially if they are directed at you. If you can be full of love, all you'll feel is love, then what they're thinking is none of your business, unless you want to offer them some of your heart energy. Hey there's a song there somewhere isn't there? *All you need is love?'*

I carried on with the massage in silence when I saw her drift into her thoughtful state.

✦ ✦ ✦

At another session a little later I asked 'Have you read Kipling's poem *If?'*

'No why?' Diana was pulled from her dreamlike state.

'I just wondered. It probably sums up everything that a human being can aspire to be when they know themselves completely, except the last line of course,' I laughed.

'What's that?'

'You'll be a man my son,' I quoted. 'But if you can get over that and realise he means being a complete human being, well it's a hairs on the back of the neck kind of thing. I've got a copy in my bag. I'll let you have it before I go.'

✦ ✦ ✦

On 16 February in London Diana gave a speech on HIV+AIDS and appealed for greater humanity to overcome prejudice against the disease. She highlighted the plight of those forced to leave their jobs through ignorance and fear and spoke of AIDS sufferers she had met, who had been abandoned by family and friends. As usual her speech came from the heart. Diana was well able to empathise with the devastating effects rejection could bring.

As she drifted through the early weeks of 1993 and approached the end of February Diana began to realise her situation had not changed very much despite the separation. In fact in some respects it was worse. Diana had been made well aware during the negotiations of the previous year that her sons were only in her life at the behest of the Sovereign. That February the Duchess of York was refused permission to fly with her daughters, Eugenie and Beatrice, to the West Indies for a holiday. According to Andrew Morton in his book *Diana: Her New Life*, the excuse given by palace courtiers was that since Diana had been disporting herself in the Caribbean sunshine in January, Sarah should not be seen doing something similar a month later. To Diana it was a signal that her own freedom, to be with her children, might be subjected to similar restrictions. She was already seeing William and Harry less than she had before the separation and she was scared that her access to them might be further influenced by her husband's family.

For all her much vaunted new independence Diana remained tied to her husband financially and was still tethered to an institution which could substantially control her freedom of action and her professional life. At about that time it was also becoming clear that a campaign to rehabilitate Prince Charles' media profile was under way and that as a consequence, elements within the royal organisation were set on hindering Diana's public role.

Given the "confederation" of royal households which made up the palace machine, it is probable the Queen was unaware of all the activities of her courtiers. Like any busy Chief Executive it is extremely unlikely she involved herself directly in all the day to day decisions of the organisation she headed. Nor that she questioned in detail every proposal put forward by senior courtiers attached to the other palaces, especially that of the heir's. Busy heads of state, like busy heads of companies, delegate to people they trust and expect them to consult only on matters of the greatest importance. Nevertheless, whoever exercised it, Diana's life was still largely under the control of others who seemed bent on damaging her future and she hated the sense of helplessness that realisation gave her. She hated as well that she had nothing, no dramatic step such as a tell-all book, available to her and with which she could wrest control into her own hands. By the end of February the new lighter atmosphere in Kensington Palace was giving way to a heavy sense of foreboding and frustration.

Diana's response to her situation was already tried and tested. She embraced once again the activities which gave her most confidence and sense of control. She committed to her work and her media profile, with every expectation she would have the public's support, should it be needed, to retain control of her sons and create the life she wanted. Under British law divorce was at least two years away and even then it would enhance her negotiating position if she could wait for Charles to ask for her agreement to the final break. The constitutional issues remained to be resolved and divorce was still considered problematic for Charles. Diana had already managed to alter opinions about a formal separation so there was good reason to believe she might bring about other changes that would free her from the mess she was in once and for all. In December 1992 Diana had declared she was "going to fight". In February 1993 Diana, the INFP Idealist, the fierce upholder of what was right and just, once again had something to fight for. The media was still the battleground and Diana set out to explore just how much independence she could force from the system.

As she prepared for yet more conflict Diana instinctively assessed the possible pitfalls. Realising the importance of the Queen to her future, Diana continued to maintain her links to her mother-in-law by taking her sons to visit as often as possible. The Princess also made it clear she was not too cheerful after her separation, or spending too much money, by dressing down and wearing more black and by cutting back on activities which might have seemed frivolous or spendthrift. Much of the time, when she was not working or out with her sons, she stayed within the confines of Kensington Palace. The press at that time was examining all aspects of royal expenditure and both the Duchess of York and Prince Charles had been criticised for extravagance. Questions were still being raised about the cost of repairing Windsor Castle after the fire in November. The Queen was responding by agreeing to plans which would raise funds by opening Buckingham Palace to paying visitors during August and September when she was usually at Balmoral.

It remained Diana's intention to present herself as a serious player on the world stage, but she was not about to commit to the long term plans envisaged by Patrick Jephson and others. Her agenda was still to pursue her future on her own terms and for the time being that meant a similar pattern of work as before her separation. Jephson described it as "absence of obvious excess"; "minimum of formality"; "quick and flexible response to topical humanitarian issues" and "readiness to communicate with her public in ways that acknowledged…the emotional dimension of her work". To prepare herself Diana set out to develop her speech-making abilities by engaging Peter Settelen, an actor turned voice coach, to help her. Peter also began helping Diana frame her speeches, so their content reflected her views and experiences more closely and their style was easier for her to present to her audience. In encouraging this and by seeking advice from a wide variety of friends and acquaintances, Diana further frustrated Jephson, who increasingly saw the ad hoc influence of too many people muddying the message he was trying to project.

✦ ✦ ✦

'"Argue for your limitations and you can be sure they will be yours,"' I quoted.

I'd been telling Diana about a favourite book of mine, *Illusions – The Memoirs of a Reluctant Messiah* by Richard Bach. It was about a spiritual master, a messiah, who decided he'd had enough of doing miracles and feeding thousands of people every day and being sworn at by people who didn't believe, so he quit.

'What do you mean quit?' said Diana.

'He came down the hill after a little chat with God, who told him he was on earth to do whatever he wanted, and told the masses – "I quit" – then he went barnstorming, flying his plane all over America, charging people five dollars for five minute flights over their homes. Shimoda his name was.'

'I couldn't do anything like that,' she frowned.

'"Argue for your limitations and you can be sure they will be yours"' I'd quoted Shimoda's words back. 'You can find a way to do anything if you really want to,' I added.

✦ ✦ ✦

The first major event of Diana's professional year was a five day solo trip to Nepal in the first week of March. Significant, because it had been sanctioned by the Government and the Queen, the tour was a manifestation of Diana's wish to become a humanitarian envoy for Britain. The event was given extra status by the presence of a Government minister, Baroness Lynda Chalker, Secratary of State for Overseas Development and a strong advocate for Diana's aspiration.

Prior to the tour, Tory grandee, Establishment figure and columnist for the *Sunday Express*, Lord McAlpine, criticised the Government's endorsement of the trip. He called it "sheer folly" and declared that the now separated Princess "no longer needs to undertake public duties that will cost the taxpayer large sums".

According to rumour, a few days prior to Diana's departure for Nepal, representatives of the media were entertained and briefed by courtiers, who quietly offered their opinion that the trip would not be a success. During the trip Diana was supposedly told by several friendly journalists that Prince Charles' camp was eager to see her fail.

On the eve of Diana's departure the Australian *Four Corners* television news program broadcast "a more complete version" of the Squidgy tape and discussed the possible involvement of the British intelligence services in its recording and dissemination. One previously "missing" section of Diana's conversation with James Gilbey quickly attracted attention from the press in other countries, but not apparently, in the UK.

DIANA: I don't want to get pregnant.
GILBEY: Darling, that's not going happen, all right?
DIANA: Yeah.
GILBEY: Don't think like that. It's not going to happen, Darling; you won't get pregnant.

Finally the entire Squidgy tape was out in the open and laid to rest, with no discernible damage to Diana's position and reputation. With it went all residual fears she attached to its existence.

The Nepal trip was an immense success on several fronts. Diana performed brilliantly and with undeniable compassion, when she made visits to the Anandaban Leprosy Mission and the homes of poverty stricken Nepalese. On occasion the press coverage of the Princess, sharing her compassion and concern, even eclipsed Baroness Chalker who was there to discuss distribution of Government aid. Diana's trip certainly eclipsed her husband's efforts elsewhere. The Prince's press coterie for a February trip to see farming in Mexico, for example, was much reduced from what he was used to and very much smaller than that which accompanied Diana. While she was away working Charles was on a skiing holiday. Noticing how few journalists were around he asked where they had all gone. "Nepal" was the answer.

The Princess's desire to play a serious role in world humanitarian affairs was not always helped by the press coverage she received. The Nepal trip was almost blighted by mischievous and misleading reports that Diana was being treated as a second class royal by her hosts. Her work was trivialised by photographs which reprised the sunshine, back-lit, pictures when she was eighteen. "Legs We Forget" was the tasteless caption. Naturally sensitive to criticism and already on the lookout for signs of attack by her opponents, Diana was sure the stories had connotations far more sinister than simple journalistic license.

Back in Britain Diana was impatient to pursue her chosen work, her way. What she wanted to do was to use her popularity and her special style of informal royalty, to bypass pomp and protocol and bring attention and caring to the suffering, whoever they were, wherever they were. Diana had meetings with Prime Minister, John Major, to talk about how she could best bring her obvious talents and resources to humanitarian causes throughout the world. She emerged from her discussions excited by his enthusiasm for her proposals. At home she began to support charities involved in helping those affected by domestic violence and eating disorders. On 18 March in London, she addressed a conference debating the Children Act and spoke of the plight of young homeless people. Her speech, underpinned by her experiences of private visits to homeless shelters, proposed it was everyone's responsibility to care for children who were on the streets. Diana, the semi-detached Princess, was gathering momentum again. Yet sometimes, in her eagerness she was caught unawares by what seemed to her a concerted effort to reduce her status and effectiveness.

When Diana's name was removed from the court circular, which listed all the upcoming "official" appearances of the sovereign and senior members of the royal family, on the pretext she was no longer an "official" royal, she was not overly disheartened. The thousands who turned up to see her unofficial engagements, compared to the relative few who showed at events performed by other members of the royal family, was sufficient evidence that the men in grey did not understand her and what she brought to her work.

Diana was certain no other member of the royal organisation shared her ability, or even understood the need to bring emotional connection to royal duties. Her certainty, bolstered by confidence born from years of popular success and enthusiasm, arising from her unattached status, led her to errors of judgement. Or perhaps over-confidence and over-enthusiasm are better descriptions. After the second IRA bombing of Warrington, on 20 March, injured fifty six and killed three year old Jonathan Bell and twelve year old Tim Parry, Diana proposed she attend the memorial service for the boys. Buckingham Palace decided the Duke of Edinburgh was the better choice to represent the royal family. Nevertheless Diana telephoned both sets of bereaved parents to give her personal condolences. She was deeply troubled when her simple gestures of concern were innocently disclosed to the media by one of the families and the consequent news coverage deflected attention from the memorial service itself. "A monumental cock-up" was how she described it later, after having her 'wrists slapped' by palace courtiers.

Even the moderate degree of extra freedom Diana was experiencing generated unexpected consequences in other areas of her life. If anything her partial liberation produced in her more frustration and impatience than when the constraints on her movements and activities had seemed permanent and unavoidable. In her work she was more inclined to be irritated with the men in grey and more sensitive to any attempt to hold her back from doing what she wanted to do. In her private life the impatience showed primarily in her attitude to her apartment at Kensington Palace. Significantly, when Charles had moved out, Diana had made only superficial changes to the decor and furnishings. She had not embarked on the wholesale redecoration her husband had initiated at Highgrove when the couple parted. It was as if she did not regard Kensington Palace as a home, but more as a temporary space until she could move on.

By late that March, the surveillance cameras, policemen, security gate and high railings, made Diana feel she was under constant observation and being restrained against her will, rather than protected from possible threats. In the circumstances it was difficult for her to pursue her relationship with Oliver Hoare. She could not be seen with him in public and when he visited her at Kensington Palace their liaisons could hardly be called private. She sometimes smuggled him through the gates hidden in the boot of her car, from where he scuttled into her apartment trying to avoid being seen by Diana's royal neighbours. Bodyguard Ken Wharfe highlighted the problem in his memoirs. He recalled rushing to Diana's room after a smoke alarm was activated at 3.30 one morning, only to find a dishevelled and embarrassed Hoare smoking a cigar on the landing.

Her sense of restriction prompted more impulsiveness from Diana and a deteriorating relationship with her protection officer. When Diana took William and Harry skiing in her favourite resort of Lech, in Austria, matters between Wharfe and the Princess suffered a further decline. After apparently retiring for the night, Diana escaped from her room in the Arlberg Hotel, by jumping twenty feet from her bedroom window into a snowdrift. At about 5.30 a.m. the following morning she returned to the hotel, rang the front door bell, greeted the surprised duty policeman who let her in with a polite "good morning" and returned to her room. None of her police detail had known she was out, probably visiting Oliver Hoare who was in a nearby resort. Wharfe was incredibly angry and gave the Princess a severe ticking off and probably, by treating her like a naughty child, hastened his own demise from her service a few months later. Such was the life of the most famous woman in the world who, at the age of thirty two had to jump out of windows in order to find some privacy. As far as Wharfe was concerned, Diana's behaviour demonstrated an erosion of the trust which was essential if he was to be able to do his job of keeping her safe. The incident marked the beginning of the end of their relationship.

Something else which happened during that holiday in Lech highlighted another developing problem for Diana. Usual practise, during such a holiday, was for Diana and her sons to appear each morning for a photo call before the gathered ranks of British and foreign press. Afterwards the royal celebrities would normally be able to go skiing or shopping without much interference. It was a tried and tested way for the journalists and photographers to get their stories and good pictures with the cooperation of their targets. The arrangements enabled Diana and her sons to enjoy their holiday without the constant presence of the press, although there were always some photographers who ignored the unwritten rules to pursue their prey onto the ski slopes, or into the boutiques. On that trip Ken Wharfe found himself dealing with a more than usually aggressive press pack. One in particular distressed the Princess by pushing too close and insisting he wanted to interview William. In the end he pushed too far and Wharfe was forced to put him on the ground, where he was swiftly joined by a friend who threw a punch at the bodyguard. The incident was a small but significant event which marked an almost unnoticed turning point in Diana's relationship with the media.

In mid-January, British newspapers had reported on a leaked document in which Lord McGregor, Chairman of the Press Complaints Commission, revealed his view that both the Prince and Princess of Wales had been "cynically manipulating the press", during events the previous year when *Diana: Her True Story* was in the news. Singling out Diana, McGregor claimed she had been "intruding on her own privacy". Some elements of the press were happy to pick up the story and report themselves as having been "manipulated" by Diana.

At the time it came out the story caused little disturbance. It was a very mild storm in a very small teacup; the press had been manipulated to about the same extent as a dog is when it rolls on its back to have its belly scratched and they knew it. The feeding of information to friendly journalists and their editors could not happen without their wholehearted consent and involvement. If "manipulation" had disturbed their moral compasses too much, they knew they could always have walked away. So it was not the abstract threshold of 'manipulation' that Diana had crossed in the summer of 1992, but a different line altogether, one which was to lead to more significant consequences than the ire of Lord McGregor, or the press purists.

Since 1990, Diana, as part of her strategy to escape from her marriage, had been giving private mini-briefings, on return flights from overseas trips, to those journalists who happened to be on board and were in her favour. In 1991 Diana selected Andrew Morton to write the blockbusting, financial bonanza *Diana: Her True Story*. After the book was published she remained in contact with Morton and provided him, through their usual go-between James Colthurst, with information for occasional exclusives and for his sequel book. On the return trip from Nepal that March of 1993, Diana had deliberately recruited another "friendly" journalist, Richard Kay from the *Daily Mail*, to be her active and supportive voice in the media. From her personal briefings, Kay was able to write exclusive stories which often found the front page. Journalism is a very competitive business. Singling out individuals for special attention and giving them opportunities to enhance their professional status and financial position was a risky thing to do. It did not endear Diana to those who had been overlooked.

Diana: Her True Story had been intended to briefly open a door onto Diana's life, so that the public could look in, through the eyes of the press, and see what was happening behind the facade. Unfortunately for Diana, from the press point of view the book showed that she was prepared to put her private life in the limelight and they were happy to oblige even when she tried to say "enough". The door was open, it was too late for her to say "I've had enough, please leave now". The incident with the photographers in Lech marked the beginnings of a new and more aggressive pursuit of Diana by some elements of the press, particularly the freelance paparazzi. Over the coming months and years Diana would suffer badly from their attentions.

The atmosphere around Diana's life at that time was poisonous. The press, politicians and to a degree some the public, had been split into two different camps, "pro" or "anti" Diana. Few were neutral. In the halls of power in Fleet Street and the royal palaces, anti-Diana meant pro-Charles. The results of their conflicting positions were seen in adversarial newspaper columns and heard in arguments and intrigues amongst the courtiers. To some extent Diana was a victim of her own success, as Charles was of his own misfortunes. Diana's star, despite some criticism, was continuing to rise; Charles', fresh from the Camillagate scandal, seemed to be in permanent decline. Press stories, focussed on their differences and invariably Diana came out best. While she continued to present her popular style on the public stage to considerable acclaim, Charles continued to inspire boredom or only mild interest with his official activities and criticism for his private life.

In the pressure cooker of that environment, at the end of March 1993, it was unsurprising to find Diana mired in a belief that there was conspiracy and threat all around. She had been using a shredder to destroy personal correspondence since 1990; her efforts to get material for her book to Andrew Morton undetected had involved her in plotting and clandestine activities; recordings of a private telephone conversation had been published around the world in strange circumstances and the press had been printing suggestions that she was mentally unstable. To Diana, naturally wary of being hurt and instinctively apprehensive about anything which might affect her future and her connection to her sons, there were many reasons to be suspicious. Her life still lay substantially in the hands of people she did not trust. They were angry at her and she knew they were using their considerable influence with the media to try to rehabilitate her husband in the public perception. It was only a matter of time before their efforts succeeded and their success would mean damage to her own image and the protection it provided her through public support.

Paramount was the uncertainty around Charles' future, for which Diana was blamed. What might happen after two years of separation was unclear. Diana would be entitled to sue for divorce. The fact that she could do so was a weapon she might conceivably use to threaten Charles' succession to the throne and his future life with Camilla. Merely being in possession of such a powerful weapon made Diana a threat, in the eyes of those who supported Charles and the monarchy, especially as they found her as unpredictable as the wind. Suspicion, fear and anger were rife on both sides and created environments in which neither side felt secure.

✦ ✦ ✦

'I need to tell you something. It's a bit difficult,' I said early during one massage session.

'What is it?' Diana's eyes opened instantly.

'Some of the other clients I see have been telling me you might be upsetting some people. It's only dinner party talk and such, just rumours, but the basic idea is you might be in danger.'

'Hmm, that fits with what I've been hearing as well,' she muttered.

I'd thought a great deal about whether to mention what I'd been told by a few concerned clients who knew of my connection with Diana. It was going better than I thought it might. At least she hadn't run screaming from the room or collapsed in tears.

'Well if you know where any nasty secrets or skeletons are buried you might want to think about giving some details to someone you trust. Like they do in the movies, and make it known you've done it.'

✦ ✦ ✦

On another visit, one evening later than usual, Diana left the room while I was packing up after the massage and returned with a couple of sheets of fax paper.

'What do you think of this?' she asked, handing them to me.

I leaned over the pages on my massage table and read a speech about eating disorders. 'It's OK,' I said, 'doesn't really say much that will help anyone. You are an expert from a point of view that a lot of people don't have. I can see what you're trying to say but I think it can be done better. I can put some notes together for you and send them by fax if you need them in a hurry. Just give me the number.'

'OK. I've been trying to come up with a way to tell people I've had bulimia without actually using the words. The press have a field day about that kind of thing and it takes attention from everything else if they can make a headline that quotes me saying "I had bulimia", any ideas?'

I thought for a while 'How about "I have it on the very best authority"? Anyone with an ounce of insight will know you mean yourself and you won't have to actually say the words.'

'Yes that might work.' She grinned as she wrote down her fax number.

✦ ✦ ✦

'You realise you're surrounded by love don't you?' I asked during another treatment as I slid my elbow up the muscle alongside Diana's spine.

'How so?' she grunted.

'Well I know you feel like people are always criticising you but there are a lot more who are really glad you're in the world. It's very easy to close down the heart because of other people's criticism and anger, but that means you don't get to the feel love of those who care about you.' My elbow slid neatly over the top of her shoulder and I moved around the table to repeat the procedure on the other side.

✦ ✦ ✦

That April Diana visited Thorpe Park with her sons for a wet but fun day out. The trip was one of an increased number of similar visits to theme parks she made that year. Critics said she made the trips for the publicity, to demonstrate the contrast between her fun style of parenting and Charles' stuffy ways and to emphasise her place in the life of her son the future King. Supporters pointed out that the contact Diana had with the Princes had been reduced by the terms of the separation agreement. It was natural she would use what time she had with them in activities they enjoyed. All the opposing conclusions represented press coverage at that time which interpreted any event involving Diana or Charles so it showed the gulf of differences between them. Which of them came out well in an article, and which badly, depended on the inclinations of the journalist and the newspaper's management. Some saw Diana sharing with her sons the kind of amusements enjoyed by tens of thousands of ordinary members of the public. Others criticised her for introducing the Princes to such unsophisticated and downmarket recreation.

With Kensington Palace feeling more and more like a prison, Diana's days out with her sons were just one way she was able to leave behind the oppressive effect her apartment was having on her. Her interest in alternative therapies and spiritual philosophies offered another and she continued to explore them, for the help they provided in countering the stress of her predicament. Diana's sister-in-law Sarah still provided information and rumours, about what was happening in the various palaces. She also shared, even exceeded, Diana's fascination with astrology and was a frequent source of predictions about what would happen next to the disenfranchised royal wives, or the key figures in their lives. The telephone was another source of support. For years the phone had been a medium Diana used for connecting to people. It enabled her to reach out for guidance and encouragement and those she phoned were used to receiving several calls a day or being party to conversations lasting hours.

Friends were essential to Diana. They listened and offered advice, but more importantly they became witnesses to her shifting thoughts and feelings as her transformation process brought new perspectives and ideas and new problems to solve. Their sympathetic presence on the end of the line, enabled Diana to verbally explore what was happening to her and bring it into a context in her mind, so that it made some sense and enabled her to continue moving forward. A friend later said, "If something was bothering her, she would talk about it over and over".

When Diana's brother, Charles, by then Earl Spencer, following the death of their father a year previously, contacted Diana and offered to rent her a country retreat at Althorp, she was elated. A house of her own in the country, within the walls of the enormous Spencer family estate was the perfect solution to many of her troubles. It would be another step to independence; a cosy home at last, to cook and clean as she used to and wanted to again. The house would have her own stamp on it and be a refuge for her and the boys; a private place to share with Oliver. The list of wonders a country retreat could offer tumbled through her mind. In a flurry of activity Diana asked for the use of the beautiful, four-bedroom, Garden House. She despatched her bodyguard to report on security and visited with her sons and interior designer Dudley Poplak to allocate bedrooms and choose colour schemes.

Within days Diana's dreams were dashed once again because of the blight her marriage had brought to her life. To make her safe at Garden House, such was her fame and status, would have required expensive and intrusive security measures which her brother thought would compromise his own family's privacy. Hurt and bitter at her own sibling's lack of understanding and support, Diana refused the alternatives he offered. His own recommendation, the fifteenth century Wormleighton Manor, seemed ideal, with its gate house for her bodyguards and walls all around. To his sister, swapping virtual imprisonment in London behind the ten foot steel railings of Kensington Palace, for incarceration in the countryside, behind the high wall of the Manor, would not have constituted the step to freedom she was desperate for.

For a while the relationship between brother and sister was strained. In a conversation with Ken Wharfe, Diana touched into the deep sense of hurt she felt from many rejections she had experienced in the past and the sense of alienation that had dogged her life, when she asked sadly "Why would anyone want all the fuss that goes with me?" It was clear to Diana that if security problems existed at Althorp, they would exist anywhere else she might try to live a normal life. That daunting thought led her to the conclusion that there could be no escape to an idyllic home of her own, until she had broken free entirely from her marriage and was able to dispense with all the constricting trappings of royalty.

The trappings of royalty gave Diana opportunities to bring attention and help to people suffering, often in lonely silence, from all kinds of problems. When she was not able to visit those who suffered, she spoke about them at conferences and other gatherings at which the media would be present because of her involvement. Coincidentally the revelations, of bulimia, self-harming, depression and marital problems, in *Diana: Her True Story* enabled Diana to offer a closer connection to her audience. Increasingly, during 1993, she felt able to share her experiences in speeches which expressed her personal and emotional perspective, but not before she had done some homework as well.

On 27 April, at London's Kensington Town Hall, Diana spoke at an international conference on eating disorders. She had vivid memories of her own struggle with bulimia and given the constant uncertainty and stress of her life then, it is likely she still used the occasional session when the strain became intense. She had studied books on the subject, given to her by Dr Maurice Lipsedge, she had also visited Great Ormond Street children's hospital and met expert Dr Brian Lask, who gave Diana more insight into the problem. Her speech was worded in a way which made it clear Diana was speaking from personal experience, when she described sufferers of eating disorders as people who, "didn't feel they had the right to express their true feelings (of guilt of self revulsion and low personal esteem) to those around them" and how this was, "Creating in them a compulsion to 'dissolve like a Disprin' and disappear." During her eight minute presentation the Princess spoke for the individual sufferer when she described eating disorders as a way of "coping with a situation they were finding unbearable" and "an 'expression' of how they felt about themselves and the life they were living." She described the illness as a "shameful friend" and shared her belief that "the ultimate solution lies within the individual." She concluded by encouraging professionals to show sufferers "how to overcome their difficulties and re-direct their energies towards a healthier, happier life."

In her speech Diana shared with a worldwide audience a problem she had addressed personally, an indication of the transformational process she was using and her aspiration for what she believed that process could bring. The full scope of Diana's speech went unnoticed by the press, which focussed only on the obvious themes it contained. Most of the reaction was positive. The problem of eating disorders was brought into the public and professional limelight and the palace postbag bulged for a while with letters from young sufferers and their concerned parents. A dissenting opinion was that of long time popular agony aunt and national treasure, Claire Rayner, who criticised the Princess for "glamourising" eating disorders. The barb hurt the sensitive Diana and it served to reinforce that part of her which always felt misunderstood. She did not understand why people chose to find fault with her well intentioned efforts. It was not the last criticism which would be aimed at her for doing her best that year.

✦ ✦ ✦

There was something strangely pleasing, I could almost say exciting, about seeing ideas and phrases I'd suggested to Diana for her bulimia speech being quoted and debated in the national newspapers. Especially since I was in the background and hidden, observing their impact. I began to recognise what kind of temptation there might be for speech writers and advisors, who had the famous and the powerful as vehicles through which to offer words to millions, words which might alter the lives of generations of people. It was heady stuff.

'The speech went well,' I said to Diana at our next session.

'Yes I really felt I was letting people know I understand their problems.'

'It came across.' I decided not to bring to her attention what I thought was the most significant point of the presentation from the point of view of her transformation. Diana had publicly and openly articulated her aspirations for herself and her own experience of bulimia. As affirmations go it couldn't have been more powerful.

✦ ✦ ✦

On another occasion I arrived in Diana's room to set up for a treatment session and found her in tears, pacing the room.

'You're upset, is there anything I can do?' She really was distressed.

'I've just heard from my brother that I can't have the house he offered me at Althorp. It's so unfair.'

'Tell me about it.'

Slowly the story emerged. Diana's brother had offered to rent her a house on the family estate. She had set her heart on having what would have become her own private place in familiar surroundings and then he had just withdrawn his offer. I thought I understood her misery and her anger, although not for the first time I wondered at the intensity of her emotional reaction. Part of my mind was analysing why she should feel so strongly, apart from the fact that she was a feelings driven INFP with a powerful emotional need for a home.

'Remember most people are doing the best they can with what they believe. It's very rare for people to intentionally hurt someone else, especially their own sister. In time, when your feelings have settled down, I expect you'll understand why he felt he needed to withdraw his offer. Is there any other way you can create what he was suggesting?'

'No,' she sniffed, 'it's just not fair.'

'If you expect life to be fair you'll be disappointed a great deal. It can be exciting, and rewarding and fascinating, but it will always be unpredictable and yes sometimes it will seem unfair. Use the situation to understand what it is the offer meant to you so you can create it through situations you can control, not have to rely on others and then be disappointed when they can't deliver what you want.'

The massage that day was of the more nurturing kind.

Diana's reaction to the loss of the dream house at Althorp made me reconsider something I'd wondered about two years earlier, when I'd guided her through the visualisation to create her future-vision. The distress she showed, when her brother withdrew his offer of a country retreat, seemed extreme, unless her need for a quiet domestic life was so powerful she really was bereft. If that was the case I suspected even more strongly that it was because of a conflict between two opposing roles she was trying to create within herself, and thereby outwardly. When I looked back at *Diana: Her True Story* and my notes on INFP and Water element types, the two distinct characteristics, homemaker and world-changer, were quite apparent. I was convinced Diana needed to integrate successfully those two sides of her nature in any vision she had of herself in the future if she was to resolve some of her problems and began to wonder how I might help her.

✦ ✦ ✦

'Stephen, what do you think about anti-depressants?' Another of her questions dropped on me unexpectedly.

I thought for a while then replied, 'If you think about what they do, basically change the brain chemistry so that people don't have access to the ideas and beliefs which make them feel depressed or angry, I think they can be a good thing as long as the one taking them is having some psychotherapeutic help at the same time. There might be a few for whom drugs are the only way to cope, but I believe the great majority of people just need help, to understand what is happening to them and with changing it, a bit like you've been doing. Drugs like anti-depressants stop people seeing their own limiting beliefs and feeling the emotions that go with them, but those beliefs and feelings don't go away, they are still there and influencing their body and health from the unconscious part of the mind. The irony is a lot of people use much more common drugs to do something similar. Caffeine, alcohol, sugar and probably cigarettes are all addictive and have mind-altering effects when used regularly, and a lot of people use them without realising they are doing it, in order to cope with situations they prefer not to look at in their lives. The problem with all of them is that they tend to hide what people don't want to see about themselves or their lives and damage their health in the process.'

'So antidepressants, helpful if there is support to get at the issues they're hiding. A nightmare if they are used as a long term solution. Or to paraphrase Bruce Willis in *Die Hard* if it's not part of the solution, it's part of the problem. Taking anti-depressants without psychotherapeutic support probably makes them part of the problem.'

'Now I'm going to wash my hands if you'd like to assume your usual position?' I grinned.

✦ ✦ ✦

At the conference on eating disorders that April Diana made the acquaintance of another speaker, the psychotherapist, social commentator and feminist writer, Susie Orbach. Within a short time, the Princess started regular therapy with the impressive and dynamic Orbach, at her North London practice. Predictably Diana told very few people of her decision, nevertheless her regular visits came to the attention of the paparazzi and soon she was being ambushed by photographers as she left the sessions with her therapist. For someone who, on a daily basis, probably experienced more scrutiny than anyone ever had before, the choice, to initiate intense, professionally guided, self-examination, was a brave and powerful step. To continue, despite the harassment of an increasingly callous and aggressive element of the media, who shouted at her to "look up" and cursed when she did not, was immensely strong.

Another strong and brave step came on a private trip to Paris that May, when Diana sent a note to Raine Spencer, at the Ritz Hotel, inviting her one-time nemesis to lunch when they were both back in London. The personalities of the two women had little in common, but they had both loved Johnny Spencer and they shared a capacity for forgiveness. In the coming years, the Princess and her stepmother would also share support, mutual understanding and witty banter as they observed the strange vagaries of their lives.

Her Paris trip was a brief spell of close to normal existence for Diana. That is if flying in by private jet; being accompanied by a bodyguard and two friends, one the wife of a billionaire the other the wife of an ambassador; enjoying a private viewing of couture dresses at Chanel; and being greeted by Gerard Depardieu in a restaurant can be described as normal. Diana was ecstatic and refreshed by the brief sense of freedom she gained from the all too short holiday; Ken Wharfe, whose skilful handling kept the visit from being spoiled by the one photographer who noticed his charge as she shopped and supped, was relieved when it was over.

Back in Britain Diana's life continued on its usual round of intrigue and anxiety. A BBC film crew was filming for the documentary that would accompany a biography Prince Charles had commissioned from journalist Jonathan Dimbleby. Due out in 1994, to mark the 25 year anniversary of Charles' investiture as Prince of Wales, the book and TV programme had already been billed as the complete rebuttal to Andrew Morton's 1992 book *Diana: Her True Story*. During filming, Dimbleby asked Patrick Jephson for Diana's input and clarification of some events especially her views on a possible divorce. Jephson advised against co-operation believing it would not be in the Princess's interests but he did eventually engineer a lunch, at which Dimbleby was able to meet the Princess socially. Diana ate heartily, laughed a lot and charmed more. In his memoirs, Jephson recalled the moment after Diana departed "in a cloud of fond farewells" when he saw, on the journalist's face the familiar dazed look he had seen on "so many others who had just received her dazzling best."

Around the same time as the BBC was busily filming its documentary at the palace, a man called Bryce Taylor was using a concealed camera to secretly photograph a leotard clad Diana, during a workout at the gym he managed in Isleworth, West London. Diana heard about the resulting pictures through a chain of concerned well wishers and an elderly lady-in-waiting. Taylor denied all knowledge when Ken Wharfe confronted him and another potentially distasteful media exposé was left hanging over Diana's head, to await its moment in the spotlight.

Diana was beginning to venture out of Kensington Palace at that time and the results were mixed. Paris had been an unqualified success. Leaving her safe but claustrophobic retreat to see her therapist and to attend an ordinary gym with her personal trainer, Carolan Brown, had led to unpleasant situations, but if she was to create the life she wanted Diana had to persevere. She had to be prepared to confront the press who awaited her.

The photographers were not so aggressive when Diana travelled to Liverpool and, with Prince Charles, attended an anniversary celebration to mark the end of the Battle of the Atlantic. When someone remarked how good the smiling and chatting Prince and Princess looked together, Charles dryly remarked "It's all done with mirrors." Part of the separation agreement made in 1992 was that Diana would be invited to participate in national level royal engagements. Although she was no longer in the mainstream of the royal family the Princess took what opportunities were offered to maintain her visible presence and to emphasise her place as mother to the two Princes, heirs to the throne after their father.

A more heartbreaking situation she kept private was the last occasion on which Diana visited the fast declining Chief Inspector Graham Smith, who had been suffering from cancer for some years and was now dying. Graham had been Diana's bodyguard before Ken Wharfe. On learning the popular "Smudger" Smith was seriously ill, Diana had invited him and his wife Eunice, to join her on an exotic holiday one year and on a cruise a couple of years later. As Graham's life drew to a close, she and Ken were able to smuggle him out of the Royal Marsden Hospital, to take him to dinner at Diana's favourite restaurant, San Lorenzo. There the three swapped stories and laughter that belied the sad end which was fast approaching. When Smith died shortly afterwards a tearful Diana attended his funeral and gave what support and comfort she could to his wife.

Halfway through the year Diana gave another high profile speech, in London, for the charity Turning Point. She drew again on knowledge gained from her work and her own experiences, when she warned about the dangers inherent in providing medication as the only help for anxious or depressed mothers. Once again Diana showed she understood very well indeed the difficulties faced by many women when she said, "it can take enormous courage for women to admit they cannot cope, that they may need help" and "sadly for others the strain becomes too much and their decision to take their own life seems to them the only way of ending their pain." More evidence of her personal knowledge was in the phrase "putting a lid on powerful feelings and emotions cannot be the healthy option".

Diana's speech, despite its slightly feminist bias, was considered and constructive. She suggested that women, who were addicted to tranquilisers or anti-depressants, lost their self-identity and could "learn how to live again" and become who they were "born to be" with specialist assistance and that they could regain "their right to fulfil their own potential and to share that with their family, children or friends".

While Diana was applauded for her words by many, there were dissenting voices, as there had been after her speech on eating disorders. Mary Kenny, described as a conservative Catholic commentator, took Diana to task for her "self-indulgent psychobabble" and for portraying women as "victims" in a world where happiness and fulfilment are demanded as a right. Once again Diana was hurt and confused by the remarks and the apparent lack of ability to understand what she was trying to convey by her speech. Her plaintive question, "What am I doing wrong?" exposed her long standing lack of confidence when it came to offering opinions on complex matters. Her inclination was to defer to those who seemed intellectually more capable and she could still be stung and hurt, especially when there was no opportunity to sit and talk with the person attacking her. Diana had yet to accept that her opinions were valid and that those who opposed them were not always right.

Diana showed more confidence when she confronted another painful issue from her past. At the time of her parent's separation and subsequent battle for custody of their children, Diana's maternal grandmother, Lady Fermoy, had spoken out in court against her own daughter, Diana's mother, and in favour of her son-in-law. Subsequently the outspoken old lady had criticised the Princess for her conduct during her marriage and even for her attire. Lady Fermoy was a close friend of the Queen Mother and a staunch traditionalist who admired Prince Charles a great deal. The matriarch had advised Diana not to marry into the royal family. Subsequently she expressed her strong opinion that since her grand-daughter had gone against her advice and married, she ought to have stayed. The Princess wanted to tell her grandmother how hurtful it had been to not receive the support and understanding of her own close relative when she had needed it. In June Diana visited her elderly grandmother and calmly but sadly told her how she felt. There was no great rapprochement between the two, before the old lady died three weeks later but for Diana, their conversation was another significant act in her struggle to lay the ghosts of her past to rest and discover her own most powerful self-identity.

✦ ✦ ✦

Through my eyes Diana's speech on women's health, and the use of anti-depressants, was another powerful affirmation for part of the vision of herself she wanted to create. I thought it would also be inspiring for anyone who could recognise themselves in the words she used. I admired what she had done, and again felt the thrill of seeing some of the ideas and words I had offered in treatment sessions and advice, being accepted by her, and shared with the world.

✦ ✦ ✦

At the end of June, Diana began reducing the number of engagements which until then had formed the bulk of her official role and identified her with more mundane public activities of mainstream British royalty. She discontinued most of the "away days", which took her out of London to perform duties such as the planting of trees and the opening of municipal buildings. Her decision seemed to signal that she might be accepting the advice of her private secretary and others, who were pressing her to prepare for a life much more independent of the royal family, by focussing on a small range of important charities and humanitarian issues. While the move to limit the time she spent out of London did enable Diana to concentrate on more serious work, it also gave her more opportunities to be with Oliver Hoare. To those who saw Diana's ultimate fulfilment in her public role, the notion that she would sacrifice wonderful opportunities for one man would have been nonsensical. The fact is they did not know what was really motivating her.

With a reduced domestic diary Diana was free to maintain a powerful media presence through the kind of large scale humanitarian project she was very well associated with by then. The assignments she undertook were often overseas, in areas badly affected by disease and poverty and in support of respected global charities, where her brief presence and tactile, caring style, could make an enormous impact. In these situations she would bring the plight of the suffering to the attention of governments and the public and prompt them to give help and money, which made a difference to a great many lives. Her activities may not have had the impact sought by those who argued for her to make long term commitments, but they were missions that gained the full and cooperative agreement and support of the Government and of Buckingham Palace.

One such mission was the trip to Zimbabwe that mid-July. The "suffering tour" as it was dubbed, had been sanctioned by the Queen in a note sent to Diana's office in May. The images of the khaki-clad Princess, opening a home for the destitute elderly and visiting a leprosy centre and an AIDS hospital, where she instinctively reached out to touch the suffering, moved many hearts. The pictures of Diana, spooning *dhovi* from giant iron pots into the bowls of starving children, at the Red Cross Nemazura feeding centre are iconic. A local journalist wrote about the Princess later "The cynical view of the press was that Diana was desperately trying to keep her role as princess alive by making such celebrity visits. Our jaundiced view melted when we saw her visit a grimy hospital where she took into her arms and hugged a young child dying of AIDS. She held hands with another, for a period of time that lasted much longer than a photo opportunity. No one in Zimbabwe had broken down the stigma of AIDS as much as Diana's empathy and close physical contact."

While Diana was undeniably emerging as a significant and effective humanitarian figure, whose efforts were backed by the Government, monarchy and major charities, she was not universally applauded. She had been working hard to put aside her Fairytale Princess identity and show the press and public her serious side. In successfully doing so, she not only exchanged trivial work for tasks with more gravitas, but she exchanged occasional trivial criticism for a more searching examination of what she was doing and why.

The press pack which accompanied the Zimbabwe trip, contained a larger than usual number of journalists from serious publications, alongside the usual tabloid hacks. The articles which appeared during and after the visit reflected the closer scrutiny Diana was being subjected to. Robert Hardman, respected correspondent for the *Daily Telegraph*, wrote "The latest tour has been a public relations triumph not just for her favourite charities but for the Princess herself." *Daily Mail* columnist, Lynda Lee Potter suggested Diana's "relentless" work with victims was her way of avoiding crucial issues in her own life. Woodrow Wyatt, for the *News of the World*, described Diana as "addicted to the limelight". The *Daily Mirror* ran a poll asking people if they thought Diana was a hypocrite, for taking luxurious holidays after serving gruel to the poor in Africa. Eighty one percent agreed she was.

This last item was probably the most hurtful and frustrating for Diana. Criticism was something Diana sought to avoid not only because it was hurtful, but because it distracted from the issues she was trying to draw attention to. Almost as soon as the pre-arranged iron pot photo opportunity was proposed she knew instinctively it might be criticised. She was proven right but she allowed herself to be persuaded and the actual experience was a heartbreaking one for her. When she distributed food to the tiny children, including one four year old boy, Tsungai Hove, who had walked seven miles to the feeding station to be given food by the beautiful smiling Princess, it was a powerful and moving moment for everyone involved, not least those who gazed up at her with wide eyes and empty stomachs.

The "Oliver Twist" style images gave some journalists the chance to fill columns of news print with personal criticism aimed at her, when they could have written about the wider picture and the charity work she was highlighting. The criticism of the Zimbabwe tour also raised one question which had already been disturbing Diana, her right to engage in worthwhile humanitarian work and public debates about important topics. Dissenting voices had already been suggesting she was a media junkie and a manipulator whose public work was merely self serving. Critics of her speeches had also questioned whether a glamorous Princess, with a luxurious lifestyle, had anything worthwhile to say about HIV+AIDS, poverty, homelessness, woman's health or eating disorders. During her years as the successful and idolised Fairytale Princess, Diana had little reason to doubt herself, or her right to share love and compassion with the hurt, the dying and the distressed. On the bigger stage, as a more serious international figure, with wider issues at stake, disapproval caused painful reactions in long dormant but still fragile parts of her make-up. In self-development terms Diana was being exposed to her own limiting self-beliefs and given the opportunity to transform them into strong and purposeful aspects of her personality.

✦ ✦ ✦

'Why can't they understand I just want to love everyone?' Diana had been pacing the room when I arrived for another treatment.

I smiled and said, 'That's a wonderful idea, you could start with Charles.' I started to unfold my massage table.

'Have you heard about Lester Levenson?' I added.

'No.' She was already letting go of her agitation.

'Lester was a scientist and very successful businessman who became so ill by the time he reached his early forties that he had suffered two heart attacks and found himself on the verge of dying and unable to leave his home. Obviously he wasn't able to do much so he spent his time trying to understand why he had become so ill. Being a scientist he started by studying books on medicine and got nowhere. He then turned to psychology and eventually spiritual philosophies. He came to the conclusion his illness was caused by judgemental thoughts he made about the people in his life. Since he couldn't get out of his home he sat day after day thinking about all the people he had felt angry at or upset about, one after the other, until he could only feel loving towards them.'

'He started with his parents and recalled as many situations as possible which had hurt him until every time he thought about his father or mother he felt love and unconditional acceptance, instead of anger or resentment for what they did or said. He thought about his girlfriend who had betrayed him with his best friend, and replaced his jealousy and anger with love, until he could imagine them together and only feel love for them both. As he let go of his damaging thoughts and the emotions that went with them, he became well, was able to leave his home and found he started to experience amazing things in his life. Not least of which was a lot of money selling his method to other people. I think he's in his eighties now.'

'A client of mine gave me a couple of his books. There is a technique he developed I think, but really all you have to do is what he did. Sit quietly and think about people who you feel bad about, one at a time, until all you feel for each of them is love and unconditional acceptance. It's an amazing experience.'

By the time I finished my story Diana was thinking hard and I was ready to start work.

✦ ✦ ✦

Holidays with her sons were usually great fun and opportunities for Diana to relax, but that August, following after the Zimbabwe trip, she was preoccupied by several situations which made her uneasy. She was, for one thing, barely two months into her intensive psychotherapy with Susie Orbach and that would undoubtedly have been throwing up all manner of emotional issues for her to deal with. Her situation at Kensington Palace had not changed, she still felt hemmed in and deeply suspicious, so the unfamiliar level of criticism from the press seemed to be part of an orchestrated attack on her. Her reaction had been instinctive when she gave sympathetic *Daily Mail* journalist, Richard Kay, forewarning of a holiday in Bali earlier that summer and precise details of her itinerary for a trip with her sons to Disneyworld in Florida and Lyford Cay in the Bahamas. To try to counter bad publicity with good coverage, in that case of her holidaying with the Princes, was a quite natural thing to do for Diana at that time, such was the challenging atmosphere which prevailed in the continuing War of the Wales's.

Unfortunately for Diana her bodyguard, Ken Wharfe, not only discovered she had primed the press about her whereabouts, but also that she had tried to mislead him when she suggested he did not need to make his usual reconnaissance for the Florida holiday, on the grounds that it was unnecessary and would cost the taxpayer too much. Coming on top of the breakdown in trust in Lech earlier in the year, the incident meant their relationship was under serious strain when they embarked for Orlando, USA on 25 August.

Diana's underhand activities made it clear she intended to use the private holiday as a PR exercise against her husband's side. In her eyes it was a legitimate opportunity to publicly reinforce her status as the mother of the Princes and her position in their lives. Her plans were frustrated when Wharfe's security arrangements at Disneyworld resulted in the waiting press pack being unable to take the photographs they needed. In her frustration and stress she became irritable and fractious.

The situation did not improve when the party moved on to the Bahamas. Wharfe was more used to trying to keep the press pack away from the Princess. On this holiday his charge seemed intent on engineering opportunities for the photographers. It didn't help the relationship between Diana and her senior protection officer when, within a few hours of the party arriving, the young Princes appeared at the separate house occupied by the team of police bodyguards ready to swim and play football on the beach, with the men. Diana, the ultimate mother and home-maker, was already sensitive to the amount of time the boys were spending away from her, at boarding school and with her estranged husband. She could not have felt happy when William 11, and Harry fast approaching 9 and their chums Andrew Charlton and Harry Soames, preferred the "police house" to spending time at the villa occupied by their nanny, their mother and her two friends, Catherine Soames and Kate Menzies.

If Diana was beginning to react during that holiday to the natural and imposed distancing of her sons, her discomfort would have been reinforced by news she received when she returned to London. Charles had engaged a young woman, Alexandra 'Tiggy' Legge-Bourke, to be nanny and companion to the Princes when they were with him. From Charles' point of view Tiggy was an inspired choice. Brought up on a huge country estate and with a love of riding, shooting and fishing, Tiggy was a more solid Earth-mother type to Diana's soft and gentle nurturer. The qualities Tiggy brought to her role matched her employer's interests and were encapsulated years later when she described what she gave the boys: "fresh air, a rifle and a horse". She contrasted her approach with what she said Diana gave her sons: "a tennis racket and a bucket of popcorn at the movies."

Nothing was simple in Diana's life from the moment she married Prince Charles. Every incident had ramifications which went far beyond seemingly similar situations in the average person's experience and the longer she remained married the more complicated things became. The tangled threads of personal need, public duty, royal expectations and constitutional roles, confused by anger, fear, suspicions and intrigue, gave a bewildering context to every event. Tiggy attracted Diana's instant personal dislike. She saw the young nanny's appointment as a challenge to the heart of her own identity, her most treasured role, as a mother. Tiggy's presence also struck at the crux of Diana's position, her status as mother and maternal influence in the lives of the future King William and his brother Harry. To Diana the nanny was both a personal insult from Charles and a threat, instigated by him, to her own future. From the moment Tiggy arrived on the scene, the dynamics of the Wales's turbulent marriage took yet another twist.

The press quickly took notice of Tiggy's presence on the scene and mischievously reported small incidents which indicated her familiarity and affection for her young charges, or between her and her employer, Prince Charles. Every incident hurt Diana deeply and fuelled her intense anger at the young woman for being there and at her husband for allowing an employee to usurp their own mother in her sons' affections. Unable to alter Charles' decision, Diana demanded to know, in detail, what Tiggy's duties were. She insisted on being regularly updated about everything the nanny proposed doing with her sons. She would not speak to Tiggy directly, but was kept informed by her butler who took messages. Over time the initial anger and anxiety faded, but like all Water elements Diana's anger and sense of injustice did not disappear but it festered, until it emerged years later in circumstances which did her no credit.

The impression that she was being manipulated and attacked was a constant in Diana's life at that time. Incidents took on a significance they probably did not warrant but which, at the time seemed reasonable to her. An opportunity to join the long list of influential figures who had given the prestigious annual Dimbleby Lecture was lost when, in Patrick Jephson's words, "the project evaporated to the accompaniment of suitably scathing and suspiciously well placed comment in establishment newspapers." Similarly a chance to lecture at Harvard was cancelled because news of it had been leaked to the press. Diana was refused permission to travel to Bosnia to meet British troops and bring comfort to refugees under the auspices of the Red Cross, an organisation with which she had strong links. Prince Charles went instead in his capacity as Colonel-in-Chief of the Cheshire Regiment on tour there. Diana's private trip to meet Irish President, Mary Robinson, in Dublin was not allowed to go ahead, for "security reasons". It seemed to Diana and those who supported her, that any engagement which might improve the Princess's international standing was automatically obstructed by the palace old-guard who favoured the Prince.

Yet Diana had notable successes that year which showed that if there was a campaign against her it was not a very effective one. Diana was invited to that year's Hollingsworth Dinner at Spencer House by Conrad Black, media magnate and then proprietor of the *Daily Telegraph*. At the function she charmed innumerable establishment figures and met and made a firm friend and admirer of Henry Kissinger, previously a Secretary of State to two American presidents and by then a world renowned authority and advisor on international affairs. A successful trip to Luxembourg, where Diana shared the platform at the British Trade Fair with the Luxembourg Crown Prince, was sanctioned by Queen. Similarly, a trip to Brussels two months later, in her capacity as patron of Help the Aged and in support of the international charity HelpAge, saw Diana moving once again amongst powerful figures from all over the world .

Kensington Palace became a venue for meetings with the ambassadors of America, Russia, Hungary, Argentina, China and Pakistan. Diana had meetings with notable figures from politics, the media and the entertainment industry. The Foreign Secretary, Douglas Hurd made it clear the Foreign Office would be happy to support her role as an informal ambassador and to facilitate her travels. On 20 October she had another meeting with Prime Minister John Major at Kensington Palace to discuss her situation and what she might achieve as a humanitarian ambassador for Britain. It seemed all Diana's wishes to be taken seriously on the world stage, regardless of her semi-detached royal status, were coming true. Despite all this Diana had, by early autumn, begun to talk about withdrawing from public life. Her reasons had nothing to do with her public role and everything to do with her private life.

Moving in influential circles and engaging in meaningful humanitarian work, were not compensating Diana for deficiencies in other areas. The constraints of her existence at Kensington Palace, the strain of the continuing conflict with Charles' supporters, constant aggressive press intrusion and criticism, were all draining her of energy and making her life increasingly intolerable. Even so, Diana believed all would have been bearable if she only had more time and space to develop her relationship with Oliver Hoare. Sadly Diana did not recognise that "more time" meant all of his time. She adored Oliver to the point of obsession and wanted his constant attention. By the latter part of 1993 Diana had determined that her public role was at the root of all the problems which stopped her relationship with Hoare from blooming. As she considered removing, once and for all, what she had come to see as the major obstacle to her dreams of happiness, other circumstances began to unfold.

That October, Oliver Hoare's wife Diane finally lost patience and demanded that her husband ask the police to trace the origin of the silent calls they had been receiving for more than a year since September 1992. The police attached tracing equipment to the phone lines. Shortly afterwards Oliver Hoare moved from the family home to a friend's Pimlico apartment to 'cool off'. His chauffeur described the relationship between the Hoare's as "like a war zone". After Oliver moved out the nuisance calls stopped.

During the same month, Diana's deteriorating relationship with her bodyguard took another step towards its inevitable finale. She confronted

Ken Wharfe about derogatory remarks he was supposed to have made about her to the press. The incident she was referring to had occurred while they were in the Bahamas. The irritated bodyguard, in response to a question "How's Ma'am?" from Arthur Edwards, *The Sun's* royal photographer, had indicated sufficient of his frustration with a shrug and "rueful grin" that the canny press man was able to interpret correctly that Wharfe was not best pleased with Diana. The Princess was not pleased either with what she regarded as her bodyguard's disloyalty. Their subsequent, unpleasant interview was another in a list of unsettling events for the two that year. A number of incidents, compounded by Diana having her own apartment secretly swept for listening devices by a private company, demonstrated to Wharfe that little trust remained between them. He was beginning to doubt he could do his job effectively under the circumstances and was becoming irritated by Diana's demands on his time and attention. During the days which followed Ken Wharfe began to wonder whether he should remain in his post as Diana's senior protection officer.

The intense pressure Diana was under during the summer had been noticed by press. The signs would have been difficult to miss. On one occasion the usually calm Diana had become so exasperated that she shouted "You make my life hell!" at an intrusive photographer. By October the tabloids were calling attention to her "angry and strained" appearance and suggesting, under headlines like "Di's at Breaking Point as Charles Wins PR War", that she was "a woman under extreme pressure" and was "increasingly emotional and unhappy" after being worn down by the "campaign against her by pro-Charles courtiers." The stories added to the strain for which they were offering only a simplistic explanation.

The reason for Diana's distress was more complex than the press imagined. At its root was her inner struggle, to recognise a coherent and worthwhile future amidst the shifting sands of events which seemed to change around her every day. She was no longer certain of her place in her sons' lives. She was unsure that success in her public life would be as satisfying to her as she once believed. It seemed that as her profile and influence increased, the possibility of an enjoyable private life receded and the backlash from her husband's side intensified. There were few stable strands in her life at that time for Diana to cling to.

✦ ✦ ✦

'I met Henry Kissinger at a very grown-up lunch the other day. He was very nice, a bit surprised when I asked him some personal questions but we got along really well.' Diana had obviously enjoyed meeting the famous statesman and finding a rapport with him.

'What do you know about Transactional Analysis?' I responded.

'Never heard of it.'

'It's a system of psychotherapy based on the idea that we all have three different mental states, a parent, a child and an adult. The parent in us behaves the way it learned from our parents or teachers, judging how things should be and what people ought to be doing and trying to make people do or be what they think is correct, like a parent tends to be with children. The child acts to other people the way it learned to in childhood. Depending on how they were brought up or taught, the child can have fun and be spontaneous; or it can be frightened, angry or upset, depending on how they usually felt when they were young.'

'The interesting part is that we each have parent, adult and child parts of ourselves available and what we use in our communications with people is prompted by the way we are treated or the way we see others. So if someone acts like an all knowing parent towards us we might act as a hurt child, or an equally knowing parent back. If we act like a child towards someone it will prompt them to be childlike with us or become parental and overbearing or protective, depending on what they learned to be from their parents.'

'The problem is that both our parent and child are reactive states, learned as we grew up and mimicked those around us, ready to be trotted out when we need them. When we communicate from the parent or child it is not an interaction, a transaction, which is based on real information and feelings we recognise and consider at the time, it's a reaction based on basic emotions prompted by past experiences. If two people are trying to communicate with what are basically unconscious, learned responses they aren't really communicating at a deep level of understanding at all. It's very superficial.'

'It's only from the adult state that we can make a real and meaningful connection with another human being, one where each person takes notice of what is said to them and how they feel about it, then chooses to communicate what will enable them to understand each other better. It takes more effort but it's more worthwhile and leads to better relationships.'

'When you tell me it was a "very grown-up do" I'm hearing that you were not feeling like an adult but more like a child. You may have had fun, but the people you were talking to were more than likely reacting to you like other children having fun, or like parents, either doting on you or judging you. Unless that is they had developed the facility to remain in their adult state and offer you a truly adult communication, and you were able to be an adult in return.'

I didn't want to put her on the spot by asking what state she had been experiencing with Henry Kissinger but I was glad to have had the chance to make her aware of something she seemed to do habitually and which would have been affecting her relationships.

✦ ✦ ✦

November started badly. On the first of the month, just when Diana was seeking stability, one of her dearest friends Lucia Flecha de Lima, wife of the Brazilian Ambassador in London, moved with her husband to his new posting in Washington. Lucia and her family had provided a haven, where Diana was welcomed as a member of what became a surrogate family. She even had her own room in their home in Mount Street. The loss of the happy domesticity and maternal advice provided by the worldly Lucia, twenty years Diana's senior, was a great blow to the Princess.

Another blow she received, on the same day her friend left, was news that her long time chauffeur, Simon Solari, was resigning to take up an appointment with Prince Charles' household. On top of the rift in her relationship with her stalwart, Ken Wharfe, these additional losses could not help but reopen old feelings of betrayal, abandonment and rejection in Diana's mind. Her growing inner strength was shown by the ability she showed in coming to terms with the setbacks, after some therapeutic weeping. She spoke to Simon, and showed she understood his reasons, for doing what he felt was best for his family and future. Lucia's departure was not the end of a friendship but an opportunity to visit the USA to continue it.

On 4 November Diana made another speech, at a lunch in aid of the charity WellBeing and dryly commented on several press stories. The *London Evening Standard* had claimed she was suffering from migraine, author Barbara Cartland had declared Diana's bulimia had taken hold again and other reports suggested she was likely to have a breakdown at any time. Diana told her amused audience that although she was supposed to have her "head down the loo" and was likely to "be dragged off...by men in white coats" she would postpone her "nervous breakdown for a more appropriate moment."

On Sunday 7 November the *Sunday Mirror* tabloid newspaper published the intrusive gym photographs taken by Bryce Taylor. On Monday another spread of the overhead shots of the leotard clad Diana working a leg-press machine was printed in the *Daily Mirror*. The outraged Princess had had enough. In private she spoke more determinedly than ever about withdrawing from public life and she consulted her lawyers. Within a matter of days she instructed them to sue Bryce Taylor and Mirror Group Newspapers.

✦ ✦ ✦

I saw Diana immediately after the publication of the gym photos and she was in a bad way, with her neck and shoulders rigid with tension, anger and fear. She couldn't believe someone had been so calculating and thoughtless. On top of being ambushed by paparazzi outside Susie Orbach's after her therapy sessions and chased by photographers whenever she went out, Diana was at the end of her tether. I hadn't seen her as low as that for a long time.

The treatment I gave softened the tight muscles but I wasn't able to say much to soothe the bitter thoughts and emotions in her mind. It was one of those sessions where just being there and caring was all I could do.

I knew there was a suggestion that Diana might have contrived to have the photos taken or have invited the episode in some way but the reaction I felt in her could not have been anything but genuine anguish and rage.

✦ ✦ ✦

'Say hello to Mr Twigg,' Diana commanded William and Harry as they came into the room. She lifted her face from the massage table and smiled at the boys. They were on exeat from school and wanted their mother's attention.

'Hello Mr Twigg, they dutifully chorused before bounding over to their mother and kissing her cheek.

'Hi guys,' I responded.

I noticed William looking at me a little warily, which wasn't surprising. He'd only seen me on a couple of occasions despite the years I'd been coming to the Palace, so I was a virtual stranger smoothing oil from the base of his mother's naked back to her neck. Harry was unperturbed and jumped onto the big double bed to have a good bounce.

'Don't do that Wills,' mumbled Diana. William had climbed under the massage bench, into the dark space made by the overhanging towels and was lying on his back on the floor kicking the underneath of the table. I had the distinct impression he wanted me finished and gone.

Five minutes later it was the boys who were banished while I completed the treatment and packed away. Diana didn't stay to chat. She had her sons to see.

✦ ✦ ✦

Diana's reaction to the gym photos was typical of her emotions-driven impulsiveness. It was clear to many that legal action, which might have resulted in Diana appearing in court to give evidence under oath, would have been fraught with dangers. On its own the history of her involvement with the press was enough to cast doubt on whether she was a complete innocent whose privacy had been seriously violated. An unexpected voice would have added to the concerns of any who doubted the wisdom of a lawsuit. Ken Wharfe made it clear he thought Diana might have "invented an elaborate sting to ensnare a newspaper and then milk the publicity – and the public's sympathy". He would be a noticeable absentee from any witness list if he was not called to give evidence for Diana. If he gave evidence which revealed his suspicions the case could have been badly undermined.

The case against Taylor and Mirror Group was settled out of court many months later without Diana having to appear on court. The case against Wharfe resulted in his relationship with Diana deteriorating even further. The pair wrote the painful final chapter of their five-year professional association in monosyllabic exchanges and lack of cooperation.

Ken Wharfe symbolised much that was distressing Diana in the final months of 1993. At the beginning of their relationship, when she had been vulnerable and scared, he was not only comfortingly professional, but caring and supportive. Over time his opinions and kind words of advice had helped her, even though he invariably advised her to stay within the royal family and, if possible, reconcile with her husband. Lately his presence seemed to distract the attention of her sons when she needed them with her, and his opinions seemed to have become more opinionated, even proprietorial. In his memoirs the police protection officer wrote he was concerned "by the growing influence of Oliver Hoare and a number of other advisors and hangers-on." Perhaps he meant in the context of how they made his job more difficult, but it seemed more personal. Within days and after another minor incident had resulted in the Princess being humiliated, and the bodyguard being irritated beyond the extent of his patience, Ken Wharfe informed Diana of his decision to resign. He spoke to his superiors, tendered his formal request to be transferred and took a short leave while the press briefly splashed the news of his departure across its pages. Within days he was gone from Kensington Palace, after five years walking a personal and professional tightrope caring for the life and lifestyle of a woman he never really understood.

When Wharfe left her side it stunned Diana for a while. He had been a permanent presence in her life for so long it was strange to be without him, and the manner of his leaving made her feel sad, angry, guilty and rejected all at the same time. His departure opened another possibility however, that of dispensing with formal police protection altogether but that would come later.

In the meantime Diana's rollercoaster life continued while she carried on working even as she contemplated leaving public life. She laid the foundation stone for a new library at Emmanuel College, Cambridge, at the invitation of the college Master, Lord St John of Fawsley. On 14 November the Princess fulfilled an engagement sanctioned by the Queen, when she attended the Remembrance Day service at Enniskillen in Northern Ireland, where six years before an IRA bomb had killed eleven people at the same ceremony. In between times she took a private interest in projects like the proposed shelter for the homeless at St. Pancras Church in North London. She also decided to announce her exit from public life during a speech she was due to give on 3 December at London's Hilton Hotel.

The final days of November saw the *Financial Times* publish an article, based on an interview with Prince Charles. He explained the work he had been doing for British commercial interests overseas and denied he was trying to redefine his job. In a thinly veiled reference to the way he had been eclipsed by his wife he complained "It's just that, since the day I got married, people have chosen to ignore the things I continue to do, day in and day out." His obvious frustration gives weight to the rumour that Charles had told his circle he wanted Diana "completely removed from public life". As November gave way to December Diana intended to make his wish come true.

As usual there were many opinions which tried to influence Diana's decision. The Queen had already spoken to her daughter-in-law about her intention to withdraw from public life and they had agreed Diana would still make herself available to join the royal family at D-Day anniversary services in June 1994. Nonetheless when, on 1 December, the Sovereign saw an early draft of the announcement her daughter-in-law intended to make she was so concerned about the potential damage it could do that she immediately sent an urgent message asking Prince Charles to attend a meeting. That afternoon Charles telephoned Diana to try to "find out more about her real purpose and whether she could find other, less resounding means to achieve it." He failed to change her mind. At an hour long meeting on 2 December the Queen and Prince Philip again tried to persuade the Princess to alter her decision to make a dramatic statement and instead scale down her appearances over several months. Diana graciously but firmly declined.

The Queen and her courtiers were clearly concerned about the impact a spectacular exit would have on the public's perception of the royal family, especially Prince Charles. Patrick Jephson also viewed Diana's plans for a dramatic and irrevocable departure as unwise. In his view the Princess would not be able to stay out of the limelight so he advised a gradual retreat without fanfare, certain she would reverse course at some point after she had time to rest and reconsider, without anyone realising what had happened. If she was determined to make a public announcement he argued, it should be a "Churchillian" statement, offering "reconciliation with her husband and his family." Without Diana's knowledge Jephson also sent a briefing note to the Queen stating his view that the Princess still had a desire to serve and his opinion that "such service would be essential to her mental equilibrium."

Even while so many were trying to persuade Diana to reconsider, Sir Robert Fellowes, the Queen's private secretary, instructed Patrick Jephson and Geoffrey Crawford, the Queen's deputy press secretary, to modify the Princess's speech, so her declaration would be less unequivocal and her reasons less damaging to Charles and the family than the first draft would have been.

✦ ✦ ✦

'What do you think of this?' Diana handed me a few pages containing another speech.

I took a few minutes to read the pages then read them again. 'This will put the cat amongst the flappy things,' I said. The speech I had in my hands was spiked with anger and resentment at the press and declared Diana's irrevocable intention to withdraw from public life. It also implied she was unhappy with the royal family and her husband.

I could see all kinds of problems in the words, phrasing and the tone of the speech I was looking at. It did not reflect Diana's adult strengths but gave voice, and therefore substance, to the viewpoint of the hurt child in her. Much of the wording was highly emotive and therefore self-centred. It was an exercise in blame and looking back to past hurts, not an explanation or strong statement of intent for the future and it didn't reflect her true feelings for the public. The words thanked people but didn't acknowledge the feelings people had shared with her or her feelings for them. Even more worrying there was no room for manoeuvre if she changed her mind, which given she was in a state of transition and transformation was highly likely. In the body-mind, personal transformation context, the speech, in the form it was then, would not be a powerful affirmation by a strong individual spoken before a worldwide audience of millions. I recognised Diana's need to escape from the confines of her situation but rather than a defining step I saw opportunity going to waste and firm steps backwards towards old beliefs and feelings.

I sat on the bed with a pencil circling words and bracketing phrases and drawing arrows to indicate where they might be better placed. I scratched out lines and scribbled in some suggestions for other words, until I realised the result was illegible.

'Can I take this away and fax you some suggestions?'

'I need it tomorrow,' Diana replied.

'That's not a problem, you're my last client today so I'm on my way home. I'll have this back to you tonight.'

Back in my apartment I wrote a new version of the speech, using as many of the words and phrases from the original as I could, but I shaped it to be closer to the Diana I knew. Unashamedly I included suggestions which reflected aspirations she might not have considered but might choose to accept. I faxed her the result late that evening.

The evening before Diana was due to speak I sent her an encouraging note by fax. *Walk tall, hold your head up and be strong* or something similar.

✦ ✦ ✦

When she eventually stood up on 3 December, at a charity event in support of the Headway National Head Injuries Association, the speech Diana gave was the product of many minds. Some of them wished Diana well and some fervently wished she would depart never to be seen again. None of them knew one of the main reasons for her dramatic announcement.

In a halting, emotional voice Diana acknowledged the help she had received from everyone she had met since entering public life. She apologised for taking the opportunity "to share with you my plans for the future". Visibly nervous but still speaking strongly she told her audience how intrusive the media attention had become and how it had affected her public duties and personal life "in a manner, that's been hard to bear." She went on to explain that after the end of the year she would be reducing her public life, focussing on a smaller range of areas and seeking a suitable way of combining a meaningful public role with a more private life. She confirmed that her first priority "will continue to be our children, William and Harry" and she acknowledged the Queen and Duke of Edinburgh for their kindness and support, and the public for their kindness and generous affection. In what became an iconic phrase she asked the public to "give me the time and space that has been lacking in recent years".

Less than a minute later, after a brief thank-you response from Jeffrey Archer, Diana left the room to a standing ovation.

The media scrutiny Diana had endured since 1981 had been unrelenting. Although latterly some of it had been with her consent, she had not wanted any of it originally and it was only by default she finally came to accept it as an unpleasant necessity. She discovered that while she could control the attention to some extent, she could not predict it nor stop it entirely. Most recently she had experienced a level of aggression, pursuit would not be too strong a word, by some elements of the press that made it impossible for her to imagine the kind of life she really wanted. Similarly she was still constrained by a marriage she would not have agreed to if she had been told the truth by her husband. Her speech, like her book the previous year, was a decisive act to give voice to some of her anger and resentment and to change her circumstances. Once again, true to her nature, she had acted impulsively but emphatically. She had not simply sat in helpless despair. Very few of those who heard her speech had any idea what Diana hoped would happen as a result.

✦ ✦ ✦

The day after she gave what came to be known as the "Time and Space" speech and what I personally referred to as the Greta Garbo speech, as in "I want to be alone", I checked out the newspapers. My private note was quoted verbatim so must have been leaked to the press. The speech had been changed yet again but the end result was much closer to what I had hoped for and contained more elements of what I had tried to suggest, a strong and balanced affirmation made before millions and echoed back to her by the press. People can move mountains with that kind of energy behind them I thought.

If she did choose to come back into a high profile role it would, like her choice to *be alive* years earlier, be at her own volition. She would not be able to fall back on blaming others for putting her in a position she did not want to be in. It was going to be interesting to see what would happen next I thought as I drove through the Kensington Palace gates shortly after the big event.

During that treatment we chatted idly about the normal and mundane things she wanted to do, things most people take for granted like sitting in the park and reading. I spoke about how much pleasure I got from cooking. It was a low level relaxed massage session and I sensed the relief in her, the release of tensions she had been holding for months of pressure cooker tension.

'Well now he knows I'm willing to give up everything for him.' Her words came out of the blue and unconnected to what we'd been talking about a few minutes before.

I didn't respond, didn't ask Diana who she was talking about. I had no idea who she was seeing and I didn't want to know. Some time ago I'd realised it was better not to know too many secrets so I finished the massage as if she hadn't spoken but my mind was already working over time.

Finally some evidence that she had been dealing with two incompatible aspirations in her vision of her future. If she really had made the speech and stepped back from her highly effective and successful public life to be with a man, it indicated her dreams and desires for her relationship with him outweighed her need to be a famous and influential humanitarian, at least at that moment.

So many things became clear as I sat later and pondered the implications of that new insight. If her need for home, family and partnership was the most important part of her future-vision then it explained why she was so angry and resentful towards her husband, Camilla and the royal family. In her eyes they had not only deprived her of the dreams she had for her life with Charles but they were still keeping her trapped, albeit the speech showed she was struggling to escape. No wonder I'd been having to deal with the physical consequences of her anger and frustration all the time.

I thought about the effects two such distinct ideas would have had on her day to day dealings with others, her staff in particular. *I'll bet they're as confused as hell* I thought *she'll have been all over the place, unpredictable, emotional, the lot.*

The only way I could foresee Diana being able to create her vision was to let go entirely of one or other of the conflicting aspects and she seemed to be trying to relinquish the public role right then, or to leave the royal family and Charles completely behind and get on with her life without them. Not so easy that last bit given her children and the constitutional issues around divorce.

Clearly though, before anything else could happen she had to have an idea, a clear vision of the future she wanted to create. Her speech indicated the main feature of her vision at that time was life with a partner, not life in the public eye – how realistic that was remained to be seen. My role would be to help her clarify her dream and stay on track and pick up the pieces if things went wrong, but at least I had a much clearer idea of what she was trying to achieve. Introducing the spiritual context into our work seemed an even better idea than it had when the year began.

If she could learn how to let go of her anger and forgive those she held responsible for her situation she might be able to move on. I was certain of one thing, anger and resentment bound her to those she blamed even more strongly than the constitutional issues or the walls of Kensington Palace. Once she let go of those feelings her vision and her path would be clearer.

✦ ✦ ✦

If Diana hoped her speech would result in some respite from the press attention she had been subjected to since marrying Prince Charles, she was soon disabused of the notion. At a press briefing for selected royal correspondents immediately after the speech the first question put to Patrick

Jephson by the representative of the Press Association was "Have we killed the goose that lays the golden eggs?" Other members of the press were still intent on pursuing the goose regardless of her stated desire for "time and space" and they had the scent of another golden egg.

Just days after the speech and amongst all the pro and con reactions, the *Daily Mirror* ran a story alluding to "one man at the moment who has been seeing Diana for some time". The *Mirror* did not name Oliver Hoare, but he was identified in a piece in *Today* a short time afterwards. Their reporter described Diana sitting in a parked car with Hoare for an hour, "her head trustingly on Mr Hoare's shoulder."

If Prince Charles hoped that Diana's speech would result in some respite from the damaging press he had been subjected to since marrying her, he was soon disabused of his notion. On 7 December a relatively minor, but vociferous, church official, the Archdeacon of York, finally opened the constitutional Pandora's Box on BBC Radio 4's *Today* programme, and in several other studios soon after, when he questioned Charles' fitness to be King. The gist of his argument, echoed in numerous headlines, was that if rumours of the Prince's adultery were true "He has broken the trust on one thing and broken vows to God on one thing. How can he then go into Westminster Abbey and take the Coronation vows?"

Both the Prince and Princess must have breathed a heavy sigh of relief after they had finished their final engagements of 1993 and were able to step away from the public stage for their Christmas break.

Diana journeyed to Sandringham on Christmas Eve, to be with her sons and the royal family for the traditional Christmas Day church service before she left to return to Kensington Palace. There she ate her Christmas lunch alone and took a swim at Buckingham Palace. The next day she flew to Washington to spend a week with her friend Lucia Flecha de Lima. She admitted "I cried all the way out and all the way back, I felt so sorry for myself."

1994

What you are
must always displease you,
if you would attain
that which you are not.

St. Augustine

"This is my life and I will live it as I choose" was the message in Diana's Time and Space speech. She started 1994 with the intention of doing just that. She was tired of living a goldfish bowl existence in which her every word and action was analysed by the press and the men in grey. She was tired of those who wanted to manipulate and control her. She was tired of the intrigue and suspicion which surrounded and enveloped her. She was tired of putting on hold that part of her life she wanted most to fulfil, normal home and normal family. She wanted the public roundabout to continue without her, for a while at least. She wanted to be left alone by the press. She wanted some peace, to be loved and cared for by a man she adored to distraction. Sadly her dreams could not be realised by simply standing up and telling the world she was opting out. It takes a little longer for some miracles to occur.

Diana's Time and Space speech, given as it was in such emotional circumstances and before witnesses, was an immensely powerful affirmation. It was, in effect, a command to her psyche and a demand that her body and mind create "a more suitable way of combining a meaningful public role, with hopefully, a more private life". Unfortunately, despite her experiences up to then, Diana did not appreciate the fundamental aspects of the metamorphic process she had begun four years earlier. In particular, even though she had experienced many changes to her outlook and her circumstances, she did not recognise that transforming the inner processes, of mind and body, was a necessary precursor to transforming her life experience. Her make-up was not drawn to the necessary self-examination that would enable her to look inward and identify those beliefs and assumptions which kept her from the life she wanted. Nor was she inclined to accumulate and develop the skills that would have helped her alter her limiting beliefs methodically and more comfortably.

Instead Diana continued to operate instinctively, responding unconsciously to her circumstances with actions driven by her emotions and needs, without asking why she felt the emotions or whether her needs represented the best she could become and the best her life could be. Just like those immortalists, who demanded "life forever in this physical body", then suffered unpleasant life and health consequences when their unthinking command disrupted a long established body-mind equilibrium based on an assumed future death, Diana's speech, her instruction to herself, was to have similarly discomforting effects for her. Achieving the future she wanted would require profound changes to occur within her. Her affirmation demanded that those changes occur rapidly. As a result, at the beginning of 1994, Diana entered one of the most challenging phases of her transformation.

From the moment she made her speech Diana was unconsciously re-evaluating everything about herself in the light of her demand for a life which combined a "meaningful public role" with "a more private life". It is true she had given a similar direction to herself when she created her future-vision in early 1990. That visualisation process had led her, in the years which followed, to give emphasis to her public role over her private needs, mainly as way of dealing with the obstacles presented by the Squidgy tape and her weak negotiating position in the royal hierarchy. Nearly four years on, at the end of 1993, Diana became distressed that her life still lacked the fulfilling private dimension she craved. She identified the causes of her problems as the constraints imposed by her position in the royal family, her place in public life and by press intrusion. She reacted accordingly, by declaring her intention to step back from the media scrutiny so that she could consider how to bring her private and public lives together. Her action was an instinctive attempt to correct an imbalance she felt intuitively, emotionally and physically.

✦ ✦ ✦

Diana's emotions were the key to her health and future wellbeing. Her anger, in particular, was a focal point for immediate problems she was experiencing and significant health and life issues that might, almost certainly would, develop over the long term. Having concluded that in my early year contemplation, I began to consider what I could do to help her. If anger was the obvious focal point for her problems at that time, it was also an entry point for the solution – that was the basic body-mind approach to health. I sat quietly considering what I knew about the emotion.

Anger equates to the liver equates to muscles in the upper chest and between the shoulder blades, just what Diana was experiencing. Anger is based on judgement, of another person or other people, the judgement that someone has or intended to hurt her. Anger is a tool, usually for avoiding emotional or physical pain. When it is part of a well functioning human being, anger is a useful resource which enables action to be taken where another emotion, usually fear, might cause inaction and therefore more hurt, more pain. Judgements are based on beliefs. So the question in my mind was 'What does Diana have to believe about herself to make her feel so angry at Charles, Camilla, the palace and the press?'

Answer – she believed they were treating her, or had treated her, unfairly and they should have known better. No! That was what she believed about those who hurt her, that was the judgement she was making on them. What she believed about herself was…she could not avoid the hurt they had inflicted or the hurt they intended to inflict – she was helpless. That was the judgement she was making on herself, that was the underlying belief – she was helpless.

If there was fear then I would expect there to be signs in her body and there were. Fear equates to kidneys, equates to the muscles at the tops of the shoulders, into the back of the neck and from the front of the spine to the crests of the hip bones and top inside of the upper legs. In turn those muscles can relate to tension and pain in the neck and shoulders, mid to lower back and through the abdomen. Kidneys are associated with water balance in the body…water equates to emotions…kidneys equate to emotional balance.

So the solution to her anger and fear was…I closed my eyes and brought an image of Diana into my mind. The solution was to change the underlying belief, to help her find another belief, one that precluded the need for resentment and a sense of helplessness.

So I came full circle. I concluded that to be truly free of her debilitating emotions Diana had to acquire a context to her life in which her beliefs, about herself and the world, would result in more positive and health giving emotions, like acceptance and understanding in place of judgement and condemnation. There was evidence she was beginning to seek those emotions and their accompanying beliefs, not by using the techniques I suggested but spontaneously and instinctively as she was driven by her future-vision. Last year she'd spoken about wanting to love everyone and I'd taken the opportunity to support her aspiration and indicate the means to achieving them. I offered her role models like Lester Levenson, who released his negative emotions and replaced them with forgiveness, acceptance and love. I invited her to aspire to the "complete man" from the poem *If* and the "man of knowing" from the *I Ching*. I was confident that at some point the qualities of caring and compassion she expressed in her work, with the sick and dying, would be transferred to all her relationships. It was just a matter of time but it could take years. The best I could do would be to continue to offer her more ideas and suggestions that would help her spiritual identity develop. I hoped Diana was still in touch with Angela Serota and other friends who, I knew, had similar views to those I thought would be helpful.

In part at least, Diana had made her Time and Space speech as a gesture to demonstrate to Oliver Hoare how deep her feelings went for him and what she was prepared to do to be with him, since he was the focus of her private aspirations at that time. By then Hoare was living apart from his wife and it must have seemed to Diana they had a chance for a future together. Unfortunately, when the possibility was tested, the reality of their individual circumstances and the intensity of Diana's need for constant, reassuring contact made it impossible. Just a few days into January, Oliver Hoare returned to his wife and Diana was returned to the uncertainty, about when the personal life she craved might become possible.

During the two months Hoare was away there had been no silent calls to his family home. Within days of his return the calls began again. Police traced them to three lines at Kensington Palace rented, according to the police report, "by the office of HRH Prince of Wales", and to Diana's mobile phone. More calls were traced later to telephone boxes close to the Palace and nearby Notting Hill. The telephone calls finally stopped after Diana was informed that the police were involved in an investigation and that a prosecution was being considered. Despite the calls Hoare and Diana continued to see each other until early 1995. It seems they were bound by a mutual obsession which overrode all reason.

Without the immediate possibility of domestic bliss with Hoare, or even constant attention from him, Diana began to explore what else life might offer her. She saw it as her right to lead the life she wanted. True to her INFP nature, Diana had made her own future a cause she was going to fight for and she would fight hard. Marriage into the royal family and the media attention which followed had trapped her in a life she would never have accepted if she had known the truth and she was incensed by the injustice of her situation. Her indignation, her resentment, was reflected in the anger she directed at anyone or any institution which stood in her way of the future she now sought. Prince Charles and the royal Establishment had already discovered the lengths she was prepared to go to when they tried to confine her into a life she did not want. In early 1994 her quest was driven by the new imperative established by her speech, her affirmation, to bring together her public and private lives but there was another theme implied by her words.

Control was a major issue for Diana, in particular control over her life and everything that happened to her. The intense distress she experienced when she felt helpless or manipulated by anyone, echoed back to her childhood. She had already demonstrated on many occasions that she was capable of extreme and impulsive behaviour to avoid any feeling that she was not in control of what was happening to her. Diana's speech was as much a declaration of her intention to take control over the events of her life, as it was of her vision for what that control should bring. That intention, to have control, now became part of the new imperative which drove her.

The exercising of control requires self-belief, or more correctly certainty. In Diana's case that certainty was her absolute conviction she knew what was best for her. She was deluding herself. Diana's perception of her needs was clouded by old beliefs that, so far, had gone unchallenged and actually diverted her from the wisest and healthiest possibilities. For example, she was only thirty two and a royal Princess. Her years, experience and status had not provided her with a facility for critical self-examination, which might have helped her question her own beliefs and assumptions. Considerable success during the past few years had enabled her to overcome much of her childhood self-doubt and replaced it with an unwavering belief in her own instincts. Unfortunately her success and therefore the source of her confidence, was mainly in the context of her work. She had very little reason to trust the same instinct when it came to her private life but she did.

Diana's instinct, her intuition, was the tenuous basis for another developing belief which began exerting its influence on her life at that time, the belief that she had a spiritual purpose to her work and her life. Her interest in esoteric and metaphysical matters had started years before when Diana began to consult astrologers she thought might be able to predict what was going to happen to her. If control is one antidote to uncertainty and helplessness, then foreknowledge is another. Her interest in astrology gradually extended to other forms of divination such as tarot and runes and developed almost into an obsession, if not a dependency. To supplement the guidance she gained from astrological readings Diana regularly cast her own set of rune stones.

By early 1994 Diana had also gained a great deal of experience in the more esoteric side of medicine and healing. At the start of her transformation, in 1989, she was using aromatherapy and some bodywork to help with relaxation and physical stress. Five years on, driven by a desire to know more about what was helping her so much and supported by her equally fascinated sister-in-law Sarah, Diana had experimented with an array of energy healing systems and alternative therapies from acupuncture to sitting under plastic pyramids. She had been regaled with an assortment of explanations for their efficacy but most notably she had begun to draw a comparison, between her experiences as a patient and her experiences of empathy and connectedness when she attended the sick and dying during visits to hospitals and hospices. In the one situation she was the recipient of caring and healing, in the other she was clearly the provider of caring and, she came to suspect, of healing as well.

For years Diana had the sense her work had a spiritual context to it. Her connection in life to her maternal grandmother had developed into a conviction she was guided by the old lady's spirit after she died. Diana's work also brought her into contact with prominent religious figures who exercised their ministries caring for the same sick, dying and disadvantaged whose welfare concerned the Princess so much and in them Diana recognised kindred spirits. By early 1994 she had studied books on religions and spirituality and had shared ideas with bishops, archbishops, priests, nuns, Buddhists, Muslims, Christians and healers of all persuasions. Already certain she had a destiny to fulfil, Diana was developing the conviction that there was a spiritual purpose to her presence in the world and the work she was able to do.

That then was the heady cocktail of beliefs and assumptions Diana brought to her life in the weeks following her powerful affirmation. Her purpose was to combine a useful humanitarian role on the world stage on her own terms, bringing care and healing to the most distressed of the world, with a fulfilling private life, which ultimately would include a loving partner, peaceful home and children. In the absence of a clear way forward she was content to keep her options open, explore some possibilities and concentrate on loosening the constraints against which she had chafed for so many years.

Diana still retained the use of a small team of office staff headed by Patrick Jephson. Early in the year she visited St. James' Palace to reassure them. Engaged as they were in untangling the Princess's official diary, which had been planned well in advance for the first six months of 1994, they were not entirely convinced their jobs were secure. Jephson, however, still anticipated Diana's return to something resembling her previous pattern of public work. He was using all the charm he could muster to maintain good relationships with charities which had been promised their patron's support and had been disappointed when she withdrew from public life. He tried to reassure them Diana would be back if they could be patient but he was not helped when newspapers publicised the Princess's occasional private visits to hospices and hospitals while, at the same time, she declined official engagements.

✦ ✦ ✦

'That's painful!' Diana exclaimed when I began working the muscles of her left thigh.

'Where? Here?' I rubbed firmly on her outer thigh.

'Ow! Yes!'

'Let's just check the other side.' I flipped the towel back from her right leg and pressed the same place. 'What do you feel?'

'Bruised. Very sensitive.'

'Okay!'

I continued the massage making sure to work the painful areas firmly enough to energise them without causing too much discomfort. I was already beginning to consider what pain might indicate. Not injury, it was bilateral so possibly fatigue from working out, but the areas affected were not in the bulk of the abductor muscles. They were in the thin, stringy parts of muscle and connective tissue about halfway between the knee and hipbone. I would have expected tenderness at the attachments, alongside the knee and at the hip, if it was exercise related.

It was when I worked her abdominal area that my suspicions were confirmed.

'Does that feel uncomfortable?' I asked as I pressed gently but firmly in the area between the crest of her right hip and the lower edge of her rib cage.

'Yes it's unpleasant. Not really painful though.'

'Right. Let me tell you what I think is going on. The area in your abdomen here is your bowel, the ascending part. It's quite solid, quite compacted. I'm going to work it and the rest of your colon just to help stuff move through. Just follow what I'm doing because you can help yourself a lot by doing this yourself.'

I traced the path of her large intestine with smooth firm massage, up the right side from just inside her hip-crest to the rib cage, directly across her abdomen, then from the outer left corner of her rib cage down towards her left groin.

'I'm not going to do too much now because it feels quite packed in there and I don't want to cause it to become inflamed.'

We continued to discuss her bowel movements in some detail while I finished the massage. As we talked I paid special attention to her hamstrings and her lower back where her spine met her pelvis. Both areas turned out to be tight and painful.

As I was packing up I gave her some feedback. 'What you're experiencing now are the effects of an imbalance in your large intestine. The muscles I brought your attention to, outer legs, hamstrings, lower back are associated with it. Now it could just be you've had too much bread and your colon has become compacted, not in any medical sense, not a medical problem unless it continues, in which case you need to see your doctor. But the fact that those muscles are involved makes me think it's part of a wider picture, to do with you trying to make some important changes to your life. This hasn't happened overnight from one or two poor meals. The muscle involvement means it's been developing for a while.'

Diana nodded, listening intently.

'Every organ in your body is associated with your emotions in some way. Your large intestine, metaphorically speaking, is associated with getting rid of old stuff, stuff you don't need in you, in your life, any more. So the situation you have here could relate to you hanging onto something you don't need, some old crap you need to let go of. Your emotions are not letting you get rid of it. It could even be a particular emotion you're holding on to and need to let go of. If that was the case I'd say it was anger, anger you've been holding in.'

'What can I do about that?' Not for the first time since her separation I noticed how much more communicative and interested in her body and her health Diana was.

'Well there is a colon cleanse you could use, it involves a special restricted diet and some supplements, mainly fibre bulking agents like psyllium husk, then a series of self-administered enemas. It's very effective from the emotional as well as the mechanical point of view. It takes a lot of caring and compassion for yourself to do it.'

'Not keen eh?' I had seen her expression and realised the procedure I described was a step too far even for the intrepid Princess who was fascinated by all things anatomical and therapeutic. 'Let me think about it and I'll see what I can come up with for you next week. In the meantime eat light, no high-starch carbohydrates, plenty of fruit, vegetables and salads with oil rich dressings, drink plenty of water. The situation might sort itself out spontaneously, just be aware that you might feel some emotional release or reactions while it's being resolved.'

The following week I arrived armed with a plan but as soon as I walked through the door of her bedroom to set up my table Diana bounded in behind me. 'You'll never guess what I've done!' she gushed.

I knew instantly, psychically. 'You've been to see Chryssie,' I laughed. Such was the connection we'd built up over the years we'd been working together that those kind of insights happened often by then but usually during massage sessions.

We chattered about colonic irrigation and the colonic therapist I was going to tell her about that same day. Someone else had made the recommendation before me and Diana had already had one session with the earthy, caring and totally dedicated Chryssie Fitzgerald. I knew from my own experience that Diana would receive more than just the skilful and caring treatment that Chryssie offered in her clinic. There would be follow up advice and sound guidance related to the body-mind connections between colon health, emotional wellbeing and practical spirituality. My client couldn't have been in better hands. Nevertheless I repeated some of the basics.

'Your gut has to maintain a healthy environment so you shouldn't have colonics too often, give yourself a chance to recover between sessions. Chryssie will advise you. You need to take care of your diet, proper food combining is best and eat yoghurt, live yoghurt, preferably organic. There's no point in having your colon washed out if you're going to put junk straight into it. You should take some time to think about the emotions you feel most of the time and which you might want to let go of. That's the key issue for you right now, letting go of situations, people and things from your life which are related to your past, while you are letting go of old stuff from your body. Make room for the new and more beneficial. You could think about what emotions you would refer to be feeling.'

Later I wondered at the coincidence of Diana seeing Chryssie at just the same time I was deciding to recommend her. I was often struck with a sense of wonder by what I saw as signs of the bigger picture in which we are all connected and all have a part to play.

I also wondered about the effects the colonics might have on Diana. I anticipated emotional releases which might result and offered silent prayers for anyone in the firing line. I knew Chryssie would help there but I was glad to know the psychotherapist Susie Orbach would be available to help Diana process any reactions.

Despite what I'd said about not having colonics too often I later discovered Diana was having them on a weekly basis and always felt refreshed and energised by her treatments. I'd been thinking that half a dozen weekly sessions would give way to perhaps once a month but I trusted Chryssie. It did make me wonder however, if regular colonics might not be a substitute for purging for some people, to replace bulimia or the overuse of laxatives.

✦ ✦ ✦

The support of the friends had been very important to Diana during the past two or three years. They had helped her in the lead up to the publication of *Diana: Her True Story*, her separation and most recently her Time and Space speech. Early in 1994 Diana took another symbolic step back from her public life by inviting the staunchest of her friends to a girls' afternoon during which she invited them to take their pick from the huge wardrobe of designer clothes she had worn for work. Perhaps it was at that party she began to notice some of them were no longer entirely on her wavelength. Many of her older friendships were rooted in her past, as an aristocratic Sloane Ranger who became a Princess. Most of those Diana knew from back then did not have her familiarity with fame or her interest in health, fitness and spirituality. They saw life from a different viewpoint to the one Diana had by then. In time there would be a noticeable loosening of the bonds which had connected them so strongly to Diana and a number of them would lose touch with her, particularly when they demonstrated they no longer understood her by offering unwanted advice or criticism.

In the early part of 1994 Diana began to develop new acquaintances amongst people whose interests and experiences more closely matched her own. Her new friends were drawn from those who were more likely to understand the demands of celebrity status, or to share her fascination with divination, spirituality or alternative therapies.

Simone Simmons, a psychic healer specialising in energy cleansing, became very close to Diana soon after they met in December 1993. Their relationship, which combined professional therapy with close companionship, lasted almost three years. The outspoken and quite irreverent clairvoyant eventually became a frequent visitor at the Palace. According to her memoirs she also spent hours on the phone some days with the Princess, apparently clocking up 14 hours on one occasion. Through Simmons, Diana explored her interest in esoteric healing and her conviction that she had abilities of her own. During the early months of 1994 Simmons provided personal healing and cleansed *negative energy* from some of the rooms in Kensington Palace. As the year progressed Diana became more comfortable with her surroundings at Kensington Palace, despite the constraints of police security and cameras. Her private rooms began to feel more peaceful and comforting and she enjoyed sharing them with friends like Simmons who had a similar outlook.

The Palace setting, with its domestic staff and plush appointments, was useful for maintaining old links and creating new relationships. Diana entertained commanding officers of her regiments to lunch; discussed ideas with old friends, and new acquaintances, from politics and the media. She spoke with leading figures such as Oprah Winfrey and Barbara Walters, who were competing to televise a major interview with the Princess and she discussed her new interests in spiritual matters and the drawbacks of fame, with fashion designers and show business celebrities. Following their rapprochement she also lunched with her stepmother Raine, sometimes at the Palace and sometimes at their favourite restaurants.

The press was still interested in Diana and she was still interested in her press coverage. Since it seemed increasingly unlikely she was going to share a future cosseted in seclusion with Oliver Hoare, Diana was considering her future anew, particularly that part which might be fulfilled on the world stage. If she chose to step back into the limelight she had to decide how she was going to handle the media in future. Press reaction to her withdrawal from public life had been largely uncritical. Prince Charles had taken some blame but the Princess was only chided gently for her self-centredness. As Diana began to consider what her new public role might be she concluded that her instincts and skill with the press meant she should be in control of her own PR. The thing she wanted to do for now was to maintain a low but positive profile in the press.

Some of the help Diana needed to ensure the media did not lose sight of her entirely, was available in the form of another acquaintance who had become a friend. Richard Kay, the *Daily Mail* journalist Diana had approached after the Nepal trip in March 1993, had become the Princess's conduit into Fleet Street and onto the front pages, especially when she wanted to put across her own versions of events being reported in the newspapers. Kay, like Andrew Morton, also guided Diana in tabloid journalism's dark art of how to respond to negative press stories and he helped write some of her speeches. In the weeks after the Princess's Time and Space announcement Kay helpfully revealed details of some of Diana's private visits to hospitals, hospices and shelters for the homeless, just to keep the media pot boiling. He also became an occasional visitor to Kensington Palace.

The trickle of leaked, feel-good, tit-bits was never likely to satisfy a voracious media appetite which had for a long time been used to a much wider smorgasbord of Diana pictures and stories. As she tried to enjoy a relatively normal private life she was followed and pestered by photographers, most notably the aggressive paparazzi. Since the golden eggs had become rarer their value had increased, if the reluctant goose could be persuaded to deliver. One good picture of Diana, shopping, smiling, crying, reacting well or badly to intrusive photographers could provide the focus for some sort of story and earn tens of thousands of pounds for the man who stole the shot. They tried to ambush her at regular venues like psychotherapist Susie Orbach's offices in North London or the Harbour Club private gym where Diana worked out almost every day. Alternatively they lay in wait for her until she left Kensington Palace to shop or visit friends, then they followed her in cars, on motorcycles or on foot, cajoling, threatening and always thrusting their cameras at her, reaching for the picture which would enhance their reputation and make them more money.

Despite the harassment, Diana's need for control made her insist her police bodyguards should be reassigned, so she could go about her life as a normal person. The ever-present protection officers had always been a very visible symbol of what confined her into and identified her with the usual royal lifestyle. Diana was determined to manage without the lifestyle and the police presence which went with it. Eventually, after much consideration and discussion, the Home Secretary decreed she would receive the same level of protection she always had but only if she requested it, otherwise Diana was on her own.

◆ ◆ ◆

After one of our sessions I gave Diana a sheet of paper describing Abraham Maslow's concept of self-actualisation which he defined as "the desire for self-fulfilment". The print-out listed the characteristics of self-actualised individuals. I had recognised some of the traits in Diana and hoped she'd be inspired to include others into her future-vision. Amongst them were "concerned with helping other people improve their lives", "value solitude and time to themselves for self-discovery" and "unconfined by conventional expectations of behaviour".

◆ ◆ ◆

By March 1994 Diana was set on her new course and ready for the challenges to come. From that month on they came thick and fast. Oliver Hoare was seen in Diana's car entering the gates of Kensington Palace and on other occasions breakfasting with her at the Harbour Club. It seemed they were unconcerned about any press stories which might appear. What did appear in the newspapers that March was an interview with James Hewitt, who had been pursued by the press since his "friendship" with Diana was revealed in 1992. Various stories during the subsequent two years had speculated on the true nature of their relationship and even suggested the Princess and the now retired army officer were still seeing each other.

According to Hewitt, it was because of the ongoing rumours and Diana's insistence that he do something to stop them, that he told his story in a tabloid newspaper that March. Apparently Diana suggested he speak to Richard Kay of the *Mail* to set the record straight, presumably because she knew she might have some influence over what was written. Instead Hewitt gave his interview to another journalist, Anna Pasternack of the *Daily Express*. Unhappily he did not tell the entire story and was held up to widespread ridicule for the obviously sanitised version he offered. The same month, during her annual ski holiday in Lech, Austria, Diana shouted at cameramen and charged down the ski slopes at paparazzi who had followed her there, screaming for them to go away. She was also shown in a pre-recorded television documentary about a shelter for battered women, taking part in a group therapy session. Every story led to more debate about the Princess's private life and when she might return to the public stage.

The wider debate in the press was mirrored within Diana as she reacted to the press stories and struggled to see a way to achieving the goal she had set herself. Her office and household staff were frequently caught unawares by what seemed like arbitrary changes in her mood. One moment she could be informal and friendly, the next haughty and demanding. On some occasions she was relaxed and easy-going, at others, in reactions characteristic of an INFP personality under stress, she flashed with anger and frustration at small infringements or minor drops in standards.

The press became as confused as Diana's staff. On 23 April journalists and cameramen were able to provide stories and pictures of Diana's low-key visit to Ulster, to meet troops of 2nd Battalion, the Princess of Wales's Royal Regiment, for which she was Colonel-in-Chief. However, even when details of her "private" charity work were revealed in advance, photographers could not be sure if Diana would cooperate or be difficult to photograph. Slowly Diana's press coverage began to turn sour, despite or because of Diana's personal PR initiative and the efforts of Richard Kay and others.

At the end of April, Diana and her two close friends, Kate Menzies and Catherine Soames, made a privately arranged trip to a tennis ranch in Malaga, Spain. On arrival they found their accommodation far below the standards they expected and they accepted an offer, from ex-pat British hairdresser George Guy, to drive them to a nearby five star hotel, the Byblos. Before she had dispensed with her police protection a trip like that would have been planned to the last detail, to ensure Diana's comfort and security. Without her bodyguards, Diana was at the mercy of paparazzi. She was recognised at the airport when she arrived and tracked back to the Byblos.

On 1 May Diana was fulfilling her promise to herself, trying to lead a normal life like anyone else by taking the sun beside the hotel pool. Lurking nearby, with his camera hidden, was a Spanish photographer, who snapped the exposed Princess when she briefly altered her position on the sunbed and adjusted her bikini top. The next day paparazzi followed the departing Diana en-masse to the airport, nearly running the car she was in off the road.

On 3 May Diana learned that "topless" photographs of her were being offered for sale for £1 million. She called Richard Kay who met her to discuss the situation and duly wrote a story about how the invasion of her privacy felt "like a rape" to the Princess, describing his source as a "friend". Unfortunately his conversation with Diana, in her car, had been photographed. *The Sun* tabloid castigated her for "hypocrisy" and "double standards". Under the headline "Two Faces of Tormented Di" they questioned how she could complain of press intrusion in her Time and Space speech and then use the press for her own ends. Other tabloids picked up the theme and in the following weeks wondered why she had taken the risk of sunbathing topless; whether she really expected to be able to act like anyone else; what she thought she was doing manipulating the press and called her mental state into question with comments about "schizophrenia" and her "Jekyll and Hyde" character.

The "topless" photographs were eventually bought by Eduardo Junco, proprietor of *Hello* magazine's Spanish sister publication *Hola!* Junco had contacted Diana's private secretary Patrick Jephson to tell him about the pictures he had been offered and the gallant Spaniard had agreed to acquire and dispose of the photos so they could not be published, thus saving the Princess from any further distress and earning her gratitude. She might have been less grateful and blushed more if she had heard her, perhaps not so gallant, saviour tell Jephson that the photographs showed: "Her Highness is not so young as she was..."

In the aftermath of that story and others Diana was described as a "rudderless vehicle", a Princess without a partner or job and with her children both away at boarding school. Sources "close" to her were reported to have said she seemed mercurial of late. She was described as "unstable at the moment" and coming across as "hyper". Journalist Ross Benson was quoted as saying "She's prone to tantrums, and she gets mood swings." More provocative commentary was to follow.

In their April issue *Tatler* magazine declared Diana's wardrobe to be "dead common." Ironically, other stories appeared during May criticising the Princess for the amount she spent on personal grooming. A figure of £160,000 was quoted as the amount she lavished on clothes, hairdressing and therapists in the year to March. It did not seem to occur to anyone that her withdrawal from public life surely meant her grooming bill would reduce in the current year. In what was to become an increasingly aggressive stance towards negative press, Diana used a pre-arranged lunch with Peter Stothard, editor of *The Times,* to explain how the figures had been leaked to journalists after her husband had mentioned them at a dinner party with friends. She then went on to horrify the editor by setting out "a complicated story" about how she had helped save a drowning tramp from the Regent's Park Canal. Perhaps Stodhart recognised the technique of casting a red herring story to distract the press from a more damaging one. He did not follow up the tip off. It was Richard Kay, recently satirised as Diana's new behind the scenes "press secretary", who revealed Diana's heroism in the following day's *Daily Mail,* to general press cynicism and ridicule.

Diana gained some respite from her embarrassing attempts at PR, when Charles replaced her under the spotlight after he was criticised for his own personal spending of nearly £275,000 more than his wife's, albeit his did include an Aston Martin. Eventually more positive media attention took the heat from both the Prince and Princess when Diana travelled to Geneva, as an official British representative to a special commission set up to advise the International Red Cross.

The responses in Diana's muscles confirmed the strain she was under and her anger and frustration at the press intrusion she was suffering.

'I think it would be a good idea to get rid of some of your anger,' I said at our next treatment session.

'What do you suggest?'

'Chryssie's partner, Keith, is a martial arts teacher. I've been working with him for a while now. He combines a range of martial arts styles like karate and taekwando with kung fu so you'll get to pound out some frustration and anger on his training pads. He'll also help you on the strength and fitness side but he's especially good at energy work with chi gong and he teaches movement meditations like tai chi and animal forms. I think you'll enjoy it and you'll get to release some of your emotions safely.'

I left it at that. As usual the rest was up to her. If she felt drawn to what I'd described she would follow it up, if not she wouldn't. That was the process of self-transformation.

✦ ✦ ✦

During that spring Diana began undergoing another phase of her metamorphosis. A new self-identity was emerging, one in which her anger and aggression was less and less inhibited by normal royal conventions or the expectations which had been placed on her. For years she had felt as if a lid was being pushed down on her to make her act the way others wanted her to. Increasingly now her anger and frustration were accompanied by a new sense of physical strength and a desire to deal directly with her tormentors and detractors.

Her new, more physical self-perception was the result of a combination of influences. Diana had already discovered what it meant to direct physical aggression at training pads during workouts with her martial arts instructor, sometimes in his far from salubrious basement gym in East London. In the more luxurious environment of the Harbour Club, Diana now met England rugby captain Will Carling, who was a self-confessed fitness fanatic. The Princess and the rugby player were soon happily enjoying coffee and conversations. Carling inspired Diana to take more interest in her body's ability to develop strength and fitness. At around the same time Diana's long serving fitness instructor, Carolan Brown, stepped away for personal reasons. She was replaced by South African Jenni Rivett, whose approach incorporated more weight training for muscle development and definition than Diana had been used to.

After she dispensed with her bodyguards, the Princess had suffered constant aggressive attention from photographers and had often been distressed and angered by it. As her body developed more power, strength and muscle bulk, she began to feel a new determination to confront those who made her life unpleasant. The paparazzi were in the front line of those and they were now in Diana's sights. Running battles were enacted, as Diana used different tactics to make things difficult for the photographers who followed and harassed her every move. Motivated by her indignation at the constraints they placed on her freedom to go about her life as she wanted, she ran away from them or ran at them, she shouted and prodded her finger at them, she held her bag in front of her face or just ignored them and at times, overwhelmed by her emotions, she just stood and wept while they snapped busily about her like terriers around a fox at bay.

If Diana expected her tormentors to understand how she felt when they pestered her she was disappointed, indeed they seemed proud of their status as the guerrilla raiders of the press pack. Two even wrote a book, *Dicing with Di*, which documented the activities of "The Loon" as they called her. Apparently she was most likely to "give the silent treatment", by which they meant standing in tears, "after she had visited one of her many therapists."

Unsurprisingly Diana was criticised for not acting in the dignified way a royal princess should when confronted by wild animals. Stories described her as "selectively mad" and "the royal bag lady". On 27 May, Lord Carteris, a former private secretary to the Queen, made disparaging comments in the *Daily Express* about Diana and the Duchess of York. Diana's reaction was to tell her friends she no longer cared what the press thought of her – "It's what you think of yourself that counts." Nevertheless an increasing number of comments alluding to Diana's state of mind were finding their way into the public domain and they must have given her concerns. She was still in a vulnerable situation and feared her mental state would be used to deprive her of her sons.

One consequence of Diana's determination to control her own life was to become even more suspicious of her husband's supporters and courtiers. She was under no illusion that she remained a thorn in their sides as they tried to rehabilitate Charles in the public perception. 1994 was the year they intended to make their big push to gain popularity for the heir, during celebrations to mark his 25 years as Prince of Wales. She need not have worried as much as she did. The men in grey were less concerned about her now she had stepped back from the public role which competed with Charles. They were happy enough to see Diana hoisted by her own petard following the "topless" photo debacle and her "loon" behaviour.

The respite Diana gained from intrusive media attention into her private life was very brief following her Time and Space speech. By May it was almost as intense as it ever had been. What might have given her some cheer was the Gallup poll which came out that month: only 12 per cent favoured abolition of the monarchy but 54 per cent agreed it should "become more democratic and approachable" like that in the Netherlands. More than half the sample questioned leant towards Diana's instinctive feeling that her more informal approach to royal duty was the way ahead.

✦ ✦ ✦

Diana was chuckling to herself when I arrived. 'You look happy. What's happened?' I grinned at her.

'I was just in a taxi chatting to the driver, his name was Joe. He was so chuffed I was in his cab and kept saying his missus would be excited.'

It made me laugh when I heard how much pleasure Diana was able to get from simple, everyday things most people take for granted.

'Anyway I got his phone number and I just called him. He was bowled over.' She laughed out loud. 'I promised to send him a photograph. It doesn't take much to make people happy does it?'

✦ ✦ ✦

Diana's Time and Space speech had been used as a stick with which to beat her for apparently maintaining a public profile despite demanding privacy. In fact there was very little inconsistency in her behaviour except, perhaps, for the occasional leaks about her 'secret' humanitarian work, not all of which were instigated by her. The problem lay in what people thought they heard her say in the speech rather than taking notice of what she actually said and intended. Specifically Diana referred to "reducing" the extent of her public life, not ending it. She spoke of focussing on a smaller range of charities in future, not stopping her charity work altogether. Finally she spoke of "seeking a more suitable way of combining a meaningful public role, with hopefully, a more private life." Since she did not know at the time how she intended to do that or even what meaningful might denote for her in the future, she did not try to specify what she might do differently but kept her options open. Of course she certainly was not going to publicly proclaim the hopes she had for a future with Oliver Hoare so the press remained unaware of a major influence on her decision.

Diana did want to retain her connections with the monarchy, partly because of her sons and partly to fulfil agreements she made with the Queen in 1992 and, more recently, when she and her mother-in-law had discussed Diana's decision to step back from public life. The Queen had promised the Princess she would be invited to participate in royal engagements at a national level. Diana had promised she would maintain her connections with regiments for which she was Colonel-in-Chief. Sovereign and daughter-in-law realised the wife of the next King and mother to two princes, both heirs to the throne, could not easily be separated from her association with the monarchy.

The Princess had fulfilled her agreement the previous year by attending the Battle of the Atlantic commemoration service in Liverpool with Prince Charles and in April when she visited troops in Ulster. In June she accepted the Queen's invitation to attend celebrations marking the fiftieth anniversary of D-Day. Despite a good degree of nervousness, given the personal hostility she felt from some members of the royal family, Diana attended the unveiling of the Canadian memorial in Green Park and joined her in-laws on board the royal yacht *Britannia* for the naval celebrations at Portsmouth.

Later the same month, on 29 June, Jonathan Dimbleby's long awaited television documentary about Prince Charles was aired on British television. More than 14 million people, nearly 70 per cent of the possible viewing audience, watched the heir to the throne explain how his marriage to Diana had failed. Nervous and fidgeting, clearly uncomfortable, Charles said he had tried to be "faithful and honourable" to his wife after making his marriage vows until "it became irretrievably broken down". He described Camilla Parker Bowles as a friend who "will be a friend for a very long time." Dimbleby explained later to reporters that Charles' comments were an admission of adultery with Camilla and that the breakdown of the marriage had occurred in 1986.

The Princess was not part of the television audience. Instead she was fulfilling a long established engagement, attending a fundraising dinner sponsored by the magazine *Vanity Fair*, at the Serpentine Gallery. The images of her, striding athletically and purposefully forward in very high heels and short, tight, low cut, black cocktail dress are iconic. The dress and Diana's plucky performance was reported by the press as a triumph.

Whether Charles' broadcast was a triumph or a disaster depended on the newspaper or the commentator who described it. *The Sun* focused on Diana, describing her appearance at the charity dinner beneath the headline "The Thrilla He Left to Woo Camilla", although two days later, when their polls showed an increase in public support for Charles from fifty-four per cent to sixty-three per cent, the same newspaper ran the headline: "Charles Rules OK". The day after the broadcast the *Daily Mirror* ran with "Not Fit To Reign", a debate that was to continue for months. One of Charles' own courtiers described the programme as a "complete whinge" and an "own goal" which affected relationships between the Prince and Princess and between the heir's St. James's Palace and the Sovereign's Buckingham Palace. Once again the men in grey seemed out of touch with public sentiment. An opinion poll showed eighty percent in favour of Prince Charles after he had shared his private anguish on television.

The interview, when Diana became aware of the details, only went part way to fulfilling her hopes for it. Her sense of injustice and her anger at Charles, required that he admit his adultery and show remorse for his actions, neither of which he did explicitly in the programme, although most who watched the tortured performance recognised the admission and regret in his words and demeanour. Diana's initial reaction to the programme was triumph and anger. Triumph that Charles had tacitly admitted adultery, anger that he had not specifically named Camilla or confirmed he had loved her throughout his marriage. Anger that he had not said sorry for the hurt he had caused his wife, although he had said the marriage breakdown was "deeply regrettable" and had caused a "certain amount of damage". Triumph that his public admission of adultery made it a virtual certainty a divorce would be granted if Diana chose to apply after the statutory two years separation was completed on 9 December.

Her own position regarding divorce had already been made clear to Charles; she intended to stay at Kensington Palace until he chose to end the marriage. She was determined not to be seen as responsible. Her lawyers were advising her that her position would be strongest if she waited for the other side to initiate proceedings and her instincts advised her that her position in the public's perception would be strongest if she did not pack up and leave of her own accord. Above all else was her concern for her sons; recalling her own childhood experience, she was not prepared to give them any impression that she had left them voluntarily. As it was she was unhappy, legally and actually, about what effects the programme, the biography which was to follow and the subsequent media debate, might have on the boys. She had her private secretary draft a letter to Charles' solicitors asking if they had known in advance what the programme contained and recording her disappointment that she had not been forewarned, so she could have taken care of William and Harry.

In fact Diana seemed to have some sympathy for her husband following her own experience with Morton's *True Story* book. Not long after Charles' appearance on television Diana acknowledged that she "admired the honesty" and that it must have been far from easy for him to be so honest about his relationship, especially in his position.

Approaching her thirty-third birthday Diana was still looking towards her future-vision although she was still unclear about how to achieve the balanced life she wanted. Certainly some of the press coverage she had received of late, criticism for appearing in public at all it seemed and yet more suggestions that her mind was unstable, were worrying for her. Charles' television appeal to the public had been successful and Diana's own place in the public's affections was in danger of being eroded. She also knew Charles' side was quietly delighted that her popularity was being reduced while the heir's was on the rise at last.

To paraphrase an old anecdote Diana was learning that if you are caught in a flowing tide of events you should not stop paddling if you want to avoid drifting backwards. She was soon going to have to make her mind as to whether she was going to paddle on into some new public role which would maintain her position of strength, or risk drifting into difficulties she might not be able to handle. There really was no alternative. A life with Oliver Hoare was not likely anytime soon and in any case Diana's main concern was still her relationship with her boys, William and Harry. With them at boarding school most of the time and with Tiggy Legge-Bourke taking care of them for half the remainder, Diana was suspicious about any situation which might reduce her influence with her sons. She did not relish being dragged back into the scheming and animosity which were sure to arise if she stepped back onto the public stage. Undoubtedly it would be assumed by the press and the courtiers that she was competing with Charles, when all she wanted to do was help people and have the public on her side when she needed it.

On 2 July, the day after her birthday, Diana travelled to Geneva for the second meeting of the Red Cross advisory commission. She had made a commitment to be involved and she tried to take part in the seemingly endless discussions and debates, but her heart was not in it. Her forte was meeting and reaching out to damaged and deprived people who needed love and caring, not talking with bureaucrats about how to make organisations more efficient and cost effective. Try as she did to concentrate, her mind was on other things.

✦ ✦ ✦

The session had progressed quite normally by the time I came to work her spine one particular day. Nothing unusual had occurred. We'd chatted briefly then become immersed in the quiet peacefulness of relaxation, contemplation and letting go. Quite suddenly I felt the unmistakable release of sexual energy from her body. It was unusual because it was not generated by any connection of that kind between us. Our relationship was epitomised by other feelings. I felt caring, admiration, affection even but I was not physically attracted to Diana at all and I was pretty sure, after the many years we'd know each other, that she didn't have any thoughts along those lines for me. I was quite sure however, that she'd experienced the surge of energy I'd noticed.

'Crikey! If you go out with that energy coming off you you'll have men following you up the street,' I laughed.

Diana giggled and said nothing but my words brought the moment to an end and the remainder of the massage continued as usual.

Driving away later I considered the incident. Apart from the most likely possibility, that Diana's daydream state had included sexy thoughts about someone, another option was that there was a body-mind shift taking place and that it was allowing more intrinsic energy, chi or prana, to flow through her chakra system. Certainly that would equate with the work on her spine and her developing sense of her body, I'd noticed her developing muscle tone and strength and recognised the work she was putting in.

'Look out world!' I muttered out loud as I negotiated the traffic to my next client.

✦ ✦ ✦

That July, with her new strength of purpose if not direction and her new body awareness from pumping iron, Diana began flexing her flirting muscles. Her warm attentiveness, humour and interest in fitness encouraged Will Carling, even though he had been married only a few weeks before. Diana added Carling to the list of attentive male admirers she would call on for company and, in the rugby captain's case, interesting sporting distractions for William and Harry. On 4 July Diana met 57 year old, urbane and charming American millionaire, Teddy Forstmann, who was seated alongside her at a dinner party hosted by her friend Jacob Rothschild. A brief and pleasant flirtation with Forstmann mellowed into a close friendship during which they shared lunches and tennis. Diana indulged herself in the fantasy that they should marry and that he would become President of the United States with her beside him. Forstmann offered genuine caring, real affection, practical help and good advice over the years they were friends.

Diana enjoyed Carling's companionship, his advice and his attentiveness, perhaps over-attentiveness would be more accurate; she enjoyed Forstmann's friendship, American charm and good humour but she was not emotionally engaged with either of them. When Diana became emotionally engaged it was from a part of her persona which expressed as a childlike victim, in need of rescue by a handsome hero. When she spent time with Carling or Forstmann she was feeling physically and emotionally stronger and more determined than she ever had. The same was not true when, as a damaged and needy young Princess, she attracted James Hewitt, or when desolate and on the verge of her separation, she had started the relationship with Oliver Hoare. Diana had not yet resolved the inner part of herself which believed a real relationship must involve mutual, unrelenting devotion. Devotion is what she still felt for Oliver Hoare and expected in return.

In late July Diana was still seeing the married art-dealer. The newfound strength and powerful self-identity she exhibited in other areas of her life by then did not translate into her relationship with Hoare. Her need, her craving, for his attention had not abated. She had tearful confrontations with him when she suspected he was misleading her about his whereabouts and even went to his home when his wife was abroad. Unhappily her visit was noticed, coinciding as it did with extra scrutiny of the Hoare family home when a tabloid began investigating a tip off about silent telephone calls.

Just a couple of weeks later, in mid-August, while she was holidaying at Martha's Vineyard at the invitation of her friend Lucia Flecha de Lima, Diana heard that a book by James Hewitt was to be published in the autumn. With a foreboding sense of betrayal she cut her holiday short and returned to the UK but was unable to stop the publication.

On Saturday 20 August, soon after she returned from the US, Diana and Oliver Hoare discovered a Sunday tabloid, *The News of the World,* was about to run a story about the nuisance phone calls made to Oliver's home for over a year since late 1992. The couple conferred and Diana approached her friend, journalist Richard Kay, for help and attempted another ruse for putting the press off the scent of a potentially damaging story. She suggested the silent calls had been made by a loyal but misguided member of her staff. Kay duly contacted Clive Goodman, royal reporter for the *News of the World*, and delivered Diana's fabricated account. That Saturday afternoon, Diana and Kay met to discuss her options and were told by an elderly gent who was passing them as they sat in a parked car, that they were being photographed. They had been spotted by another journalist.

On Sunday 21 August, Goodman's five page article ran in the *News of the World* under the headline "Di's Cranky Phone Calls to Married Tycoon". The piece gave a very detailed account of when the calls were made from telephones in Kensington Palace and call boxes nearby. He suggested Diana and Hoare were having an affair, something which had been suspected for some time. Perhaps the most damaging part of his story from Diana's viewpoint was his allusion that her behaviour indicated she was mentally unstable. The article included Richard Kay's rebuttal story about the calls originating from a concerned member of staff and attributed it to a "friend and advisor" close to the Princess.

Reference to friends "close to the Princess" had been Kay's usual way of protecting Diana as his true source when he wrote his exclusives from information she gave him. Knowing his meeting with Diana the previous day had been photographed Kay had no choice but to quote her directly in his piece in the *Daily Mail* on Monday 22 August. Under the headline "What Have I Done to Deserve This" Diana refuted the suggestion she was having an affair with a married man and declared she did not even know how to use a parking meter let alone a phone box.

During the weeks which followed, aided by Richard Kay, Diana tried desperately to present herself as the victim of shadowy figures in the Establishment who wanted to harm her by making out "that I am mad". Indeed she had every reason to be concerned about suggestions she was unbalanced and that she had been involved in an illicit and obsessive affair with a married man. Potentially she stood to come off badly if either case was made against her. She was still married, no agreement, financial or otherwise had been made regarding a divorce and she was worried about ongoing contact with her sons. Knowing about the upcoming Hewitt book only made matters seem worse.

Her efforts at damage control merely added fuel to a blazing fire. Newspapers referred to her increasingly desperate and unbelievable explanations as "neurotic nonsense" and "bizarre". By September the tabloids had inflated the supposed number of "crank" calls to 300. By October Diana was attracting ridicule for offering one highly questionable excuse after another, only to have them dismantled almost as rapidly as she set them up. Even her ex-lover James Hewitt waded in by telling a Sunday tabloid he had also received silent calls during the summer of 1993 and that he was "very sorry for her". As soon as the story broke Diana had asked her current lover, Oliver Hoare, to make a statement to the effect that they were not involved in an affair. He had declined and Diana felt betrayed yet again.

Harmful allegations were being made against her and Diana had no balancing public profile to soften their impact on her reputation when, that September, she left for Geneva for the third meeting of the Red Cross advisory commission. As she sat with her eyes glazing over, listening to the droning voices, the Princess was becoming more and more inclined to put her vision of a balanced life on hold and return to the world stage as a leading humanitarian light. She was not inclined to continue attending any more committee conferences. Declaring herself unwell she left the meetings early, returned to her hotel and began preparing for her flight home. Within a few weeks she would resign her place on the commission.

As he sat with the Princess in her hotel suite Patrick Jephson, took the opportunity to talk about her future and outlined a plan he had been developing for some time. Early in his appointment as private secretary Jephson discovered he had responsibility for The Princess of Wales's Charities Trust, which had been set up in 1981, at the time of Diana's marriage. For years the Trust's modest income, from investments and occasional donations, had enabled Diana to make small payments to charities. During 1993 Jephson was already thinking the Princess, then separated, might be able to use the Trust as a vehicle for a new working role. To test his idea and its potential for fundraising, he had successfully negotiated a mutually beneficial arrangement which saw Diana and her Trust associated with the West End premiere of the Harrison Ford film *The Fugitive.*

During 1994 he had been developing plans to make the existing trust the core of a large organisation, backed by sympathetic and influential figures from the worlds of industry, finance and the media. His sophisticated concept would, he believed, offer Diana the funds and almost unlimited opportunities "to involve herself in whatever branch of humanitarian activity caught her fancy."

When he sketched out how the organisation could work Diana was excited and enthusiastic. During their conversation and over the following weeks she eagerly offered ideas for fundraising events and projects the trust might support. Jephson set about developing the idea further. He saw a genuine opportunity for Diana ahead, a future he believed she wanted and he was delighted to be playing a part in making it possible for her.

✦ ✦ ✦

I'd been sensing a strange kind of confusion in Diana during several sessions by the time I went to see her in September. I was fairly sure it was related to the conflict I suspected in her future-vision. Stepping back from public life might have given her time to think about how to bring together her private and public lives but I was certain she hadn't clarified what she wanted yet. The continuing tensions in her body confirmed it even if the fact that she was still married didn't.

I was also concerned about the implications of the Oliver Hoare phone call stories and thought it might have some bearing on the state of body and mind I was noticing. While it was not my business and I had no opinion about it one way or the other, it seemed highly likely that Diana was involved with the married art dealer in some way. Of interest to me was what must have been in her mind to be able to make such calls and as often as was suggested. It indicated at the very least a manifestation of the victim mentality she had assumed some areas of her life. In many ways she was challenging that assumption of helplessness but her behaviour with the phone calls suggested she wasn't doing so in her personal relationships with men. The phone calls indicated an obsessive attraction in which any mature self-perception was completely suppressed by childlike needs.

If Diana had stepped back from public life to demonstrate her feelings for a married man she was obsessed with, and I now suspected she had, it seemed to me she was a long way from bringing together the conflicting parts of her self-identity and future-vision. Looking back at what had been reported about her relationship with Charles I saw the same kind of childlike subordination of her own needs and interests for someone who was unavailable to her. I was determined to offer her a situation in which she might find the opportunities, to resolve any issues she had around relationships and bring together her aspirations for the private and public lives she wanted.

In my bag I had a three page proposal, which I gave her before I left after that session. The paper described a scenario I believed would answer a great many of her needs. In essence I proposed a Spencer Trust, to distinguish it from her royal identity in the event of a divorce, through which Diana could engage in world improving humanitarian endeavours with whatever degree of involvement she desired. My argument was that she could choose any role which suited her at any time, in such an organisation. With the right team behind her she could be figurehead, executive, hands on ambassador or hands off observer, whatever suited her inclinations and abilities and her personal circumstances. If she wanted to she could focus on her private life and only be involved in the trust at a minor level, or she could, at a time of her choosing, step forward and be at its head, driving it as a high profile and very active participant. Her international connections with politicians, charities, business leaders, show-business celebrities and media figures would make it an enormously effective and influential global entity. In a nod to my own self-interest I also proposed the organisation could support research into alternative therapies and education in holistic health practices and that I would be happy to be involved with that part of things.

Driving away from Kensington Palace I wondered again whether I was becoming too involved and too attached to the outcome of my efforts.

✦ ✦ ✦

In a curious coincidence, during the second half of 1994, several other people proposed the idea of an organisation through which Diana could operate and fulfil her global humanitarian ambitions, outside the purview of the palace system.

Unaware that The Princess of Wales Charities Trust already existed, Andrew Morton produced a five-page discussion paper which, in part, suggested an "umbrella organisation for her charitable interests." Diana's friend, film maker David Puttnam, organised a lunch at Claridges, where Diana discussed the idea of setting up a Princess of Wales Trust with "the great and good of TV and movies."

All the effort, the energy, the creativity and the enthusiasm, Diana's as well as that of well-meaning friends and staff, did not result in the powerful and influential organisation they envisaged. While the ambitious ideas resonated to the caring side of her, the side driven to help people and make a difference, they did not speak to the romantic idealist within her. Still driven by the affirmation which demanded she create a balanced future for herself, Diana, was unable to commit to what seemed like complicated, long term projects. Instinctively she realised they might hamper her search for something she wanted more than a place on the world stage, a partner's love and constant presence in her life.

There were other reasons Diana did not pursue the far reaching proposals suggested to her at that time. She was very confident in the tactile, direct and informal hands-on work she was familiar with but she was unnerved by the idea of a more remote, intellectual or executive role in a large organisation. Her experiences in Geneva at the Red Cross meetings had only served to reinforce her view. In some ways she still regarded herself as "dim" She did not have the confidence, or inclination, to embark on big schemes that could require abilities she was not sure she had.

She was also well aware that Charles' side wanted her to stay out of public life altogether. Instinctively she knew that setting up a Spencer, or Princess of Wales, Trust would have constituted an unacceptable hostile act. With many influential figures from the media, finance, business, charities and even politics arrayed alongside her and offering their help, Diana was already in danger of being accused of attempting to attract a rival court. The Princess was still a member of the Windsor royal family and mother to two Windsor Princes. Instinctively she shied away from what could have inflamed an already difficult situation. The stakes were too high to take such risks.

During that September Diana did take her first step back onto the public stage but she did only what she was best at. As personal favour to Michael Adler, chairman of the National AIDS trust, she opened a new AIDS clinic in London. When he promised there would be no press present Diana responded by telling him a media presence would suit her – "the more the better."

In the autumn Diana visited the USA again in one of half a dozen trips she made that year. The country and its people were becoming increasingly familiar and attractive to her and she, in turn, was welcomed and admired when she went. On that particular visit Diana attended a glittering dinner with other celebrities in New York, before a private jet, loaned by her friend Teddy Forstmann, ferried her to Washington where she stayed for three nights with her dear friend, wife of the Brazilian Ambassador, Lucia Flecha de Lima. In the US capital Diana had a full itinerary of prestigious meetings. She discussed charity work with Elizabeth Dole, wife of Presidential hopeful Senator Dole and she joined leading political figures at a dinner, given in her honour, by Katherine Graham, owner of the *Washington Post*. At the British

Embassy Diana had a private meeting with Hilary Clinton before lunching with notable figures who included General Colin Powell. The Princess returned home on a high, full of excitement about the new path beckoning her forward. The call of celebrity status and a meaningful public role was becoming stronger in face of all the criticism she had received since her semi-retirement. The call would be impossible to ignore when other events unfolded in the weeks which followed.

On 3 October, Anna Pasternack's book *Princess in Love* was published, to widespread ridicule for its style and content. James Hewitt was berated by the tabloids in brutal headlines. Depressed and shocked he took refuge in France where, for a brief while, he contemplated suicide as preferable to being hounded by the press. The royal family was embarrassed by the book and subsequent commentary, which suggested it had made them a laughing stock and hastened the end of the House of Windsor. Diana let it be known, through newspaper stories by Richard Kay and others, that the book was a product of Hewitt's "fevered imagination" and she was hurt by his invasion of her privacy. She also maintained she and Hewitt had never been lovers. The tabloids helped the public decide for itself by giving over page after page to the most lurid details of the book, which immediately became a best seller.

Prince Charles fared little better when his biography, by Jonathan Dimbleby, was serialised in *The Sunday Times* on 16 October and published a short while later. The book offered Charles' unhappy impressions of his childhood and upbringing, and managed to embarrass and anger his parents. Overall the 620 page tome, product of two and a half years research, was seen as a hand-wringing, self-justifying PR exercise. Amongst the critical press commentary which followed was the suggestion in *The Economist* that the book merely confirmed the Crown was "an idea whose time has passed".

Charles' book contained little about Diana personally and no direct criticism but it did describe her bulimia and hysteria extensively and offered them as the main reasons for the failure of the royal marriage. Diana saw little remorse and less vindication for herself than she had in the TV documentary, particularly in regard to Charles' relationship with Camilla Parker Bowles. The suggestion that Diana's mental state was to blame for the ultimate breakdown of the royal couple's relationship was hurtful and sinister, given her sensitivity to any agenda which might affect her future.

When Andrew Morton's new book, *Diana: Her New Life,* was published in November it did not help matters. Covering the years since his original offering of *Diana: Her True Story,* its contents seemed to portray Diana as damaged, weak and neurotic.

The books by Dimbleby and Morton projected an image of the Princess from years before onto the canvas offered by the newspapers in late 1994. Diana had changed considerably by then but the books, added to stories about her aggressive attitude towards the paparazzi and her obsessive behaviour around Oliver Hoare, once again raised doubts about her mental state which could not be ignored. In October, mainly in response to the damaging portrayals of her, Diana recommitted her energies to that side of her life which had always been an unqualified success and a lifeline in the past – her public role caring for the damaged and distressed of society. It seemed appropriate to begin her return to work with low-key visits to two high security psychiatric hospitals, Broadmoor and Carstairs. At Broadmoor, when she sat in on a private session of the patients' council, which included men considered to pose a serious threat to the public, Diana was immediately greeted with laughter and warm appreciation for her natural informality.

Similar warmth was expressed on a more glamorous stage in Paris that November, when Diana was involved in three days of fundraising work in support of French children's charities. After visiting projects in some of the most run down areas of the city, she was given a standing ovation by 900 diners at a grand banquet in the Hall of Mirrors at the Palace of Versailles.

With her triumphant trip to Paris and a public statement confirming her return to public life Diana was back in the limelight with a bang. She shared her hope that, with the Queen's approval, she would be closely involved in the 125 year anniversary celebrations for the Red Cross due in 1995.

While the last month of 1994 ran its course, Diana was able to contemplate the attempt she had made to pursue her life and build her future as she wanted. She had done exactly what she said she would when she stood before her audience a year earlier. She had "reduced the extent of her public life". That year she undertook only 10 official engagements against 198 in 1993. If she had still been seen, in the newspapers and magazines, as frequently as before, it was mostly as a result of intrusive and aggressive press attention. It was true that Diana offered some voluntary contributions of her own to the coverage. She condoned leaks about her 'secret' and unofficial humanitarian activities, in order to bring attention to them and she tried to manipulate the press coverage of stories she thought would damage her. In the main, she had not invited the majority of the coverage and the attention she received reinforced her view that the press stood in the way of the balanced life she craved.

Throughout the year Diana had been seeking a way of "combining a meaningful public role, with hopefully, a more private life". She had yet to find the formula which would make that possible but she had not given up. Her powerful affirmation would not allow her to ignore her desire for a quiet and fulfilling private life. Her failure to completely reorganise her lifestyle and bring about the balance she sought, in less than a year, owed more to her instinctive recognition that the time was not right and she had other priorities which needed her attention. She was virtually forced back into active public life to counter negative media attention that would have undermined her position as the separated wife to the heir and mother to the Princes.

In her Time and Space speech Diana had acknowledged her commitment to charity work and her desire to "focus on a smaller range of areas in the future." Against advice from Patrick Jephson, Diana had already reduced, to very few, the numbers of charities she patronised. Her private secretary felt she should maintain her power base at home and continue her work beneath the royal umbrella. The Princess was driven by a bigger vision which was consistent with her INFP personality. She wanted to focus on causes with global dimensions, where she believed her celebrity status and presence could make a substantial difference to people's lives and help improve the world. She also wanted to be free to respond, intuitively and rapidly, to requests for her help, rather than be tied to long term plans. Diana's vision of her future, both the working element of it and her private life, required that she be completely independent of the palace organisation which she felt was antagonistic to her and free of her marriage. That then was her ultimate aim but for now, after her experiences of the year just ending, she realised it could not be achieve while she remained married to her husband.

On 9 December the clock ticked off two years since Diana and Charles' separation had been officially announced. Diana was free to apply for a divorce on the grounds of an irretrievable breakdown of her marriage. She did not do so. She still felt strongly that it was for her husband to request that the marriage should end. Her lawyers agreed and advised her to wait for the other side to open negotiations so they could make the financial and practical arrangements which would secure her future. Until the issue was resolved Diana was determined to stay at Kensington Palace and perform her humanitarian role on the world stage in the way only she could. There she would be highly visible and safe, as mother to the Princes William and Harry and as a strong and popular figure, whose interests could not be dismissed without the risk of public disapproval.

Well aware that she needed the press to restore her position and maintain it, Diana was confident she would succeed in harnessing the so called "Fourth Estate" to her aims. By late 1994 she had been on the media front line, as a subject for press scrutiny, for thirteen years and she had an instinct for what the press wanted. They wanted her in the limelight and she was prepared to place herself there again but this time on her own terms. If the media was to have what it wanted, she would have what she needed and she was prepared to go to greater lengths than ever before to get it. Diana had already made a point of courting newspaper proprietors, editors and journalists on the assumption that they would print supportive stories about her once she had a chance to meet and speak with them, to show them who she really was and what she was trying to do. She was still hurt and confused when she discovered an article was even mildly critical or contained small inaccuracies. During 1994 she had tried her hand at press manipulation using tactics she had been taught by friendly journalists and she had started to lie.

In Diana's eyes there was nothing inappropriate about lying to the press when it came to her private life. In her experience they seemed to show as little regard for the truth as they did for her feelings and those of her children when they offered their lurid and embellished versions of stories about her to the public. Why should she not tell them whatever would put them off the scent or take them in the direction she wanted them to go?

After six years of self-transformation Diana had not only gained an unfailing confidence in her ability to outperform her husband in public but she had become hugely combative. She assumed she would be able to outmanoeuvre any of Charles' supporters who might try to derail her popularity. Her aggression, however, was no longer targeted at Charles himself but at the Establishment figures behind him.

Diana's relationship with Charles had undergone its own transformation since they were separated. The Princess was less angry at Charles and Camilla; her soubriquet "The Rottweiler" for the older woman had not been used since the Prince and Princess were separated two years before. The Prince was noticeably happier and more relaxed those days, according to people close to him. Since their separation the royal couple had fallen into a pattern of regular face to face meetings, alternating the venue between Diana's home, Kensington Palace and Charles' new apartments at Colour Court in St. James's Palace. What was difficult to begin with – Diana was distinctly tense although calm before she saw her husband – became easier and more cordial. After visiting her husband in his apartments Diana often visited her staff in the same palace complex and always had positive remarks to make about his attitude to fatherhood. The couple had achieved a dialogue they had been unable to share when they were together.

As cordial as their private relationship became, Charles and Diana could be nothing but competitors for public opinion on the world stage. Diana's step back from public life had given Charles and his courtiers some breathing space and they had tried hard to raise the Prince's profile and popularity, the last thing they needed was the most consummate performer in history occupying the same stage. Diana's decision, not only to return but to stride back, with even more impact than before, was bound to be seen as provocative and Diana was concerned at what the result might be. Unfortunately she had little choice but to risk the wrath of the men in grey and anyone else who gave their allegiance to Charles and the monarchy.

The Catch-22 for Diana, was that her high profile and influence on the world stage created, at one and the same time, a risk which endangered her and the situation which kept her secure against risks. As a result her position, at the end of 1994, seemed to be even more precarious than ever.

The risk to Diana came from her position as the key to Charles' status and position in public life. Ironically, the Princess who had been seen by the men in grey as inconsequential in the big scheme of Charles' life had become an essential factor in it. Her presence on the public stage, cast her husband and virtually everyone else in the royal family for that matter, into the shadows, so his path back into the hearts and minds of the British people was made more difficult. Diana's mere presence, as wife to the heir and the mother of his children, affected the, as yet unresolved, issue of Charles' succession to the throne and compromised his future with Camilla. Diana was certain she was seen as an obstacle, if not a downright threat, to Charles' aspirations and to the monarchy itself. Now that divorce was possible, with all the inherent complications it might cause for the heir and the royal family, it was possible that some of the imagined threats to her safety might become reality. Damned if they did and damned if they did not, comes to mind. Might it not, in some misguided person's eyes, be preferable to have a widowed heir rather than a divorced one? Diana was not blind to the possibility that her life could be at risk and that taking a highly visible and influential public role would only increase the danger she might be in. But she had no choice.

Despite her concerns Diana had proven to herself time and again during the past few years that public sympathy and support, gained through hard and much admired work on a highly visible world stage, was what kept her safe. Safe from personal attacks to her reputation following questionable behaviour, for which had always been forgiven. Safe from attempts to wrest her from her place beside her beloved sons and the work she felt destined to do. A red rag to the Establishment raging bull it may have been but Diana's public role was essential to her if she was to create the life she wanted. Charles's side had always had no option but to take notice of public opinion and Diana's popularity. In her new situation Diana instinctively recognised that her future was implacably tied to her public role and the more successful she could be the better.

✦ ✦ ✦

She rarely spoke about her husband and Camilla by the end of 1994. I hoped it meant she was beginning to replace her anger and resentment towards them with forgiveness and compassion. I doubted that they had enjoyed much of what had happened to them in the last thirteen years since Charles married Diana. I felt sad for them but my concerns were for my client. The constant diet of fear, anger, rage at times and resentment could do nothing but erode her health, bit by bit. I realised she used her anger, to alleviate her fear and doubt about the future but I was worried it was becoming a habit and she would still be eaten up by anger even when there was nothing left to be angry about.

Shortly after Charles had been interviewed by Dimbleby on TV, Diana had muttered something about the way she'd been treated and trotted out an angry mantra she hadn't used for a while, "I am the mother of his children."

As I walked past to put more oil on my hands, I rested my hand gently on her shoulder, a conciliatory gesture which enabled me to challenge her, without it seeming aggressive or confrontational "Yes, and he's the father of your sons."

I knew she felt she had been treated unfairly and was driven to confront those who seemed intent on perpetuating the injustice. It was her way of dealing with her feelings of helplessness, when what she really wanted was someone to take care of her and make decisions for her.

During the year I'd suggested she stop all her therapies and treatments, including mine, for a month, to find out where things stood in terms of her health and outlook. I wanted her to step back from another roundabout which might have become part of the problem, instead of part of the solution. I don't know if she discontinued any of her other therapies but she insisted I keep visiting.

✦ ✦ ✦

As the clock ticked down to the end of the year Diana attended some of the usual royal occasions so she could be with her sons. At the same time she contemplated the year to come, with her mind full of suspicions and concerns and the awareness that she might be facing her toughest time yet. Perhaps she recalled her own prophesy, made when she was a child, "I knew my life was going to be a winding road." Her life also promised to be a busy one, she had already instructed her staff to plan the most ambitious schedule of public engagements she had ever undertaken.

1995

Courage is resistance to fear,
mastery of fear,
not absence of fear.

Mark Twain

A mantle of power and influence enveloped Diana when she strode back onto the world stage in Paris at the end of 1994. The implications of her return to public life sent shivers of down the spines of many in the British Establishment who feared the harm the Princess could do to the royal institution they supported. As they contemplated Diana's busy and wide ranging schedule for 1995 they were filled with even more alarm.

The monarchy, the royal family and Prince Charles in particular, had already been much reduced in the public's perception, by questions about cost and relevance and by damaging personal revelations which cast doubt on the Prince's character and suitability for the role of King. According to those who supported Prince Charles, much of the blame for their diminished popularity belonged at Diana's door. It was, they argued, the disclosure of her unhappiness with her husband and his family which had caused the media spotlight to shine so harshly onto Charles, the Windsors and the institution they represented, with the result that all were now under intense and critical scrutiny.

Diana's withdrawal from public life at the start of the previous year had been greeted with a collective sigh of relief by Charles' supporters and the grey men at St. James's Palace. They set out to restore the heir's battered reputation and expended considerable efforts to make 1994 a revival year for him. It had not worked. One year was not enough. At times it seemed they were making headway but a steady stream of poor press and negative public reaction to his PR campaign had cancelled out the good impressions Charles occasionally gave. The result, at the start of 1995, was little change to the public's general perception that he was profligate, ineffective and responsible for the breakdown of his marriage to Diana.

With the Princess now back on the same platform Charles was trying to command, his palace courtiers were fearful that her presence would damage him, and the monarchy further. Time and again they had seen her suck the vital oxygen of publicity from her husband's important role and areas of interest, to her own less relevant efforts and causes. They had experienced her amazing, and to them quite mystifying, ability to generate popular affection and support. Many times Diana had acted in ways which should, they believed, have mortally damaged her reputation and credibility, yet she seemed to brush off all criticism and come back stronger, with more sympathy than ever. If anything, her transgressions reflected more adversely on Charles, who was blamed for not being the paragon of patience and virtue he was supposed to have been when he married his beautiful Princess. In every one of the past five years Diana, the inconsequential young woman, who was originally supposed to be just a minor piece in the royal organisation, had topped opinion polls and been voted the most popular member of the royal family. To many in the British Establishment at that time Diana was worthy of their rancour, deep suspicion and fear.

Ironically, the object of their distrust and apprehension was also fearful as her year commenced. In early January Diana had just returned from a skiing holiday in Vail, Colorado. Her plans for a trip to the sun, in South Africa, had been changed because the Queen was due to visit the country later in the year, underlining once again that Diana's life was bound by royal interests and not her own preferences or needs. Nonetheless, she had enjoyed the week she spent with wealthy businessman Mike Flannery and his family in their luxurious chalet. A brief period of domesticity, during which she "mucked in with everyone else", according to her personal trainer Jenni Rivett, who had arranged the trip at short notice and accompanied her, was just what Diana had needed. The respite it gave her from the troubles of her royal existence had been welcome but now, contemplating the coming year, she was becoming increasingly concerned.

When I pondered the first session I was due to have with Diana that year I was wondering what more I could do to help her. She had come so far already. What amazed me was how tough she had become. Her self-belief and strength of will were astonishing, even if she sometimes wept and raged with frustration. It had been a long time since I'd detected any signs of the suicidal tendencies that had been prominent when we'd first started working together six years before. I was under no illusion though. The notion of surrendering her life, like her bulimia, had become part of her psyche and might emerge again if she was confronted with extreme circumstances but I doubted that she'd succumb. I knew she'd developed resources by then that she hadn't had before, so she would probably be able to cope with almost anything. If she ran into problems she knew enough to seek professional help.

As far as I could judge, Diana had several resources which enabled her to continue striving towards her future-vision. None of them could be relied upon to endure and I hoped she would discover better in due course but what she had were powerful and effective at that time. The first was her role as mother to her sons. There were signs that they would soon be drifting outside Diana's sphere of influence but for the time being they were a significant part of their mother's future-vision and her inspiration to pursue it. It was a natural process of course and I wondered how she would deal with the situation when they began to distance themselves from her.

Another ability she'd acquired was the capacity to confront frightening situations with aggression but that ability was grounded in anger and the combination of the emotions and her reaction was a corrosive mixture which was not conducive to optimum health and well-being. I wondered how long she would have to use them as a way of dealing with the constant grinding strain of her life. I hoped not much longer but it was clear she was not ready to replace them with the spiritual perspective I believed would serve her better in the long run so they would have to suffice. Still, I had laid some foundations and time would tell whether she would be able to incorporate the compassion and love she shared in her work into her everyday life and all its various situations.

Diana's third resource was her absolute certainty that she would find a partner who would provide all she wanted to complete her life. Her future-vision demanded it and it was clear to me she was driven more powerfully by her desire for a fulfilling love relationship than by her desire to make the world a better place. Indeed I'd tried to suggest that we all affect the world just by our presence in it, so the only obligation she might choose to accept was to make the world a better place by making her life the best it could be. However she interpreted "best" was up to her, I pointed out, and nothing to do with other people's expectations. She didn't buy my reframing of one of her strongest beliefs about her destiny but I hoped she might come round to it. It would certainly take some of the weight of self-obligation she carried on her shoulders if she did. What worried me a lot was that she was placing so much store on finding the perfect partner, a soul mate who would fit into her life like a piece in a jigsaw.

My own observations, which I also shared with Diana, suggested that personal relationships, as much as any other situation, were opportunities for self-understanding and sharing love and intimacy. Perhaps, after learning what she needed to from those relationships which hadn't worked, she would attract someone who was a very close fit to her ideal partner. If the stories about her relationship with Oliver Hoare were true, however, her image of an ideal partner needed to be examined and altered. It seemed to have changed very little since she was the teenager who married Prince Charles. I'd tried to suggest to her that her idea of a perfect man was based on old beliefs, about herself and relationships, which no longer applied. I knew she hadn't been able to accept what I was talking about, which meant she would probably continue to attract men who could not fulfil her needs or who fulfilled the needs of her poor self-image only too well. I suspected she'd have some painful times ahead before she found happiness in that area but her hope of finding the love she sought drove her on.

I didn't have a plan for how to work with Diana as we entered 1995. *Wait and see what we're dealing with,* I told myself. The foundations which she'd put in place, in her beliefs and thinking, were already bringing about changes. We would just have to see, in the due course of time, where they took her life and her health and deal with the outcomes as they arose. I was certain she'd be in a better place and better shape than she would have been if we hadn't met. In the meantime, I'd continue to offer my support and try to make the journey easier with massage and gentle guidance when the path became difficult.

✦ ✦ ✦

The problems Diana was facing were like nobody else's despite their superficial similarity to those confronted by many other women. The scale and complexity of Diana's difficulties involved layers of complication which frequently made her despair of finding a way out of her nightmare. In principle, her circumstances seemed commonplace enough. Like countless others before her she was in an unhappy marriage and, like those others she wanted to be free to pursue her life as she wanted. The remedy for most people was to obtain a divorce. Divorce, however, was not necessarily a remedy that would help Diana at that time and even if it turned out to be, it was not as readily available to HRH the Princess of Wales as it was to the average person. Diana's marital situation was not commonplace at all.

To begin with her husband was no ordinary person he was the heir to the throne. Divorce for him had more profound implications than for most people and he was in no hurry to add problems to those he already had by taking steps which would bring about the final break in his marriage. There were matters of public perception to be considered if he was seen to initiate a divorce from his high profile and more popular wife. There were constitutional issues to take into account as well. Divorce might not have threatened Charles' succession and future role as Sovereign but if he wanted to marry again it could have thrown the monarchy into a disagreement with the Church of England, which was already looking askance at an heir who had been publicly reflecting on his preference to be "defender of faiths" rather than The Defender of the Faith, as required by the Coronation oath he would be expected to take.

The royal couple's children added more than the usual complications to the matter. William and Harry were not ordinary boys but royal Princes and heirs to the throne after their father. As a result, under British law, Diana's contact and influence over her children's futures was subject to the Sovereign's agreement. In reality the Queen was unlikely to risk public disapproval by obstructing the extremely popular and unpredictable Princess's access to her beloved sons. But a divorce could have opened an entirely new set of circumstances that would affect the Princes, such as where Diana might choose to live if not in the UK and who she might marry. In those cases the Queen might have felt compelled to assert her rights.

Then there was the matter of Diana's public profile. Marriage to Charles and into the British royal family had exposed her to unprecedented levels of media exposure. By 1995 she was the most famous woman in the world and instantly recognisable everywhere except the most remote places on earth. No sensible person could imagine that divorce would make her invisible overnight. In simple terms Diana had nowhere to hide even if she wanted to. If she did the unthinkable and walked away, leaving behind her sons, her luxurious lifestyle and her highly regarded humanitarian role, someone, somewhere would undoubtedly recognise her and alert the press.

That then was the situation which filled Diana with anxiety at the start of 1995. She could not create the life she wanted while she was married to

Charles, that much was clear. What was not clear was whether a divorce would be offered to her or how she would respond if it was. Even if a divorce was eventually agreed it would have to be an arrangement which helped rather than hindered her in achieving the future she envisioned for herself, a future that included her sons, her work and a proper marriage based on love, otherwise it would be no better than her present.

It would have been easier for the Prince and Princess if there had been someone in Diana's life who could replace Charles, someone who could offer her the loving relationship and home she craved with the possibility of more children and a chance to continue some kind of humanitarian role in the world. If such a person had existed he would have to have been very wealthy, an acceptable stepfather for the Princes and extremely comfortable with his own place in the scheme of things he would be exposed to. If such a person had existed Diana would have carefully considered what, if any, public role she was prepared to play from the safety and security of a new marriage and peaceful home, preferably with another baby on the way. Such a person did not exist at that time.

On the face of it Oliver Hoare had seemed ideal and Diana, who adored him, had stepped back from public life a year ago to explore what future they might have together. It was true he moved in the right circles and could, conceivably, have been accepted by the royal family as a suitable stepfather to the Princes but it turned out he was not very wealthy – his wife was. More significantly his failure, a few months before, to support Diana's assertions that she was not responsible for the silent calls to his home, had made Diana uncertain of her feelings for him. By the early weeks of that January their relationship was starting to cool, even though he had been seen climbing into the boot of Diana's car on one occasion, presumably so she could drive him into Kensington Palace unseen. In the circumstances, her lack of certainty about Hoare and what might become of her own future without him, reinforced Diana's decision to return to the work which had always offered her stability, a comforting environment and some confidence that she was in control of at least part of her life.

Around mid-January another event occurred to add to Diana's concerns. Camilla Parker Bowles and her husband announced their intention to divorce and raised in Diana a new level of intense speculation about her own future. Camilla free to marry Charles had significant implications for Diana. If her husband and Camilla married then Diana's sons would become stepchildren to a woman she detested. Diana still had painful memories of how she had felt when Raine married into the Spencer family and even though the Princess and her once hated stepmother had become friends, this new turn of events caused Diana to worry for her boys. She did not know which would be worse, Camilla as a stepmother hated by her sons or Camilla as stepmother beloved by her sons.

Diana's concerns, however, went beyond the maternal anxiety she felt for William and Harry. Diana's position, as mother to the young heirs, was an important factor in her current situation, which at least was being held in a sort of tense equilibrium, a balance of power that provided her with some sense of security. Her status, her mother's role, gave her a degree of protection against more overt hostility which might otherwise have been directed at her. It also added to the pressure she could bring to bear when she wanted to confront the constraints the royal organisation tried to impose on her. The mere possibility that Camilla might usurp her position and so upset the delicate balance of power, potentially added to the dangers Diana faced. She had already seen her influence and position eroded to some degree by Charles' appointment of Tiggy Legge-Bourke as the boys' nanny and companion. By comparison, the news that Camilla would soon be free to marry increased the threat and added to Diana's sense of disquiet.

✦ ✦ ✦

When I worked on Diana for the first time that year I was fascinated by the physical transformation her body had undergone since we first started working. She was leaner and more muscular, especially in the shoulders and legs. No doubt the latent muscle development, from swimming so much since childhood, had been accentuated by her work in the gym with her personal trainers and Will Carling. I could see and feel the strong physique she had acquired to underpin her more assertive mental stance in the world and how it helped her deal with so many of the situations which threatened to engulf her. Not for the first time I was struck by the amazing phenomenon of the body-mind process in action.

Once again though, I was saddened by the fact that she had been driven, by fear and anger, to become antagonistic. It seemed an indictment of the system into which she had married that someone so full of the desire to give and receive love should have learned to cope by becoming aggressive.

All part of the great scheme of things my own inner guidance prompted me as I shrugged off the tendency to become angry on Diana's behalf.

Balancing Water with Earth, I mused as I worked on her. By then I was so familiar with every muscle and joint that my hands worked automatically to reduce the tension and tightness, at least as far as I could. There were still areas which would not change until her mental attitude altered. Still, it was odd that I was not entirely focussed on what I was doing but gave myself up to pondering the Chinese elemental significance of her physical transformation. Nevertheless I did, and concluded she was automatically balancing aspects of her pre-dominantly Water nature with its opposite, Earth. Emotions, in particular fear, were being balanced with physicality and its inherent power to change situations immediately with direct action.

Sad she doesn't know that Water will always win in the end over Earth, eroding away even the hardest rock. The gentle power of the most life enabling emotions, like love and compassion, will always overcome physical alternatives.

Eventually, I reminded myself.

What was strange and gave me much to think about after that session was that I didn't feel inclined to share my insight with Diana. Somehow there didn't seem any point in trying to explain the esoteric concepts which might have guided her to another way of seeing her situation.

When I thought about that later, I realised that up to then I would automatically have shared my thoughts with her if she'd been open to them. Clearly she no longer was or I was no longer able to sense when she was receptive. It was the first indication I had that our work together might be coming to an end.

As usual Diana's only recourse, her only antidote, to the threat she felt she was under, was to confront her rivals and outwit them in the one arena where she held all the cards, the arena of public opinion. Fearful she may have been but she was still combative and was responding to challenges with considerable aggression. At the beginning of February Diana embarked on her first major engagement of the year. Filled with the sense that very important matters, affecting her future and even her life, were slipping from her grasp, she embarked on a four day visit to Japan. There she performed brilliantly on behalf of charities associated with the disabled, the young and the aged. She spoke a few words in Japanese during a speech in which she offered her personal sympathy to those affected by the Kobe earthquake, which had occurred just three weeks before. As president of Great Ormond

Street Hospital, she played a role in the formalising of links with Tokyo's National Children's Hospital.

In his memoirs Patrick Jephson recalled the suspicions he faced in the royal palaces from those who opposed Diana's public role. Her answer was to excel at the work she did. From all of her many solo engagements Diana had received nothing but praise from grateful British diplomats across the world for the good will she generated for Britain and, ironically, for the prestige she gained for its royal family. Accompanied, as she always was, by an enormous press entourage, Diana was welcomed by heads of state and important figures in almost every country and inevitably, when she met them, she charmed them. In Japan in 1995 the story was the same, the Princess did not put a foot wrong, although one particular incident in which she placed her feet even more correctly than usual was recalled later, in his memoirs, by Patrick Jephson.

The story is one of many which illustrated Diana's professionalism, attention to detail and her awareness of how to benefit personally while performing her exemplary public role. Diana was preparing to meet the Emperor of Japan and his family when Jephson witnessed her trying on several different pairs of shoes. It seemed like a frivolous and pedantic exercise to discover which would make her tallest, even when she laughingly explained "I'm already taller than the Emperor, but it won't do any harm to look just that bit taller!" Only much later was Jephson to understand the full importance when she explained that protocol demanded she curtsy below the Emperor's eye line, then she handed her private secretary a newspaper. The photograph it contained showed the stunning result when a very tall, very athletic and very beautiful Princess in a tight skirt and very high heels curtsied deeply.

While she was in Japan Diana's long running dispute with Bryce Taylor and Mirror Group Newspapers, over the intrusive gym photos published in 1993, ended with an out of court settlement in the Princess's favour. The terms of the agreement did little financial damage to Taylor, or the newspapers involved. Compared to the sums the gym manager received for the results of his subterfuge, only a small donation was paid to charity. The Mirror Group paid all legal costs and handed over the offending photographs. What meant more to Diana was the apology the *Daily Mirror* carried on its front page and the vindication it represented for her stance against press intrusion into her privacy. What meant a great deal more to her lawyers and concerned supporters was that she narrowly avoided being cross examined in court by a very able QC about her dealings with the press.

By the time Diana returned to the UK after her Japan tour she was entangled in a difficult psychological dilemma. On the one hand she was extremely comfortable and totally confident when engaged in her public role. There she knew she brought a genuine healing presence to the most disadvantaged and did well by her charities and the British Government while adding to her own public profile which would keep her safe. On the other hand she was feeling increasingly uncomfortable with what seemed to be happening behind the scenes, where she could not be seen by the world's media and the ordinary people who supported her and where she had little control over events.

Diana knew she was viewed with suspicion and animosity by her husband's followers and some others who proposed that her activities on the world stage might damage the monarchy. She knew the ill-feeling resulted in active obstruction of her public role. Patrick Jephson frequently had to deal with the whispering campaign of disapproval and the minor but irritating obstructions or argue strongly for prerequisites, such as royal travel facilities for her official engagements, to which Diana was entitled. Ironically the hostility and concern was directed at her despite all the evidence which showed it to be unwarranted, at least in regard to the damage she might do to the royal institution. The Princess's every triumphant appearance in public, especially on the world stage, automatically enhanced the reputation of the British monarchy and thereby the Windsors, even though her separation agreement had removed from her any official identity as the Queen's representative abroad. Also, the very institution she was supposedly harming was the same one her son William was due to head when he became King after his father. Logic should have indicated Diana was a positive asset to the royal family and one unlikely to be seeking to harm it, yet she was still deemed by some to be a risk whose public role should be strongly discouraged if not actively impeded.

It was hard to see any reasons for the enmity except personal dislike of Diana, an opportunistic attempt to benefit Prince Charles by attacking her role, or a genuine belief that she was involved in some complex conspiracy to displace Charles as the future King in favour of her own son. It is possible that Diana's own outspoken and critical opinions, about the royal family's public performances and her husband's suitability for what she called "the top job", all shared candidly with many media figures, friends and celebrities, might have given ammunition to those who wanted to suggest she was a threat to Charles's succession and the Windsors' future. Wherever the hostility originated, the result for Diana was an escalating level of fear for her future and even her own safety.

In time her fear was labelled "paranoia" by some who either could not fully understand Diana or the position she was in, or who were incapable of caring. The irony was that the same label of paranoia could well have been affixed to some of those who attached it to Diana. Overheated imaginations on both sides gradually created an atmosphere of mutual suspicion which fed on itself and caused Diana immense difficulties that year. In fact, when considered from her viewpoint, Diana's intense anxiety can be seen as a very understandable reaction to what was an extremely unpleasant situation.

Since she was quite young Diana had been wary of other people as a result of her childhood experiences and later because of her personality. By the time she met Prince Charles she was reluctant to share her thoughts and ideas openly, except with a few very close friends. Her natural inclination to be on her guard was reinforced into outright distrust when she entered the royal environment, where she encountered disturbing undercurrents of intrigue and suspicion on many levels. Early on, she sensed that Charles and his friends were not entirely honest with her about his relationship with Camilla Parker Bowles. Diana had been proven correct in her suspicions.

Then there were the ever vigilant security measures and the legions of staff, present during almost every waking hour. The constant scrutiny naturally gave rise to an inclination to conceal and hide as much as she could from prying eyes and to an increased sensitivity to possible breaches of trust. Her concerns were justified by the leaks of stories from "sources close to the Princess" which found their way into the press. Not long ago she had apparently caught Paul Burrell, her junior butler at the time, looking through private papers on her desk and she had become convinced other domestic staff regularly rifled through her waste paper bins.

For years Diana had lived and operated in a hostile royal environment, where subterfuge was the norm rather than the exception. For her own self-protection she had become embroiled in similar behaviour. Ever since 1991, when she had secretly facilitated Andrew Morton's book, she had been using a shredder for private correspondence and assumed she was under almost constant surveillance, although she did not know by whom. By early 1995, with the hostile men in grey seeking ways to reduce her status and public profile, she was adept at deception in order to keep "the enemy", as she called her opponents, guessing about her intentions and plans.

Media interest added another dimension to Diana's distrust of those around her. For the past fourteen years, since she was connected with Prince Charles, she had lived with the knowledge that information about her was a commodity, with monetary value if sold to the press. Anyone linked to her, friends, staff and even acquaintances with the briefest of associations were potential sources of betrayal. Already Diana had suffered many embarrassments, the most recent being from James Hewitt's tell-all book a few months earlier. By 1995 every relationship was coloured by the possibility she might not only be humiliated but harmed as well. Information about her was not just trivia which shaped tabloid tales for the general public's titillation, it was ammunition which could be used by those who were hostile to her. Sources "close" to her, who shared their tit-bits about her private "mood-swings" and "tantrums", added weight to more damaging stories about her mental state, which could have affected her entire future.

In February Diana's suspicious nature proved to be well founded when Oliver Hoare's former chauffeur, Barry Hodge, sold his story about his employer's relationship with the Princess to the *News of the World*. It was a double blow which struck at Diana's reputation and her dreams. The story was a damaging one, especially coming on top of the phone calls scandal, because it added to the impression that the Princess was obsessed with a married man. The consequences for her private vision of the future was perhaps more painful when Hoare again refused to support her and declined to comment, as he had during the phone calls scandal a few months earlier. Hoare's disloyalty made Diana finally acknowledged he was not going to be part of her future but it also magnified her perception that she was beset on all sides and might be betrayed by anyone. The news, on 3 March, that Camilla Parker Bowles was divorced, merely added to the strain Diana was under and increased her scepticism about almost everyone around her.

For years Diana had habitually and automatically compartmentalised her life, sharing only parts of herself with her friends, staff and acquaintances, until none of those who spent time with her knew all that was going on in her life. Even her closest friends admitted they did not know who else she might be seeing or talking to, or what she might be planning. The result was often surprise, anger or embarrassment when press stories revealed, to friends and staff, situations they had no knowledge of. In effect Diana's secretive nature, exacerbated by her royal life, isolated her from genuinely close friendships based on trust and mutual sharing, until her belief that she was not understood become self fulfilling.

By 1995 Diana's precarious position and strong belief that nobody could truly appreciate the situation she was in, led her to become even more secretive and increasingly sensitive to any signs of disloyalty. Her friends noticed that Diana became more prone to irritability and aggression when they offered advice or comments, which she saw as criticism and disloyalty. Of course it was difficult for them to offer worthwhile advice. They did not know the full picture and it was unlikely their own life experiences would have enabled them to fully appreciate all the personal, professional and constitutional complexities of Diana's life or what she was aiming to achieve. In the event, Diana expected unquestioning loyalty and acceptance whatever she did. Her attitude seemed to be "if you're not for me then you're against me." Friends, who had known her since she was a teenager and seen her at her most vulnerable and weak, were unlikely to be able to view her as the strong and confident woman she felt herself to be by that time, especially since she could still seem like the moody and capricious young woman they remembered from the past.

People tend to respond to the model implied by the way they are treated, either by acquiescing to it or confronting it. If someone is treated as a weak person they will either react weakly or demonstrate aggressive strength. Diana wanted her friends to treat her like a powerful and capable person even if, at times, in her uncertainty, she acted anything but. By that March Diana had already fallen out with her old friend and co-conspirator on the Morton book, James Colthurst, when he tried too hard to persuade her to accept help from NLP expert and motivational guru Anthony Robbins. Other friends were permanently or temporarily side lined for similar transgressions. That month Diana fell out with long time friends Kate Menzies and Catherine Soames during a skiing holiday in Lech, Austria. They had made known their disapproval when Diana received phone calls from Will Carling. Diana rarely explained why she distanced herself from her friends. Explaining her feelings was inconsistent with her personality type and entirely consistent with her inclination to avoid direct confrontations. She either dropped the person who offended her or picked up their relationship after a brief hiatus, as if nothing had happened.

The situation was not made easier by how Diana reacted to the strain she was experiencing. It was part of her INFP personality that under extreme stress she became irritable and nit-picking about small things. Her new friend and psychic therapist, Simone Simmons, who also had differences of opinion with Diana which resulted in periods of estrangement, later recalled mood swings, tantrums and despondency which might last for days. But she also remembered Diana as a sweet natured, funny and caring friend. This kind of paradoxical behaviour was most obvious when it came to Diana's work. In public she was invariably the poised professional; cheerful, charming and sensitive to others but in private, when the curtain had fallen between her and the audience of press and public, she could be temperamental, difficult and sometimes unkind. Very few were able to understand her changeable behaviour or deal with it with equanimity.

Understanding Diana as she was then required an appreciation of her unique personal circumstances, married to Charles and constrained within the royal family and the situation she was experiencing at the time. With the demise of her relationship with Oliver Hoare, Diana's future-vision was momentarily lost and she was left without the comforting presence of a partner while dealing with a very hostile palace environment. The pressure on her was so great that she risked slipping back into old patterns of thinking and coping. In a mature and courageous response Diana sought professional help at that difficult time. She was still being treated by Susie Orbach but she also arranged a four hour session at Kensington Palace with Canadian bulimia expert Peggy Claude-Pierre. Claude-Pierre's later comment about the interview "She was hurting because she couldn't express who she was" was particularly insightful about Diana's situation.

I grinned at the policeman who peered in through my car window as I sat filing my nails. He didn't ask and I didn't explain that my work required very short nails with smooth edges and that the unusual blood flow to my hands all day, every day, because of my work, meant my nails grew very strong very quickly. They needed constant attention to stop me scratching my clients. Indeed I'd once, jokingly, suggested to Diana that she take up massage to improve her nails which she used to gnaw to the quick. But that was a long time in the past and her changing self-perception had resolved that particular issue.

The policeman was checking me out after I'd arrived at the Palace early and parked, as I sometimes did, about a hundred yards away from the gates on a small car parking area. Despite knowing me and my car well by then, they still came to make sure I wasn't up to anything nefarious. Conceivably I could have had a bomb laden terrorist in the back or someone examining the security arrangements. After a few friendly words the bobby returned to his colleague at the gate and I returned to my musings.

I was wondering how Diana's life would have to unfold so that she could balance her amazing public work with the personal life she wanted and if there was any way I could help her make it happen. Given her circumstances, it didn't seem possible while she was married and working so hard. I came back to a conclusion I'd come to before. Sometimes the body has to go through a serious crisis before its most profound healing is triggered, sometimes a life has to go through a serious crisis before it can change course and overcome what is blocking the best future possible. I hoped the crisis Diana required, if I was correct in my analysis, would not be too painful. I didn't know at that time just how prophetic my thoughts were.

Around then Diana took the time to write down her own personal description of what she wanted to do with her life. The document she produced did not describe the future-vision she had created in her guided visualisation years before, so when she shared it with her private secretary, Patrick Jephson, he did not know the complete picture Diana had in mind when she penned the words. In particular he would not have known that alongside the working life he was employed to facilitate, she envisioned a private life with home and family, or that her personal life was probably more important to her than her public role. As a result, when he read her description, he found it represented what he had come to judge as her usual "muddled thinking".

The document did not reflect his own opinions that Diana should focus for the long term on "a few well-defined objectives" chosen from her UK based humanitarian interests. He had also urged her to stay within the royal system because he believed she would lose much of her credibility as an influential humanitarian if she left. In her written comments about the "inflexibility" of her diary and desire to "deal with many countries" Jephson saw a lack of self-discipline and a desire for glamour over substance, when they actually represented a reluctance to commit to long-term projects that would deny her the chance of a fulfilling marriage and home life.

He was able to sympathise with Diana's desire to use her "healing interests and abilities" and make a "contribution on the world platform". He also recognised that she wanted a chance to "address increasing world problems" but he was not as sympathetic to her wish to avoid having others take the praise for her efforts or "being used as a puppet".

Had he known her personality type better, Jephson might have noticed that Diana's aspirations were couched in terms associated with her emotions based make-up and intuitive perception of the world, rather than the unemotional, logical planning he preferred. If he had known her better he might have recognised her frustration, at being trapped in an unappreciative and hostile royal organisation that nevertheless benefited from her presence. With more knowledge he might even have noticed old childhood patterns of thinking emerging in her words because of the strain she was under. In the end, he decided she was merely describing a situation that would fulfil an insatiable requirement, for what he later called "reassurance, popularity and recognition" and referred to her document only when the opportunity arose to "nudge her in a particular direction that might prove rewarding."

The significance of Diana's personal manifesto, in terms of her personal transformation, was that it highlighted the extreme imbalance which had arisen once again between her highly successful public role and her unsatisfying personal life. Without a personal relationship that offered the possibility of a safe home and more children with a man she loved, she was only able to focus on the other side, the public side, of the future she really wanted and with that disparity she could not become happy. Diana's craving for a happy family life and meaningful relationship would have a significant effect on events which occurred over the following year.

As the strain increased, Diana's household staff underwent a radical reorganisation similar to that which had seen many of her close friends fall by the wayside. Her long serving butler departed and then her chef was replaced. Paul Burrell, now one of the most trusted people in her life, became the mainstay of Diana's domestic and personal arrangements, her "rock", as she called him. In his memoir Burrell wrote "My role began to evolve in 1995 into personal assistant, messenger, driver, delivery boy, confidant...." With Burrell's devoted support Kensington Palace became

Diana's redoubt. She forayed out to exercise at the gym and perform her special brand of magic in the public eye. Within her fortress walls she shared time with selected friends and connected with others by innumerable and prolonged telephone calls. Burrell became her gatekeeper.

During the months of spring and summer Diana focussed much of her time on her work. During March detailed briefing notes and other information from Mike Whitlam, CEO of the British Red Cross, added to her increasing interest in the problems caused in many areas of the world by antipersonnel land mines. The issue had been raised first in 1991 and was considered again in 1993, during discussions about her work following her separation. In 1995 the momentum towards what would become one of Diana's most famous and controversial campaigns was maintained.

In late April Diana travelled to Hong Kong where, on a trip sponsored by millionaire David Tang, she visited projects which involved cancer treatment, the homeless and drug rehabilitation. At a gala dinner her presence prompted donations totalling a quarter of a million pounds which were channelled through her Charities Trust to the Leprosy Mission and other charitable organisations operating in Hong Kong and China. Patrick Jephson later called the trip "a model of how her working life might have evolved."

Jephson was not so impressed by Diana's continued courting of high profile figures from business, the media and the world of entertainment although even he had to admit she used her own celebrity status to good effect. On 9 June Diana returned David Tang's generous support in Hong Kong by travelling to Venice, to attend his exhibition promoting Chinese artists and in the process she raised funds for London's Serpentine Gallery. Later in June she attended a gala concert to raise money for Ty Hafan, a children's hospice near Penarth, Wales. She had only become it's patron that March but had soon persuaded opera star Luciano Pavarotti to appear at the fundraising event.

When, in turn, the great tenor asked her to go to Modena, Italy, in September, to Pavarotti's own concert in aid of his War Child project and children affected by the Balkans conflict, she was happy to be amongst the celebrities there. In mid-June Diana was in Moscow where she visited Tushinskaya Children's Hospital, which benefitted from her support by receiving new equipment. In Moscow she was also awarded the international Leonardo Prize for important sponsors of charity. In July Diana faced other members of the royal family again at the 50th anniversary celebrations to mark VJ day. Unknown to her it was to be her last official royal family engagement.

Her powerful public appearances and the acclaim she was receiving on the world stage energised and comforted Diana for a time, but when she was alone they merely served to highlight even more the vast chasm which separated her from the future she sought. Without a companion to offer love, support and a comforting embrace she was even more inclined to see the darker side of her life and be distressed by what was lacking. When she was not working, the strain she felt was immense and those friends and acquaintances who were with her during private moments noticed her anguish, or her fluctuating mood and emotions.

The tension she was under was captured in the portrait of Diana painted that summer by British artist Henry Mee, who had been commissioned by the British Red Cross. "Diana was raw", Mee claimed, "On several occasions her eyes were red (from crying all night)." The resulting portrait was unveiled in late September and evoked, for many observers, memories of the iconic black and white photograph of Myra Hindley, the infamous Moors murderer.

In early August the British tabloids revealed Diana's friendship with Will Carling. In a story provided by Carling's former personal assistant, Hilary Ryan, the closeness which had developed between the famous rugby player and the Princess was portrayed as a romance which involved "secret trysts", although the article was unable to establish that there had been any physical intimacy between them. Diana's friend at the time, Simone Simmons is adamant that the Princess could not have been attracted to a man so much shorter than her, no matter how muscularly attractive and knowledgeable about fitness and health. royal chauffeur, Steve Davies, who caddied for Carling agreed he and Diana probably had not had an affair. Friends of the Princess concurred. Diana had been unable to keep the nature of other relationships secret from them and she always insisted Carling was nothing more than an ardent admirer.

The probable truth was that Diana had been her usual open, caring and flirtatious self, during her conversations at the Harbour Club with the handsome rugby star. Apparently she was especially empathetic with Carling and when she detected that her friend's marriage was in difficulties she raised the topic and offered advice. Carling, like Prince Charles and others before him, was flattered by the Princess's thoughtful concern and probably misconstrued her interest. Diana certainly recognised the attraction he felt for her and was happy to enjoy his close friendship and their mutual flirtation. In her romantically arid and embattled life she wanted friends to be constantly available and would often call several times a day for telephone conversations. For Carling, an attractive man she admired, Diana even had a dedicated SIM card for her mobile phone calls with him and used pet names, calling him "captain" and sometimes answering her phone as Mrs Carling. Encouraged by the Princess's attention, his personal assistant said he had been "running after her like a puppy". The rugby player submitted to the frequent demands on his time and became enmeshed in Diana's complex life just when his relationship with his wife was struggling. In the circumstances it was only too easy for an affectionate and often flirtatious friendship to become embellished into a torrid romance by the tabloid license to thrill.

Comments made by Carling and his wife to the press when the story emerged, were not used to help the situation blow over, quite the contrary. Julia Carling, a TV presenter, formerly in PR, publicly blamed Diana for her marital problems and was not inclined to be understanding. Obviously referring to Diana's relationship with Oliver Hoare she commented in the *Mail on Sunday* "This has happened to her before" and the Princess was branded a marriage wrecker. A contrite Will Carling admitted publicly that he had made a mistake by allowing himself to be flattered by Diana's interest in him and had hurt his wife as a result. He promised not to see Diana again.

In the meantime, slightly battered by the unexpected press mauling she had received over a relationship that never was, Diana was about to find herself involved in the real thing. On 1 September she went to the Royal Brompton hospital to visit Joe Toffolo, husband of her acupuncturist and friend Oonagh and met his Pakistani heart surgeon, Hasnat Khan. According to Oonagh, when she recalled the meeting later, it was "love at first sight." Apparently Diana agreed. Her first words after Khan left the room were "He's drop dead gorgeous." During the two weeks after their first meeting Diana visited Joe in hospital as often as possible and talked to his surgeon on many occasions. She recognised they shared the same dedication for caring for the sick and revelled in the feeling of connection to him she felt as a result. Her attraction to Hasnat Khan grew when she realised he was completely unimpressed by her glamorous image and wealthy lifestyle.

✦ ✦ ✦

It wasn't the first time I'd experienced the disconnection which was obviously occurring. In fact I was experiencing the same thing during my work with other clients as well but with Diana it was more noticeable because of the intensity of the bond I'd shared with her for so long. In part it was happening because she was becoming less receptive to the solutions I was offering her. There was something else though – I was tired, physically and emotionally and needed a rest. Also, my personal self-transformation process, which had continued unabated through all the years I had been working with Diana, had brought me to another moment of decision about my own life.

When I asked myself if it was time to step back from the work I loved and try another path, my answer each time was more clearly 'Yes!'

The bodywork I used was still quite effective, for Diana as well as my other clients. I was still able to release the tension in her muscles and help her deal with the stress she was under. As always I was amazed at her resilience and saddened that she had to be so resilient. There wasn't much more than the bodywork by then though and it was becoming increasingly mechanical. I was reluctant to tune it at any other level or to offer solutions I believed would help her, or perhaps she was reluctant to hear them. Whatever it was, I noticed the difference in the work and she probably did as well.

I remembered a client I'd had some years before. She was a bit, let's say, hyper. Anyway I saw her quite late one evening and she was more distracted than usual. Kept talking to her husband, wanting to know who was on the phone, that sort of thing. I was tired and instead of focussing more, to bring my attention to what I was doing, I winged it and for the first time ever just went through the motions without engaging my heart. After the massage she looked me straight in the eyes and asked me "What was that?"

Shame is a great teacher and I felt ashamed then. With Diana at that time I was finding it difficult to remain engaged in the work I was doing for her. I didn't want to experience the same shame again and it made me think even more about stepping away from her.

✦ ✦ ✦

Within a few weeks Diana asked Khan if she could speak to him privately and from late summer, according to Simone Simmons, they held "Intense conversations at Kensington Palace..." Their relationship blossomed over the months which followed. Diana became a frequent visitor to the hospital while Khan was on duty, often late at night. She comforted his patients, some just recovering from surgery and they walked the quiet wards together. They talked at the pubs he enjoyed or over fish and chip suppers at a simple local restaurant and Diana was impressed by his warmth, wit and intelligence. She was totally smitten and, as was usual for her when in a relationship, she began to build visions of her future around the gentle, soft spoken surgeon.

As Diana's relationship with Hasnat Khan was developing other significant events were taking place. Late that summer a journalist and producer, Martin Bashir, who worked for the BBC's flagship current affairs programme *Panorama*, contacted Diana's brother, Charles. In a meeting at Althorp, Bashir told Charles Spencer he was investigating MI5 activities in relation to the royal family and was concerned about "dirty tricks" aimed at Diana. In what came to be regarded by many well placed commentators as a very calculated manipulation, Bashir apparently used faked documents and clever psychology to persuade Diana's brother, then the Princess, that she was under threat. The solution he offered for the situation was for her to go public, in an interview with him on national, prime-time television.

To understand why Diana might have even considered such a dramatic step it is necessary to realise that Bashir approached her at a time when she was feeling more vulnerable than she ever had and more confrontational. Her heightened levels of fear and suspicion were not merely the results of old childhood doubts given new life by a fanciful imagination and over active emotions. Her apprehension and distrust, especially of the security services, was based on what she regarded as real, tangible evidence accumulated over a number of years. Evidence that seemed to support her conviction that she was under surveillance, was being attacked on the media battleground and that her life might genuinely be at risk as a consequence of the problems she posed.

As far back as 1986 Diana had become aware that the heavy hand of royal influence could cast a sudden shadow over her life. Her bodyguard at the time, Barry Mannakee, had been abruptly moved to other duties after being accused of allowing his relationship with Diana to overstep its professional boundaries. When Mannakee had been killed in a traffic accident the following year Diana was convinced he had been killed for his transgression.

James Hewitt was convinced he had been followed on a number of occasions during his relationship with Diana and had asked her what he should do. Little more than thirty months after Mannakee's death, a private telephone conversation between Diana and James Gilbey was tape recorded, in suspicious circumstances and eventually offered to the tabloid press. In his memoirs, Ken Wharfe, Diana's senior protection officer during the time of the ensuing Squidgy tape scandal recounted his recollection of the affair and the results of his own investigation into it.

Wharfe confirmed the internal security services had undertaken a full investigation and all the parties involved had been identified. He therefore knew who had made an original master recording of the conversation and why it was made but was unable to divulge who it was for legal reasons. According to Wharfe the original recording was transmitted regularly so that it could be picked up by amateur radio enthusiasts, who were known to scan for private chats late at night, on the assumption Diana's damaging conversation would "eventually end up in the hands of the media." At least two taped copies of the re-broadcast conversation were apparently made by different radio hams on different days and offered to tabloids.

Wharfe also confirmed that Diana was aware "the intelligence services routinely monitored the daily lives of the royal family" but he personally did not know, until much later, "that they routinely taped the Princess's telephone conversations." He declared that his department, the Royal Protection Department, was "categorically not involved in this surveillance". It can reasonably be assumed that the Camillagate tape of Prince Charles' intimate conversation with Camilla, made around the same time, and another of private conversations between the Duke and Duchess of York, came about in a similar fashion.

The subsequent exposure of the Squidgy tape in August 1992 was equally shrouded in mystery. More than two and a half years after the tape was originally obtained by a British tabloid, which did not use it, extracts were published in the USA, then worldwide, virtually forcing publication in the UK. Seven months later, in March 1993, one of the most damaging parts of the taped conversation which had been withheld, was revealed in Australia, again ensuring it found its way into the public domain in the UK.

In June 1992, when the royal family was desperate to prove she was involved with Andrew Morton's sensational book *Diana: Her True Story* and pressing her to denounce it, Diana told James Colthurst that Prince Philip had personally threatened her with the exposure of another secretly taped conversation. That time she was supposedly discussing arrangements for the newspaper serialisation of the offending book. The tape was never produced and Diana was told to forget it had been mentioned.

Ever since Morton's book was published in 1992, Diana mental state had been raised in some sections of the press and she was sure that was due to the influence of Charles' friends and supporters. The damaging assertion was prominent in coverage of Prince Charles's television interview with Jonathan Dimbleby and the Oliver Hoare silent calls debacle a year before. On that occasion records of the police investigation mysteriously became available to the tabloids. When Patrick Jephson asked for copies of the police report and a list of the calls, he was promised they would be made available to him. They never were, nor was an explanation of how the press obtained details of the official investigation.

Andrew Morton later wrote about the apparently well established practice at that time of bugging phone calls emanating from in and around Kensington Palace. In his book *Diana: In Pursuit of Love* he describes the experience of a police officer who made a private call from an official phone "at the end of the Palace drive". When he replaced the receiver the phone immediately began to ring. On picking it up the officer heard his own words being replayed back down the line. Diana always denied making the hundreds of calls which had apparently been made to Oliver Hoare's home, although as a compulsive telephone user she was clearly responsible for some of them. It is entirely possible she believed someone, who sought to damage her reputation, was responsible for making extra calls in a considered attempt to create doubt about her mental state and judgement.

That then was the background which made Diana's psychological state so receptive to Bashir's persuasive stories of listening devices in her apartment, friends not to be trusted, paid informers on her staff and MI5 dirty tricks aimed at her. The journalist was easy to talk to, he seemed caring and understanding and Diana was thoroughly convinced by what he told her, especially since it confirmed so much of what she already believed.

Soon after she heard Bashir's offer of a TV interview Diana was canvassing the opinions of selected friends about the idea, without telling them any details about who had suggested it. Some, like Clive James and David Putnam, advised her firmly against what they thought was her own inspiration. Others, like the Duchess of York, who was by then a firm friend and collaborator, were enthusiastic.

On 24 September, while Diana pondered on the possible benefits of reaching out in person to millions of ordinary people in their own homes, the Will Carling issue was raised again in the press. The *News of the World* reported that Carling, despite his promise not to see Diana again, had been seen visiting Kensington Palace and had met Diana at the Harbour Club. The story neglected to point out that the Princess was not at home when Carling was delivering rugby shirts for William and Harry and that the encounter at the gym they both belonged to was quite by chance.

Julia Carling went on the attack and in her statement, "It hurts me very much to face losing my husband in a manner which has become outside my control", implicated Diana in the separation the Carlings announced less than a week later. Diana responded by denying any involvement in the breakdown of the marriage and said she thought Carling had acted like a "fool". Her protestations did not deflect the tabloids which slated Diana. According to *The Sun* she was a "homewrecker" and *Today* weighed in calling her a trophy collecting, "bored, manipulative and selfish princess". *The Daily Express* questioned whether any marriage or man was safe from the wife to the heir to the throne.

The attack on Diana, especially coming so soon after the Oliver Hoare revelations, was particularly worrying. She had been forgiven for many transgressions by her sympathetic public, who saw her as a victim of a heartless Prince Charles and cold royal system but there was a good chance she would not find them so tolerant of a calculating husband-stealer. The idea of reminding them, in a television interview, who it was who had been so badly done by, became more appealing. She probably would have been even more determined to have her say on the airwaves if she recalled Charles telling her, before they were married, that he only chose married women as girlfriends because they were "safe". Threats to her life were all very well and needed to be dealt with, but unfairness and injustice which resulted in her being thought ill of – now there was an even better reason for telling people what she really felt.

By the end of October Diana had secretly agreed details for a *Panorama* interview with Martin Bashir. Initially the project had been proposed as a documentary style presentation about her life, views and charitable work. By the time they settled on the fine points it was to be a very different personal sharing of her thoughts and feelings. Diana was absolutely confident in her ability to make a personal connection with her audience so that the interview would convey what she wanted to tell the public. She was convinced she would see similar reactions of sympathy and support to those she had received after the Morton book three and half years before and her Time and Space speech two years previously. Even Charles had received a massive surge of support and understanding after his Dimbleby interview, Diana believed she could expect a lot more.

There was another factor in her decision. Hasnat Khan was in her life and Diana was already projecting her own notion of a life with him as the other, balancing half, of her future-vision. Her programme would be an opportunity to clear up outstanding issues from the past and set out a clean slate, one on which she would be able to write the next chapter of her life backed by public support. It would also be an opportunity to provoke Charles into action on the divorce and to warn those who might mean to harm her just when she was getting close to her dream.

The fact that her husband had not sought a divorce so he could marry Camilla was suspicious to the emotions driven, deeply romantic Diana, who was prepared to make great sacrifices to be with someone she loved. Perhaps it meant Charles was in no hurry to marry the woman he said he cared most about, possibly because he had someone else. Diana was already harbouring doubts about Tiggy Legge-Bourke. Alternatively, perhaps he expected something to happen which would make divorce unnecessary. That very month Diana had written a note about her concerns and given it to Paul Burrell for safe keeping. Her letter clearly indicates the stress she was under and states how much danger she believed she was in. It concluded "My husband is planning 'an accident' in my car, brake failure and serious head injury in order to make the path clear for Charles to marry." Burrell's own memoir says the note was written in October 1996, but that is now regarded as an error on his part.

On Sunday 5 November, Guy Fawkes Day, Martin Bashir and a few colleagues were allowed through the gates of Kensington Palace. The police on duty would have been notified in advance of their visit but not the reason for it. Bashir was not, at that time, a famous figure on television so he would not have been recognised. Diana had made sure there were no household staff on duty to observe and opened her own front door to allow the BBC film crew to bring their equipment into her apartment, where they were soon set up. Three hours of film was recorded during which Diana, her eyes ringed with black liner that matched her dress but contrasted with her pale face, answered a wide range of questions about her marriage, her relationship with Prince Charles, her hopes and her fears. The questions did not surprise her. She had prior knowledge of them all and had been able to prepare her responses in advance. Only a handful of people were aware of the recording, none of Diana's acquaintances or palace staff was amongst them. Well aware that the project would be stopped in its tracks if the palace courtiers discovered what she intended, Diana had kept her plans completely secret from everyone.

On 13 November, as they waited to leave Kensington Palace for another visit to Broadmoor special hospital, Diana told Patrick Jephson she had "done an interview for TV." When he heard she had made a recording for *Panorama*, the highly reputable BBC current affairs programme, Jephson realised the Princess was not talking about a harmless piece of PR but a much more serious project and his heart sank. As the details emerged during their one hour drive to Crowthorne, Berkshire, Jephson discovered the extent to which he and the Palace had been deceived. The documentary was to be aired in a week's time and there was not time to stop it or to influence its content. Questions he put to the Princess about the programme revealed little about its content and generated even less confidence that she had considered any of the financial, constitutional and legal implications he would have raised, had he known. As her private secretary subjected Diana to what he called a "tentative interrogation", her responses to his questioning went from patient, through evasive to flustered until she fell back on what he called her mantra "It's terribly moving....Don't worry, everything will be all right..."

With Diana's agreement, Jephson telephoned Buckingham Palace from the car and outlined the basic details of what he had just discovered to the Queen's press secretary. Knowing that the Queen was now aware of the programme Diana telephoned Bashir to tell him he could announce the interview. On 14 November, Charles' birthday, the BBC released the story of their impending exclusive to the media.

A week of intense pressure ensued as Palace courtiers and even Diana's own lawyer, Lord Mishcon, cajoled, threatened and attempted to reason with the Princess, trying to discover what the interview contained. Diana resisted every effort, merely repeating to her private secretary that "Everything will be all right."

The programme, aired on the evening of 20 November while Diana attended a fundraising dinner for a cancer charity, was fifty-five minutes edited from the original 3 hours of recording. In a calm and measured voice Diana responded to questions ranging from her relationships with her husband, James Hewitt and Oliver Hoare to her bulimia and mental state. She gave her views on the monarchy, the royal system, Charles' position as heir and how she saw her own role by comparison. The greater part of her views were measured, thoughtful, insightful and frequently sympathetic of the difficulties faced by Charles and the royal family, who had found themselves dealing with her postnatal depression, lack of confidence and bulimia during the early days of her marriage. She was also disingenuous and occasionally downright untruthful, about some matters such as her part in the Morton book and the circumstances surrounding the Oliver Hoare silent phone calls.

Overall it was a fascinating performance, difficult to watch for those who knew Diana as a friend or foe but extremely moving for many of the huge international audience which tuned in. In the days which followed the broadcast she received 6,000 letters of support, many of them from women who sympathised and were grateful for her inspiration. Polls showed the public response to be overwhelmingly positive. Seventy five per cent of those who responded to a Gallup survey said she was right to appear on television, eighty-five per cent agreed she should be given a role as an informal ambassador for Britain, something she said in her interview that she aspired to. Seventy-seven per cent did not agree that revenge was her motive and thought she only wanted to put her side of the story. Seventy-four percent found her strong and eighty-four percent believed she had told the truth.

There were negatives as well. Nearly thirty-three per cent said the Princess was manipulative and twenty-five percent regarded her as unstable, an issue Diana had dealt with at length and indicated was of major concern for her. Another damaging statistic for Prince Charles showed that after the interview was aired, forty-six per cent regarded him as unfit to be King, an increase from thirty-three per cent in the summer of 1993.

Public commentary, all without any knowledge of Diana's real motives for agreeing to the programme, was almost universally critical from friends and foes alike. So it was that the press and others picked up on a small number of issues and Diana's performance, while they seemed to ignore or discount the overall context and tone of her interview.

The press saw revenge on Charles and Camilla and determination to damage her husband's succession, as her reasons for giving the interview.

Even her friend Richard Kay wrote of "the stench of revenge" in his *Daily Mail* piece. Soon another theme emerged to coincide with comments by Charles' friend Nicolas Soames that Diana "showed the advanced stages of paranoia". Perhaps he forgot she was seeing a psychotherapist on a regular basis. Downing Street quickly distanced itself from the remarks of the Tory Defence Minister, making it clear his words were a personal opinion only. The Minister rapidly made a statement saying he was not questioning the Princess's state of mind but, by then, other commentators were doing just that. William Deedes, for the Establishment newspaper *The Daily Telegraph* suggested Diana's performance seemed to confirm "her reputation for being unstable." A chilling remark by Piers Morgan, editor of *The Mirror* also summed up the feelings of the tabloid press about how they would treat Diana in future, "She had no right to claim privacy after what she said."

From Diana's viewpoint the letters of support and the polls fully justified her decision. She had revealed her innermost thoughts and feelings to the people and dealt with all the issues which had prompted her to speak out. She had expressed her concerns about those who opposed her and who might want to harm her by speaking of her "enemies" at the Palace. She had made her case, to the public and the Palace, for what she wanted; a place in her sons' lives and a chance to be a "Queen in people's hearts" as an ambassador for Britain doing what she did best, offering love and caring to ordinary people. She also made it clear she did not expect to be the British Queen and she admitted adultery with James Hewitt, in a quid pro quo for Charles' admission about Camilla, surely that would be enough to make him act and set her free. Diana had also indicated what she expected her husband to do. By saying that it was not her wish to divorce, she made it clear to Charles that he must make the first move. With another telling phrase the Princess issued a barely veiled warning, "She won't go quietly, that's the problem. I'll fight to the end, because I believe that I have a role to fulfil, and I've got two children to bring up."

Two days after the *Panorama* programme was aired Diana was in Argentina, on an official tour which saw her demonstrating what she meant by an informal ambassadorial role for her country. She flew into Buenos Aries less than fourteen years after a brief and bitter war between Britain and Argentina over the Falkland Islands, which remained a source of continuing diplomatic hostility. The Argentine tabloids were unimpressed by Diana's visit, seeing her as a symbol of an outdated monarchical society they deplored. Headlines screeched warnings about "The Adulteress Di..."

and "The Seducer Lady Di..." while those due to meet her appeared less than enthusiastic. A fundraising dinner was not sold out and a Welsh community she was due to visit promised she would be treated just like any tourist.

Within two hours of her arrival Diana was changing opinions fast and showing, once again, that the press was often well out of tune with public opinion, even in Argentina. She visited a centre dealing with child paralysis and rehabilitation of the disabled. There she comforted a nine year old little girl with paralyzed legs and gently stroked the hair of a three year old little boy while she chatted with him through an interpreter. Susana de Vila, president of the centre, told reporters "Diana talked with the patients much more than protocol demands. Outside the centre, crowds of well-wishers mobbed the Princess's car shouting "Lady Di! Lady Di!"

Back in the UK on 25 November Diana was shocked and bewildered by the atmosphere she discovered. She had expected a reaction to the *Panorama* interview, perhaps similar to that which followed the Morton book, or her Time and Space speech but the scale of hostility and disapproval surpassed anything she had imagined. Many of her friends criticised her and told her she had made a terrible mistake. In echoes of her childhood, she was hurt by their lack of understanding and support, despite that she had ignored their advice and not told them all the reasons for her decision. The hostility directed at her by palace courtiers and Establishment figures was palpable and Diana was soon desperately afraid that the wind of change she had sought to sow might instead reap a whirlwind of damage, rather than bring about her dreams.

✦ ✦ ✦

The *Panorama* interview was my release. When I considered what I'd seen in Diana's performance I realised I could move on. Leaving aside the stage management and soundbite comments, and it was quite difficult to not be shocked by Diana's appearance and her delivery of some of the pre-prepared remarks, I saw enough evidence that she was capable of finding her own way without my help.

Primarily I saw another powerful affirmation, similar to her Time and Space declaration and other speeches, but on an even greater scale. This time however, she was being more open about her problems and taking responsibility in front of millions of witnesses for actions she had been criticised for. I thought it was hugely significant that she'd been as sympathetic and understanding of Charles and the royal family's situation, without apologising for being afflicted by depression and bulimia. There was nothing to apologise for, she had not known how to handle her problems better at the time, any more than Charles, the royal family and the men in grey had known how to deal with their frustrations with the Princess.

I knew Diana had harboured a great deal of resentment for the treatment she received from her husband and his family but I didn't see that in her demeanour or hear it in her words during the programme. It was a good sign. Neither did I see the attack on Charles that the following day's press suggested was behind her words. I saw a reasonable opinion, thoughtfully offered, I saw irony and some self-deprecation in the comments about the marriage and Camilla. I also heard a clear statement of intent about the future she wanted, at least that part which involved her work. Again I was worried that she might be focussed too much on her public role and be neglecting the personal side of her life but I understood her choosing not to discuss that on prime time television.

As far as I was concerned the woman on television was far removed from the one I'd met nearly seven years before. Regardless of any issues she might still have been facing she was strong and capable and as likely to find her solutions whether I was there or not. The process of self-transformation was well under way driven by a powerful future-vision. I hoped she had envisioned some of the higher and more life enabling qualities I'd suggested, if so they would become part of her reality in time. As things stood, the process would continue without me and I would probably be able to observe the results in the papers or on TV.

Personal development is neither predictable nor convenient and I'd been noticing a tendency to want more for my clients than they wanted for themselves, or were ready to receive. The same was true for Diana so it was time for me to step back and follow my own path.

✦ ✦ ✦

Soon after their return from Argentina Patrick Jephson sat down with Diana and outlined a hastily drafted plan to bring her back into the royal fold and under what he later called "the benign control of the Queen's household." He had already been in touch with the Queen's private secretary and told him that "the Princess had shot her bolt" and was finally ready to accept "the firm but compassionate intervention" of Buckingham Palace "to keep her out of harm's way." During their meeting Jephson went over his plan with Diana, detail by detail. She seemed to him shell-shocked by "the enormity of what she had done." His memoir indicates that the Princess seemed to acquiesce to all his suggestions, which would comprehensively place her offices, financial arrangements, future role and press representation firmly under the control of the Queen's staff rather than Charles'.

On 29 November, Jephson and Diana met with the Queen's private secretary, Sir Robert Fellowes, to discuss the plan and received a guarded and non-committal hearing from the man who was also Diana's brother-in-law.

On 30 November, not much more than twenty four hours later, Diana was photographed outside Brompton Hospital, after midnight, by a *News of the World* photographer who had been tipped off about her presence. Impulsively she used the photographer's mobile phone to give a twenty minute interview to his paper's royal reporter, Clive Goodman, and explained she often made late night visits to comfort terminally ill patients. By doing so Diana diverted attention from the real reason for her visit, to see Hasnat Khan but paid the price of later press coverage, in the *Evening Standard*, which criticised her for her lack of judgement and "willingness to abandon protocol and infuriate Buckingham Palace."

While Buckingham Palace considered its options Diana was beginning to recover her confidence. On 7 December she made an emotional speech about the plight of the young homeless, at a charity lunch for Centrepoint. Sharing the platform was Labour's Shadow Home Secretary, Jack Straw, who went on to castigate the Tory Government for its policy towards the homeless. Diana's presence and polite applause, was reported in the press as a tacit endorsement of the Opposition's criticism of the Government and evidence of the Princess's political naivety. To Diana the censure was another example of the lack of understanding which always seemed to blight her life and her work and it started a resurgence of the combative stance she had momentarily lost. As far as she was concerned the needs of the disadvantaged were paramount and anyone who championed them deserved her support. Naive it may have been but she could see no reason to do otherwise, even if it did anger or embarrass the Government. It would not be the last time Diana would be criticised for placing human need over political niceties.

On 11 December Diana was in New York causing gasps for the tight, low cut dress she wore at a glittering gala dinner where she received the United Cerebral Palsy Foundation, Humanitarian of the Year award from her friend Henry Kissinger. In his address to the gathering of 2,000 prominent political and social figures Kissinger declared that, although she was there as a member of the royal family, "we are honouring the Princess in her own right who aligned herself with the ill, the suffering and the downtrodden." In her ten minute response Diana dedicated her award to caring professionals and suggested more recognition should be given to government's role in humanitarian work. She spoke of the need for more kindness and love, in the "sad world" and dealt with a heckler who asked "where are your children?" The Princess's cool response "In bed!" gained her the longest ovation of the evening.

The event in New York raised $2.1 million for research into cerebral palsy. Diana had shared the evening with her staunch ally and friend, Liz Tilberis, who had been appointed honorary lady-in-waiting. The courageous New York editor of *Harper*'s magazine was fighting an inspiring battle with cancer at the time and was to die in 1999.

While Diana was wowing her audience in New York the Queen was taking opinions from her courtiers, church leaders and the Government about the Wales's marriage. On 12 December she informed the Prime Minister, John Major, that she would write to the Prince and Princess of Wales urging them, in the best interests of the country, to agree to "an early divorce".

In mid-December, Hasnat Khan was identified by the *News of the World*, as a close friend of Diana. The tabloid's story described Khan as the inspiration for Diana's late night visits to Brompton Hospital where, the newspapers declared, they shared a platonic and professional relationship. It was a near miss and Diana must have been aware that it was only a matter of time before the real nature of her liaison with Khan was revealed and her life became even more complicated. Once again, while she continued to wait for a reaction from Charles to her *Panorama* interview, Diana would have been struck by the injustice of her situation.

An entire string of tabloid stories during the year had mischievously suggested there might be a connection between Prince Charles and Tiggy Legge-Bourke, the young woman employed to take the role of surrogate mother to William and Harry, as something more than an employer/employee relationship. Paternal pecks on the cheek from Charles and Legge-Bourke's weight loss were put down to a growing attraction between them. Even Richard Kay, Diana's journalist friend, had written in July that year "The word is Tiggy is slimming to please Prince Charles."

Diana had been given what she regarded as reliable information about a hospital visit which made her certain her sons' nanny had terminated an unwanted pregnancy. The Princess already suspected her husband of prevaricating about a divorce because he might no longer want to marry Camilla but had turned his sights on the woman who was just four years younger than Diana. Add that the Princes seemed a little too happy with their nanny and William, who started at Eton that September, was growing up and possibly away from his mother. Diana then, was angry and ripe for mischief when, on 14 December, she attended the same staff Christmas party as Legge-Bourke and whispered, "So sorry to hear about the baby," in her ear.

As cruel as the remark was and it undoubtedly hurt its recipient who was already having to contend with tabloid gossip of her own, it also indicated the degree of vulnerability and suspicion Diana felt at that time. Following the *Panorama* interview Diana was all but a pariah to the rest of the royal family. The reasonable relationships she had managed to maintain, with the Queen's sister, Princess Margaret, for example, had been damaged beyond repair.

Patrick Jephson noted "her paranoia had reached new heights" and his memoir recalled Diana telling him someone had tried to 'take a pot' at her in Hyde Park and insisting, on more than one occasion, that her apartment was bugged. Once, when he expressed doubts, she showed him signs of disturbance to the floorboards and fresh sawdust under a carpet. His attempt to put her mind at rest, by reminding her that the rooms had been rewired recently, was not successful.

It might seem that Diana was showing signs of paranoia at that time but if that condition is defined as, "suspicion and mistrust of people or their actions without evidence or justification", it has to be asked whether anyone in her situation, at that time, would not have been similarly fearful. Jephson himself wrote later of the "thickening climate of whispering directed at her" within the royal palaces and the atmosphere of hostility and outrage he had to deal with. The press frequently insisted that Diana was angering the courtiers, her husband or the Queen. The truth of the matter is it would have been more irrational to have been unafraid in the intense, hostile and isolated situation she was in. The alternative to her fear would have to have been an irrational level of trust, that the powerful figures arrayed around her actually had her best interests at heart at that time. Whether she was paranoid or simply filled with intense and justified fear, Diana was entitled to question much of what she saw and heard and interpret it as evidence that she was under threat.

On 18 December Diana received two letters, one of which raised her suspicions and indignation to levels which would cause a dramatic change in her future-vision. The first was from Tiggy Legge-Bourke's lawyers, demanding an apology for the slur she had made on their client's reputation and insisting that the Princess withdraw her "false allegations." Diana ignored that communication but could not dismiss the other, which was from the Queen.

In the only letter she apparently wrote to Diana in all the time she had been in the royal family, the Sovereign urged the Prince and Princess of Wales to end the country's uncertainty and seek an early divorce. What amounted to a royal command generated a series of emotions in Diana. First was a childlike sense of rejection. Expulsion from the family, admittedly one she did not enjoy being a part of, was hurtful. Next came the feeling of betrayal. Just three weeks before, in her confusion and contrition, she had offered herself to the embrace of the Queen's own household, true it would have been a constricting embrace and Diana no longer desired it but she was desperately vulnerable and had needed understanding and love. The Queen's letter made it clear that she had been talking to the Government and leading figures in the Church, exploring a different course of action entirely than the one her courtiers seemed to be considering. Diana was indignant that she had not been consulted as well, then angry. After so much prevarication and so many doubts about whether a divorce could even be contemplated for the heir and his wife; after all the questions about the succession and the Church and constitutional issues, divorce was suddenly possible – not only possible but required.

Diana's emotions were magnified when, very soon after receiving the Queen's letter, she opened another from Prince Charles and found his personal request for a divorce couched in words almost identical to those used by his mother. Diana sensed a Windsor conspiracy. The Spencer in her replied by return to the Windsor matriarch and her son. The Princess told them she wanted to take some time to consider her options before responding to their request. Shortly afterwards she informed the Queen she would not be accepting her invitation to spend Christmas with the royal family at Sandringham. Even small rebellions against royal protocol were better than complete capitulation and helplessness.

✦ ✦ ✦

On Wednesday 20 December I saw Diana for the last time. While I worked she chatted quietly about her trip to New York, which she referred to as "very grown up." I laughed inwardly and kept quiet. Someday I hoped she would see herself as entirely grown up but that was a change for her to make in her own time.

Not long afterwards I wrote her a letter explaining that the time had come for me to step away and follow my own path. I expressed my admiration for what she had achieved and wished her well for the future. I told her there were other massage therapists who could be just as effective as I and I told her of my plans to write a diet book which would not mention her at all. After I posted the letter, its envelope marked in the way which would ensure it reached her unopened by staff, I felt comfortable with my decision. I didn't expect any response, and received none, which was as it should be. It proved to me that the natural end of our relationship had come. There was nothing more to say or do.

In some ways I was glad I was no longer involved in Diana's immensely complicated life. I was sickened by some of what I'd seen and heard – the circumstances which had nearly destroyed a beautiful and loving young woman and the treatment she received from people who I'd hoped would have known better. I suppose that was the point, they didn't know better so how could they be blamed but sometimes you hope and it's disappointing when your hopes are not fulfilled. I'd had enough too, of the fears I was unable to help her with and the secrets I didn't want to hear. I'd had enough of noticing imperfections in a remarkable woman and seeing solutions she wasn't ready for. From a distance I was able to appreciate just how astonishing Diana was and how much more amazing she might become. I hoped she would amaze me by the amount of happiness she enjoyed and the love she was able to share in a home with a man she adored as well as, if she chose, on the public stage. I felt she had a long way to go but I was confident she would manage it if anyone could.

✦ ✦ ✦

On 24 and 26 December Diana had appointments with her psychotherapist Susie Orbach; Christmas Day she spent alone. A few days later she departed for a holiday in the Bahamas accompanied by her personal assistant Victoria Mendham. It was not a happy holiday. She had little in common with the twenty-six year old employee and too much on her mind to be patient of the differences between them. No doubt they were both glad when the holiday ended.

Despite her gritty responses to the Queen, Diana was hurting badly and in need of support and comfort. She would have been grateful therefore, when the Prime Minister, John Major, called on her just before Christmas to offer sympathy, they may even have discussed her work. It is unlikely they would have talked about her personal life. She had been in discussions with the British Government about how she might use the attention and acclaim she attracted to further British interests. A formal role had been ruled out by mutual agreement but Diana still hoped for official backing for her work, especially now her royal status was in doubt.

As the year came to a close Diana was still patron of more than 100 charities and was acclaimed world-wide for her humanitarian work. During 1995 she had fulfilled 127 engagements of which ten, a higher proportion than ever before, had been abroad and she was focussing more and more on a global role. What would she do if she did not have royal status?

Gradually a new thought was taking shape in Diana's mind, what if she did not have the high profile, exhausting, day to day effort it took to bring caring and compassion to the sick and dying? Diana's ideal role model was Mother Teresa of Calcutta who she did not need glamorous accessories to care for people. In fact she had told Diana that healers, such as they both were, had to suffer for their work. Hasnat Khan did not need the trappings of royalty to carry out his work. He was unimpressed by that side of Diana's life, even concerned about it impinging on his ability to do his job. He wanted nothing to do with her fame and media attention.

Perhaps, the thought entered quietly, almost unnoticed, to be with him in the future she should really step off the world stage and not set foot on it again. She wanted more children and she wanted Hasnat Khan, perhaps now that she was no longer wanted by the royal family she could really do as she pleased. At that point of course she would have thought of her sons and was once again been dragged back to the reality of her situation. She had no doubt she would have to fight to be able to stay close to them and fighting meant a highly visible public presence. With that the determination that had driven her for the past few years would have kicked in and the quiet thought, the unthinkable idea, would have sunk back into her unconscious mind, gone for now but not erased.

As Peggy Claude-Pierre had commented earlier in the year:

"She was hurting because she couldn't express who she was."

PART FOUR

END GAME

What I do is me –
For this I come into the world.
Gerard Manly Hopkins

When Diana returned to the UK at the start of 1996 she was still very distressed by the Queen's command that she divorce. Simone Simmons recalled "Diana fell apart" and was constantly in tears. That January a posse of paparazzi photographed her sobbing by her car after a session with her therapist Susie Orbach. John Junor, writing in *The Mail on Sunday*, asked "Is she indeed perilously close to a complete breakdown?" Diana's answer was given shortly afterwards, at a lunch where she was the guest of hour. Declaring herself "very stable" Diana was obviously back in fighting mood and this time the battle was not just to be with Charles' men in grey and his Establishment supporters; it was with the Windsors.

During the preceding years, especially since the separation, the Queen had supported Diana's independent public role, at least by not opposing many of the engagements and trips for which the Princess required permission from the Sovereign as well as the Government. Now the heir's mother had issued what amounted to a royal command to her son and his wife to divorce as soon as possible. Diana had demurred, she had always maintained in public that she did not want a divorce and now she told her husband and mother-in-law she wanted time to consider her options. She also wanted some assurances before she would publicly agree to the Windsor's request, so for the time being the divorce was stalled.

Diana was aware of how significant the Queen was in any divorce arrangements. Access to William and Harry, questions of whether the Princess could retain the title Her Royal Highness and if she could continue to live at Kensington Palace, even the amount of any financial settlement, were all in the Queen's purview. For Diana, the personal issue of who would ultimately be seen by the press and public as responsible for the breakdown of the marriage and its final ending, was very significant as well. She had been holding out and pressing for Charles to ask her to divorce so she would be exonerated and blame would fall where she believed it was rightfully due, on her husband and his mistress Camilla. Now the Queen had commanded and her son had dutifully complied the result would not salve Diana's sense of injustice and answer all those who suggested she was to blame or that her mental state was the reason the marriage did not work. By her intervention, the Queen compounded her family's complicity in making Diana's life as a Princess that much more painful than it needed to have been by their lack of understanding and support when she needed it.

So now Diana saw she had to fight the Windsors and it could not be an open conflict. She respected the Queen and did not want to make an opponent of her because of the influence she wielded. The Sovereign was grandmother to William and Harry and in the final accounting, the guardian of their destiny. She was also the ultimate arbiter of what public role Diana would be permitted to take if she wanted to stay in Britain and have access to her sons. The Princess needed to maintain contact with the Queen, so she could not overtly criticise the monarch or act against her. Nevertheless her mother-in-law must be made aware that Diana could not be treated lightly.

Neither did Diana want to damage the royal family, as some were suggesting she had been attempting to do. Her sons were Windsor Princes after all and their future lay within the family. No, what Diana wanted was what she had been struggling to bring about for the past six years, since she had created her future-vision. She wanted her life, her way and under her own control. Entering 1996, her determination to make a balanced and complete life meant resisting the life-crushing influence of the Windsors with every resource she could muster on the battleground she knew best, the battleground of public opinion.

One of the resources Diana was relying on was Patrick Jephson. During her negotiations with the Windsors she needed to maintain the public's support. Her private secretary was the one person who knew how to ensure she had that support, by arranging the successful charity engagements and overseas humanitarian trips on which it was founded. Jephson, however, had been struggling with grave doubts about his role in Diana's working life. By the start of 1996 he had been working with the Princess for eight years and was becoming increasingly unhappy about her behaviour and what he thought were her motives.

During the preceding year or two Jepshon had noticed, with increasing alarm, a new degree of ruthlessness, even meanness that had entered Diana's dealings with her staff. He had always struggled with her emotional personality and quite prided himself on his ability to manipulate her into doing what he thought was best for her and the monarchy but her treatment of her employees rankled. It seemed to him she was now demanding impossible standards of loyalty which, when they were not forthcoming, resulted in a freezing out of dependable members of the domestic and administrative staffs. She seemed to use cruel ploys to test individual's allegiances and then used their apparent failures as reasons to dispense with their services.

Jephson was, in any case, considering his own future by then. He had been happy to believe that his work for Diana was also of value to the monarchy but now he was becoming convinced that was no longer the case. He had been upset by Diana's subterfuge in delivering the *fait accompli* over her *Panorama* interview and he was horrified by her callous remark to Tiggy Legge-Bourke. He also believed he saw signs that Diana was about to strike out at him and he was afraid of the damage she could do to his career prospects. Despite his instinct, that Diana was beginning to question her need for him, Jephson was shocked when he received an anonymous, prank pager-message, "The Boss knows about your disloyalty and your affair". Other staff members had received similar messages in the past and Jephson was certain they all came from the Princess. Diana's denial did not persuade him he was wrong about the origin of the "nasty little message" and he immediately informed her he thought it was time for him to move on.

Her private secretary's decision to leave was a bitter blow to Diana just when she needed him, both for his organisational abilities with her work and for the level-headed counselling she expected during the divorce negotiations. She was, by turns, frightened, indignant and angry. She knew he did not understand her and she was suspicious of where his ultimate loyalties lay but she had come to rely on him completely in that area which was essential to her future, her public role. As far back as 1993 she had been made aware of an approach Jephson made to David Putnam, about the possibility of a job and the incident had led her to ignore both men for a while. Jephson also thought Diana should work within the royal organisation and had never made any secret of his preference, even while he helped her create a more independent role. His recent efforts to broker an arrangement that would see Buckingham Palace exercise an even greater control over her life had almost seen her agree to a step she would have regretted for the rest of her life but she needed him now, as the end-game approached and she saw her future beckoning.

On 22 January, after a period of bitter exchanges during which Diana rejected Jephson's offer to aid in a smooth transition of his work into other hands he left, full of anxiety about the reprisals she might take over his perceived disloyalty. Around the time her private secretary departed and stories of his disaffection hit the newspapers, Diana found herself dealing with two more potentially difficult situations which required staff experienced in media affairs. The Christmas party incident with Tiggy Legge-Bourke was revealed in the tabloids and Hasnat Khan was identified by the *News of the World* as Diana's possible love interest, after they had been seen sharing dinner in Stratford-upon-Avon with Khan's uncle and aunt.

Within two days of Jephson's departure Diana engaged an experienced press consultant, Jane Atkinson, to advise and handle her media profile. Atkinson later recalled the initial interview when Diana "told me how she was canny with the media" and also said she had "a strong sense of self-preservation, a sixth sense of what was right for her." Atkinson, who saw the Princess as a challenge, was given the job of protecting Diana's media image during the divorce negotiations but found the job increasingly difficult. Her client was "quite secretive" and "She felt she couldn't trust anyone, and she needed to have control." It came as a surprise to Atkinson therefore, when she arranged a series of meetings for Diana with newspaper editors at Kensington Palace, to find the Princess had already met and even dined with many of them.

One person Diana did trust was Paul Burrell, her butler. He was one of the small team which remained to provide Diana's household and administrative needs during that time but he was the only one whose loyalty she was certain of. He had been tested on many occasions already and had undertaken every task, no matter how much it interfered with his own private life, with the utmost devotion. Burrell became her co-collaborator and confidante in most matters where she needed unquestioning loyalty and commitment. He listened, comforted when required and offered advice on everything from personal relationships and press coverage to the divorce negotiations.

Until her divorce was finalised Diana was still suspicious of almost everyone and living with the fear that some harm might come to her. Driven by her future-vision and the series of affirmations which supported it, the Morton book, the Time and Space declaration, *Panorama* and her private manifesto, she was determined to bring the two threads of her ideal personal and public lives into one completely satisfying reality.

What might constitute an ideal public role was under review. Hasnat Khan was the focal point of her personal life. The future Diana envisioned with him was already shaping her thoughts about what she might do to make the world a better place. Knowing how much he detested press attention and any intrusion which would affect his work Diana was already considering how to adapt her humanitarian work to fit in with a life with the surgeon. In a pattern similar to that which she showed in her relationship with Oliver Hoare, Diana had already started learning everything she could about Hasnat, his work and his background. She studied books on anatomy and articles about heart surgery and she accepted an invitation to visit Pakistan from Imran Khan, the famous Pakistani cricketer who was married to Jemima, the daughter of Diana's friends Annabel and Sir James Goldsmith.

In Pakistan Diana intended to help raise funds for Imran's Shaukat Khanum Memorial cancer hospital but she also wanted to discuss more personal matters with Jemima, who had converted to Islam and moved to Lahore when she married. The trip was scheduled for mid-February and was kept secret until the last moment. Before she went Diana had an important meeting to attend with the Queen which, it was hoped, would clarify what was to happen after the divorce.

In the middle of the morning of Thursday, 15 February the Sovereign and the Princess met at Buckingham Palace to discuss the divorce. The Queen's deputy private secretary was there to keep a record of what was said. By the time they all sat down in the Queen's private sitting room the Princess had already conveyed quite a lot. Her "demands" had appeared in the tabloid press. Details of the meeting were recounted by Diana to Burrell and later recalled in his memoirs. She made it clear to her mother-in-law that she had never wanted a divorce and "none of what has happened is my fault". She also registered how hurt she had been by the letters from the Queen and Charles requesting the divorce be rushed. As the discussions progressed Diana agreed that the divorce could go ahead but raised her concerns about her future, pointing out that she had worked for the family for sixteen years and "do not want to see my life taken away". She added "I have real concerns for the future, and all the answers lie with you, Mama."

According to Burrell's account it was at that time the Queen said she "would like to decide things in consultation with Charles" and that Diana's title after the divorce and whether she could retain the appellation HRH, were matters for discussion with the Prince. Diana's recollection was that the Queen suggested "Diana, Princess of Wales" as the most appropriate title but the matter was left in abeyance, pending discussions with Prince Charles, as were those to do with access to William and Harry and Diana's occupation of Kensington Palace when in the UK. Nowhere is it recorded that Diana discussed her plans for Hasnat Khan with the Queen.

Her personal aspirations for Hasnat did not feature either when, very late in the day, Diana notified the British Foreign Office she was travelling to Pakistan but they could not have failed to notice the tabloid's assertions that the surgeon would be joining her. On 18 February Diana's trip was revealed to the public under the headline "Diana's Love Trip Secret" despite the fact that Hasnat would not travel with her. The Foreign Office had few concerns about Diana's private life, they were much more nervous about her connections with Imran Khan than they were about his namesake Hasnat. At that time the popular ex-cricketer was setting out his plans to establish an opposition party to run against sitting Prime Minister Benazir Bhutto on an anti-corruption platform. Diplomats were concerned her visit might be considered as support for the Pakistani Government's opponent. Their fears were increased when Prime Minister Bhutto was not invited to a fundraising dinner at which Diana was the guest of honour and the Princess declined an invitation to change her plans and stay in Bhutto's guest house.

Political and diplomatic sensitivities were becoming less and less important in Diana's viewpoint by then. Humanitarian issues and affairs of the heart were the focus of her life and her trip. Dressed in simple but stunning examples of the beautiful Pakistani national dress, the *shalwar kameez*, she reached out to the sick and dying and took the opportunity to familiarise herself with the country where Hasnat Khan's parents had their home. She hoped she had made a good impression.

Back in the UK, on the afternoon of 28 February, Diana met with Charles to finally agree the main details of the divorce. Immediately afterwards she authorised a press release which stated that she had agreed to Prince Charles' request for a divorce, thus making sure the world knew who had ended the marriage. The statement also detailed the points Diana said had been settled. She would be involved in all decisions regarding her sons, she would continue to live at Kensington Palace and she would relinquish the HRH title and "be known as Diana, Princess of Wales." As the statement was being distributed to the waiting media Diana was telephoning the Queen to confirm her consent to the divorce.

Buckingham Palace quickly issued its own statement to rebuff Diana's assertion that decisions had been made. The Windsors insisted that there had been only requests which "remain to be discussed and settled." Diana responded, making it known that she had merely wanted to give "the image of a strong woman…in control of the message". She then proceeded to leak her version of what was said in her meeting with Prince Charles. The resulting story, by her friend Richard Kay in the *Daily Mail*, gave the impression Diana had been pressured into relinquishing the HRH title. The Palace hit back, claiming Diana had lied, declaring "The decision to drop the title is the Princess's and the Princess's alone." Diana was so upset at the attack she dropped out of the final gala event on 29 February to mark the 125th anniversary of the British Red Cross, where she was to be the guest of honour.

The public spat, between the Princess and the Windsor's, served Diana well in her efforts to ensure public support. By her unilateral declaration of what were supposed to be confidential matters, she made it known she must be treated carefully. She provoked a Palace response that saw the plucky Diana publicly reprimanded by the Palace organisation, which was already seen as cold and unfeeling towards her. The public was also given the impression that the Queen, aided by Charles, intended to spitefully remove Diana's HRH status.

The issue of the HRH title was not an insignificant one. To most observers it seemed that without the prefix Diana would lose much of the status on which her public role, and the adulation she received, was based and she was therefore desperate to hang onto it. In fact she was already considering a complete change in her working life that might make the Royal title unnecessary. The HRH part was already fairly superfluous anyway. If the name Diana was spoken to almost anyone on the planet at that time, they thought of only one person, the Princess who loved and cared for the sick and dying. The tag "of Wales", with or without the HRH attached, became less than an afterthought for most ordinary people. It could have been handy to hang onto until she chose to stop using it but whether she succeeded in retaining the tile or not, making the Palace fight her for it in the tabloids was only ever likely to elicit public sympathy for her. Keeping the enemy guessing was a favourite ploy of Diana's and she had years of practise to draw on.

Probably the most significant thing for Diana about the HRH title was that if she lost it, protocol would require that she curtsy, as a mark of respect, to Windsors who had been obliged to bob or nod to her in the past. Given her feelings about the family and their behaviour towards her, she felt little respect for most of them and was reluctant to be placed in a difficult position. She would have seen it as a great injustice if she had been. Her make-up meant she always put human and personal issues over those of protocol or correct form. Her personality type ensured that she would go to great lengths to resist any such unfairness. In the end a compromise was reached and encapsulated in a later Palace statement. Diana would be treated "as a member of the royal family" and be invited to state and national occasions where it would be as if she still retained the HRH title.

By spring of 1996 the divorce negotiations and Diana's working life were both moving slowly. The engagements Patrick Jephson had planned for her before he left were almost completed and the small, inexperienced office team which remained was not able to maintain anything like the same programme the Princess had been used to. It did not really matter. Diana was fully involved in her struggle with the Windsors, perhaps too involved. That April, Diana indulged herself in a little mischief at their expense when she let the press know which restaurant was to be the private venue for the Queen's 70th birthday party. The party eventually went ahead at a different location but much of the pleasure of it was probably lost in the last minute changes.

A little instant karma might have been observed in the events of 22 April, when a news story about Diana's visits to Brompton Hospital exposed her to ridicule and criticism. A coincidence of events had resulted in a television crew filming a heart operation the Princess had been invited to witness. The subsequent incongruous images, of Diana wearing mascara and earrings with her surgical gown and mask, were flashed around the world. Castigated and mocked at the same time, for transgressions from poor hygiene and poor taste to publicity seeking, Diana was hurt by the misrepresentation. She was also worried about the effect of the story on her relationship with Hasnat Khan. By then she was seriously considering a future with the surgeon and the incident added to her concerns about anything that might deter him from marrying her They were managing to keep their romantic connection secret, partly because they met in ordinary places like cafés and pubs where the Princess would not be expected and partly because Diana was learning to use wigs and make up to avoid recognition and press attention. But there was little doubt in her mind that Hasnat was very worried about being caught up in the media scrutiny that was regularly directed at anyone involved with her and the idea that she might lose him gave her considerable cause for anguish.

In the months which followed her panning in the press Diana maintained a low profile and waited, impatiently and nervously, for her divorce arrangements to be finalised. One engagement she did not avoid that June however, was another visit to her favourite country, the United States. In Chicago she spent three days raising funds for cancer charities and experienced a reception of such enthusiasm, wherever she went, that it must have lifted her flagging spirits at a time when she was feeling isolated and under attack at home.

Back in the UK the trip was hailed as another Diana triumph but unhappily for her media consultant, Jane Atkinson, the *Daily Express* commended her specifically for her part in making it so successful. Her client, the Princess, ever watchful and very determined that she should be the one to receive any plaudits for the effort she put into her work, soon made her displeasure known. Atkinson's explanation, that she had nothing to do with the story, was backed up by the newspaper's editor but from then on Diana took direct control of her own media strategy. Atkinson was used as a spokesperson on occasions, while Paul Burrell and other members of her small Palace retinue were instructed to leak stories to journalists or contact newspaper editors, often while Diana listened in on a phone extension.

During her tenure Atkinson was probably not aware of the informal media team Diana had gathered around her. Apart from close contacts with several newspaper editors, like Piers Morgan of the *Daily Mirror* and Stuart Higgins of *The Sun*, she had developed a friendship with Martin Bashir, producer of her *Panorama* interview. Bashir had begun advising Diana on media matters soon after the programme was aired. That April, when it was revealed the BBC man had probably used false documents to help him persuade Diana to take part, the Princess refused to condemn him and maintained contact. Bashir's role, he was soon helping to write speeches for the Princess, somewhat displaced Diana's friend and long time conduit into Fleet Street, Richard Kay. Nevertheless Kay overcame his disappointment and remained close to Diana, continuing to offer advice and his connection with one of Britain's most popular British newspapers. It was through Kay that Diana pitched the improbable story, at the end of June, that Buckingham Palace was insisting she should retain her HRH title because the mother of the future King must have appropriate status. How much influence her story had on events is unknown. By that time only minor details of the technicalities remained to be settled but she did, in practical terms, retain the status if not the title.

With a final agreement so close and most of their personal differences aired and dispersed during the negotiations, Diana and Charles began to discover a new relationship, as friends. When the Prince called at Kensington Palace unexpectedly, two days before his wife's thirty-fifth birthday, Paul Burrell later described them as relaxed and cordial after greeting each other with laughter. It was to be the first of many amiable chats between the two, once the barrier of their impossible marriage was removed.

Three days after her birthday, on 4 July, the final divorce settlement terms were presented to Diana. Her lawyers had kept her informed of every detail so there were no surprises. Her place and influence in her son's lives had already been agreed. As mother to the Princes she would be a senior, if detached, royal figure, so she would still need to seek agreement from the Foreign Office and the Queen for any working trips overseas but she would be entitled to use aircraft from the Queen's flight for official travel and the state apartments at St. James's Palace for entertaining. The financial settlement would make her independently wealthy if she was careful and she could continue to live at Kensington Palace where her office would be located but she was barred from engaging in any commercial ventures from which she would gain personally. The couple also signed a confidentiality agreement.

Four days after receiving the details, Diana formally agreed to the terms. After a brief delay, so the announcement would not coincide with a state visit by Nelson Mandela, details of the settlement were reported in the press on 13 July. On 15 July, Diana and Charles together took the penultimate step to ending their marriage when they were granted a *decree nisi*. Diana immediately began taking her own steps to create her future-vision.

A little more than twenty-four hours after she received her decree Diana issued an announcement that she was cutting her ties to around a hundred charities including the Red Cross. She would retain her connections to only five which would see her involved with the homeless, sick children, HIV+AIDS, leprosy and the ballet. Sympathetic press coverage for "Her Royal Humiliation" and "The Final Betrayal" following the divorce announcement, rapidly turned to criticism when it was calculated how much her defection could cost those charities she had "ditched". Diana instructed her spokesperson, Jane Atkinson, to issue a statement explaining the decision was "entirely because of her loss of royal status" which meant her support would no longer "be beneficial to those charities." Atkinson pointed out how illogical it was to say Diana's status would not help one group of charities while she still retained her relationship with another but once again the media consultant was not fully in the picture developing in her client's mind and the statement went out anyway.

Diana was exhausted, frustrated and in a hurry. She had been waiting years for the freedom to follow her own path and now she had it. For many months she had been contemplating the public work which might fit with her dream of a life with Hasnat Khan and it did not include more than one hundred demands on her time and energy. She was becoming increasingly dissatisfied with the glamorous aspects of her work and felt almost as much of a puppet to the charities she served as she had been to the royal family.

Her vision was clear; she wanted her work to be less structured, more spontaneous and with room for a private personal life. Her destiny was to work on a global scale and make the world a better place. In her haste to move on she was not inclined to consider too carefully the needs of charities which had already benefitted from her hard work for so many years, nor the press which had driven her decisions for just as long. Even public approval might not be essential to her plans. Certainly she wanted to retain public support if she could, not least because a significant part of her humanitarian work was to help charities raise cash but just then, what she wanted more, was to clear her path to the life she felt was long overdue.

Diana was sure that the withdrawal of her HRH status was a spiteful parting shot from the Windsors and she had been upset and tearful when she discovered she had lost on the issue. Her riposte was to try to divert blame for her decision to relinquish so many charities onto the royal family, citing the loss of the title as her reason. It was true the title might have been helpful in her "focus on a smaller range of areas" to quote from her Time and Space speech but she was not even sure she wanted to be affiliated to those few charitable organisations she had retained. She already had a new major project in mind for her future humanitarian work and unlike most of her others it was one which could make a truly global impact. She was sure the public would understand and support her when they heard about it.

The horror of antipersonnel land mines had been revealed to Diana as early as October 1991 when she was on the Afghan-Pakistan border visiting a hospital funded by war correspondent Sandy Gall's Afghanistan Appeal. There she saw children and adults being fitted with prosthesis, to replace limbs they had lost in mine explosions. There can be no doubt her gift for empathetic connection would have given her a real sense of their anguish. In his book *Diana: In Pursuit of Love*, Andrew Morton records what Diana told her friend James Colthurst at the time, about the irony of the situation. It struck her that if she had made the trip when it was scheduled, for the previous year, she would have "skimmed through it" without being affected as much as she was. Instead, she noted what was happening but saw no opportunity then to become involved. She was helping Andrew Morton write *Diana: Her True Story*, at that time, concerned about the Squidgy tape and preparing to fight for her future. Like many events in her life, a seed was sown and it bore fruit much later.

The possibility of supporting the Red Cross's work for landmine victims re-emerged in the winter of 1993, when various proposals were being considered as she and Patrick Jephson tried to shape a public role which would suit her shifting aspirations. At that time, within days of her surprise Time and Space speech and temporary departure from public life, Jephson recalls Diana "rejected it out of hand." No doubt if she had embarked on a campaign then, especially one which would have been heavily influenced by Jephson's tendency to consider the larger royal organisation's requirements, it would have been short lived or effective in a completely different way.

Instead the seed was re-awakened in March 1995 and then nurtured by Mike Whitlam, CEO of the British Red Cross, who began sending Diana briefing notes and videos about his organisation's work associated with land mines in the world's warzones. Thus prepared it only remained for another co-incidence to bring the seed to maturity. In the early summer of 1996 Diana's friend Simone Simmons returned from a trip to Bosnia with horrifying pictures of what antipersonnel land mines were doing to people there.

"Do you think I could make a difference?" asked the Princess.

"If you can't, nobody can," came the reply.

Simmons' intervention came at a perfect moment. A moment when Diana was seeking to put her public profile behind a global campaign that would make the world a better place, a moment when she was being liberated from the shackles of her royal life and a moment when she was ready to confront more controversial issues. By helping with the land mines problem Diana also saw she could shape her role with it to fit the life she anticipated with Hasnat Khan. First though there was the matter of her divorce to finalise.

On Wednesday 28 August the Prince and Princess of Wales were awarded their decree absolute and their marriage finally came to an end. Diana was free to make her own life.

From August she contrived an almost normal life for much of the time. She walked openly on Hampstead Heath with Simone Simmons and enjoyed regular dates with Hasnat Khan. She queued and shopped, unnoticed by ordinary people and the press, having perfected the art of disguise and what Simmons called "hiding in plain sight." An array of excellent wigs, shaped and styled by her hairdresser, with different make up and sometimes plain lens glasses, enabled her to blend in when she accompanied Hasnat to smoky jazz clubs in Soho and Camden. Her lover stayed at Kensington Palace more often and Diana revelled in the freedom to be herself. A single sighting of the lovers together, by a *News of the World* photographer who spotted them meeting near the Brompton Hospital, could not spoil what was an idyllic period in Diana's life but she wanted more, she wanted the future she had set her heart on.

As she sought to explore the boundaries of her freedom Diana seemed, to the press and other observers, to be leading a life that was unfocused and frivolous. In September she attended the funeral in Greece of a young man, a cystic fibrosis sufferer, she had befriended at the Brompton Hospital. In October she went to Rimini, Italy to receive a humanitarian award from the Pio Manzu Centre. She paid little attention to the few charities to which she was still affiliated and her neglect upset some of those who counted her as a friend as well as an important patron. There seemed to be no pattern and no purpose for the woman who had been so prominent on the world stage.

In fact Diana was doing a great deal at that time with distinct purpose; it simply was not as obvious as it had been. That September, while *The Times* published a story about her "tarnished" image and other newspapers wondered what she was up to, Diana was taking another symbolic stride away from her past by planning a charity auction of many of her designer dresses. Nearly all the dresses had identifiable and therefore historic connections with times and events when she was HRH the Princess of Wales and it gave the garments considerable monetary value. The idea was attributed to Prince William and would raise a small fortune for the recipients of her generosity when the auction was held.

Diana's trip to Rimini that October enabled her to meet another award recipient, Dr Christiaan Barnard. Diana befriended the famous South African heart surgeon and asked him if he could help find a job for Hasnat Khan. She revealed she wanted to leave the UK and marry the man she loved, with whom she wanted to have "two little girls". South Africa was her preferred destination because her brother was there. Barnard visited Diana twice in London and met Hasnat at London's Grosvenor House hotel. The pioneer of open heart surgery later recalled that Hasnat knew Diana loved him very much but "he couldn't handle the publicity."

South Africa was not the only possible location for the new life Diana envisaged with Hasnat. Australia and America were other options where he might work as a surgeon and be a wonderful stepfather to William and Harry, while she created hospices around the globe and worked to rid the world of land mines.

That autumn Diana invited Mike Whitlam from the British Red Cross to a series of discussions about what role she might take to help his charity's work on the antipersonnel land mine issue. Despite the Red Cross not having made Diana's short list a few months earlier Whitlam, who knew Diana quite well, recognised she was serious about her commitment to the campaign. He willingly offered his advice and collaboration.

As the landmine project was taking shape Diana visited Sydney, Australia, at the end of October, to attend a fundraising ball in aid of the institute named after Hasnat Khan's early mentor, the surgeon Victor Chang. The four-day trip was a mixture of success and failure. Diana visited hospitals and helped raise $1 million for the charity. James Whitaker, royal correspondent for the *Daily Mirror* described her as "magnificent". But she fell out of love with Australia, which she felt was "primitive" and isolated, when compared to London, New York or Washington, according to Paul Burrell's memoirs. It clearly was not going to be somewhere for her future-vision to take shape. Her impression was not helped when some of the charity's sponsors apparently tried to gain financially from her presence. Ever cautious about her image and by now aware of the constraints of her divorce agreement, Diana was not amused.

Nevertheless Diana had momentum, the landmine campaign and her relationship were coming together nicely in her plans and it all seemed perfect, until an unexpected blow almost destroyed everything. The *Sunday Mirror* splashed a story linking Diana romantically with Hasnat Khan. The "world exclusive" may have been largely true. She was, as it said, in love with the heart surgeon who was described as "shy" and "caring" and she did want to have his children but the revelations were untimely. Knowing how much Hasnat detested publicity Diana reacted with a rather too vehement denial of the story. She told Richard Kay it was "bullshit" and how amused she had been at the very idea she was in love with the man who was only a "friend" she knew professionally. Kay's subsequent article in the *Daily Mail* of 4 November condemned the *Sunday Mirror* story and claimed Diana was concerned about its effect on her sons. The surgeon in the spotlight was upset by the publicity and hurt by Diana's public comments but the press backed off and the romance survived so the dream continued.

Even a fatal rift in her relationship with Fergie that same month could not halt Diana's impetus towards her ideal life. Sarah had been a stalwart friend ever since her own separation from Prince Andrew and her country home had been a sanctuary for Diana many times in the preceding months. The transgressions which ended their relationship centered, unsurprisingly, around the media. In the autobiography that followed Fergie's own divorce earlier that year, she made a few unflattering references to Diana. Later, during her publicity tour, there were some unguarded answers to questions about the Princess. In all they were enough to see the cheerful redhead sidelined forever.

That December Diana's plans moved several steps forward. She agreed to be the guest of honour at the UK charity premiere of the movie, *In Love and War*, by her friend, film producer Sir Richard Attenborough. The film was based on Hemingway's book about the futility of war. The charity which would benefit was the Red Cross appeal for victims of antipersonnel land mines.

At the same time Diana was consulting with the British Foreign Office about her first trip abroad to publicise the campaign against the horrifying weapons. Her Red Cross sponsors suggested Cambodia, then Afghanistan. The Foreign Office agreed to Angola in January 1997. More negotiations were facilitated by Lord Attenborough, who helped Diana arrange for a BBC film crew to follow her to the "killing fields", as she called those areas most blighted by land mines, for a documentary.

With her work and her relationship developing well enough for Diana to be able to see her future-vision becoming a reality, she was able to view her ex-husband much more sympathetically. Charles had taken to dropping into Kensington Palace unexpectedly for tea and a chat and, on one occasion, for use of the toilet. At one time they had been unable to spend even a few minutes together without painful words being spoken. Now they were relaxed together and both benefited as their wounds healed. In mid-December Diana sent a sympathetic letter to the Prince after his mentor, Laurens Van der Post died. Her thoughtfulness was much appreciated. That Christmas time they were heard laughing together in the headmaster's study at Eton where they were both attending the annual carol service at Prince William's school.

✦ ✦ ✦

As she entered 1997, after a Caribbean break, the emotions Diana was experiencing most were love and hope. The charity auction of her dresses was announced and she had her ground-breaking trip to Angola to prepare for. Hasnat Khan was the love of her life and she had already spent a little time at the homes of some of his family members in Stratford-upon-Avon. Helping with meals and washing up afterwards seemed just like the times she had enjoyed with James Hewitt at his mother's home in Devon. Diana was feeling confident and all seemed set fair to the future she longed for.

Her first foray amongst the antipersonnel land mines of Angola in mid-January, also placed Diana in a political minefield and in the middle of the perennial war between those with commercial interests in armaments and those who opposed them. While the press and commentators marveled at her composure and compassionate handling of victims in the heat and dust of Africa, Lord Howe, back home in the UK was condemning her as a "loose cannon" for her political naivety. Diana, whose focus as always was on individuals and her personal connection with them and not Government policy or diplomatic relations was used to being misunderstood by those who did not share her viewpoint. Nevertheless, her experiences on that trip, with all the child amputees, the mutilations and with one particular little girl Helena, whose intestines were spilling out from wounds caused by a land mine, made Diana less than patient with politicians.

"Idiot minister," Diana muttered when she heard of the junior defense minister's comments. The only journalist within earshot was a fellow campaigner, the venerable news man, William Deedes, the same man who barely a year before had written of Diana's "mental instability". He did not report the words in his *Daily Telegraph* articles but wrote of the land mines crusade as a "watershed" for her and described how she did not need interpreters to be able to communicate with the victims she met – "Diana had her own way of breaking through the language barrier."

Diana's offense had been the speech she made when she arrived in Angola "to assist the Red Cross in its campaign to ban, once and for all, antipersonnel land mines." Her Foreign Office briefing had made the Tory Government's policy clear. It had contributed £21 million to clearing mines and was committed to a two-stage process for stopping their use. In the first instance they wanted to promote the use of "smart" weapons which would self-destruct after a time, the second step would be a global ban. Diana's intervention was not welcomed although, following the publication of iconic pictures of her walking through a cleared minefield wearing a Perspex mask and flak jacket, the official message was adjusted to suggest her comments had been broadly in line with policy.

More supportive comments came, significantly, from Labour Shadow defense spokesman, David Clark, who said Diana "should be applauded for what she's doing." Since late 1994 Diana had enjoyed occasional private meetings with the Opposition leader Tony Blair, the introduction having been made by one of her legal team, Maggie Rea, who knew the Blair family. Blair recognised Diana as symbolic of the New Labour concepts he was promoting to his colleagues and she, in turn, was impressed by his vision. She would eventually enjoy more support from him and his party for her informal ambassadorial ambitions and the anti land mines campaign.

Not long after she returned from her Angola mission Diana's friendship with Simone Simmons ended after another difference of opinion. This time it was not to be restored. The woman whose urgings had encouraged Diana to make her most powerful humanitarian commitment never had contact with her again.

The loss of another close friend, however, was not as distressing for Diana as the potential loss of her lover. On 9 February the *Daily Express* carried the latest in a series of tabloid stories about Diana's relationship with Hasnat Khan and their love-life seemed about to unravel. His father, Rashid, was quoted as saying "He is not going to marry her." He continued "We are looking for a bride for him...preferably she should be at least a Pakistani Moslem girl." Hasnat's mother, Naheed, said media attention was "ruining his life."

The *Express* article served only to heighten Diana's sensitivity to what she instinctively knew was occurring in the relationship. She was aware that Hasnat became very upset when subjected to any press attention and almost unconsciously she had been sensing a subtle shift in their relationship. Her automatic response, as she felt a distinct loosening of the intense connection she needed with her lover, as she had always needed in her relationships with men, was to press Hasnat for more time and attention. The result, of her many hand-delivered messages and too frequent phone calls while he was at work, was the opposite of what she needed and hoped for. Hasnat, like his father, was becoming certain that a marriage would not work out. Unaware the surgeon was feeling so doubtful and with old fears of abandonment and panic starting to emerge in her thoughts, Diana became more determined to prove she would make a good wife.

Bad press was the last thing Diana needed just then and to avoid negative reaction from the tabloids she belatedly withdrew from a project in support of Elton John's AIDS Foundation. Diana had agreed to write the foreword to a book, *Rock and Royalty*, and had donated a family portrait of her with William and Harry. Only later did she become aware that book would also contain pictures of naked men and might cause offense to the Queen and could potentially damage Diana's public image and her relationship with those who had ultimate control of her sons. The project's celebrity sponsors, designer Gianni Versace and singer Elton John, were extremely upset when she pulled out and also cancelled her intended appearance at their gala book-launch. As a result Diana became estranged from two more good friends and supporters.

At the end of February Diana enjoyed a little tabloid tit for tat when she initiated legal action against the *Sunday Express* and its editor in chief, after the newspaper published an article stating she would benefit personally, to the tune of £1 million, from her dress auction. The story was incorrect and Diana won a settlement of £75,000 and an apology on the front page. The editor, Richard Addis, offered to pay the money direct to a charity but was forced to pay it to Diana, thus depriving him of the face-saving option. "She did that to punish us" recalled Addis later.

The press coverage was better in mid-March when Diana visited South Africa and was photographed with President Nelson Mandela. Her main mission in Cape Town was to see for herself what the country could offer her and Hasnat Khan, if they were to move there. Diana's brother, Charles, was already living in the country and they were able to spend time together, healing past misunderstandings which had distanced them.

In the same month Diana refocused attention on the anti land mines campaign and took a step to mollify those who saw her as a 'loose cannon'. She had taken advice from her friend Bill Deedes and agreed to moderate her hard line by supporting de-mining, the clearing of antipersonnel land mines from areas where they had been scattered and highlighting the effects of mines on their victims. At a charity lunch she made an award to former army captain, Chris Moon, who lost a leg and a hand clearing mines for a project in war torn Mozambique. Diana called him "a symbol of bravery."

Diana's vision of her future always had a third constant element, her relationship with her sons and that spring she attended William's confirmation service at Eton with Prince Charles. Notable absentees from the ceremony were any members of Diana's immediate family, omitted because she did not expect it to be anything more than "brief and straightforward" and Tiggy Legge-Bourke, who had been invited but was then asked not to attend. Observers noted the ease between Charles and Diana when they posed for photographs and left in the same car.

On 2 May Britain's Labour Party won the general election by a landslide and Diana's hopes for more Government support for her role as an informal humanitarian ambassador for Britain increased.

Diana was hoping to give and receive support when, early that May, she made one of her frequent visits to hospitals which provided treatment for people with addictions and eating disorders. On that occasion she was at Roehampton Priory and sat in on a group session where she openly discussed her own history of bulimia, hoping it would help others and that she might learn more about herself in the process. Someone tipped off the tabloid newspaper, the *Daily Mirror* and its editor, Piers Morgan, contacted Diana to give her the opportunity to put her side in the piece he intended to print. The article's main angle was the revelation that Diana had suffered from bulimia since she was a teenager. Despite having been betrayed yet again she agreed to speak, then gave Morgan a forty-five minute interview on condition she would not be quoted directly.

In the subsequent story, which appeared in the *Mirror* on 8 May, Diana confirmed she had finally overcome her bulimia problem three years before, when she woke up one morning and thought "I've had enough of everyone treating me like absolute rubbish; I must stick up for myself". Her account was entirely consistent with the emergence of her new physical and mental strength in mid-1994 and her process of self-transformation since 1988, which gradually allowed the damaging coping strategy and its underlying low self-esteem, to be replaced by a more effective self-image and ways of dealing with her problems. In her interview Diana went on to show great self-awareness when she acknowledged the bulimia would "always be in the back of my head." Ever since she started her journey of self-improvement Diana had taken opportunities to gain more information and help from professionals. The previous year she had sought insight in a brief session with the Canadian specialist Peggy Claude-Pierre even while she had been seeing therapist Susie Orbach, whose sessions had ended that spring after more than two years.

Diana went on to say how strenuous exercise helped her control her anger and emotions and enabled her to "get rid of all the stress and rages". Speaking about the questionable benefits she received from psychotherapy she gave an insight into her awareness of people around her who, perhaps, were not being as helpful as they believed. She said "Everyone knows how to treat you when you are vulnerable. But if you show any sign of strength then it is they who end up feeling intimidated. And they try to squash you back to where you were."

Strength and determination is what Diana took with her when she quite suddenly travelled to Pakistan again on 22 May. The overt purpose was to help Imran Khan raise more funding for his cancer hospital in Lahore but the hidden motive was to visit Hasnat's family. With her entire future invested in her love affair with the man she called "Mr Wonderful", Diana was intent on gaining his family's approval for the match she desperately wanted. By that time Diana was completely confident in her ability to alter even the most negative opinion by sitting and talking to whoever professed not to like her. She assumed, because it had been the case with so many cynical newsmen and politicians over the years, that showing who she was in a personal meeting would be enough to bring anyone onto her side. After an hour and a half with Hasnat's parents and a dozen or so of his relatives she was sure she had succeeded in convincing them "she was a nice girl" as her friend Elsa Bowker described the mission.

Back in London Diana quickly told friends that the marriage was possible. "They loved me" she said "they didn't mind at all that I'm not a Muslim." Unfortunately she had not told Hasnat she intended to speak to his family and he was upset and angry at her. The couple quarrelled and gradually their relationship began the dreadful decay Diana had experienced before. Friends who witnessed her devastation after arguments or misunderstandings, were worried by the torrents of tears and despair they saw her suffering. For Diana it must have seemed like another betrayal, not public this time but a betrayal of the heart. She had been so sure Hasnat understood her.

It was in that environment of pain and panic, a week after visiting Pakistan, that Diana felt betrayed and misunderstood once more, by someone she believed should have known better. By then it was normal for her, with all her experiences and evidence acquired, to assume that anyone she interacted with might say something to the media which would cause her embarrassment or even significant problems. As wary as she had become in every relationship, she had to trust some people sometimes and so she was particularly devastated and angry when those she trusted let her down. Towards the end of that May *Hello* magazine published the first of a two-part interview in which Diana's mother, Frances Shand Kydd, shared with the world her private thoughts about her daughter. The tabloids quickly picked up on various comments and another feeding frenzy began at the expense of Diana's reputation and privacy. The result was a rift in the already strained relationship between mother and daughter that was never healed.

Whatever tears Diana shed over any situation by that time in her life they were short lived and soon replaced by anger and aggression. As she had said at the Priory earlier in the month, she was tired of being treated like rubbish and intended to stick up for herself. A telling comment during her *Panorama* interview indicated who could expect her to confront them when she said "you see yourself as a good product that sits on a shelf and sells well, and people make a lot of money out of you."

Diana knew her mother had a drink problem and lacked sympathy for her inability to deal with it. The press had reported it widely when Mrs Shand Kydd was arrested for drunk-driving the previous November and had lost her license. The royal correspondent for *The Mirror*, James Whittaker, explained that after a good lunch she was "prone to giving colourful and unguarded interviews and comments." With her patience already stretched Diana blamed not only her mother but *Hello* for publishing the article. When she discovered her mother had been paid £30,000 for her interview Diana was even more disgusted. Initially she considered suing, as she had over the *Express* piece earlier in the year. Instead she cancelled some arrangements that would have given the magazine special treatment at two upcoming charity events and made her "shock" and "bitter disappointment" clear in a *Daily Mail* article.

At the same time as she was reacting belligerently over her mother's failure, Diana was provoked by another family incident, this time involving her son William. The tabloids revelled in the situation when Tiggy Legge-Bourke, accompanied by the fourteen year old Prince, was photographed pouring champagne at his school's open day. Legge-Bourke was there because neither Charles nor Diana had time in their schedules and William was not given any alcohol but the lack of sensitivity to possible adverse press coverage annoyed both his parents. Diana was the most vociferous and made her feelings known through the press. Her comments about the young woman who had apparently "harmed" William and been "foolish" and "thoughtless" were featured heavily. Perhaps realising she had overdone it Diana then tried to backtrack and blame the press for views they attributed to her. Eventually a luckless member of her staff, administrator Michael Gibbins, was held responsible for everything and Diana avoided another possible lambasting by editors who were becoming increasingly annoyed with her inconsistency and unsporting tactics in their perpetual game of tabloid ping-pong.

With all the hullabaloo it might have gone unnoticed when Tony Blair's new British Government announced, on 22 May 1997, that they were imposing a unilateral ban on "the import, export, transfer and manufacture of all forms of antipersonnel land mines." Other policy changes included destruction of all stocks, a moratorium on their use by British Forces, negotiations for an international ban and help with clearing mines "already laid across the world." In his announcement, Foreign Secretary, Robin Cook, said "Every hour another three people lose their life or lose a limb from stepping on a landmine. Thousands of young children who ran onto a landmine are left unable to run ever again. Land mines have limited military use, but create unlimited civilian casualties." Diana, who knew more than most about the children who would never run again, punched the air with delight when she saw the announcement on television.

Children running and playing was unlikely to have been on Diana's mind when, on 3 June, she used the state apartments at St. James's Palace for a charity event in aid of English National Ballet. At the performance and dinner that evening she sat with Mohamed Fayed, the controversial owner of the famous Harrods department store. Fayed was a long time acquaintance of Diana's and friend of her late father and stepmother Raine, to whom he had given a directorship on the board of Harrod's International.

The Egyptian-born son of a schoolteacher, Fayed had made a fortune from imports, shipping and property. By June 1997 he owned the Ritz Hotel in Paris and had won control of Harrods after a battle with his bitter rival 'Tiny' Rowland. A report on the takeover, by the Department of Trade and Industry, called into question Fayed's business practices and background. All his subsequent attempts to gain British citizenship were unsuccessful and he reacted by revealing that he had paid Conservative members of Parliament to ask questions on his behalf in the House of Commons.

The function that evening was not the first occasion on which Fayed had supported Diana's charities. He had been a generous contributor to other causes in the past and she had attended a fundraising dinner Fayed had given at Harrods to aid the work of Hasnat Khan's teacher and mentor, Sir Magdi Yacoub. In her after-dinner speech at the St James's Palace event, Diana announced that Harrods would be sponsoring the English National Ballet's new production of *The Nutcracker*. Fayed claimed he had promised Diana's father he would keep an eye on her and he was generous in fulfilling his vow. For years he had sent birthday gifts to William and Harry; every Christmas he sent Harrods hampers to Kensington Palace and he regularly invited Diana and her sons to holiday at his homes in Switzerland, Scotland and the south of France.

She had, up to then, declined all his invitations but she did visit him sometimes when she was in the department store. During their conversation on that June evening Diana mentioned that her plans for a summer holiday with her sons had fallen through. She had apparently been invited to the Hamptons by an old-flame, now established friend, Teddy Forstmann but security fears had made it impossible for her to get permission to take the Princes. Immediately he heard of her problem Mohamed Fayed repeated the standing invitation to join his family in Saint-Tropez in July. Shortly after extending the offer he ensured he would be able to provide his guests suitably luxurious accommodation, if Diana accepted, by completing his purchase of the 200 ft yacht *Jonakil*, for an estimated £15 million,

Before she could take any break in the sun, however, Diana had more work to do, a lot more work. The British Government had responded to the anti land mines campaign, after she added her voice to it and now she wanted to continue the momentum. On 12 June she made a major speech at a conference in London, co-hosted by the Mines Advisory Group and the

Landmine Survivors Network. Once again Diana took the advice of Bill Deedes and focused her words on the issue of mine-clearing and the effects of mines on their innocent victims. Reinforcing comments made by the Foreign Secretary in his announcement of a ban, Diana spoke of how she had been affected by her experiences in Angola, in particular with the children maimed by the indiscriminate weapons. Less than a week later she was in Washington DC speaking on the same subject, supporting an accelerated programme of mine-clearance and aid for victims.

In New York, the day after her Washington speech, Diana managed to spend some time with Mother Teresa of Calcutta, at her convent in the Bronx. The frail and ailing nun managed to leave her wheelchair briefly to stroll arm in arm with the woman whose work was inspired by their meeting years earlier in the back streets of Calcutta. The revered Mother Teresa was an increasingly powerful role model for Diana, whose joint ambition by then was to emulate her heroine by opening hospices around the world, while she continued the work to bring about a global ban on antipersonnel land mines.

Before she went to Washington and New York, Diana had attended the London preview party for the upcoming charity-auction of her dresses. At another similar event in Manhattan later in the month Diana was jostled by the excited crowd and Christie's UK chairman Charles Hindlip steered her through the throng with a hand on her bottom. The tabloids were quick to comment about the "tactile" assistance and Diana later mentioned how people kept calling her Di and shouting for her to "sign this." It was all "awful" she said later, "so familiar". At the time no one noticed her distaste. Observers commented on how she "knocked herself out, talked to everyone" and the press coverage was glowing.

For the land mines campaign Diana was able to draw on the guidance and wisdom offered by Bill Deedes to keep her from more trouble with politicians and those to whom she was a "loose cannon" in the arms arena but she had no similar figure to offer advice on other matters. If Patrick Jephson had still been at the helm to organise her engagements and guide her affairs, it is almost certain she would not have had the situation in New York to contend with, or a number of others which her inexperienced and poorly managed staff were unable to foresee.

Increasingly Diana was creating problems for herself because she insisted on handling her own PR and had engaged staff which did not include anyone capable of standing up to the strong personality she had become. Her make-up meant she wanted the control but she was incapable of Jephson's objectivity. Instead she reacted, emotionally and intuitively, to events as they arose and it was causing difficulties with her press coverage, like that she had received over the Legge-Bourke incident and her mother's *Hello* interview. It is even likely Diana would not have accepted Mohamed Fayed's invitation to Saint-Tropez that year if Jephson or someone of his calibre, had been available to offer strongly worded advice and arrange an alternative holiday.

As it was, even if Patrick Jephson had still been with her, Diana would probably not have been able to avoid the next episode which saw her criticised by the press and politicians alike. That month she made a spontaneous decision to take William and Harry to see a film, *The Devil's Own*. The movie had a 15 certificate which meant William scraped through, his fifteenth birthday having been just two days before but Harry was squeezed in illegally by dint of his mother's pleading with the cinema staff. The subsequent *furor* seemed like more karmic come-uppance to balance her tirade at Tiggy Legge-Bourke for the Champagne incident. Where Tiggy was criticised for exposing William to the demon alcohol, Diana was castigated for taking the Princes to see the "Devil" movie, which was widely thought to glamorise the Irish Republican Army and for taking Harry to a film he was too young to see legally.

Perhaps the conversation she had afterwards, with Father Gelli, the curate of St Mary Abbot's Church, Kensington, would have helped her understand the curious metaphysics of personal transformation. The Father had written a letter of support to Diana after the IRA movie story hit the press and she subsequently asked him to tea at Kensington Palace. Whether or not he explained that setting out on a spiritual path, as Diana most definitely had by that time, was likely to draw challenges aplenty, they did speak of many other matters from Sufism to exorcism. One topic in particular intrigued Diana, Father Gelli later recalled. With Hasnat Khan still very much in her mind obviously, Diana wanted to know if Christians and Muslims could be married in church.

A few days after her movie experience the dress auction netted millions of pounds and a mixture of good and ill will for Diana. The latter was something else which could have been avoided with better advice. When she decided to share the proceeds of the sale between the Cancer Research Fund at Royal Marsden Hospital and AIDS Crisis Trust, she was probably once again being led by her preference for the personal over correct form and for the global over the home grown. In that case she had a friend in America, Margeurite Littman, who ran the AIDS Crisis Trust. With that charity in the USA and the Royal Marsden in Britain the project had an attractive transatlantic flavour but by her decision Diana rejected one of her few remaining British charities, the National AIDS Trust. The auction was held and exceeded all expectations but by that time the British AIDS charity was on the verge of bankruptcy. It was a hard pill to swallow for National AIDS Trust chairman Michael Adler, who later said of Diana, "if you are a patron, you have responsibilities which go with patronage that you must fulfill."

Whether she was aware of Adler's criticism or not, Diana was acting on behalf of yet another charity when she was the guest of honour at a fundraising dinner for the Tate Gallery on the evening of her thirty-sixth birthday. According to her brother Charles, who was one of the 500 guests who paid to be at the event, she "sparkled". She also sparkled when she had dinner at Harry's Bar in London's Mayfair and hit the dance floor at Annabel's nightclub with another friend she knew well through her charity work, millionaire Gulu Lalvani. The electronics magnate, 22 years her senior, was one of two men Diana was seen out with during that summer. The other was long time friend from her gym, property developer Christopher Whalley, with whom she had lunch on a few occasions. Significantly Diana made no attempt to keep the meetings hidden from the press, with the inevitable result that the tabloids speculated on whether one or the other might be a new romance. Diana's friends speculated on whether she was attempting to save her much more secret relationship with Hasnat Khan by misdirecting the press or trying to make him jealous.

Jealousy was almost certainly in Diana's mind a few days after her birthday, when she watched a television documentary about Camilla Parker Bowles, her rival for her late husband's affections throughout their marriage. The presentation of Camilla's life and her romance with Prince Charles, was part of a concerted campaign to shape public opinion about their relationship and Diana was shocked by her own emotions when painful incidents from the past and difficult situations from the present were brought to her mind. It was especially painful to hear the assertion that Prince Charles had never really loved her. As much as she was personally hurt by the suggestion she also worried how it would affect William and Harry. Her sons after all were still within the royal family and spent half the time with their father, which meant Camilla would soon be influencing them if she was not already doing so. In a phone call to her astrologer Debbie

Frank Diana shared her distress and showed her growing capacity for insight when she said "All the grief from my past is resurfacing."

With the documentary came the news that Charles was to host Camilla's fiftieth birthday party at Highgrove on 18 July. Within days of hearing the news Diana ensured she would be out of the country on that date, by accepting Mohamed Fayed's invitation to join his family in Saint-Tropez. In his memoir Paul Burrell recalled how Diana had agreed, hours after lunch at the RAC Club with her stepmother, Raine, in the first week of July.

Less than a week before she was due to depart for France with her sons, Diana took William with her when she attended a private meeting with Prime Minister Tony Blair at his country home, Chequers. After they discussed how his Government might support her future role as a goodwill and humanitarian ambassador Diana was ecstatic and told friends, "I think at last I will have someone who will know how to use me." Tony Blair's opinion was equally enthusiastic. In Diana he saw elements of his own political vision. "Whatever New Labour had in part," Blair wrote in his autobiography, "she had in whole." He also acknowledged the ability at the core of Diana's work and what he believed she did with her gift "We were both in our ways manipulative people, perceiving quickly the emotions of others and able instinctively to play with them."

It was the ability to perceive the emotions of others which enabled Diana to connect so intensely with people, whether they were sick and suffering or in a relationship of a more conventional intimacy. So it was that she was already aware but unwilling to acknowledge, that her relationship with Hasnat Khan was coming to an end. Four days after being uplifted by her summit at Chequers, Diana was crushed by disappointment when Hasnat told her they could not see each other again. Months of media and family pressure and his anger at being kept in the dark about her visit to his parents in Pakistan in May, came to a head when he read a *Sunday Express* story stating that he and Diana were "unofficially engaged." He accused her of leaking the story and over her protests of innocence declared, regretfully, their relationship was finished. Why Diana would leak such a tale to a tabloid with which she had been engaged in a running battle all year, is an unanswered question but in truth it did not matter. Hasnat Khan was unable to overcome the twin difficulties of their cultural differences and appalling press scrutiny, no matter how much love they shared.

Hard blows, even when they are anticipated, are hard to take and for twenty four hours Diana was inconsolable. The man she had felt such a close connection with and who was a cornerstone of her future-vision had stepped out of her life. Old feelings of rejection and doubt flooded in briefly but they passed more quickly than they had after previous losses. Diana was stronger by then, with a clearer self-identity and a perspective based on past survivals that could see beyond the current despair. She was also a mother who was obliged to show a mother's strength, even at the most trying moments. On Friday 11 July, the day after her relationship with Hasnat Khan ended, Diana wiped her tears, gathered her bags and her sons and embarked on a Harrods helicopter bound for Stansted airport, where a company jet whisked them to Nice Airport and the sunshine.

A short limousine ride brought Diana and the boys to the port of Nice from where they were taken on the short cruise along the coast to a mooring just off-shore from the Fayed's luxurious beach-front compound at Saint-Tropez. Soon they were ensconced in the guest villa with their own cook, maids and swimming pool. Not much later they were swimming from the deck of the *Jonakil* and the boys were jet-skiing in the Mediterranean. The security, provided by ex-Royal Marines and the family atmosphere suited Diana perfectly. In business Mohamed Fayed was ruthless, even brutal, in private he was warm, generous, loving and rather given to bad language and crude jokes. Diana, no shrinking violet herself when it came to coarse humour was comfortable in his company and got on well with Fayed's wife, the Finnish born ex-model Heini. The presence of the Fayed children gave Diana added pleasure.

Within twenty-four hours of her arrival small boats filled with paparazzi and journalists were swarming amongst the three Fayed yachts, the 200 ft *Jonakil*, the schooner *Sakara* and the converted U.S. Coast Guard cutter *Cujo*. The British press had at least two angles to exploit in their coverage of Diana's holiday. First was the controversy surrounding Fayed himself and whether it was wise for Diana to be seen in his company, especially accompanied by her sons, both heirs to the throne. The second angle was how Diana would behave as 18 July and Camilla's birthday party approached. The pressmen were already primed to interpret any activity on Diana's part as significant in some way.

With the party a few days away the Sunday tabloids ran with headlines which were sure to annoy Diana and her host. *The Sunday Mirror* had "Di's Freebie" while many of the others recalled Fayed's background, in particular the "cash for questions" scandal which was referred to by one paper as a "systematic campaign of bribery" intended to "subvert" the work of the British Parliament.

Mohamed Fayed and Diana shared a special and dubious distinction – they were both rebels against the British Establishment. With little interest in political matters, a history of confronting authority and an increasing determination to enjoy her freedom as a single woman regardless of press attention, Diana quickly reacted by providing photo opportunities which showed her lack of concern at the criticism and support for her friend. When *The Sun* published a headline, "Di's Amazing Cuddle", alongside a picture of Fayed with his arm around Diana's waist and her hand on his shoulder, she had already telephoned a journalist to explain that Fayed had been a friend for many years and his offer to have her and the two Princes share his family's holiday had saved her sons from spending the summer in Kensington Palace. Piers Morgan of the *Mirror* later confirmed he had offered to pull his people out of Saint-Tropez after two days but had been assured by Diana's office "that won't be necessary." Richard Kay's piece at that time described Diana's defiance and aggressive self-justification.

It was somewhat appropriate that Diana's most dramatic confrontation with the press during that holiday occurred on Bastille Day, when the French celebrate their rebellion against royal absolutism. Dressed only in a one piece tiger-print swimsuit and accompanied by a security guard she jumped into a launch and approached the *Fancy*, a fifty foot motorboat containing a number of British tabloid journalists and photographers. Once there she gave them an impromptu interview and spoke about her life and concerns now she was divorced. During the ten minute conversation Diana told the hacks that her sons were upset by the press attention and had been trying to persuade her to live abroad. She complained that her land mines campaign was being treated unfairly and she took the opportunity to confirm her support for her father's "best friend" Mohamed Fayed.

Diana was described later by one reporter as being confused but it seemed to be the press pack which was more uncertain. In the articles which followed her chat one hack said she was relaxed, another that she was upset while a third described her as distraught. None recognised the strong self-image that had to have been present for an ex-bulimic to act so assertively while dressed so simply. Her parting shot "You're going to get a big surprise at the next thing I do!" gave them sleepless nights trying to work out what the mischievous taunt meant.

One person who did not witness the incident was Mohamed Fayed's son Emad, nicknamed Dodi, who arrived just in time for that evening's traditional firework display. He would have seen the media coverage and pictures the following day, however, and been able to meet the beautiful and strong-minded woman who acted so decisively to support his father and family.

To begin with Dodi treated Diana politely and deferentially. They had met socially before but not in circumstances which had enabled them to get to know one another well but within two days of meeting again that summer they could be found engaged in quiet and earnest conversations. Dodi impressed Diana by his kindness towards William and Harry and the easy relationship the boys seemed to enjoy with the man even his best friends called a "boy" or a "kid" at heart.

There can be little doubt that their rapid attraction to each other in Saint-Tropez, France, was reminiscent of Diana's instant connection with Prince Charles sixteen years before in Petworth, England. Hard-wired into Diana's brain, and well developed now by years of work with the sick and distressed, was a facility for empathising with the deepest undercurrents of other people's emotions. In Charles she had instantly recognised and responded to the "sad man" within him; with Dodi she would have sensed a similar sadness and reacted with the same concern and natural sympathy. Few men would be able to remain unmoved or unflattered by the gentle caring that Diana freely shared in such circumstances, in this case more freely because he was the beloved son of her host. Dodi, because of his own past and personality responded with a gentle consideration which reciprocated Diana's. The connection between them would have been instinctive and instantaneous and in all probability both would have been quick to identify it as a kind of love they had not experienced before.

In the beginning however they felt a growing bond and explored friendship. Dodi was accompanied in France by his fiancée, the model Kelly Fisher, who had been installed on one of the yachts offshore. Diana was with her sons. Dodi spent much of his time with them but visited his wife-to-be every night, explaining his father wanted him to keep his royal guests amused. The press pack hardly noticed Dodi at all. One freelance photographer admitted "We thought he was a sailor." The reporters were distracted by their own agenda, the second angle they sought to develop during the holiday, Camilla's upcoming birthday party at Highgrove. When the day finally dawned, only a very poor journalist would not have been able to contrive a story which interpreted Diana's sporting in the sun and sea as an attempt to steer the spotlight away from Camilla's big day. Pictures of the swim-suited Diana and stories of her blatantly grabbing the limelight duly filled the tabloids pages.

On 20 July, her vacation over, Diana left early with the Princes to return to Kensington Palace. When she and her sons eventually made it home at midnight, after their plane was delayed with a fault, Diana told Paul Burrell her holiday was "wonderful" and "normal". The following day she received huge displays of roses and a beautiful Cartier watch worth several thousands of pounds from her new admirer, Dodi. To her astrologer Debbie Frank, Diana described her time in France as "the best holiday ever" and admitted "I've met someone". Few others who knew her heard about Diana's attraction to Dodi until they read about it in the newspapers weeks later.

A few days later, after she returned from a trip to Milan where she attended the funeral of Gianni Versace and was reconciled with Elton John, Dodi called to ask Diana out to dinner. She asked him when, he said "tomorrow night." She asked where they would be going, he replied "Paris." According to Paul Burrell she was beside herself with excitement after they arranged for the helicopter to pick her up. This was a new experience. A man was pursuing her and money seemed to be no object, time seemed to be no object. Apparently he had all the time in the world to dedicate to her. Significantly, when Diana left Kensington Palace with her Versace shoulder bag packed for the weekend, she left William and Harry with Paul Burrell and the nanny.

When she called Kensington Palace from The Ritz in Paris that weekend, Diana was "like a sixteen-year-old" with excitement and happiness when she told her butler about another gift, a diamond studded gold watch, Dodi had given her. "I've never seen anything so beautiful" she squealed. Dodi was doing what he did naturally, treating a woman he liked with kindness, undivided attention and generosity. Diana had never felt so special. After a weekend made even more idyllic because it was unspoiled by paparazzi or journalists, the two friends, now feeling even more attracted to each other, returned undetected to London.

By the end of July William and Harry were with their father and the rest of the royal family at Balmoral and Diana was free to be indulged to her heart's content. The "flexible diary" she had envisioned in her personal manifesto two years before was a reality. She was answerable to no-one and happily agreed to join Dodi for a five day cruise off Sardinia and Corsica on board *Jonakil*.

They started that cruise as friends and returned as lovers. Towards the end, a paparazzo, acting on a tip off, managed to capture their romance in a photo which turned out to be worth hundreds of thousands of pounds when it was auctioned to the tabloids. Dodi and Diana, as immersed in their discovery of each other as they were in the warm waters off the island of Corsica, where they were photographed kissing and embracing, were blissfully unaware of the intrusion and blithely unconcerned about whether the world knew about their love or not.

In each other they had found an almost perfect match of personalities and needs. It was uncanny. Dodi was the child of a marriage which ended in acrimony when he was four. Although his father had custody, the small boy had little contact with either parent, being brought up by relatives and servants while Mohamed Fayed travelled extensively building his business empire. As a child he was given gifts more than love and attention and was regarded as an academic failure. At the age of thirteen he spent a single year at a Swiss boarding school after which he lived for five years in his father's Park Lane apartment. During that time he received little formal education although he did get his own Rolls-Royce with chauffeur and bodyguard when he was fifteen.

Six months at Sandhurst military academy when he was nineteen saw him become an officer and he served briefly as a military attaché in the United Arab Emirates Embassy in London until he succumbed to the sybaritic life style of a full time playboy. By his mid-twenties Dodi was mixing with a crowd who lived fast and well. His tastes ran to sports cars, cocaine and beautiful women, mostly models and actresses, who he pursued with extravagant gifts and idealistic devotion. He had few interests that would have enabled him to make his own living and enough money to support the excesses he had become used to. His father supported him and tried to help him develop a career in the one area he was attracted to, the film business. Credits as executive producer on a few successful movies belied his input on the projects which was minimal in every case.

By the time Dodi met Diana he was forty-one, had been divorced from a wife he was married to for eight months during his early thirties and had no children. Past girlfriends and business colleagues recalled a man who was a loner and who tried to impress with lavish gifts. Shy, sweet, thoughtful, kind, gentle, introverted, attractive, generous and appealing, a liar without guile, were words used to describe him. He was financially dependent on his father and apparently overspent his estimated $100,000 a month allowance on a regular basis as he acquired a collection of five Ferraris and a reputation for high spending coupled with a lack of accountability for the many debts he left in his wake. According to his fiancée, Kelly Fisher, he had also provisionally agreed to marry her on 9 August, five days after he and Diana were photographed in their loving embrace.

Whether she was aware of any of his background or not, it would probably have been irrelevant to Diana who relied entirely on her intuition when it came to assessing anyone and she had already made an intense emotional connection with Dodi by the time they spent that week together. In Emad 'Dodi' Fayed, Diana would have recognized the similarities between them not the differences. She would have sensed and reached out to the deep sadness and need beneath the childlike exterior and understood it completely. She would have seen him as someone she could look after.

With her belief in fate and pre-destiny, Diana would have been quick to see positive omens in their unexpected meeting and immediate attraction. She would also have been quick to assess their compatibility and to find possibilities for the future. Her own series of relationships with men had taken her through a distinct learning curve and resulted in a clear idea of the man she wanted to be with.

Charles had been emotionally cool, intellectually incompatible and unavailable for the kind of relationship she needed. James Hewitt had been the archetypal "rescuer" to her "victim" of a loveless marriage, a lover who showed her she was still attractive and worthy of romance but no more compatible emotionally than her husband. She also looked to Oliver Hoare to rescue her from the royal life she did not want and saw in him some similarities in outlook. He was sixteen years older, warm, caring and ultimately unable to deal with the strength of the love she wanted to share with him. Then there was Hasnat Khan, the man who up to then had come closest to her ideal. When they met she no longer needed to be rescued. She was breaking free of her old life by herself. He had been attracted by her spirit, her compassion, which matched his own and her loving nature but he could not handle her fame, her complexity or the intensity of her need for him.

None of the men who had stolen her heart in the past and then rejected it were able to share with Diana what she wanted most, mutual devotion and a bond which surpasses what most people mean when they speak of love. All, to one extent or another, had been limited by commitments on their time or emotions, or simply by their perception of the state of love, from making the connection which Diana assumed she would share with her life partner. So none had withstood the tests applied by daily life and they had moved on.

By 1997 Diana was experiencing on an almost daily basis, a phenomenon which most people do not even acknowledge, let alone feel even though they are capable of it. In her work she connected so deeply and profoundly to the sick and dying she touched and held that she sensed their emotions and felt their pain. To her it was a spiritual tie to individual human beings that gave and brought healing to both. In her relationships with men she had experienced a similar bond with Charles, James and Oliver but in each case it was distorted by her own need for attention and acknowledgement. As she had been transformed inwardly by her journey of the past eight years and learned to give more freely of her gift for caring, the connection she felt with Hasnat had come the closest to what she expected with a lover but even her link to him had been lost in the end. The sense of loss Diana felt when she parted from anyone with whom she had been linked at that profound level, was like a hollowness inside her, an emptiness and longing which she assuaged to some extent by her work.

With Dodi she almost certainly felt that intense spiritual connection again but this time it was from a completely different self-perception than on any other occasion and because of that their relationship had the potential to succeed where none of the others had. Diana would not have been able to explain what was happening or analyse it but she would have known it intuitively and she would have responded.

That August Diana was stronger and more certain of her ability to create the life she wanted than she had ever been before. Her strength was reflected by a change in the way she saw herself. She was no longer a victim but a woman, with substance and worth, who wanted a partner with whom she could share her future, not one who gave purpose to it. She no longer needed to be rescued by a gallant knight who would carry her away to some quiet home where he would look after her and give her more children, while she cared for him, supported his career and did modest good works of her own. She absolutely believed she could change the world and make it a better place, on her own if she had to. She still wanted more children and a peaceful home, a sanctuary she could share with a man she loved but what she wanted most from him was his support for what she felt driven to do and above all she wanted his unfettered time to experience the connection which would complete them both. In Dodi she would have seen such a man.

When Diana's friends recalled how she was, at the time of her relationship with Dodi, they spoke of radiance, happiness and fulfillment such as they had never seen in her before. Her own words to a friend reflected how she felt "I'm so strong now, I fear nothing, nothing." Dodi's friends and relatives had similar memories of him.

On 5 August, as Diana was getting ready to return to London, the British Foreign Secretary, Robin Cook, endorsed Diana's campaign against antipersonnel land mines campaign and her proposed trip to Bosnia that month, in the *Daily Mirror*. He was quoted as saying she had "captured public attention over a weapon that strikes hardest at civilians."

On 7 August, the day before Diana was due to leave for Bosnia the newspapers which had not been successful in acquiring the photographs of Diana and Dodi's loving embraces in Corsica, began running spoiler stories about their romance. That evening, after supper in Dodi's Park Lane apartment, Diana emerged and was confronted by about fifty photographers. She seemed completely unconcerned about their presence. Over the next few days the tabloids, encouraged by Mohamed Fayed's spokesman Michael Cole, depicted Dodi as an "ideal husband" and "gentle soul."

During the next few days in Sarajevo, Diana toured the "killing fields" with Bill Deedes, her butler and a huge press pack. The sights and stories of those affected by the weapons she abhorred were heart rending and she made every effort to bring them to the world's attention. Deedes described the half hour Diana insisted on dedicating to each victim because she knew they needed the opportunity to be heard. He commented later "It was brilliant. She was impressive." Despite her hard work the press wanted to know about Dodi. One incident during that trip to Bosnia epitomised Diana's cynicism about the tabloids and probably hastened a decision she was to make a few days later. As she tried to give a pair of prosthetic feet to an amputee, a *News of the World* reporter called out "Isn't it wonderful news about Dodi? What's it like to be in love again?"

Throughout the trip Dodi provided an antidote to the horrendous scenes Diana saw each day by speaking to her as often as possible via their satellite phone. "She laughed and laughed with him," recalled Sandra Mott who was Diana's liaison on the trip. Even as he offered encouragement and they shared laughter, ten pages of photographs of them together in Corsica were published in the *Sunday Mirror*. The page one shot on Sunday 10 August was entitled The Kiss. According to the accompanying article, which waxed lyrical about happiness at last in her lover's arms and referred to Dodi as a "generous caring spirit", an engagement seemed likely soon. Bill Deedes, who accompanied Diana home the following day on a jet, loaned by billionaire George Soros, recalled she studied The Kiss and the press coverage and was "not at all resentful of the pictures that had been taken."

By the time she was back in the UK, however, the tabloids were beginning to change their tune about her lover. Over the next week Dodi's past, then his present caught up with him. Details of financial problems with ex-girlfriends and American Express hit the headlines with warnings to Diana to be careful with her money. News of his cocaine habit followed, with tales of sexual inadequacy and alleged threats of violence to old girlfriends. The anti-Dodi bandwagon gathered pace and vitriol when his now ex-fiancée, Kelly Fisher, emerged to sell her story of the broken engagement and to announce a lawsuit, for failure to pay her the "premarital support" he had promised if she gave up modeling.

From perfect husband material Dodi became an "Oily Bedhopper" whose "Dodgy" past made him a target for a vile and sustained tabloid attack during which barely concealed racism was combined with salacious comments alluding to his sexual relationship with Diana. To avoid the pressure and regain some equilibrium, Diana and Dodi kept as low a profile as possible at the Fayed estate in Surrey and in London. If she had any misgivings she did not mention them to friends but doubts might have formed part of the reason for the couple' s helicopter hop to see one of Diana's favorite psychics, Rita Rogers, in Derbyshire on 12 August. Their readings were satisfactory enough to persuade Diana to send Dodi a pair of her father's cufflinks, probably the same ones she had given to Oliver Hoare and which he had returned when their relationship ended. Her friend, Elsa Bowker, later said "They were her most precious possession. I couldn't believe she gave them to Dodi so quickly."

As the media pressure mounted, Diana escaped to Greece with her friend Rosa Monckton, on a Harrod's jet. Before she departed, on 15 August, she spoke to her stepmother on the phone and told her how blissfully happy she was, "having really one of the best times of her life and Dodi was very much a part of it" Raine recalled. Rosa Monckton recollected later that during their five days away they spoke about Hasnat Khan more than Dodi and Diana expressed concerns about the younger Fayed's extravagance which made her angry, "I don't want to be bought" she said "I want someone…to make me feel safe and secure."

Safety and security was something her lover could offer almost as well as the royal family it seemed. With his father's blessing and active encouragement, he had the fabulous Fayed wealth at his disposal to surround Diana with bodyguards and whisk her from one place to another by private jet, helicopter and limousine. She barely touched the ground after returning from Greece on 20 August 20 before she was back on board *Jonakil* with Dodi, cruising between Nice and Sardinia.

As they enjoyed the sunshine and more shopping in Mediterranean resorts, Diana's reservations about her lover's extravagance seemed to fade along with any remaining doubts she might have had about their long term future together. If she had ever started out to enjoy a summer fling on the rebound from Hasnat Khan and it is highly unlikely that she did, since casual sex and throwaway romance were not in her make-up, things were rapidly becoming more serious by the time the voyage ended. Her relationship with Dodi had been endorsed by her psychic, her astrologer, whose charts showed them to be compatible and by her own intuition which was never questioned. He offered her something she had never had from any man, his unequivocal and undistracted attention and time, time to be together in the intense union of body, mind and spirit she instinctively sought but had never achieved. Driven by her powerful future-vision Diana was almost certainly considering what permanent place Dodi might have in her life even as he handed out cigars to *Jonakil's* crew to celebrate the first anniversary of her divorce from Prince Charles on 28 August.

Other factors in her contemplation would have been the persistent tick of her own body-clock and yet another betrayal by the press that seemed to indicate how futile it was to expect any fulfillment from her public role. On 26 August the magazine *Le Monde* had published an article based partly on a face-to-face interview with Diana and partly on responses to written questions submitted the previous June. In the piece she spoke of the importance of touch to her work, "it isn't premeditated", her bitterness at her treatment by the British press and her preference for life abroad where "I'm taken for what I am." Insight into her personality came from other remarks "No one can tell me what to do. I work by instinct. It's my best adviser." The observations which were included about her land mines campaign were the ones which pitched her into hot water. The article included comments which praised the Labour Government for its position and quoted her as saying "Its predecessor was hopeless."

The resulting *furor* back in Britain was predictable. Conservative grandees took umbrage and warned her to stay out of politics and the press criticised her. The *Daily Express* called it "her most ferocious political row." For several days, from the sun-baked decks of *Jonakil*, surrounded by paparazzi in boats following every move, Diana tried to respond to what she saw as a "stitch up" by *Le Monde*. She instructed her office to release their copy of the draft article she had authorized, to prove it had been altered to include the "hopeless" quote. *Le Monde* shot back that she had used the word in the face-to-face interview but confirmed they had added the offending quote after Kensington Palace had agreed what was supposed to be a final version. No wonder then, that friends who saw press photos of that cruise, described her body language as "wrong" and undemonstrative towards Dodi.

Diana's anger was intense but more significantly, her determination to be her own person without hindrance from anyone was increased. Her thoughts turned to the possibility of a future that did not rely on dealings with the gatekeepers of public opinion, the press. When she left with Dodi for Paris on 30 August she had changed her plans from the original intention to go straight back to London that day.

In Paris they were harassed continuously by a large pack of aggressive paparazzi and had difficulty going anywhere in the city with the expectation of enjoying themselves. By the evening Diana was tired and stressed and beginning to react as she usually did, with irritation. Dodi became more and more protective as her mood deteriorated.

At around 6.00 p.m. UK time, 7.00 p.m. local time, while she waited for Dodi to take her to dinner, Diana called her friend Richard Kay in London. During their conversation, recalled in his book *Diana: the Untold Story*, she told him she had decided to "radically change her life." She went on to describe the plans she had discussed with Dodi and his father which would see her conclude all her obligations to her charities, including the land mines campaign, by that November. Fayed money would finance a charity for victims of antipersonnel mines and she had already begun to explore with them how she could open hospices around the world for the dying, along the lines of Mother Teresa's work. She would live as a private person and Kay gained the distinct impression Dodi was to be a significant part of her future. They were, he wrote, "blissfully happy" and marriage "was possible." Shades of Diana's old self-doubt and past struggles entered the conversation when she suddenly said "But I sometimes wonder, what's the point? Whatever I do, it's never enough for some people." Then she brightened and spoke about how much she was looking forward to returning to London the following day, when she would be able to spend a few days with William and Harry before they returned to school.

In her conversation that evening, with Richard Kay as her witness, Diana articulated every detail of the future-vision which had taken nearly eight years to crystallize into a genuine possibility. Eight years of challenges and confrontations and rejecting what was not the vision, of privacy with a man she loved, a man who would be able to take care of her; a family to belong to and the possibility of more children; work she was driven to do to make the world a better place, her sons, love, happiness and peace of mind at last. Diana was on the threshold of it all. Six hours later, at 12.26 a.m. on Sunday 31 August, the Mercedes S280 in which Diana was a passenger, smashed into pillar thirteen of the Pont de l'Alma underpass at almost 100 miles per hour.

An off duty doctor, Frederic Maillez, stopped to provide first aid and had to push his way past the pack of excited men who surrounded the car taking photographs. "It was like a scene out of the annals of Hell," he said later recalling the blaring horn, tangled wreckage of the car and its dead and dying human occupants lit by flash after flash, from the cameras of the milling paparazzi. If her half open eyes and bewildered mind had been able to register anything at all, that hell would have been the last thing Diana was aware of.

Three and a half hours after the accident the Princess of Wales was pronounced dead. Her brain had been badly damaged by the impact and she had suffered colossal damage to her pulmonary artery, which was ripped from her heart causing massive internal bleeding and a series of major cardiac arrests. In the end Diana's heart stopped and her heart chakra, the energy centre associated with love, compassion and charity, ceased to play its part in the ebb and flow of universal life force that fills us all.

READING SUGGESTIONS

The following books contain ideas which have influenced my own approach to body-mind self-transformation. For more information see the website:-

www.dianahertransformation.co.uk

Moshe Feldenkrais, *Awareness Through Movement* (Thorsons: 1991)

Bruce Lipton, *The Biology of Belief: an introduction to Epigenetics and how your mind influences your health* (Hay House: 2011)

Richard Bandler and John Grinder, *Frogs into Princes: an introduction to neurolinguistic programming* (Eden Grove: 1990)

Deane Juhan, *Job's Body: a handbook for bodywork* (Barrytown Ltd: 2002)

Desmond Morris, *Manwatching* (Triad Works: 1978)

Candace Pert, *The Molecules of Emotion* (Pocket Books: 1999)

John F Thie DO, *Touch for Health: a practical guide to natural health using acupuncture, touch and massage to improve postural balance and reduce physical and mental pain and tension* (Devorss & Company: 2006)

Dub Leigh, *Zen Approach to Body Therapy: From Rolf to Feldenkrais to Tanouye Roshi* (University of Hawaii Press: 1987)

BIBLIOGRAPHY

Andrew Morton, *Diana: Her True Story* (Michael O'Mara: London, 1992)

Jonathan Dimbleby, *The Prince of Wales* (Little Brown: London, 1994)

Andrew Morton, *Diana: Her New Life* (Michael O'Mara: London, 1995)

Andrew Morton, *Diana: Her True Story, In Her Own Words* (Michael O'Mara: London, 1997)

Richard Kay and Geoffrey Levy, *Diana; The Untold Story* (Daily Mail: London, 1998)

Simone Simmons, *The Secret Years*, (Michael O'Mara: London, 1998)

Sally Bedell Smith, *Diana: The Life of a Troubled Princess* (Random House: London, 1999)

James Hewitt, *Love and War* (Blake: London, 1999)

Patrick Jephson, *Shadows of a Princess* (HarperCollins: London, 2000)

Trevor Rees-Jones, *The Bodyguard's Story* (Warner Books: London, 2000)

Ken Wharfe, *Diana: Closely Guarded Secret* (Michael O'Mara: London, 2003)

Paul Burrell, *A Royal Duty* (Penguin: London, 2004)

Andrew Morton, *Diana: in pursuit of love* (Michael O'Mara: London, 2004)

Tina Brown, *The Diana Chronicles* (Arrow Books: London, 2007)

Lightning Source UK Ltd.
Milton Keynes UK
UKOW030617230812

197974UK00002B/2/P